The King's W

The King's Wife

FIVE QUEEN CONSORTS

Robert Gray

SECKER & WARBURG
LONDON

First published in Great Britain in 1990
by Martin Secker & Warburg Limited
Michelin House, 81 Fulham Road, London sw3 6RB

A CIP catalogue record for this book
is available from the British Library

ISBN 0 436 19986 6

The lines quoted from Richard Cobb's *A Classical Education* (p. 347)
are reproduced by kind permission of the Hogarth Press Ltd;
those from James Pope-Hennessy's *A Lonely Business* (p. 363)
by kind permission of Weidenfeld & Nicolson Ltd.

Typeset in 11/14pt Linotron Sabon by
Hewer Text Composition Services, Edinburgh
Redwood Burn Limited, Trowbridge, Wiltshire.
and bound by Hunter & Foulis Ltd, Edinburgh

For my mother-in-law, whose present *Françaises, Reines d'Angleterre* gave me the idea for this book; for my own mother, who has always made everything possible; and for Charles and Susanna Swallow, in whose bounty likewise there has been no winter.

Cover your heads, and mock not flesh and blood
With solemn reverence;

Shakespeare, *Richard II*, Act III, Scene 2

Contents

Illustrations

Introduction

These paths have been trodden before. Between 1840 and 1848 Agnes Strickland and her sister Elizabeth, who preferred to remain anonymous, produced no less than twelve volumes entitled *Lives of the Queens of England*, a collection that included consorts and regnants alike. What the Misses Strickland may have lacked in critical rigour they more than made up in energy and enthusiasm, so that – one registers with delight – their books sold extremely well. In consequence there was no problem of selection: the sisters covered every queen available in as much detail as they could dig up, before moving smoothly on to a further eight volumes dealing with the *Lives of the Queens of Scotland and English Princesses connected with the Regal Succession of Great Britain*.

Their somewhat less energetic successor has conceived his book first and foremost as an entertainment: witness the absence of footnotes and bibliography. Not, let it hastily be emphasised, that historical accuracy has been carelessly sacrificed; rather that readers are requested to take the academic underpinning on trust in the cause of avoiding undue solemnity. Pending the development of a huge popular market like that created by Agnes Strickland, it has been necessary to limit the number of queens under consideration to five; and if asked upon what basis they have been singled out, the author replies with firm and level gaze that he chose them simply because they appeared to him to be interesting. Should the questioner persist, to the extent of demanding what unifying principle animates the essays, the honest answer, delivered with gaze only marginally less firm and level, must be that there is no such principle, beyond an attempt to consider the queens concerned as flesh and blood rather than as ornaments of state. It cannot even be said that there are obvious connecting threads between one queen and the next. How could there be, when, for instance, more than four hundred years separate Eleanor of Aquitaine's death from the birth of Henrietta Maria in the succeeding section?

It is tempting to claim that the book does something to rectify the masculine domination of history, a bias that persists not necessarily through any lingering sexist prejudice but simply because for centuries the actions of women were barely recorded. Certainly the lives of the queen consorts present an exception to this rule: over the last thousand years they have been more fully and continuously documented than those of women in any other category. It would be futile, though, to pretend that the experience of queens has been in any way typical of women as a whole. Those eager to trace the development of the feminine consciousness will find no enlightenment within these pages, beyond incidental confirmation of Saki's dictum that it takes all sorts to make a sex. Nor does this book attempt to analyse how the constitutional position of queen consorts evolved. In practice, the status of the King's wife, like that of all wives, depended upon the balance achieved in each particular marriage, a matter quite unpredictable even in the prolonged dark ages of theoretical male ascendancy.

What remains after these disclaimers, it is hoped, are five lives which are not only fascinating in themselves but which also offer unfamiliar and sometimes far from flattering perspectives on well-worn episodes in English history. Moreover, for all the variety of time and circumstance, certain themes do reappear in different chapters of this book. There is, first, the lottery of royal marriage: the ordeal of being plucked, perhaps while still a girl, from familiar surroundings for delivery to the dread intimacy of an unknown husband in an alien court. There is, next, the difficulty of establishing and maintaining domestic harmony under conditions where commonplace family quarrels are liable to become state crises; likewise, of bringing up children to be both royal and well balanced. There is the challenge of rivals, whether mistresses or ministers, for the King's favour. There is the uncertain loyalty of courtiers who follow the rising sun, and of crowds that cheer by rote.

Above all, these histories afford examples of feminine resilience. None of the queens in this book led a life which it is possible to envy. Eleanor of Aquitaine's power urges were disastrously foiled;

Henrietta Maria's life was wrecked by the Civil Wars which ended in her husband's execution; Catherine of Braganza became a hapless matrimonial victim; Caroline of Brunswick lurched crazily between scandal and disgrace; Queen Mary saw her joyless sacrifice to royal propriety wantonly rejected by her eldest son. Yet all these women, in their very different ways, rose above the wreckage; and all of them, save Caroline of Brunswick, outlived their husbands.

Death itself, however, does not exhaust the tribulations of royalty. Whereas the sins and follies of the general are allowed to fade into merciful oblivion, those of kings and queens stay permanently on display. The foibles of those who have been set upon the throne merely by the chance of heredity or marriage present an irresistible temptation to the uncharitable. Historians tyrannise over extinct royalty without fear of retaliation, rather as an absolute monarch lords it over his subjects. Such arbitrary judgement may be inevitable; it is also wholly unjust. Queen consorts do not become especially culpable or ridiculous because their faults are public property, any more than those who censure them gain virtue from being unknown. 'Use every man after his desert,' said Hamlet, 'and who should 'scape whipping?' That is a pertinent text for a biographer, even if Hamlet himself was not noticeably forbearing when it came to arraigning the Queen.

Eleanor of Aquitaine

c.1122–1204

I

Eleanor of Aquitaine was the most famous woman of her time, an imperious, dangerous figure who crowded her long life with drama and adventure. She remains the only person to have been Queen in turn in France and England, a double distinction from which, through the terrible force of her will, she contrived to extract a double share of tribulation. Yet notwithstanding her remarkable career, the most extraordinary thing about Eleanor is that, dead for nearly eight hundred years, she has only achieved her apotheosis in the last fifty.

For seven centuries the main lines of her character had seemed clear enough. Eleanor's memory was preserved in two guises, positive and negative versions of one compelling image. She was a powerful, capable and very beautiful woman; alternatively, and no less absorbingly, she was the Demon Queen. Matthew Paris, writing within fifty years of her death, propagated the first view. 'She was an admirable woman,' he considered, 'at once beautiful and accomplished.' 'A very able woman of great tact and experience,' echoed the historian Bishop Stubbs six hundred years later. The Demon Queen tradition, on the other hand, while it denied neither the beauty nor the accomplishment, insisted that these qualities had been perverted to evil ends. On this account Eleanor appears as ruthless, vindictive and scarifying. In the Middle Ages she was credited with a close family kinship to the Devil; in Shakespeare's *King John* she appears as a 'canker'd grandam'. This vision of her character still persists, as witnessed by Katharine Hepburn's shrewish performance in *The Lion in Winter*.

In particular, the Demon Queen was a woman of voracious sexual appetite. Even in Eleanor's own time monastic chroniclers were adept at encouraging the reader's worst suspicions about her love-life, albeit then tending, infuriatingly, to retreat under cover of some pious phrase like '*melius tacenda sunt*', 'these matters are better left in silence'. They became rather less shy after her death. A French chronicler, Aubrey de Trois Fontaines, complained around 1250 of 'the promiscuity of that woman, who did not conduct herself like a Queen, but offered herself almost as common property'. Stories of Eleanor's moral delinquency were always popular in the haunts of virtue. In the seventeenth century another French monk recorded his conviction that '*elle ne pouvait vivre sans homme*'. The Victorians, in adverting to these matters, generally concentrated on Eleanor's failings as a mother, cloaking their darker imputations in classical allusion. The Queen, it was coyly asserted, resembled the Roman Empress Messalina. In France Michelet drew his comparison from native folklore. Eleanor appears as '*la véritable Mélusine, mêlée de natures contradictoires*'. Melusina was a Poitevin water-sprite who refused to see her mortal husband on Saturdays, for the excellent reason that she reverted to being a mermaid on that day.

So Eleanor was remembered until, after the Second World War, her shade fell among female historians, notably the American Amy Kelly, whose study *Eleanor and the Four Kings* was published in 1950, and Régine Pernoud, whose biography appeared in France in 1965. Amy Kelly's book, in particular, was written with a zest and a flair that drew strength from her encyclopaedic knowledge of the twelfth century. It created an Eleanor for our times: a dashing, magnetic woman who contrived, by sheer force of personality and talent, to set herself above the trammels of the brute and masculine medieval world. The model proved irresistible, tempting other historians, even some male ones, to throw caution to the winds. (An honourable exception should be made of E. R. Labande, whose rigorous and scholarly account of Eleanor has unfortunately been confined to the pages of an obscure academic journal, the *Bulletin de la Société des Antiquaires de L'Ouest, 4ième série, II*, Poitiers, 1952.) With breathtaking confidence, considering the gap of eight centuries, Eleanor's mind has been re-examined, her ambitions descried, her psychology laid bare. If the patient were actually present on the couch it might seem foolish to venture so far; in the field of historical biography such presumption can always be passed off as imaginative reconstruction.

Out of this process Eleanor has emerged transmogrified into a kind of prototype feminist heroine. Nothing, it follows, could have been beyond her. 'Through Eleanor', a French historian called Rita Lejeune has written, 'a new character made a triumphant entry into French literature and French society: Woman. The woman of the world, but also the cultivated woman, both of them pursuing their civilising mission.' Eleanor is no longer Messalina, the depraved empress; she is Minerva, the goddess of wisdom. More specifically, this paragon has been presented as a knowledgeable and discriminating patroness of the troubadour poets. In a puff of smoke the Accomplished Beauty stands revealed as the Important Literary Influence.

Such conjuring tricks, however, are apt to induce scepticism among the nastier kind of children, invariably, of course, the boys. They fear that the wool has been pulled over their eyes. They would like to see the performance again, in slow motion.

To begin at the beginning, then. The first point to make about Eleanor is that she was not merely 'of Aquitaine'; she was sole heiress of the whole vast duchy, and of Poitou into the bargain. Indeed, in her childhood she was attended by so much material good fortune that one can hardly be surprised if the Furies singled her out for special attention later in her career. She was born, around 1122, the daughter of Guillaume X, Duke of Aquitaine, which is to say that she was a member of one of the most cultivated, if also one of the most notorious, houses in Europe. There was a younger sister, Petronilla, but a brother called Aigret died in infancy, so that Guillaume X's death in 1137 left Eleanor, around the age of fifteen, as mistress of the entire western side of France between the Loire and the Pyrenees. She was beautiful – '*perpulchra*' one chronicler called her, as though seeking to assure his readers that he is not just dealing in the flatteries routinely due to princesses. If a poem based on the recollections of William the Marshal, who knew Eleanor well in later life, is to be believed, she was also 'charming', 'welcoming' and 'lively'. Altogether, in 1137 she must have appeared as alluring a matrimonial catch as the world can furnish.

In fact, Eleanor's background was both more flawed and more interesting than the polished surface might suggest. At the beginning of the tenth century her family had simply been Counts of Poitou, but as they acquired further overlordships to the south – Perigord and Limoges in the tenth, Guyenne in the eleventh century – their interests naturally moved in the same direction. They looked towards Toulouse, Provence, and across the Pyrenees into Spain. In particular Guillaume IX, Eleanor's grandfather, determined to bring Toulouse, the communications centre of southern France, under his aegis. He married the daughter of the Count of Toulouse, and seized the county twice (1098–1100 and 1114–20) without ever securing permanent control. Despite this failure, the ambitions of the Dukes of Aquitaine remained concentrated in the Mediterranean world. Theoretically, it is true, they owed allegiance to the Capetian kings in Paris, but this overlordship was a mere vestige of the hegemony which the Franks had once established over the whole Roman province of Gaul, and long since lost. The French King was a distant figure, useful enough to cite in legal argument with rival feudatories, of no import whatever in the day-to-day running of the duchy.

It would be quite wrong, simply because we know the end of the story, to consider France as it exists today the inevitable culmination of some inexorable historical process. Perhaps it *was* inevitable that northern France should be united, whether under the Capetians or under some great feudatory like the Count of Anjou or the Duke of Normandy. But the south – Provence, the Auvergne, Toulouse and, by association, Aquitaine – seemed destined for quite distinct development. It was separated from the north geographically by the Massif Central, verbally by a different language, structurally by a social organisation far less deeply penetrated by feudalism, and culturally by a civilisation which retained something of the genius, as well as the liberty and licence, of the pagan classical world. The narrow clerical circle that surrounded the Capetian King in Paris discovered in Aquitaine everything that was reprehensible. The ungodly in that remote province dedicated themselves unabashedly, and all too successfully, to the celebration of pleasure; the godly drifted into every species of heresy under the patronage of a nobility consumed with hatred and jealousy of the Church. The Dukes of Aquitaine, moreover, snapped their fingers at Paris. Like the Counts of Anjou and the Dukes of Normandy, they allied themselves with or against their theoretical sovereign purely as interest dictated. How could they regard him with deference when their own territories were so much larger than the meagre royal domain in the Ile de France?

Yet the vast extent of their lands, though it conferred prestige, also brought problems to the Dukes of Aquitaine. The duchy was more or less ungovernable. Around the centres of Bordeaux and Poitiers, where the Dukes possessed personal estates, their power counted for something; between these cities were tracts over which baronial families like the Lusignans and the Talifers lorded it in total independence. To the east, in the Auvergne, and in the extreme south, on the foothills of the Pyrenees, it was impossible to tell where Aquitaine began or ended. In most of the duchy ducal authority was for all practical purposes non-existent. The land might be fertile, the salt and wine trades might flourish, but it was their subjects, not the Dukes themselves, who prospered.

Perhaps that was why the ruling house of Aquitaine showed itself so eager for foreign adventures, particularly in Spain. For the Dukes, the Pyrenees hardly existed as a barrier. Duke Guillaume VIII had led the 'Spanish crusade' against the Muslims in 1063 and married his daughters into the ruling houses of Castile and Aragon. Duke Guillaume IX joined his Spanish relations in expeditions against Islam, on one occasion (1115) penetrating as far south as Cordova. He married the King of Aragon's widow as his second wife, and bestowed his daughter upon an Aragonese prince. Eleanor, therefore, grew up in a family associated far more closely with the Mediterranean world than with northern France. As for England, she would not have given it a thought, unless she heard the jest of the Bordeaux merchants, that English wine could only be drunk with closed eyes and through clenched teeth. Fate would draw Eleanor far away from her native country, but essentially she remained a woman of the south.

No doubt she was also influenced by the memory of her extraordinary grandfather. Duke Guillaume IX of Aquitaine was one of the most remarkable men of his time. This had nothing to do with his political or military prowess. As a ruler he achieved little; as a crusader he contrived to get his army cut to pieces. He was, however, a poet of genius, often called 'the first of the troubadours' for his part in reintroducing the vernacular lyric to Western Europe. ('Vernacular' in his case meant the *langue d'oc*.) In many ways he brings Byron to mind, though very much the Byron of *Don Juan* rather than the self-dramatising creature who wrote *Childe Harold*. Guillaume had the same scathing wit, the same directness of attack and rapidity of thought, the same impatience with convention, and the same negligent ease with hideously difficult verse forms.

He also shared Byron's contempt for domestic virtue. Why, he declared, he was such an accomplished lover that he could easily have made a living from his skill: he never left a woman without her begging for more. Such braggadocio would be intolerable but for the sense that Guillaume is laughing at himself, no less than at his mistresses, for becoming ensnared in the merciless play of passion. He shows himself piercingly aware of his folly in chasing the pleasures which imagination conceives. 'It has been my fate', he wrote, 'that I have never been able to enjoy what I have loved: it has always been thus, it will ever be thus, for the moment I act my heart whispers "All is in vain."' But Guillaume resolutely declined to be gloomy. 'He made everything into a joke and made his listeners laugh uncontrollably,' William of Malmesbury noted with evident disapproval. Guillaume even turned his crusading misadventures into rhymed couplets that kept his audience in stitches. One might discern an essentially religious spirit behind Guillaume's determination that nothing in this life is worth taking seriously, were his shade not on hand to deride such a notion. 'May God let me live long enough to get my hands under her cloak' was the only sort of prayer that he liked to publicise.

He cared no more for the Church than for any other organisation; indeed, he was excommunicated for the depredations he wrought thereon. His charity was aroused by the abbey of Fontevrault in Anjou, but then he had every reason to be grateful to an institution that harboured both his cast-off wives. In later life Guillaume purloined the wife of one of his barons, the Count of Châtelleraut in Poitou, and lived with this woman, the aptly named Dangerosa, in open concubinage, heedless of the ecclesiastical censures heaped upon him. He had her portrait attached to his shield, remarking that he wished to bear her in battle as she had so often borne him in bed. Marriage to Dangerosa was hardly possible, but to content his mistress he arranged that his son should marry her daughter. From this union Eleanor was born, and later in her life she would make the most of her mother's connections among the baronage of Poitou. As for Guillaume IX, no doubt he felt more than the usual measure of grandpaternal pride in Eleanor; he had, after all, played more than the usual grandpaternal part in her origins. Eleanor might just have remembered him for she was about five when, in 1127, he finally laid down what he called 'the burden' of gallantry and pleasure, not without some hope that the Lord might, in spite of everything, number him amongst His own.

Guillaume X did his best to carry on in his father's vein. He got himself excommunicated for interfering with the appointment of bishops and supporting an anti-pope. He patronised the troubadour poets. Yet he never cut the same dash as his father. Saint Bernard, that fierce champion of ecclesiastical orthodoxy, reduced him to a prone and foaming wreck simply by brandishing the Host before his face. It is difficult to imagine that Guillaume IX would have been impressed by such a routine ecclesiastical gambit.

Eleanor's mother died in about 1130, when she was eight, which may have left the young girl somewhat over-exposed to the masculine world of her father's court. Perhaps she sometimes followed Guillaume X on his peripatetic way about his huge duchy, though tradition places her childhood firmly in the Bordeaux region, whether in the town itself or at Belin, thirty miles to the south. Bordeaux was on the line of linguistic division between the *langue d'oc* and the *langue d'oeil*, and Eleanor would have grown up at ease in both languages. During her childhood she would not have been regarded as a princess of any especial importance: in 1137 her father was only thirty-eight, so there was every chance that he would marry again and produce a male heir. This nearly happened, for negotiations were concluded for a match with Emma, daughter of the Vicomte de Limoges. The prospective bride, however, was carried off by the Comte d'Angoulême, and Guillaume X had failed to find a replacement when he contracted a fatal malady on one of his regular pilgrimages to the shrine of Saint James of Compostela in Santiago. He was buried there before the high altar, and Eleanor became the Duchess of Aquitaine.

As he lay dying in Spain, Guillaume X had cast about for means of safeguarding his daughter, alike from turbulent barons within and rapacious enemies without Aquitaine. He decided that the best hope of guaranteeing her inheritance was to seek the protection of the French King, the overlord for whom he had shown such scant respect in the days of his health. Louis VI had done something to increase Capetian prestige, but in power and personal possessions he still remained feeble compared with his great vassals. On the other hand, the French King's position at the summit of the feudal hierarchy meant that the rulers of fiefs like Anjou, Normandy and Champagne could not menace a territory under his protection without calling into question the right by which they themselves maintained their authority. So there was sound practical sense behind Duke Guillaume X's dying instructions that Eleanor should be committed to the care of Louis VI, that the King should be responsible for finding her a husband, and that in the mean time he should enjoy the revenues of Aquitaine.

These dispositions, however, were also proffered as a bait. Guillaume would have known perfectly well that the French King might in any case have claimed rights over Eleanor as her feudal superior during her minority. Doubtless the dying Duke's real intention, in acknowledging this fact, was to persuade Louis to seize the occasion to marry Eleanor to his own son and heir, the Dauphin. Louis was not called 'Le Gros' for nothing; the probability was that he would not live much longer, and that, if Guillaume's plan worked out, Eleanor would soon be Queen of France.

And so it proved. The French King sent his heir post-haste down to Bordeaux. The Dauphin Louis travelled with a large escort of courtiers and knights, partly, of course, for reasons of prestige, but also because there was concern about the danger of being attacked in so unruly a province. In the event, apart from one minor scuffle, the cavalcade was required to devote itself to feasting rather than to fighting. The fifteen-year-old Eleanor and the sixteen-year-old Dauphin Louis were duly married at the church of St André in Bordeaux on 25 July 1137, after which they beat a hasty retreat northwards. Many lords of Aquitaine, fearing that their independence might be compromised by the marriage, had conspiciously absented themselves from the wedding, and Suger, Louis VI's faithful counsellor who had accompanied the expedition from Paris, feared a surprise attack. Not until Louis and Eleanor reached the castle of Taillebourg, some eighty miles north of Bordeaux, would they have been able to relax. Forty-two years later one of Eleanor's sons would cover himself with glory through his capture of this same castle. He would not, however, be a son of Louis.

In 1137 Eleanor can have had few forebodings, swept along as she was in such an exciting rush of events. In April of that year she had been a young princess of uncertain prospects; four months later she was Duchess of Aquitaine and married to the Dauphin; a few weeks more and, with the death of Louis VI, she became Queen of France. Her husband was handsome, virtuous, and by all accounts madly in love with his wife. As for Eleanor, she was still too young and inexperienced to draw any immediate dissatisfaction out of such a cornucopia of good fortune.

2

Perhaps it was Eleanor's life in Paris that set off the first stirrings of discontent. The reader must banish all images of the modern city with its associations of splendour, elegance and pleasure. In 1137 Paris was only just beginning to expand from the island in the middle of the Seine where the Romans had formerly established a walled citadel. The royal palace where Louis and Eleanor lived was at the west end, and the cathedral, precursor of the present Notre Dame, at the east end of the island. In between were countless other churches. Eleanor, who had been brought up in an atmosphere of robust indifference to the Church and its anathemas, would have found herself surrounded by ecclesiastics. On the north bank of the Seine, it is true, a commercial city was burgeoning: in fact in the very year that Eleanor arrived the market moved there, to a site where it would flourish for eight hundred years before giving way to the Pompidou Centre. But if Eleanor let her eye drift to the west of the market, she would have seen nothing but a desolate marshland where no effective drainage was undertaken before 1150. The contrast with her native Bordeaux cannot have been favourable. On the south side of the Seine little patches of building clustered around the abbeys of St Victor, Ste Geneviève and St Germain des Prés; and out of the schools attached to these foundations the future university of Paris was beginning to develop. It is customary to refer to the atmosphere of intellectual excitement that prevailed, for this was the time when Pierre Abélard was shocking the orthodox with his exaltation of reason at the expense of blind faith. Nothing that we know of Eleanor, however, suggests that she would have cared a straw for theological contention, or for that peculiar brand of terminological hair-splitting in which medieval philosophers delighted.

Paris was her husband's world. Louis went back to his clerical tutors with a will. It was remarked how he hated to claim any precedence over the monks. He had originally been intended for the Church before the sudden death of his elder brother unexpectedly propelled him into a role to which he was less well suited. In many ways a sympathetic figure, he remained a tangle of scruple and conscience. 'He was a man of kindliness and simple mildness,' the Welshman Walter Map recalled after Louis's death, 'and showed himself so affable to any poor man . . . that he might have been reckoned an imbecile.' On the other hand, 'he was the strictest of judges, though often with tears, stiff to the proud and ever fair to the meek'. It was characteristic of Louis that when on one occasion he discovered that he had ordered a house to be built on a poor man's land he immediately commanded its demolition.

Such transparent goodness and humility may or may not have impressed the granddaughter of Guillaume IX. Louis's naivety could appear almost wilful. There is a story from later in his life of a great lord finding him asleep in a wood guarded by only two knights. When the interloper remonstrated with the King for exposing himself to danger in this way Louis was unperturbed. 'I sleep alone, perfectly safe,' he said, 'because nobody bears me a grudge.' Such innocence might be interpreted as evidence of a natural goodness of heart, or it might just seem plain exasperating. Louis, in fact, was far from simple-minded, but he did lack force and effectiveness. To a woman of courage, energy and power his fervent piety might easily appear as drivelling religiosity. Even Louis's adoration of herself may have struck Eleanor as irritating rather than flattering. John of Salisbury, who saw the King and Queen together after twelve years of their marriage, remarked on the almost puerile quality of Louis's passion.

Nevertheless, a slavishly devoted husband does present opportunities to a strong-minded wife, not least when he is King of France. Moreover Eleanor remained Duchess of Aquitaine in her own right. The hope, of course, was that she and Louis would have a son under whose rule France and Aquitaine would eventually be united, but this prospect did not materialise. There was an early miscarriage, but thereafter year succeeded year without any further pregnancy.

Eleanor was left with time on her hands, and she was never the type to shine in the role of demure and submissive helpmeet. Her influence on her husband is difficult to prove but easy to deduce, for Louis VII's actions in the first few years of his reign manifest a ruthless aggression quite out of character with the rest of his career.

The first straw in the wind was the sudden departure from court of Louis's mother, Adelaide of Savoy, in the autumn of 1137. Perhaps this development had more to do with the failure of the Queen Mother's intrigues against the Abbé Suger than with any plotting by her daughter-in-law. Nevertheless, the absence of the Queen Mother can only have increased the power of the Queen. Soon afterwards, when the barons of Poitou rose in revolt, Louis reacted with quite unwonted fury. The rebellion was crushed and the miscreants treated with the utmost harshness: according to one account Louis even hacked off the hands of captured rebels with his own sword. The Abbé Suger found himself obliged to rush from Paris to mitigate the ferocity of his formerly docile charge. In general Suger had pursued a peaceful policy towards the King's feudal dependants. Provided they did formal homage to Louis, the Abbé was rarely inclined to meddle any further in their affairs. Now, though, it seemed that Louis was bent upon a more active and ambitious course. Suger did not like the change. In 1140 he laid down his charge and retired to his abbey at St Denis.

Next year Louis led an expedition against Toulouse, an attack which appeared to have more to do with the traditional preoccupations of the Dukes of Aquitaine in that area than with any conceivable interest of the Capetians. Soon afterwards Louis, quite extraordinarily given his clerical background, became involved in a bitter clash with the Church as a result of having appropriated revenues from vacant bishoprics. It was precisely thus that Eleanor's father and grandfather had earnt themselves clerical anathemas. The dispute intensified later in 1141, when the see of Bourges became vacant. Louis pressed the claims of one Cadurc, who had replaced Suger as Chief Minister, whereas the canons of Bourges elected a Cluniac monk called Pierre de la Châtre, and appealed to Rome when the King refused to recognise their choice. The Pope supported the canons, declaring that Cadurc was altogether unworthy of ecclesiastical office, and adding for good measure that the King of France was 'behaving like a foolish schoolboy'. That was too much for Louis, who swore a mighty oath on the appropriate relics to the effect that Pierre de la Châtre should never be installed in Bourges. Pierre, meanwhile, had taken refuge with Thibault Count of Champagne, brother of King Stephen of England and a powerful feudatory whom Suger had always been especially careful to conciliate. Thibault had formerly been a friend of Louis's, had indeed accompanied him on his journey down to Bordeaux to marry Eleanor. Since that time, however, the King appeared to have changed utterly.

Before long the Count of Champagne had further, more deadly, cause to reflect upon the new domineering attitude of the Capetian court. The trouble originated, like so many of the world's ills, with a broken marriage. Thibault's niece was the wife of a lord called Raoul de Vermandois, who had risen high in favour at the royal court in Paris after the retirement of Suger. It rather looks as though he may have owed his elevation to the Queen, for he suddenly announced his intention of casting off Thibault's niece in order to marry Eleanor's sister Petronilla. There was no difficulty about drumming up a few friendly bishops to annul his first marriage on grounds of consanguinity. The rejected wife, however, inconsiderately refused to accept this ecclesiastical verdict. Instead, she fled to her uncle Thibault who appealed to the Pope against the decision, using the formidable Bernard of Clairvaux as his advocate. The response from Rome was gratifying. Raoul's first marriage was declared to be valid; the errant bishops were suspended; and Raoul was excommunicated.

Louis, or Eleanor, reacted savagely, determining upon a retributory invasion of Champagne. The ensuing war was conducted with the utmost brutality. Thibault's subjects were obliged to flee as his lands were mercilessly devastated. In one particularly horrifying incident at Vitry (known to this day as Vitry-le-Brûlé) some 1,500 people, including women and children, were burnt alive in a church that had been set on fire by Louis's command. The atrocities brought down Bernard of Clairvaux's thunder on the King's head. 'From whom but the devil', he wrote to Louis, 'could come the advice under which you are acting, advice which causes burnings upon burnings, and slaughter upon slaughter?'

In fact Bernard probably had a very shrewd idea about who was counselling Louis. He had long known the house of Aquitaine and judged its fruit to be rotten; and he was never a man disposed to give the benefit of the doubt to the female of the species. While pondering on Louis's moral deterioration he was struck by an argument that had momentous implications for Eleanor's future. 'I ask you,' he wrote to a Cistercian friend, 'how has he [Louis] got the effrontery to try so hard to lay down laws for others about consanguinity when it is clear that he himself is living with his cousin in the third degree.' Actually Louis and Eleanor were related in the fourth degree, but the error was not so important as the fact that the most renowned ecclesiastical figure in Europe, already widely acknowledged to be a saint, was casting aspersions upon the validity of the King's marriage. Evidently the matter was under discussion in France at this time, for the Bishop of Laon was busily researching the precise degrees of propinquity between the King and the Queen.

Such an investigation may have stirred Louis's religious scruples. The possibility that his marriage was unpleasing to God would explain why the first few years of his reign had been so disastrous. His nature had been wrenched out of its natural groove: the prospective monk found himself ruling like a bloodthirsty tyrant. Bernard of Clairvaux did not hesitate to tell him that he had been following the counsels of the Devil. If his marriage was invalid, was it not all too likely that the Devil had assumed the form of the woman whom he loved?

That Bernard held Eleanor responsible for Louis's transformation from obedient son of the Church to vengeful warrior is clear from the account of his meeting with the Queen on 11 June 1144, at the consecration of the new choir which Suger had built at St Denis. It was Eleanor, not a whit cowed by Bernard's reputation as the unbending champion of the Church, who sought the encounter. Perhaps she was eager to measure her personality against the man who had so dramatically overawed her father. Perhaps she was pushed forward by Louis. Most likely, though, she was genuinely worried by the matter which she broached, her continuing failure to produce an heir. According to one chronicler she was by this time in despair of having children; and after seven years of barren marriage any expedient would have seemed worth a try. The confrontation between the beautiful young Queen, who lived most decidedly for this world, and the fierce ascetic ready to suspect her of every evil, cries out for detailed description, but unfortunately we know only of Bernard's admonitions. The saint would not grant the favour of his intercession with the Almighty in the matter of an heir without insisting that Eleanor should use her influence beneficently in affairs of state. 'Strive for peace within the kingdom,' he told her, 'and I promise you that God in His infinite mercy will grant you what you request.'

Louis, at least, appreciated the wisdom of taking Bernard seriously. Notwithstanding his oath to the contrary, he agreed that Pierre de la Châtre should be installed as Archbishop of Bourges, thus opening the way to reconciliation with both Thibault and Rome. The Pope withdrew his anathemas, though he still refused to recognise the marriage of Petronilla and Raoul de Vermandois, who remained adulterers in the eye of the Church until the convenient death of Raoul's first wife. Thus the peace settlement represented the complete failure of the policies which Louis had pursued to such extremes. On the credit side, though, Eleanor *did* give birth to a child in 1145. It was a daughter, but no doubt she had omitted to compound with Bernard on the point of the infant's sex. One day this girl, Marie, would marry the son of Thibault, on whom her parents had vented so much spleen. Meanwhile, her birth did nothing to allay Bernard's efforts to improve Eleanor. 'Put an end to your meddling with affairs of state,' he commanded her.

Whether or not Eleanor continued to meddle, she was at least soon removed from the affairs of France. Suddenly from the east came an opportunity for Louis to redeem himself for all his failings as a Christian king. In December 1144 the Turks captured Edessa, at the north-eastern limit of the Latin estates in the Holy Land. This coup left Antioch, and ultimately Jerusalem itself, under threat. Louis VII was the first to answer the call for help. Perhaps significantly it was at Bourges, where Pierre de la Châtre was now installed as Archbishop, that the French King chose to announce his intention of leading an army to the Holy Land. This royal example did not immediately kindle much enthusiasm, and only when Bernard of Clairvaux brought his burning moral fervour to bear in a sermon at Vézelay (Easter 1146) did the crusade begin to inspire Louis's subjects. Another year and more passed in making preparations before the heterogeneous band of soldiers and pilgrims assembled at St Denis for the ceremony of departure on 8 June 1147.

Curiously, as some thought, Eleanor was to accompany her husband; and many other women, by no means all wives, followed her example. Later, after the crusade had proved a fiasco, ecclesiastical chroniclers discovered that the presence of women on such a sacred mission was an outrage that really left the Almighty with little choice but to chastise his followers with disasters. 'Camps are called "castra" from the castration of impurity,' explained William of Newburgh with more than doubtful etymology, 'but our camps are not chaste, for there the lusts of many were raging through ill-starred licentiousness.' Yet women had accompanied the first crusade without imperilling the success of the enterprise. And William of Newburgh himself, in accounting for Eleanor's presence, suggests that Louis was inspired by the best of matrimonial motives. 'The Queen had, at first, completely bewitched the young man's affections by her beauty. On the eve of setting out for that famous crusade he felt himself so strongly attached to his youthful wife that he resolved not to leave her behind but to take her with him to the Holy War.' A less charitable explanation might be that Louis was terrified by what she would get up to in his absence. Clearly, if he held her responsible for the disasters of his reign, he would not care to leave her to her own devices in France. Rather, the Abbé Suger was brought out of retirement and put in charge of the kingdom, a restitution that in itself demonstrated Louis's dissatisfaction with the previous drift of policy.

Eleanor, however, was evidently not a passive victim of Louis's decision that she should accompany him on the crusade. Far from moping at the prospect of leaving behind her infant daughter, she eagerly plunged into the business of raising men and supplies. Various deeds and charters witness to her having made several grants to monasteries at this time, presumably in return for ready cash. Among them was an assignment of fifty shillings a year to Fontevrault, the first record of her interest in the abbey with which she would become closely associated in later life. Apparently her efforts to recruit for the crusade were successful, for the barons of her native land of Poitou and Gascony were especially well represented among those who took the cross. That was just as well, as their presence on the crusade was also the best guarantee that Aquitaine would be peaceful while its Duchess was away.

Eleanor would have been excited by the prospect of an adventure after so many dreary years in the Ile de France. As a child she must have heard many a tale of her grandfather's crusading experiences, and her enthusiasm would have been heightened by the fact that her uncle, Guillaume IX's son Raymond, was now King of Antioch. Raymond was only eight years her senior, and might have kept her out of the succession to Aquitaine had he not decided at an early age to seek his fortune in the east. Perhaps he had been a hero of Eleanor's childhood: at all events he had made sure that he was not forgotten in France by sending rich presents from Antioch to the court in Paris. This family connection of Eleanor's conceivably had some influence on the choice of route which the crusaders took. King Roger of Sicily had professed himself willing to transport Louis's army to the Holy Land in his own ships and at his own cost, but this offer, which would have saved immense hardships, was refused. It was believed that Roger had designs on Antioch, and his alliance would have involved a tacit rejection of Raymond.

A crusade is an irresistible subject for romantics, and biographers of Eleanor have avidly seized on every scrap that might present her in a heroine's role. In particular they have gleaned the following passage from Nicetus Acominatus, the Byzantine historian:

> There were in the army women dressed as men, mounted on horses and armed with lance and battle-axe. They kept a martial mien, bold as Amazons. At the head of these was one in particular, richly dressed, that went by the name of the 'lady of the golden boot'. The elegance of her bearing and the freedom of her movements recalled the celebrated leader of the Amazons.

Nicetus was only born around 1150, so this passage, which reads like legend and which in any case makes no specific mention of Eleanor, was written many years after the event.

The truth is that, with the exception of the notorious incident at Antioch (of which more in a moment), very little is known about Eleanor on crusade. Perhaps there was not much of interest to report.

Eleanor doubtless enjoyed the constant stimulation of new sights and new places on the four-month overland hike to Constantinople, for ever afterwards she showed a remarkable readiness to travel. Yet the discomforts must frequently have been severe. Apart from the hazards of climate, food was scarce because the Emperor Conrad, also on the crusade, had led his army on the same route as the French only a short time before. And it is a commonplace that travelling under trying conditions hardly conduces to matrimonial harmony. Nevertheless, Louis and Eleanor reached Constantinople on 11 October 1147 without any discord vitriolic enough to have reached the ears of the chroniclers.

The wealth and glory of Byzantium, replete with every luxury and refinement, must have made Paris seem dim and provincial in comparison. Eleanor met the Emperor Manuel Commenus, a man whose striking good looks, effortless accomplishment and easy social grace did not entirely mask the hint of corruption within. The majesty of the Emperor, and the fulsome reverence with which he was treated, offered Eleanor a new vision of power; and no doubt the granddaughter of Guillaume IX responded eagerly to the seductions of a court far too sophisticated to trouble itself with conventional morality. But there was hardly time for such impressions to take root: within three weeks the crusaders were moving on. Their route originally lay due east, until a messenger arrived with the news that Conrad's preceding army had been cut to pieces on that road. Louis ordered a change of direction, skirting the western coastline of modern Turkey and cutting south through the mountains to Pergamum, Smyrna and Ephesus, thence eastwards to the port of Adalia on the southern coast. From there the odyssey was to continue by sea.

On Christmas Eve 1147 a sudden and fierce storm turned the river by which the army was camped into a flood that carried away tents, stores and equipment. On 6 January, as they neared their destination of Adalia, the French columns became so stretched out in the mountainous terrain that the vanguard lost touch with the rearguard. The Turks, who had been lurking in the surrounding hills, attacked and inflicted heavy casualties. Louis only narrowly escaped with his life; how close Eleanor was to the action history does not record. In the end the journey from Constantinople to

Adalia took as long as that from Paris to Constantinople, and
even then the crusaders discovered that there were not enough
ships available to carry everyone to the Holy Land. A group had
to be left behind, and was duly massacred by the Turks. All told,
the journey can have done little to enhance Eleanor's respect for
her husband. Events would show that by the time the royal couple
reached Antioch the iron had entered deep into her soul.

Eleanor spent just eleven days in Antioch, but they were long
enough to ruin her reputation for centuries. The charge is that she
conducted a passionate affair with her uncle Raymond of Antioch
under the very nose of Louis VII. The accusation, however, appears
far from proven, even though there are two excellent accounts of what
occurred in Antioch, by John of Salisbury and William of Tyr. Both
were well informed chroniclers, alive at the time, albeit they wrote
about the drama respectively twenty and forty years after the event.
Eleanor emerges for once out of 'the dark backward and abysm of
time' into the full glare of history – and still she remains elusive.

At least it is certain that Louis and Eleanor had the most almighty
row at Antioch. Raymond gave the crusaders a hearty welcome,
plying them with choice and expensive presents. There was, however,
an ulterior motive behind his generosity. He wanted Louis to help him
ward off the Turkish threat to Antioch by making a surprise attack
on Edessa, the fall of which had, after all, originally sparked off the
crusade. Perhaps he also hoped to take Aleppo, the main centre of
Muslim power in the region. But to Raymond's consternation Louis
would have no truck with such plans. He had made his vow, he said,
to go to the Holy Sepulchre in Jerusalem, and only after that vow
had been fulfilled would he listen to Raymond's ideas. Eleanor, on
the other hand, was clear that they had not brought an army over
three thousand miles from Paris just to pay pilgrim visits to the Holy
Places. She sided with Raymond, who did not hesitate to exploit her
sympathy against Louis.

'When Raymond saw that he was getting nowhere,' William of
Tyr reported, 'he began to pour scorn on the King's plans and
openly to plot his downfall. He attempted in fact, whether by
force or by dark intrigue, to carry off the King's wife, and she,
being one of those fatuous females [*una ex mulieribus fatuis*] was
quite agreeable to this design.' William of Tyr plainly had it in for

Eleanor. 'Both before and after this episode she showed herself to be a light-minded woman who in despite of her royal dignity conducted herself as though heedless of matrimonial law and forgetful of the connubial bed.' That is an aspersion rather than a definite charge. William of Tyr appears as a misogynist eager to blacken a woman who, at the time when he was writing (c.1180), had entirely fallen from grace.

John of Salisbury, who saw Louis and Eleanor together within fifteen months of the Antioch drama, adopted a more measured tone. Omitting any reference to Raymond's political motives, he concentrated solely on the Prince of Antioch's relations with his niece.

> The attentions paid by the prince to the queen, and his constant, indeed almost continual conversation with her, aroused the king's suspicions. These were greatly strengthened when the queen wished to remain behind, although the king was preparing to leave, and the prince made every effort to keep her if the king would give his consent. When the king made haste to tear her away, she mentioned their kinship, saying it was not lawful for them to remain together as man and wife, since they were related in the fourth and fifth degrees.

Here was an ingenious ploy of Eleanor's, to turn the whispers which had been made in France against the validity of the marriage to her own advantage in Antioch. But was her riposte actually anything more than a spontaneous flare of anger in the midst of matrimonial combat? As far as one can tell at a distance of eight centuries, it seems unlikely that she really had an affair with Raymond, or that she seriously envisaged staying with him in Antioch. What on earth would she have done there? If, after months of travelling with a husband for whom she felt no affinity, she rejoiced to see her uncle, that was only natural. Raymond was Louis's opposite in every way, a glamorous swashbuckling figure of whom his father, Guillaume IX, would surely have been proud. He was handsome, strong and courageous, ever prepared to put his life to the hazard, ever prepared also to take his pleasure in between these buffets with fortune. Cut off as he was from the world into which he had been born, it was obviously a delight, and surely an innocent delight, to meet the formidable adult version of the little girl whom he had known in Bordeaux. On the other hand, Louis's withdrawn, diffident nature, poles apart from Raymond's bluff uncomplicated charm, would have been galled to watch his wife blossom under her uncle's regard. To make matters worse she was even siding with Raymond over matters of military policy, as if women could possibly comprehend anything of such matters.

So there was reason enough for Louis's jealousy without having to postulate adultery on Eleanor's part. Raymond was a well known womaniser, it is true, but he combined this reputation with that of a chivalrous gentleman. His interpretation of honour would have been lax indeed if it had allowed him to seduce, or be seduced by, his own niece, however readily such lubricious notions invaded the minds of clerical chroniclers. Yet he may well have sown some disruptive ideas in Eleanor's mind. He too was a member of the ruling house of Aquitaine, and no one would have been better qualified to remind Eleanor that she was Duchess of that province in her own right. If she was unhappy with Louis she could always fall back upon her own hereditary titles and responsibilities.

No doubt it was this consideration that made Louis's advisers so alarmed by Eleanor's threat to leave the King. Let John of Salisbury take up the story again:

> Although he loved the queen almost beyond reason, he consented to divorce her if his counsellors and the French nobility would allow it. There was one knight among the king's secretaries, called Terricus Gualerancius, a eunuch whom the queen had always hated and mocked, but who was faithful and had the king's ear like his father's before him. He boldly persuaded the king not to suffer her to dally at Antioch, both because 'Guilt under friendship's guise could lie concealed' and also because it would be a lasting shame to the kingdom of the Franks if in addition to all the other disasters it was reported that the king had been deserted by his wife, or robbed of her. So he argued, either because he hated the queen or because he really believed it, moved perchance by widespread rumour. In consequence she was torn away and forced to leave for Jerusalem with the king; and, their mutual anger growing greater, the wound remained, hide it as best they might.

On that bleak note Eleanor disappears altogether from history for another year. During that period Louis engaged in an unsuccessful siege of the friendly Muslim town of Damascus, dreamt of future crusades, celebrated the Easter of 1149 in Jerusalem, and generally did nothing to promote the prestige of a Christian king, whether in the eyes of the Turk or of the Queen. Plainly he wrote to Suger about his matrimonial difficulties, for the minister sent him some cooling advice. 'If the Queen gives you offence,' the Abbé wrote from Paris, 'conceal your resentment as best you can until such time as you shall both have returned to your own estates, when this grievance and other matters may be attended to.' Suger does not specify any sexual impropriety on Eleanor's part; it was only much later that the wild legends began to proliferate. There would be tales that Eleanor had been the lover of Saladin (who was ten in 1148) and of one Gilbert de la Parrée (who was seventy). The proposition that Eleanor was, like so many wives in every age, at once faithful and discontented, made no appeal.

The unhappy couple set off home from the Holy Land, in separate ships, after Easter 1149, but the voyage only extended the chronicle of misfortune. Skirting the coast of the Peloponnese they fell in with a squadron of Roger II of Sicily who was now, after Louis's quarrel with Raymond of Antioch, accepted as a friend. While Louis had been in the Holy Land, Roger had become embroiled in a naval war against the Byzantine empire. It is not precisely clear what happened, but there was some kind of skirmish with the Emperor's fleet, in the course of which Eleanor's ship was captured. Louis perforce went on without her, landing somewhere on the heel of Italy (22 July 1149) without any idea of what had become of his wife. Luckily, at least for Eleanor, the Sicilians counter-attacked and managed to rescue her. 'After many peregrinations by sea and by land the Queen by the grace of God reached Palermo,' Louis reported to Suger, 'and hastened safely and joyfully to us.' It may be that Louis somewhat exaggerated Eleanor's delight at the reunion; on the journey to Rome she most uncharacteristically fell ill, and had to rest at the monastery of Monte Cassino. Romantic biographers like to imagine that her distress had been occasioned by the news of her uncle's death, for Raymond had been slain in battle at the end of June. It is also possible that she was pregnant.

At Tusculum, just south of Rome, Louis and Eleanor stayed with Pope Eugenius III, whom they had last seen at St Denis as they were setting out on the crusade. This meeting is the best-documented event in Eleanor's life, for John of Salisbury was present as a papal chaplain. Evidently the couple's marital troubles were broached, for the Pope laboured hard to resolve them:

> He reconciled the king and queen, after hearing severally the accounts each gave of the estrangement begun at Antioch, and forbade any future mention of their consanguinity: confirming their marriage, both orally and in writing, he commanded under pain of anathema that no word should be spoken against it, and that it should not be dissolved under any pretext whatever. This ruling plainly delighted the king, for he loved the queen passionately, in an almost childish way. The pope made them sleep in the same bed, which he had decked with priceless hangings of his own; and daily during their brief visit he strove by friendly converse to restore love between them.

Eugenius proved no less, but unfortunately also no more, successful than Bernard of Clairvaux in his attempts to procure an heir to the French throne. Eleanor gave birth 'shortly after' her return to Paris, but once more it was a girl. Possibly the child, who was called Alix, had been conceived before the meeting with the Pope: otherwise one is driven to the melancholy conclusion that Eleanor and Louis could only procreate under high ecclesiastical sanction.

It is easy enough to declare one's good intentions when in a mood of spiritual exaltation before the Vicar of Christ, rather harder to stick to them amidst the pettinesses and frustrations of everyday existence. One might guess that Eleanor had been further irritated by the role of injured and adoring husband that Louis had adopted before the Pope, and wonder whether his devotion was quite so evident when there was no one but the Queen to impress. Back in Paris Eleanor found no consolation whatever in the birth of her second daughter. 'Hell is a place of punishment,' wrote Walter Map later in the twelfth century, 'and the court is only milder than hell, in that those whom it torments are able to die.' At a mere twenty-eight Eleanor could hardly hope for such remission. But she was never one to mope: her unhappiness manifested itself in scathing contempt. The way Louis behaved, she declared, she thought she had married a monk not a king. Nor did it escape her attention that, as Duchess of Aquitaine, she was one of the very few medieval women in a position to do something about her plight.

3

Eleanor's hopes of escaping from Louis were enhanced by the death of Suger early in 1151. The Abbé had always counselled the King against casting away a wife whose vast dominions might one day come under direct Capetian control. Poor Louis, though, had to live with Eleanor, who doubtless discerned that her best chance of release lay in making herself as unpleasant as possible, and waiting upon events. As it happened opportunity almost immediately presented itself in the persons of Geoffrey Plantagenet, Count of Anjou, and his eighteen-year-old son Henry. The Plantagenets were very much the rising power. Geoffrey's marriage to Matilda, daughter of Henry I of England, had given him an interest in both Normandy and England. He had succeeded in establishing himself as Duke of Normandy before passing on that title to his son Henry in 1150. As for England, though the Plantagenet claim was temporarily in abeyance it was far from being abandoned. So when Geoffrey and Henry arrived in Paris for a peace conference in August 1151 Eleanor was at her most welcoming.

Father and son alike were of the handsome, virile, energetic and power-hungry type who contrasted so markedly with Louis and who always seemed to appeal to Eleanor. According to Walter Map, who knew Henry well in later life, Eleanor was 'secretly reported to have shared the bed of Louis with Geoffrey', who had been a fellow crusader. Another chronicler, Gerald of Wales, adds the titbit that Geoffrey, whether or not as a result of this experience, warned his son never to have anything to do with Eleanor. Probably such stories were yet further examples of the malicious gossip that attached to Eleanor; certainly, if Geoffrey ever gave such advice, Henry most signally failed to profit from it. There had once been talk of marrying Henry off to Eleanor's elder daughter Marie, but now he and his putative mother-in-law plotted their own alliance. Gerald of Wales reports a rumour that the Queen of France and the young Duke of Normandy became lovers at this first encounter in Paris, though opportunities for anything beyond flirtation must have been limited at the peace conference. The real point was that they came to a firm political understanding.

At the start of the conference Geoffrey had been in an ugly mood, treating Bernard of Clairvaux, who was once more acting as peacemaker, with such contempt that the saint felt bound to prophesy the imminent demise of his tormentor. For some reason, though, Geoffrey suddenly changed tack and became conciliatory. Could this change of heart have been caused by the knowledge that Aquitaine might shortly be added to the rapidly expanding Plantagenet lands? Geoffrey's good humour, whatever its cause, was short-lived. In September news reached Paris that he had died of a fever on the way home. St Bernard's anathemas had once more proved their power. Nearer to Eleanor's heart, Henry was now Count of Anjou as well as Duke of Normandy. With the English throne also a possibility, an intoxicating prospect opened out before Eleanor. If she married Henry their joint domains would cover the whole western side of France, and eventually their rule might stretch from the Pyrenees to the Scottish border.

Around this time Louis, still quite ignorant of Eleanor's plans, decided that he no longer cared to prolong his marriage. Possibly Eleanor had helped him to this conclusion with concentrated doses of matrimonial venom. The King's advisers and relations unanimously recommended that he should repudiate the Queen. The Menestrel of Rheims, though admittedly writing a hundred years after the event, reports the counsel given to Louis with gusto. 'The best advice we can give you is to let her go, for she is a devil, and if you keep her any longer she will be the death of you. What is more, you have no heir.' The lack of a son, indeed, might easily be taken as a sign that the marriage was unpleasing in the sight of God. A manuscript note found in a monastery at Auchin states that the King put away his wife on the advice of St Bernard. Some such high authority, one might think, would have been required to convince Louis of the nullity of a marriage which the Pope himself had but two years previously expressly declared valid, 'both orally and in writing'.

Then, as now, the Church had ways and means of getting round such details. By the end of 1151 all was set for an annulment. Louis and Eleanor visited Aquitaine, and French officials in the duchy were replaced by those owing loyalty to Eleanor alone. Then at Beauregency near Blois a council of French bishops, including that same Archbishop of Bordeaux who had married Louis and Eleanor fifteen years before, formally declared the marriage void on grounds of consanguinity. Eleanor's great-grandmother, it transpired, had been a granddaughter of Louis's great-grandfather. The trumped-up nature of the proceedings was obvious enough; nevertheless, to Eleanor the decision must have come as a glorious relief. At last she was free: of her tedious husband, of the censorious French court, of the oppressive ecclesiastical atmosphere of Paris. She was also free, it should be added, of her two daughters, but if that was a cross she bore it with fortitude.

Her sense of release would have been heightened by the reflection that her liberty had been achieved against formidable odds, entirely through her own policy and tenacity. Not for nothing did Gervase of Canterbury call Eleanor 'an exceedingly shrewd woman sprung from noble stock, but fickle'. The reward of her fickleness would be a husband who appeared infinitely better suited to her, and who brought with him the prospect of an assemblage of territories that mocked Capetian pretensions to rule in France. Eleanor, in short, had put herself in the highly dangerous positon of having attained exactly what she most desired. Out of her ambitions and out of her success centuries of Anglo-French conflict would be bred. What might have concerned Eleanor rather more, had she but known it, was that she had also sown the seeds of ruin in her own life.

Louis let her go without inflicting any conditions, careless of the fact that his abhorred queen was still, to the uninitiated, as alluring a matrimonial bait as she had been fifteen years before. Even on the road to Poitiers, immediately after leaving Louis, Eleanor was obliged to escape the unwanted attentions of two suitors. Henry Plantagenet's younger brother Geoffrey, who was already beginning to worry, with some reason, about how much of the family property Henry would leave for him, attempted to seize her forcibly and had to be beaten off by her escort. Then word came that Thibault of Blois, second son of that Thibault against whom Louis had waged war in 1143, was also lying in wait for her. This attempt was easily frustrated by a change of route, but Eleanor must have been made aware that life could be dangerous for a woman with no husband and one huge duchy.

Certainly she showed no desire to prolong her second spinsterhood, and no coyness in her approach to Henry. A messenger went out from Poitiers to the young Duke of Normandy, informing him that she was now free, and pressing him to marry her. Gervase of Canterbury was a commentator who suffered from few illusions regarding Henry's motives. 'The Duke, seduced by the nobility of this woman, and above all driven by a lust to possess the titles which attached to her, straightway took some companions with him, followed the shortest route, and in a very short time achieved the marriage that he had, already before, greatly desired.' The wedding, which took place on 18 May 1152, was not celebrated with any particular splendour lest the preparations should have warned potential enemies of what was afoot. Whoever conducted the ceremony did not trouble to point out that Eleanor's second marriage offended against the laws of consanguinity to the same degree as her first.

The news of the marriage was received with consternation in Paris. Louis, we are told, suffered greatly, as well he might have done. Apart from his personal feelings in the matter, as King he was bound to oppose the development of a rival power in western France. Louis continued to call himself the Duke of Aquitaine, but that was a meaningless gesture. He meant to make his point more forcibly. Within a few weeks he had put together a formidable coalition against Henry and Eleanor. There was King Stephen of England, his son Eustace, Henry's brother Geoffrey Plantagenet, still worrying about his inheritance, and Henry of Champagne, who hoped to gain Aquitaine through his marriage to Eleanor's daughter Alix. The aim of this group was to destroy Henry and divide up his lands amongst themselves; and as they marched into Normandy few would have betted against their chances of success. No one, perhaps not even Eleanor, yet understood that Henry was the most effective and dynamic prince of his age. Not Louis, nor Geoffrey, nor King Stephen, nor all three together, were remotely a match for him.

Under threat, Henry struck with such lightning rapidity that he left several horses dead on the road from exhaustion. After feinting a move towards Paris he suddenly switched his attack on to his brother Geoffrey, who speedily surrendered. Then, with calculated coolness, he abandoned his continental possessions and crossed the Channel to pursue his claims to the English crown. His luck held on every front. Louis fell ill with a fever and had to retire back to Paris, while in England Eustace, his rival for the succession, suddenly died from a surfeit of eels. King Stephen, a broken man, openly acknowledged Henry as his successor and obligingly died in the following year (1154). That December Eleanor crossed a stormy Channel with her triumphant husband, and the two of them were crowned King and Queen of England in Westminster Abbey.

At this point French historians invariably break off to indulge in descriptions of the fog, rain and cold of England, their prose weighing heavily with the implication that the climate of the northern isle struck a chill into Eleanor's warm and passionate southern soul. They could well be correct: evidently she had never felt much enthusiasm for the northerly clime of Paris. The important question of climate aside, however, it is likely that Eleanor would have regarded England as an essentially peripheral interest. English historical atlases often show the Angevin empire coloured in red, as though it represented some early attempt at English colonisation. The truth was quite the opposite. Henry and Eleanor were French princes who happened to have acquired a kingdom to the north of the Channel. England was valuable to them because it conferred the prestige of a crown, with revenues to match. For that reason Henry sought to govern it as efficiently as possible, and since he was an administrative genius his reforms have received copious attention from English historians. The success of his efforts, however, only meant that England was the more tightly incorporated into a political system that had its heart in Normandy and Anjou.

During a reign of thirty-four years and eight months Henry spent just over a third of his time in England, Wales and Ireland; and Eleanor, though she was occasionally required to stand in for her husband, was only in England for a total of about six years during the first nineteen of the reign. During this time she made three long visits, between December 1154 and June 1156, between March 1157 and November 1158, and between January 1163 and March 1165. She was also in England from January to September 1160 and in October 1167, but from the latter date to July 1174 no record has survived to indicate that she came at all. By that period she was no longer minded to do her husband's business.

If Eleanor had imagined when marrying a nineteen-year-old (she was thirty) that she might be able to bend him to her will, or at least share in the work of government, she soon discovered that she had been most profoundly mistaken. Henry was the sort of man certain to attract women and no less certain to make them unhappy. His very frame radiated power. Sandy-haired like all the Plantagenets, slightly above medium height, immensely strong, with a bull-like neck and ruddy countenance, he could not strictly have been called handsome. Yet all eyes were drawn to him. So natural was his authority that he could afford to disdain the outward trappings of kingship. He had no time for ceremony, cared not a whit for what he wore, and undermined attempts at courtly grace with his caustic wit.

On good days this lack of side made him approachable and beneficent: an especially attractive facet of his character was his generosity to servants. But should his will be crossed, or should he suspect his confidence betrayed, his rages could be terrible. On one occasion he is reported to have flung off his clothes in an extremity of fury and writhed around on the floor chewing the straw. For all that, and though he pursued his aims with a ruthlessness quite unrestrained by any spiritual consideration, he never glamorised violence. Nor was he in any sense a philistine. He spoke Latin fluently and understood nearly all Western European languages. 'With the king of England,' wrote Peter of Blois, 'it is school every day, constant conversation with the best scholars and discussion of intellectual problems.' Both physically and mentally Henry's salient characteristic was energy. To keep his vast domains in order he had to be continually on the move, and it was said that he could travel four or five times further than the next man without stopping. Even when business did not compel him to travel he still spent much of his time in the saddle, for he had a passion for hunting. When he did finally dismount he would pace about ceaselessly, never sitting down except to eat.

A woman might as well seek to contain a whirlwind as to dominate such a man. Henry rarely shared his deepest thoughts with anyone, and he certainly did not look for advice from his wife on affairs of state. In his mind Eleanor had served her political purpose when she brought him her lands; for the rest, although he might require her to represent his authority when he was away, he treated her simply as a child-bearing machine. In the 1150s she was almost always pregnant. Already in August 1153 she had given birth to a son, an event which must have caused some grinding of the teeth in Paris. This little prince, called William, died three years later, but by that time the succession had been secured by the birth of another son, Henry, in March 1155. Three more children, Matilda, Richard and Geoffrey, followed in the next three years. Eleanor never had reason to complain that her second husband was a monk; indeed she probably realised early on that she had cause for concern on quite the opposite score. Walter Map records that an illegitimate son, another Geoffrey, had been born 'at the beginning of his reign', the mother being 'a common wanton who shrank from no impurity'. In fact, this child may have been born before Henry's marriage to Eleanor. The Queen, though, could never have been in any doubt about her husband's proclivities.

The 1150s were a decade when all Henry's political activities were crowned with success. He consolidated his hold in every part of his dominions, acquired Brittany, and left his titular overlord Louis VII apparently helpless before the relentless encroachment of his power. The French King had remarried in 1154, but this second match again brought forth only two daughters. Henry did not miss the opportunity thus presented: by a marriage treaty in 1158 his son Henry, aged three, was betrothed to Louis's infant daughter Margaret. There now seemed every chance that Eleanor's descendants would occupy the throne that she had relinquished, and that the whole of Western Europe might be combined under a joint Angevin-Capetian dynasty. After the treaty was signed Louis showed his acceptance of the entente by accompanying Henry on a progress through Normandy and Brittany. He was even heard to declare that there was nobody whom he esteemed so highly as the King of England, a remark which caused a monastic chronicler to observe that wonders will never cease. One would like to know if the subject of Eleanor was taboo between the two monarchs. The thought of his ex-wife still seemed to lie heavy on Louis's mind, for even at this low point in his fortunes there was one humiliation that he would not swallow. When, as was customary in the case of infant betrothals, he handed over his infant daughter Margaret to be educated by Henry, he insisted that the girl should not be placed under Eleanor's care.

Yet Eleanor now appeared as a strangely diminished figure compared with the harpy that Louis had known. Whether or not she felt pride in Henry's achievements, she never participated in them. If Henry required female counsel he went to his mother – and there was no question of *this* Queen Mother, the Empress Matilda, meekly retiring from the scene on Eleanor's appearance. Matilda, in fact, lived on until 1167. Even when Eleanor found herself with neither husband nor mother-in-law at hand, as when she acted as Regent in England during 1160, her power was minimal. Henry's expertise was in setting up systems of government that ultimately depended on no one but himself, and he established a professional administration that ran in his absence independently of great lords and the Queen. Eleanor never had a chancellor or a secretariat of her own; her duty, when she acted as Regent, was simply to lend her nominal authority to the decisions of Henry's counsellors.

Moreover, notwithstanding her pregnancies, she was expected to move wherever her sovereign lord commanded. So, after the birth of Matilda in June 1156, she must needs post immediately to Normandy; then to Saumur in August and to Bordeaux at Christmas, after which, pregnant again, she returned to Normandy in February 1157. In 1158 she made a continuous progress through England, hardly interrupted by the birth of Geoffrey in September. In December, though, she was once more in Poitou, summoned by Henry in order that her authority as Duchess should be associated with the siege of Thouars which he was undertaking. Christmas was spent at Cherbourg before dashing down to Blaye, just north of Bordeaux, in January.

Of course Eleanor could not have imagined when she married Henry that her life would be static, and she was never shy of travel. All the same, it must have been hard to find herself permanently peripatetic at her husband's whim. Even in her native Aquitaine Eleanor counted for nothing beside her all-powerful lord. Whereas she treated her uncle Ralph de Faye as her deputy in the duchy, Henry preferred to run Aquitaine through Normans and Englishmen. It never occurred to him to worry that he might be giving his wife a common cause of dissatisfaction with the local barons.

Nevertheless, Eleanor would surely have been pleased when, in 1159, her tyrannical husband took up the old claim of her house to

Toulouse. Henry even followed the traditional Spanish policy of the Dukes of Aquitaine in forming an alliance with Raymond Berengar of Barcelona. Subsequently he gathered together a huge force, but the expedition against Toulouse turned out to be the first check in his hitherto uninterrupted run of success. Louis VII, who in 1144 had himself eagerly supported Eleanor's rights in the county, now rushed to the assistance of the Count of Toulouse. Henry, despite the overwhelming superiority of his forces, hesitated to make a direct attack on his feudal overlord. The campaign ended with nothing more to show for the huge expenditure than the capture of the neighbouring county of Quercy. In Eleanor's story the episode was important because it heralded a renewal of the conflict between her first and second husbands. This struggle would yield opportunities for getting even with Henry that she was unable to resist, though in the end her vendetta would bring nothing but ruin to her sons and affliction to herself.

In the 1160s, however, she was still bearing children, although now her pregnancies occurred at somewhat longer intervals. A daughter, another Eleanor, was born in September 1161; another girl, Jeanne, in September 1164. It is noticeable that Eleanor's fourth, fifth, sixth and seventh children by Henry were all born in September or October, that is, nine months after the Christmas holidays. It seems that by now her contacts with Henry were chiefly restricted to the great religious festivals. The couple's last child, John, was born nine months after Easter, on Christmas Eve 1167, when Eleanor was forty-five. In the mid-1160s the King and Queen did not always see each other even at Christmas. Evidently the eleven-year age gap between them was beginning to tell. As yet, though, there was no outward sign of disloyalty on Eleanor's part. She did not, for instance, try to exploit the King's difficulties with Thomas à Becket. Indeed, one of Becket's supporters wrote to the Archbishop warning him against Eleanor: 'You can hope for nothing from the Queen – she puts all her trust in Ralph de Faye, who attacks you as much as ever.' It was not to be expected that Eleanor, with her family background, would suddenly step forward as a champion of the Church, even to undermine her husband.

Yet the long periods of separation between husband and wife eventually produced the inevitable consequence. For the first decade of his married life Henry, if he had mistresses, at least contrived to manage them with discretion. Around 1166, however, he fell in love with a younger woman, Rosamund Clifford, and this was a passion which he made no effort to conceal. Legend has it that Eleanor reacted with fury, though the tradition that she murdered Rosamund, or at least compassed her death, is surely an offscouring of the Demon Queen mythology. That is not to suggest that she was indifferent to Henry's infidelity, or that she eschewed the satisfactions of a jealous and vindictive wife. Revenge to Eleanor, however, would surely have seemed both sweeter and more effective in the realm of power politics than in the conventional domestic domain. And as it happened the political situation was simultaneously developing in a manner that gave Eleanor the opportunity, for the first time since she had married Henry, to act independently.

4

In August 1165 Louis VII, by then married to his third wife, at last fathered a son, the future Philippe Auguste. The event was celebrated in Paris with great joy, though with hindsight it might be argued that Philippe's birth, by putting paid to the Plantagenet ambitions implicit in the betrothal of the young Henry to Louis's daughter Margaret, postponed the unification of France by several hundred years. Louis soon showed himself far more determined to protect his son's inheritance from the Plantagenets than he had ever been on his own behalf, whereas Henry II, his principal dynastic aim shattered, thought increasingly in terms of dividing his possessions among his children. In fact he had made provision as early as 1159 that Richard, then aged two, should inherit Aquitaine, a disposition that may explain the particular interest that Eleanor always took in this son. (By contrast John, the youngest child, was packed off to Fontevrault as soon as possible, and scarcely had any contact at all with his mother before the age of twenty.) Aquitaine, however, was always a special case, and an exceedingly troublesome one at that. In 1168 Henry, fed up with the fractious barons of the duchy, and perhaps anxious to keep the Queen out of England while he pursued his affair with Rosamund, decided for once to give Eleanor her head in governing her duchy. He took the precaution, however, of appointing the Earl of Salisbury as her military adviser.

The experiment got off to an ill-starred beginning. The Lusignans, a powerful Poitevin family who, like so many of their kind, resented any form of exterior control, set an ambush for Eleanor and Salisbury. In the ensuing skirmish Salisbury was killed, and Eleanor only managed to escape thanks to the courage and swordsmanship of the Earl's nephew, a young man who later achieved fame as William the Marshal. The episode proved the first important step in his career, for Eleanor, 'valiant and courteous lady that she was', not only paid his ransom but 'bestowed upon him horses, arms, gold and rich garments, and more than all opened her palace gates and fostered his ambition.' It appears that Henry was not alone in his susceptibility for the young of the opposite sex.

In 1169 Louis VII and Henry made a peace under which Henry finally carried out his intention of portioning out his territories among his children. Young Henry received his father's own inheritance of England, Normandy, Maine and Anjou; Richard, the duchy of Aquitaine; and Geoffrey, Brittany. All three boys then did homage to Louis as their overlord.

The apportionment was foolhardy, for Henry's and Eleanor's sons had already shown themselves to be unworthy of any trust. Henry, the eldest, was shallow, spoilt, dissipated and idle, the sort of youth who wins a reputation for generosity and charm by spending his father's money. To those who profited from his largesse he appeared as 'the beauty and flower of Christian princes'; to less partial observers he was 'as wax' in his inconstancy, 'a restless youth born for the undoing of many'. Richard, the next in age, was a sterner and more formidable character, who would become a great warrior. But his soul was steeped in cruelty. The image of crusading hero has survived, yet the gallant soldier was a man who could cold-bloodedly slaughter three thousand prisoners when faced with a victualling problem. Geoffrey, the third boy, was dismissed by one chronicler as 'a son of iniquity and perdition'. Another writer, Gerald of Wales, considered that he would have been 'one of the wisest of men, had he not been so ready to deceive others. His real nature had in it more of bitter aloes than of honey; outwardly he had a ready flow of words, smoother than oil . . . [but] he was a hypocrite, who could never be trusted

and who had a marvellous gift for pretence and dissimulation.' The
fourth son, as yet without an inheritance, was John, whose meanness
and viciousness have emerged unscathed from recent attempts at
rehabilitation. Whether the fault lay in breeding or nurture, Henry
and Eleanor had produced a quite exceptionally unpleasant quartet
of sons. Possibly the girls were less odious: little is known of them
beyond the fact that one discontented troubadour considered that
Matilda offered some compensation for having to attend the dreary
Plantagenet court in Normandy. Henry duly married his daughters
off as best he could, always outside the orbit of France: Matilda
to Henry of Saxony in 1168, Eleanor to Alfonso VIII of Castile in
1179, Jeanne to William II of Sicily in 1177.

It soon became clear that, in dividing lands among his sons, Henry
had no intention that his own powers should be diminished. In his
eyes the titles which he had conferred were purely nominal. As the
boys grew older they increasingly resented their status as puppets,
and we may be sure that Eleanor did nothing to extinguish their
mounting sense of grievance. In 1169, however, they were still too
young to be manipulated into open rebellion.

Besides, Eleanor had every reason to be content. During these
years Henry was much distracted by his quarrel with Becket, first
by the difficulties of dealing with the live Archbishop, then by the
consequences of having created the dead martyr. Eleanor was left
almost entirely to her own devices; indeed she may not have seen
Henry at all for two years after Christmas 1170. As for England, it
seemed that she had abandoned it for ever after a flying visit in the
autumn of 1167 to see off her daughter Matilda before her marriage
to Henry of Saxony. At last Eleanor enjoyed what perhaps she had
always wanted, a position of power in her own duchy. The record
shows that she proved a thoroughly competent ruler. For nearly five
years after her escape from the Lusignans, Aquitaine and Poitou were
relatively quiescent. No doubt the local lords were as glad as Eleanor
to be spared Henry's attentions, for they disliked his interference in
their affairs as much as she disliked his behaviour as a husband.
Eleanor, moreover, was naturally at home with the baronage of the
duchy: after all, on her mother's side she belonged to it. Nor did
she lose any authority when her son Richard was formally installed
as Duke of Aquitaine in 1172. The boy was only fourteen, and to

Eleanor he was always '*carissimus*', 'most dear one'. She would go on calling herself Duchess of Aquitaine and Countess of Poitou for the rest of her life.

According to the more enthusiastic of Eleanor's modern admirers, this period when she ruled independently was a time when her court became a magnet for the troubadour poets. The first objection to this theory is that she never had a court in the sense of a fixed institution. To govern Aquitaine and Poitou Eleanor must have been constantly on the move: in 1172, for example, we happen to know that she was in Bayonne and Limoges. The idea of a static court serving as a cultural centre just does not conform to the realities of medieval life. Nevertheless, recent writers, especially women, have been seduced by the notion of Eleanor surrounded by brilliant and admiring poets. Extraordinary determination and faith have been devoted to maintaining this vision. Should a word composed in either England or France during Eleanor's lifetime be deemed of merit, it is a fair bet that someone will have attempted to prove that it was written under her auspices.

This exercise is rendered comparatively easy because the troubadours invariably felt themselves bound to discretion about the identity of their loved one. Thus if Jaufre Rudel sighs for his '*amor de lonh* [distant love]' it is simple enough to postulate that he had Eleanor in mind. But literary historians have not stopped there. They have claimed that the Arthurian legend was further enriched through her interest and that the Tristan story became more widely known through her court; after all, '*la supposition n'a rien d'invraisemblable*'. This technique of the negative proposition is almost indefinitely extensible. '*On ne voit bien*', writes one French historian, '. . . *où Chrétien* [de Troyes] *avait composé . . . si ce n'est pas à cette cour d'Aliénor.*' Even when works have been totally lost historians still cannot resist speculating that Eleanor was responsible for them. Nor are the Queen's protagonists content to allot her a passive role in the twelfth-century literary renaissance. Fluent as Eleanor would undoubtedly have been in both the *langue d'oc* and the *langue d'oeil*, she has been regarded as the vital link between the cultures of north and south, the intermediary through whose influence the profane ideals of the Provençal poets were adapted into the more staid northern tradition of historical narrative. The result of this synthesis, the argument runs, was a new art form, the historical romance, wherein appears a new kind of hero, no longer just the successful tournament thug, but now the 'verray parfit gentil knight'.

If Eleanor achieved all that she certainly achieved a great deal. The awkward fact remains that there is precious little concrete evidence of her having any interest in literature at all. The technique of the negative proposition could equally well be applied the other way about: there is nothing demonstrably false in the hypothesis that Eleanor was indifferent to poetry. The literary connections of other contemporary monarchs can easily be established. Alfonso VII of Castile, Count Raymond V of Toulouse, Counts Raymond I and III of Provence and Alfonso VI of Aragon – all these rulers had fully attested associations with troubadours. Yet when historians try to link Eleanor with poets they are largely forced back on to supposition. It is not enough to say that her grandfather and father were devoted to literature, that her son Richard composed lyrics and that her daughters by Louis VII acted as patrons. If definite proof exists in the case of her ancestors and descendants, why is it not more abundant with Eleanor herself?

There are, indeed, indications that she was associated with the poet Bernart de Ventadorn during the 1150s. A short biography of Bernart tells us that 'he was a long time at her court, and fell in love with her and she with him', but this is a thirteenth-century text. In his works Bernart made only one definite reference to Eleanor, in which he inaccurately refers to her as *'la reina dels Normans'*. To Henry II, by contrast, he dedicated several poems. In the eagerness to put Eleanor at the centre of every literary movement it is often forgotten that her husband was renowned for his love of books. Bernart did, however, address poems to a mysterious 'Aziman' or 'loved one', and there have been literary sleuths determined to believe that Aziman and Eleanor were one and the same. This seems most unlikely, for two of the Aziman poems, expressing a decidedly carnal love, were dedicated to Henry II. Surely Bernart would hardly have presumed to beguile a friendly monarch with rhapsodic effusions of lust for the Queen.

The obvious deduction, unromantic though it may seem, is that Bernart had been entertained at court, and presented poems to his hosts in gratitude. The troubadour poets were grateful by profession:

they often came from the lesser gentry and looked to the court as a means of rising in the world. That was probably the reality behind the contacts between Eleanor and Bernart de Ventadorn.

The same kind of explanation would account for her relations with another poet, Benoît de Sainte-Maure, who inserted a panegyric of a

> *riche dame de riche rei*
> *senz mal, senz ire, senz tristece*

into the middle of his *Roman de Troie* (c. 1160–65). He can hardly have had anyone but Eleanor in mind, and no doubt with his reference to her

> *Beauté e chasteé ensemble*

he meant to defend the Queen from the rumours that were still circulating fifteen years after the episode at Antioch. Here at last, then, is a poem that may have been composed under Eleanor's patronage. Yet a poet looked for support wherever he could find it: the insertion of flattery into his work does not of itself suggest that the person flattered was interested in literature. Indeed, if the *riche dame* had been so inclined we may be sure that Benoît would have mentioned the fact.

The one work certainly dedicated to Eleanor is Wace's *Roman de Brut*, a verse reworking of Geoffrey of Monmouth's *Historia Regum Britanniae*. This dedication, however, could well have been made at Henry's request. Wace was very much the King's man, whose loyalty was eventually rewarded by a canonry at Bayeux. He wrote the *Roman de Brut* to celebrate Henry's assumption of the English throne, at a time when the King may yet have retained some interest in pleasing his wife. The dedication would have been an ideal way of associating Eleanor with the country of which, through his efforts, she had just become Queen.

Another fact used to demonstrate Eleanor's connection with literature is her appearance as a character in a book entitled *De Amore*. This was a treatise on the nature of love written by one Andreas Capellanus in the 1180s. The author owes much to Ovid and duly sets forth his somewhat cynical precepts for service in Cupid's wars.

In one section of the book various great ladies, Eleanor among them, give their opinions on such matters as whether the love of a younger or an older man is to be preferred, what presents may be received from a lover, or what should be done with a lover who breaks the vow of secrecy. (Answer to this last: he should be treated extremely rough.) Eleanor is credited with answers to three such questions, or six if she is also the person referred to anonymously as 'the Queen'. Her daughter Marie of Champagne plays a more important role in these debates, not surprisingly since Andreas was probably one of her chaplains. There have been scholars prepared to believe that these 'courts of love' actually took place, and that Andreas Capellanus was reporting an historical event. Yet, while no one would wish to push scepticism so far as to deny that well born women of the twelfth century gossiped about love, to maintain, with some academic heavyweights, that they advanced their opinions in formal tribunals is surely to strain the limits of credulity.

The interesting point about the concepts of love put forward in *De Amore* is that they completely reverse the values normally obtaining in the male-dominated feudal world. Men appear as the supplicants, forever sighing after the object of their desire; women stand forth as the arbiters of male destiny. It has been suggested, however, that Andreas's intentions were really satirical. He was close to the court of Paris as well as that of Champagne, and his book could well have been designed to amuse an audience familiar with the life histories of those concerned. Eleanor's answers seem to bear out this interpretation. Henry II's wife is supposed to have judged that a woman should prefer a worthy older man to a rascally younger one. Moreover, if she was intended to be recognised as 'the Queen', her opinion that love can never exert any power between husband and wife, and that consanguineous marriages are taboo, would also have carried ironic undertones.

That Eleanor herself had nothing to do with the contents of *De Amore* is further suggested by the only date cited therein, 1 May 1174. By that time Eleanor was far removed from any concern with gallantry. The last Christmas for many years at which she appeared as Duchess and Queen was that of 1172. She spent the festival with Henry at Chinon – their first recorded meeting for two years – and no doubt the King was satisfied to witness at first hand the effective way in which she had governed Aquitaine. How satisfied Eleanor felt with him is another matter, for Henry was beginning to assert himself in *her* duchy again. Apparently, though, she disguised her discontent. Then at Limoges in 1173 there occurred an event which, though in one sense it represented a triumph for Eleanor, in another underlined her husband's dominance. The satisfactory aspect was that Raymond of Toulouse did homage to Richard as Duke of Aquitaine, thus fulfilling the old ambition of Duke Guillaume IX to bring Toulouse under control. What would have pleased Eleanor and her barons rather less, however, was Henry's insistence that Raymond of Toulouse should also do homage to the young Henry. The idea that the Duke of Normandy and the King of England (as the young Henry had been designated) had anything to do with Toulouse would have been anathema to all who prized the independence of Aquitaine.

There was an odd occurrence at this Limoges meeting. Count Raymond took Henry aside and warned him that his family was plotting to depose him. Despite this, Henry gave no immediate indication that he mistrusted Eleanor. He allowed Richard and Geoffrey to return to their mother from Limoges, while he himself travelled north with young Henry. A few days later, however, he can have been under no illusion at all as to the peril in which he stood. Young Henry, furious that his brother John had been given castles in his territories, escaped from his father's charge and ran off to join Louis VII at Paris. Shortly afterwards Geoffrey and Richard also reached the French court, apparently sent there by their mother. The extraordinary truth was beginning to emerge. The Queen appeared to be working with her first husband to destroy the empire of her second.

Whether there was any direct communication between Eleanor and Louis, or whether they just instinctively knew each other's minds, is impossible to tell. What does seem clear is that someone – and who but Eleanor possessed the experience and ability? – had achieved the remarkable feat of organising simultaneous rebellion throughout the Angevin dominions, in Normandy, England, Touraine, Maine and Poitou. The very efficiency of Henry's government had everywhere antagonised local lords who found their power and revenues diminished with the inexorable rise of royal authority. Nowhere was this phenomenon so marked as in Eleanor's Poitou, where hatred of foreign rule had become venomous. A local lordling called Hugh de Chauvigny spoke for many when he exclaimed that he loathed all Englishmen. Henry's policy was to govern through servants who had no ties of birth with the province to which they were posted. For a few years, under Eleanor's administration, the menace of foreign domination seemed to have receded. But now that Henry had come through the crisis created by Becket's murder, the Poitevin lords must have dreaded a return to the more invasive government of the early 1160s. Ralph de Faye appears to have been a key figure. As Eleanor's uncle he was able to ensure that the selfish manoeuvring of dissident barons was orchestrated with the machinations of the Queen.

Henry faced utter ruin. The co-ordinated series of revolts caught him completely by surprise. For a while there was little he could do but get the Archbishop of Rouen to deliver a lengthy lecture to Eleanor.

> We all of us deplore [the bishop wrote] that you – a prudent wife, if ever there was one – should have parted from your husband . . . Still more terrible is the fact that you should have made the fruits of your union with our lord the King rise up against their father . . . We know that unless you return to your father you will be the cause of general ruin . . . Return then, O illustrious queen, to your husband and lord . . . or else, by canon law, we shall be compelled and obliged to bring the censure of the Church to bear upon you.

No more than her grandfather, however, was Eleanor likely to be disconcerted by ecclesiastical fulminations.

The flaw in her position was that she lacked the lieutenants to execute her plans as efficiently as she had devised them. And Henry, for all his difficulties, was still Henry, the most formidable figure of the twelfth century. He knew that he had created an administration that could function independently of feudal loyalties. Far from panicking at the sudden collapse of his universe, therefore, he waited unperturbed at Rouen while his enemies closed in upon Normandy. He was even cool enough to order his hounds to be sent over from England. But his outward calm was deceptive. Every treasure that he possessed was pawned to raise mercenaries. With these troops he struck with swift and deadly effect. Early in November 1173, having seen off the threat to Normandy, he swept down into Poitou and attacked the lands of Ralph de Faye. Several castles fell to his army, and Eleanor, at Poitiers, found herself obliged to flee.

She struck to the north-east, as though making for Paris. How Louis VII might have received her is one of those interesting questions that history unfortunately failed to resolve. Almost on the edge of Louis's lands a detachment of Henry's troops encountered a small group of Poitevin knights, whom they made prisoners. One of the 'knights' turned out to be a woman; and the woman, it transpired, was Duchess of Aquitaine and Queen of England. The game was up for Eleanor. Perhaps she had been betrayed: at any rate her capture was a singularly happy chance for Henry. Without her leadership the great revolt diminished into a series of local troubles, bothersome enough but controllable one by one. Young Henry was not a man to hold out long against his father, and Richard was still too young to be formidable. The King's power was restored; the Queen was doomed so long as he lived. He lived another fifteen years.

It is not difficult to imagine what might have been the fate of, say, a wife of Henry VIII had she conspired against her husband in the manner of Eleanor. Henry II was relatively merciful by comparison. For eight months Eleanor was kept at Chinon, until Henry took her to England in July 1174. But when the King returned to the continent that August Eleanor remained in England.

To French historians the fate of being forced, against one's will, to live in England is self-evidently durance hard and vile. An Englishman, however, may be allowed to suggest that, though Eleanor was under restraint, she did not suffer imprisonment of any insupportable nature. That she eventually emerged from her long confinement with undaunted will is rightly cited as proof of her tough fibre. It might equally be taken as evidence that she had not, in the circumstances, been badly treated. The Pipe Roll accounts show that she was held under the guardianship of trusted servants of Henry, but if the places where the Queen's expenses were paid are any guide to her whereabouts she was far from being confined in any one place. Apparently she spent a considerable time at Salisbury and Winchester, but there are also references indicating her presence in Buckinghamshire and Berkshire.

For a brief moment in 1175, when the papal legate was in England,

Henry flirted with the idea of having his marriage annulled. Eleanor, after all, was as closely related to Henry as to Louis VII. After the Church had separated them, she might follow the example of her grandfather's wives and take the veil at Fontevrault. But Henry, shrewd politician that he was, soon abandoned this idea. He knew that he could never trust Eleanor again; at the same time, though, he would have been aware of the difficulties of persuading her to accept permanent incarceration in even so worldly a convent as Fontevrault. It was safer to keep her as a captive wife than to set her loose as a dangerous divorcee. For a lecherous man, moreover, there is nothing more convenient than a wife who is out of commission: the situation at once maximises opportunity and minimises the risk of commitment. 'Once he had imprisoned his wife Eleanor,' explained Gerald of Wales, 'he who had formerly practised adultery in secret, now did so without concealment.' Rosamund Clifford probably died around 1176, but Henry was not inconsolable. Ugly rumours flew about that he had seduced, among others, Alice, a daughter of Louis VII who had been placed in his care after her betrothal to Richard.

For almost ten years after Eleanor's disappearance from the political scene Henry and his sons managed to work together without overt conflict, demonstrating that so long as the Angevins remained a united family they were a match for any opposition. This, of course, was not at all to the liking of the great barons of Poitou, although their underlings would have profited from the restoration of order. A wail of regret went up for the Queen who had been their leader:

> Tell me, Eagle with two heads, tell me: where were you when your eaglets, flying from their nests, dared to raise their talons against the King of the North Wind? It was you, we learn, who urged them to rise against their father. That is why you have been plucked from your own country and taken to a foreign land. Your barons have cheated you by their conciliatory words. Your lyre has assumed strains of sorrow, your flute the note of affliction. In the old days, with your taste for luxury and refinement, you enjoyed a royal freedom: you abounded in riches of every kind: your young companions sang their sweet songs to the accompaniment of tambourine and cithara. You delighted in the melodies of the flute, you rejoiced

in the harmonies of your musicians . . . Return, O captive,
return if you can to your own lands . . . The day is truly
coming when you will be set free by your sons and return to
your own land.

It is interesting to hear of Eleanor's delight in music, and of the
atmosphere of sensual luxury which she had cultivated in Poitou.
But if the writer imagined that her sons would contrive to release
her from Henry's custody he overrated their abilities.

The young Princes had been too well trained in the science of
selfishness to maintain a solid front with their father indefinitely.
In 1183 the self-destructive Angevin pattern threatened to repeat
itself, this time with the dimension of brother against brother added
to that of sons against father. Young Henry and Geoffrey associated
themselves with the rebellious barons of Aquitaine in order to rob
Richard of his inheritance, while the new King of France, Philippe,
showed himself as eager as Louis VII had been to foster and profit
from these divisions. A full-scale war was only avoided through the
providential death of young Henry in May 1184. The Prince, whose
life had been so futile, succeeded in making a pious end, asking those
attending him to plead with his father for his mother's release.

There are indeed signs that, with the relaxation of political tension,
Eleanor was kept on a looser rein. When her daughter Matilda of
Saxony came to England in 1184 Eleanor was allowed to see her at
Winchester; and the Pipe Roll records that the very considerable sum
of £28 was spent on the Queen's clothes, including various items for
her maid Amaria. Afterwards she attended the Christmas festivities at
Windsor, where Henry apparently gave her a gilt saddle. Next year,
1185, the King, in order to bring Richard to heel, ordered Eleanor
to Normandy where Richard was obliged to hand Aquitaine back to
her. This transaction turned out to be nothing but a charade: within
a short time Richard was again in charge of the duchy. Eleanor did,
however, take advantage of her visit to France to endow Fontevrault
with a hundred *livres*.

In 1187 Richard, partly inspired perhaps by his mother's youthful adventures, committed himself to take up the cross. Before he
could think of leaving, however, he needed to be sure that he was
officially recognised as his father's heir. His brother Geoffrey had
died in 1186, so that now John was the sole remaining rival for

the entire Angevin inheritance, unless one counted Geoffrey's infant son Arthur. Henry, though, remembering the troubles that had followed his earlier attempt to bequeath his kingdom, refused to give Richard any guarantee about the succession. The upshot was that Richard took up arms and in 1189 succeeded, together with Philippe of France, in dictating terms to his ill and prematurely aged father. 'God grant that I may not die until I have had my revenge on you,' Henry snarled as he gave his son the formal kiss of peace. Two days later he was no more. His lifetime of triumph had ended ignominiously. He was buried not, as he had wanted, in his favourite monastery of Grandmont in the Limousin, but at Fontevrault, the house with which Eleanor was closely associated. Such an obscure place, commented Gerald of Wales, 'was by no means suited to such great majesty'.

5

It is to be hoped that Eleanor received the news of her husband's death with appropriate expressions of grief and dismay. The figure who emerged from the long years in the shadows, however, could hardly have been further removed from the broken-hearted widow. The impression is rather of long pent-up energies being suddenly discharged with tremendous force. It seems that during Henry's strife with Richard Eleanor had again been placed under closer surveillance. Richard, as soon as he succeeded, commanded that his mother should be released. But William the Marshal, arriving at Winchester to execute this order, found the Queen Mother already at liberty, 'and more the great lady than ever'. Sheer force of personality, concentrated rather than dimmed by captivity, had caused her guardians to relent: no one wanted this formidable woman as an enemy under the new regime. 'No matter how bestial and obdurate a man might be,' the admiring Richard of Devizes once commented of Eleanor, 'that woman could bend him to her will.' Like many medieval women, like many modern women also for that matter, Eleanor attained her apogee in widowhood. She was already sixty-seven in a period when fifty was considered old, but she did not mean to let that stand in her way. Her daughter Matilda died that July, the fourth of her children to predecease her. Eleanor herself still had very far to travel, in every sense.

No one had formally appointed her Regent, but equally no one dared to object when she assumed responsibility for the government of England pending Richard's arrival from the continent. Her main concern was to secure the acceptance of Richard as King, and to this end she ordered every free man in the country to swear an oath of loyalty to him. To make the new order popular, she commanded the release of prisoners, especially of those who had offended against Henry's harsh forest laws. This measure, she could not resist adding, was undertaken 'for the good of Henry's soul'. Her long confinement, she said, had taught her 'how hateful prisons are'; it was 'a most delightful refreshment to the spirit to be liberated therefrom'. William of Newburgh, unimpressed by these sentiments, commented that this opening of the prison doors merely set a lot of villains on the loose.

In August 1189, Richard landed and met Eleanor at Winchester, but mother and son were so close that the arrival of the new King involved no diminution of her influence. They travelled together to London for Richard's coronation, which was a very grand occasion, although it is interesting that Eleanor's robes cost only seven pounds and sixpence, just a quarter of the allowance she had received in captivity. Yet the delights of power are not to be measured in money alone. Eleanor did not miss an opportunity to settle old scores with the Church. When a papal legate presumed to approach Canterbury without her permission he was instantly expelled from the country.

Richard's sole use for England was as a treasure-house for the crusade. He spent four months fleecing his kingdom in every conceivable way and then returned to France. Eleanor did not follow until February 1190. She was the one ally whom Richard could trust absolutely, and he needed her in England to see that everything ran smoothly in his absence. His great problem was his brother John, who could never be trusted to be anything but treacherous. Richard's initial solution was to buy him off with huge grants of land. John was given five counties, but on condition that he swore to stay out of England for three years. At this point Eleanor made a bad mistake. When she reached France she persuaded Richard to release John from his oath to keep away from England. Perhaps she imagined that Richard's Chancellor, William Longchamp, had the country well under control; or perhaps she was incapable of believing that her youngest son was as bad as people said. In any case, John would not then have appeared as a long-term threat. If, as seemed likely, Richard married and produced a son, the security of the succession would reduce the scope for nuisance-making.

In this century it has become received wisdom that Richard was a homosexual, though there is little or no evidence for this beyond the words of a hermit who warned him to 'remember the destruction of Sodom and abstain from illicit acts'. The destruction of Sodom, however, was a routine part of medieval jeremiads and did not necessarily imply any particular form of vice. Contemporaries animated against Richard's ravishing propensities; and he had at least one illegitimate child. The main difficulty about his marriage was that he had been betrothed at an early age to Louis VII's daughter Alice, a choice which was no longer agreeable to him politically, quite apart from the whispers that Alice had given birth to a child by his father. Eleanor was so determined that Richard should not marry Alice that, once in France, she held the unfortunate girl captive. Clearly her recently proclaimed hatred of prisons was of limited scope. The match between Richard and Alice, however, could not be called off without causing mortal offence to Alice's half-brother King Philippe of France. It seemed wiser to wait until Philippe was away on crusade before bringing to a definite conclusion Richard's negotiations with King Sancho VI of Navarre for the hand of his daughter Berengaria.

Richard himself said farewell to Eleanor at Chinon on 24 June 1190. He had decided to take the sea route to the Holy Land, a choice perhaps influenced by his mother's tales of the disasters she had encountered in Asia Minor forty-two years before. After this parting from her son Eleanor disappears entirely from our view for a while. She is next encountered at Lodi, twenty miles south-east of Milan, on 20 January 1191, together with the Princess Berengaria. It seems possible that the sixty-eight-year-old Queen Mother had crossed the Pyrenees to finalise marriage negotiations in Navarre. It is certain that she set out over the Alps in mid-winter to deliver the bride to Richard in Sicily. The chronicler Richard of Devizes reported the further progress of the party; though the terms of his eulogy might be questioned, the triumphant march of his phrases well conveys the awe which Eleanor now inspired in her contemporaries:

> Queen Eleanor, a matchless woman, beautiful and chaste, powerful and modest, meek and eloquent, which is rarely to be met with in a woman; who was sufficiently advanced in years to have two husbands and two sons crowned kings, still indefatigable for every undertaking, whose power was the admiration of her age, came to Pisa.

Richard sent ships to meet the party at Naples but Eleanor, perhaps remembering her youthful misadventures in the Mediterranean, preferred to stick to land for as long as possible. Finally, on 30 March 1191, she reached Reggio, where Richard greeted her and took her across the straits of Messina into Sicily. Surely now, her mission accomplished, she would be content to rest awhile with her children. As well as Richard, her daughter Jeanne, Queen of Sicily, was there to greet her – Jeanne whom she had last seen fourteen years before as an eleven-year-old girl. Eleanor, however, was not given to sentimentality, save where power and dominion were at stake. Three days in Sicily sufficed her. After that she took ship to Salerno, and then travelled to Rome, which she may have reached just in time to see the consecration of the new Pope, Celestine III. Eleanor had business with the Vicar of Christ. First, she ensured the recognition of Henry's illegitimate son Geoffrey Plantagenet as Archbishop of York, thus putting another potential claimant to the English throne out of consideration. Secondly, she obtained a special legateship for Walter of Coutances, whom Richard had just appointed his Justiciar in England.

Richard and Eleanor wanted Walter of Coutances to have this extra authority because they were worried about what John might be getting up to in England, and with good reason. In the autumn of 1191 John took advantage of William of Longchamp's unpopularity by siding with the baronial opposition and chasing the Chancellor out of the kingdom. He seemed on the brink of seizing power. No less worrying from Eleanor's point of view, as she returned from Rome to spend the Christmas of 1191 in Normandy, was the news that King Philippe of France had come back early from the crusade. Unlike Richard, Philippe had won no glory in the east, but Eleanor knew that this personal failure would only sharpen his eagerness to profit at the expense of the still-absent hero. She issued orders putting all the Plantagenet frontier garrisons on the alert. The precaution was well justified by subsequent events, for Philippe soon stationed forces on the borders of Normandy. At the same time, intent on sowing division between the Plantagenet brothers, he offered John all Richard's continental dominions if he would redeem Richard's promise and himself marry Alice, who was still imprisoned at Rouen. John, tempted by the Capetian bait, had raised an army of mercenaries in England and was about to cross the Channel to claim his prize.

It was a serious crisis, which Eleanor met with address and authority. She quickly decided that her first priority was to prevent John from ever crossing the Channel. Having delivered herself of a stinging rebuke to King Philippe for lowering himself so far as to attack the territories of a man on crusade, she took ship to England in February, oblivious of the hazards of the winter crossing. 'She was quite determined, with every fibre of her being,' wrote Richard of Devizes, 'to ensure that her younger sons remained true to each other, so that their mother might die more happily than their father had done.' Eleanor now abandoned any illusions she might once have nursed that she could deal with John through force of maternal influence. Instead, she summoned meetings of the barons in Windsor, Oxford, London and Winchester, and made them swear loyalty to Richard. John was summarily forbidden to leave the country on pain of losing all his English lands and revenues. By sheer strength of personality Eleanor succeeded in carrying the day. King Philippe, meanwhile, had discovered that his barons, perhaps influenced by Eleanor's remonstrations, refused to engage in his projected invasion of Normandy. Richard's inheritance had been safely preserved. Nothing now remained to Eleanor, it seemed, but to hand over the government of an orderly and peaceful empire to her returning son.

Unfortunately, though, her son did not return. If Eleanor ever thought in terms of retirement, her dreams were shattered at the end of 1192 by the news that Richard had fallen into the hands of his enemies on his way back from the crusade. At first the only intelligence was that the King had been captured by Leopold Duke of Austria and subsequently delivered to Henry VI, the Holy Roman Emperor. That was information enough for John, who immediately began to behave as though his brother would never return. Not daring to confront his mother directly, he crossed the Channel and demanded that the Norman barons acknowledge him as Richard's rightful heir. When they refused, he posted to Paris and reiterated his willingness to give away territory in return for recognition as ruler of the Plantagenet domains. Then, while King Philippe attacked Normandy, John used French cash to raise the Flemish mercenaries who were to make him master of England.

'My brother John', Richard loftily remarked upon hearing of his treason, 'is not the man to conquer a country if there is anyone to offer the feeblest resistance.' Such disdain no doubt came the more easily to him because he had total confidence in his mother's ability to deal with the situation. Once more the survival of his cause depended on Eleanor's strength and resource, and once more she did not fail him. She again demanded that the English barons should swear an oath of allegiance to Richard; she ensured that vital castles were kept in repair and readiness; she called out a general muster of the people to guard the coast facing Flanders. Most of John's troops, when they came, failed to make a landing, and those that did were immediately arrested. John himself, however, slipped through the net and took refuge at Windsor, which was immediately put under siege.

At the same time Eleanor worked frantically to secure Richard's release. Two English abbots were despatched to Germany to discover his whereabouts. They eventually found him in the Rhineland, from whence, on 14 April 1193, Richard addressed a letter to 'his dearest mother Eleanor, Queen of England'. (Apparently he had quite forgotten his wife Berengaria, who was staying in Rome.) Richard thanked Eleanor, as well he might, for all her labours in his behalf, and reported that he had made 'a mutual and indissoluble treaty of love' with the Emperor. Unhappily, though, as far as the Emperor was concerned this love expressed itself in the demand that Richard should pay a ransom of one hundred thousand marks to secure his release. It was Eleanor whom the King honoured with the ungrateful task of raising this colossal sum, ordering that all the monies should be entrusted to the Queen, or to those nominated by her. Eleanor taxed both clergy and laity to the bone; when the proceeds proved insufficient, she taxed them again. She was goaded by the fear that, should the ransom not be paid, Philippe of France would make a counter-bid for Richard, and that the Emperor would deliver her son to Paris as a prisoner.

To relieve her feelings Eleanor wrote to the Pope to let him know exactly what she thought of him for failing to support a crusader in his time of travail. Probably it was Peter of Blois, her secretary, who actually penned these missives, the same Peter who had once served the Archbishop of Rouen and in 1173 perhaps written that dignitary's homily recalling Eleanor to her matrimonial duty. Yet the letters to Rome read very much as though the passion behind them came from Eleanor herself, the culmination of an anti-ecclesiastical prejudice that had matured over a lifetime. 'Eleanor, by the wrath of God, Queen of England', she styled herself, and proceeded to live up to that beginning:

> The Kings and Princes of the earth have conspired against my son, the anointed of the Lord. One keeps him in chains while another ravages his lands; one holds him by the heels while the other flays him. And while this goes on, the sword of Saint Peter reposes in its scabbard. Three times you have promised to send legates and they have not been sent. If my son were in prosperity we should have seen them running at his call, for they well know the munificence of his recompense. Is this the meaning of your promises to me, made with so many protestations of friendship and good faith? Alas, I know today that the promises of your cardinals are nothing but vain words. Trees are not known by their leaves, nor even by their blossoms, but by their fruits. In this wise we have known your cardinals.

Eleanor's fury did not preclude the use of pathos. In Richard, her letter went on, she had lost 'the staff of my age, the light of my eyes'. She described herself as 'worn to a skeleton, a mere thing of skin and bones, the sap consumed in the veins, the tears all but dried in the fountains of the eyes'. There was strength enough, however, in her menacing peroration. 'The fateful moment draws near when the seamless robe of Christ shall be rent again, when Saint Peter's yoke shall be broken, when the Church shall be split asunder.' As a prediction it was only about three and a half centuries premature.

When the ransom money had been raised, Richard instructed that

Eleanor personally should accompany the treasure, all thirty-five tons of it, to Germany. The date of the reunion of mother and son had been fixed for 6 January 1194, at Speier, but at the last moment the deal with the Emperor was undermined by just the hitch that Richard's supporters dreaded. King Philippe and John were also offering one hundred thousand marks in an attempt to persuade the Emperor to keep Richard as a prisoner until the end of the year, by which time they hoped to have taken over the Plantagenet dominions in France. Eleanor, however, did not despair. She knew that the Emperor Henry VI nurtured wild dreams of universal power, and that he was not at heart a friend of the Capetian. Putting these two facts together, she persuaded Richard to gain his freedom by doing homage for all his lands to the Emperor. Such an oath would mean little or nothing in practice and it might actually be turned to Richard's account as the basis for an alliance with Henry VI against Philippe. It was an inspired gambit, for which the Emperor instantly fell. Richard was finally released on 4 February 1194 at Metz, and those who witnessed his reunion with his aged mother were moved to tears.

Elsewhere the event inspired other emotions. 'Look to yourself,' King Philippe warned John, 'the devil is unloosed.' In March Richard and Eleanor reached England and received a magnificent welcome in London. Next month the Queen Mother was present when her son was recrowned in Winchester cathedral. She had every cause for pride and satisfaction. Almost alone she had held the Angevin possessions together in the teeth of misfortune. Had she died then, she must have died happy and full of honour.

For five more years, indeed, Eleanor moved in the eye of fortune. She was finished with England now, though when she sailed from Portsmouth after the Winchester coronation Channel storms blew her back one final time on to the island with which her fate had been so capriciously linked. By the middle of May, however, Richard and she were in Normandy, where their triumphal progress continued. At Lisieux John came crawling to his brother for forgiveness, doubtless calculating that Eleanor's presence offered the best hope of deflecting Richard's wrath. So it proved. Richard bestowed his pardon like a rich man scattering coins before a beggar. 'You are a mere child,' he told his brother (who, in fact, was nearly thirty), 'you have been ill-advised and your counsellors shall pay for it.'

If Eleanor was indeed responsible for the rehabilitation of John, she had by that one act put at risk all her valiant work in defence of the Angevin possessions. Possibly she still hoped that Richard and Berengaria would have children, though there were already signs that this marriage, for which she had worked so hard, was a failure. If Richard remained childless, John could claim to be the rightful heir: his only possible rival was Arthur, the infant son of Eleanor's third boy, Geoffrey of Brittany, and his widow Constance. For some reason Eleanor had no time for Constance, who had contracted a second marriage with the brutish and ambitious Earl of Chester. Perhaps she considered that this match had put Constance beyond the Plantagenet pale; perhaps she simply disliked her daughter-in-law. Eleanor displayed equally little enthusiam for Arthur, though in this case she could plead sound political motives: the accession of a minor would bring with it the threat of disorder. Yet the matter of the succession must have seemed remote in 1194. In all likelihood Richard would rule for many more years. The Queen Mother was too old to concern herself with hypothetical problems.

At last Eleanor began to withdraw from government. Richard was thirsting for vengeance upon the perfidious Philippe, and even she accepted that there could be no place for an old woman amidst the rigours of military campaigning. Between 1194 and 1199 little record of her has survived. Probably she spent much of her time at Fontevrault, a religious community which specialised in the spiritual care of its noble and royal patrons. Not that the abbey was exclusive: it included a strict order of contemplative nuns, a house for lepers, a small group of priests and monks, and a society of reformed prostitutes. Despite the presence of both sexes (strictly segregated of course), there was a pronounced feminine bias, reflected in the fact that the head of the community was always a nun, albeit a nun of impeccable aristocratic background. Eleanor would have been treated with extreme deference, and no doubt in her case religious exercises were optional. Nor should we imagine her as entirely cut off from the outside world. Recognised as a powerful influence upon Richard, she was the natural medium through whom grievances might be aired to the King: thus the records show the monks of both Canterbury and Reading seeking her intervention on their behalf. Chinon, one of the nerve-centres of Angevin government, was nearby; and Eleanor must have followed with satisfaction the repeated successes that her warrior son gained over the French King. Twice Philippe only narrowly escaped capture, and by 1199 it seemed that Richard was poised to inflict a death-blow upon the Capetian. Then in a moment the course of history was deflected and Eleanor's world turned upside-down.

For all that historians delight to rake up profound causes for decisive changes, it was a single chance arrow that set in train the course of events that destroyed Angevin rule in France. Early in 1199 Richard was besieging the town of Chalus, in the Limousin, when he was struck in the shoulder by a shot from the battlements. At first the wound seemed slight, but the shaft of the arrow broke as the doctors attempted to extract it. Gangrene set in and Richard knew that death was upon him. His first thought was to send for Eleanor, who arrived in time to be with him at the end. He had always been her favourite son, and perhaps his character, with its strange compound of courage and brutality, generosity and vindictiveness, passion and cynicism, owed something to her own. His sudden death must have been the kind of shattering blow that calls into question the whole meaning of existence. Eleanor's daughters by Louis, Marie of Champagne and Alix of Blois, had also recently died, and five months after Richard's burial at Fontevrault another daughter, Jeanne, the former Queen of Sicily, was interred in the same abbey. Was Eleanor fated to outlive all her ten children? None of them now survived except her namesake the Queen of Castile, and John. All her losses, though, were subsumed in the loss of Richard. 'The light of her eyes and the staff of her age' were gone. What remained for her now, it seemed, was a melancholy decline into the grave.

Eleanor, however, had been born a fighter, who always responded as eagerly to the siren voices of power as to the call of motherhood; and at this juncture it was hard to tell the difference between the two. Richard was dead: *ergo*, John needed her help; *ergo* her energy rose up once more to meet the challenge. She would bear it out even to the end, though her last years, like some unrelenting Greek tragedy, brought the ruin of everything for which she had striven.

As the tragic convention demands, the new reign began on a deceptively encouraging note. It was announced, whether truthfully or no, that Richard had named John as his successor. Richard, indeed, had scarcely been buried before Eleanor was addressing herself to the task of ensuring John's acceptance. Her vitality was staggering for a seventy-seven-year-old woman. Using Richard's mercenaries she seized Angers, only ten miles from Fontevrault, out of the grasp of John's chief rivals, her grandson Arthur and his detested mother Constance of Brittany. Then, hardly pausing for breath, Eleanor set off on a five-hundred-mile progress through Aquitaine in order to drum up support for John's rule. She was at Poitiers on 4 May; Niort, La Rochelle, Saint Jean-d'Angély and Saintes in June; Bordeaux on 1 July; on her way north again at Tours on 15 July; and finally with John at Rouen before the end of that month.

Throughout her journey she sought to buy the loyalty of the towns by granting them charters which guaranteed their privileges. In one of the deeds executed at this time she referred to 'King Henry, our very dear husband of gracious memory', bearing out that there is no forgetfulness like that of a widow. At Tours she forced herself to kneel before the arch-enemy Philippe of France, so that, by doing homage for Poitou and Aquitaine, she should establish beyond argument the credentials of her house. Constance, meanwhile, had been conducting a rival campaign on behalf of Arthur, but in the battle between the two mothers Eleanor emerged as the clear winner. Even John was constrained to be appreciative. 'We desire', he declared, 'that she [Eleanor] shall have Poitou throughout all the days of her life . . . and that she shall be lady not only of those territories which are ours, but also of ourself and of all our lands and possessions.' This was good policy as well as filial duty. As long as Eleanor was actively involved in the rule of her lands the danger of revolt was reduced. John himself, moreover, had been surprisingly effective during this period. By the end of 1199 Philippe of France, who had not hesitated to support Arthur's claims after Richard's death, was negotiating for a truce.

In the discussions that ensued the old project of a marriage alliance between the Capetians and Plantagenets was renewed, though this time the Plantagenets were to provide the bride. The thoughts of Eleanor and John turned towards the family of her namesake daughter, the Queen of Castile. This Eleanor had eleven children, including two unbetrothed girls of marriageable age, one of whom would do very well as a bride for King Philippe's son, the Dauphin Louis.

Incredibly, the ancient grandmother now decided to dash down to Castile herself in order to secure one of the Princesses, quite regardless of the fact that it was the middle of winter. Perhaps she imagined, with an old woman's vanity, that she alone possessed the authority to bring off the match. Perhaps she simply wanted to see her daughter again, though this was an urge she had successfully repressed for thirty years. Her motives remain an enigma. Conceivably, though the suggestion is fanciful, she was impelled by some atavistic instinct: in her infancy, after all, when her family's fortunes had seemed to lie in the south, her grandfather and father had crossed and recrossed the Pyrenees without a thought. Or, more fanciful yet, did the prospect of marrying the grandson of her first husband to the granddaughter of her second husband awaken some obscure redemptory urge? She was far too experienced politically to believe that the match would assuage King Philippe's determination to destroy the Angevins, but she might still have divined that the union of the Capetian and Plantagenet lines represented the final hope of bestowing some lasting significance on her own chequered existence.

Eleanor's journey to Spain began inauspiciously, for she was kidnapped by Hugues Le Brun, a member of that same Lusignan family who had tried to seize her thirty-two years before. For an old woman in a hurry there was nothing to be done but to accede to the Lusignan demand that the territory of La Marche should be transferred to themselves. Evidently Eleanor did not brood over this misfortune, for by the middle of January 1200 she had crossed the Pyrenees – she seemed to have a penchant for tackling mountain ranges in mid-winter – and arrived in Castile. Here, by some whim, her choice alighted on the Princess Blanca, though she was the younger of the two eligible sisters. Eleanor gave out as her reason that the elder sister's name, Urraca, would be too difficult for the French to pronounce, but it is more likely that she discerned some special quality in Blanca. If so, her judgement was proved abundantly correct, for Blanche of Castile would become one of France's greatest queens, and the mother of Saint Louis, one of her greatest kings.

To the unlucky Plantagenets, however, Eleanor's final gift was John. The weight of good fortune that accompanied the beginning of this Prince's reign proved more than he could sustain. In the summer of 1200 he provoked his enemies by marrying Isabella of Angoulême, a beautiful girl, aged only fourteen, who was already betrothed to Hugues Le Brun, the kidnapper of his mother. There may have been some rough justice in this choice, but it was never good policy to annoy the Lusignans. Eleanor recognised this, despite her recent humiliation at their hands. In 1201, 'during my illness' as she wrote to John (was age at last beginning to tell?), she had met another of the clan, Amaury of Thouars, and exerted herself to make him a friend. 'As a result,' she told her son, 'he has promised to do everything he can to bring back to your obedience the lands and castles that some of his friends have seized.' John's rash marriage, however, once more stirred the Poitevin barons to revolt, and instantly Philippe of France moved to exploit the situation. Espousing the Lusignan cause, and cleverly linking it with that of Arthur, he launched an attack on Normandy at the beginning of 1202. At the same time he offered Arthur the hand of his daughter in marriage, and received his homage for Maine, Anjou and Touraine – even for Poitou, for which he had previously recognised Eleanor's claims. In addition, Philippe provided Arthur with a contingent of knights with which to enforce his authority.

It was perhaps Arthur's Lusignan allies who gave the youth the fatal idea on which his life was to founder. The capture of Eleanor! Just as Hugues Le Brun had gained La Marche by kidnapping her, so to seize her again would be to remove the main prop of John's continental possessions. Arthur's troops moved into Poitou in the summer of 1202. Eleanor, at Fontevrault, only grasped the danger when it was too late. She attempted to fly to the security of Poitiers, but found herself trapped in the small town of Mirebeau. Her grandson's plan appeared to have succeeded completely. Eleanor, though, had not lived eighty years to surrender tamely to a teenager. She managed to send off urgent pleas for help to John, eighty miles away at Le Mans, before retreating into the town's citadel with a few loyal soldiers. Playing for time, she opened negotiations and bargained long and hard. Perhaps Arthur was restrained by feelings of chivalry towards his grandmother; if so, it was a gesture that he would live (but not very long) to regret. John, arriving with astonishing speed within forty-eight hours of receiving Eleanor's message, caught the over-confident besiegers completely by surprise. The ensuing battle was the greatest military triumph of his life, and prompts the thought that he might have fared much better if he had been obliged to rescue his mother more often. Arthur, his sister, the two most important Lusignans, and several other rebel lords were captured. John had won himself a chance to repair the damage done by his marriage and to re-establish his rule in France.

How that opportunity was wasted, and how John, instead of seeking reconciliation, rekindled the rebelliousness of his French barons by the murder of Arthur and other atrocities, does not properly belong to Eleanor's story, unless she shared in her son's holocaust of vengeance. Certainly she failed to restrain John at Mirebeau as he crammed his noble captives into ox-carts, their heads chained to the beasts' tails. Eleanor was no stranger to the horrors of war; she had never shown any love for Arthur; and she had a score to pay off with the Lusignans. If history tacitly acquits her of any complicity in John's savageries, it also fails to record that she pleaded for mercy.

After Mirebeau Eleanor retired once more to Fontevrault, but no longer to placid and honourable retirement. Death comes too late for some. Eleanor was obliged to watch helplessly as Philippe of France, profiting from the universal revulsion against John, seized the chance for which he had waited so long, and systematically dismembered the collection of Plantagenet possessions that a later age dignified with the title of the Angevin empire. Only Eleanor's own Aquitaine, too distant for simultaneous envelopment, escaped Philippe's grasp. Aquitaine, indeed, would remain part of the patrimony of the English Crown for another two and a half centuries, an isolated and ironic memorial to an alliance that had originally been contracted with quite another aim. For Eleanor had married the Duke of Normandy, not (in 1152) the King of England; her ambitions had been concentrated in France. It was a grim morality tale, therefore, that the relentless advance of Philippe's armies through Normandy should have been matched by the slow ebbing of life from the indomitable old woman who, in the days of her youth and beauty fifty years before, seemed to have destroyed the Capetian claim to rule in France.

By the end of 1203 only Rouen and a few odd patches remained to the Plantagenets in Normandy. In March 1204 Richard's mighty fortress at Château-Gaillard fell, almost undefended, to the French King. By then John had already fled to England. To the last Eleanor, isolated amidst the cataclysm, kept her grip on affairs as well as she could: in 1203 we find her granting a commune to Niort in an attempt to secure its loyalty. She must have known that Philippe's armies would move south after the conquest of Normandy. But the Furies, sated at last, spared her from witnessing the loss of Poitou. Her tumultuous life reached its utmost mark in the spring of 1204. Philippe entered Poitiers on 10 August.

They buried Eleanor at Fontevrault with the husband she had fought and the son she had loved. The nuns duly repaid the charities that their patroness had lavished upon them with an unblushing encomium. 'She enhanced the grandeur of her birth by the honesty of her life, the purity of her morals, the flower of her virtues; and in the conduct of her blameless life she surpassed almost all the Queens of the world.'

There is much in that 'almost'. Eight hundred years later we might conclude that Eleanor of Aquitaine was a brave rather than a good woman, who lived her life with magnificent energy and spirit, but who very decidedly chose to place her treasure where, as we are assured, moth and rust corrupt, and thieves break through and steal. Her bones, like those of so many eminent French monarchs, were scattered to the winds at the Revolution, but her effigy, sculpted not many years after her death, still survives in the sombre abbey setting at Fontevrault. An idealised figure rather than a true likeness, it presents a beautiful if somewhat long-faced woman in flowing dress reading what is conventionally assumed to be a book of prayers. Whether the Eleanor who lived so vitally among the shining lights of this world was greatly sustained by such literature is quite another matter.

Henrietta Maria

1609–1669

I

Henrietta Maria was very Catholic and very French, attributes which generally serve well enough in this world – in the next one also, no doubt – but which were, nevertheless, conspiciously inappropriate for a seventeenth-century English queen. Her character, moreover, compounded her difficulties. Quick but not clever, opinionated but ignorant, she was no more capable of seeing anyone else's point of view than of doubting the correctness of her own. Perhaps if she had married a masterful monarch in control of his kingdom her inability to understand or to adapt to English ways would not have mattered. Her very real qualities – her gaiety, spirit and loyalty – might have flourished unchecked and her faults passed unnoticed beyond the narrow circle of the court.

Unfortunately Charles I, with whom destiny united her, was neither masterful nor in control. His instincts were those of an absolute king but, outside the paintings of Van Dyck, he never convincingly sustained the role. Upright and honourable in his personal dealings, in politics he was a devious incompetent. Henrietta's tragedy was to be caught between those two poles in her husband's character. Her life was enriched by his private virtue, and wrecked by his public inadequacy. The marriage, after a disastrous beginning, turned into a genuine love-match. Yet Charles and Henrietta gained their domestic happiness in a world which was collapsing around them; and it must be said that Henrietta's shallow certainties and her passionately delivered support for her husband hastened the plunge towards catastrophe.

In one sense only was Henrietta prepared for her role: from the very start of her life she had been much exposed to the vicissitudes of royal existence. Before she was six months old her father, Henri IV, arguably the greatest, certainly the most distinctly French of French

kings, had been assassinated. Henrietta not only lost a remarkable
father: she fell under the control of a disastrous mother. Henri IV
had agreed to marry Marie de Medici on the evidence of a flattering
portrait, and discovered too late that he had united himself with a
fat, humourless, meddlesome and foolish woman whose ostentatious
devotions did not include any serious attempt at marital harmony.
Henri was the most likeable of men, but he never succeeded in
charming his second wife. Marie de Medici resented him bitterly,
not merely for his numerous infidelities but also – perhaps more – for
his dogged persistence with the business of lawful procreation. Only
by drenching herself in scent had she been able to endure his sweaty
attentions, which eventually yielded six children, three boys (one of
whom died in infancy) and three girls. Henrietta, born in November
1609 and received with some disappointment on the grounds of her
sex, was the youngest. When Henri was killed in the following May
Marie de Medici found it impossible to muster even a conventional
show of grief. Joyously celebrating her unexpected release from the
matrimonial yoke, she assumed the regency for her nine-year-old
son Louis XIII and proceeded to unleash her incompetence upon
the affairs of France. The intoxications of power left little time for
maternal duty, which she discharged chiefly by letter.

So Henrietta spent her early years under the care of the royal
governess Madame de Montglat, living in the beautiful surroundings
of St Germain-en-Laye to the west of Paris, with occasional forays
to Fontainebleau, St Cloud, the Luxembourg and the Louvre. It was
a happy, even an idyllic childhood. Less fortunately, the modified
rapture expressed when Henrietta had been born a girl hardened
into a disastrous indifference to her education. She learnt, as French
children learn in every age, that France is the centre of the universe.
She became convinced, as all Catholics must be convinced, that there
is but one true Church. These precepts, however, constituted the sum
of wisdom imparted to her. Otherwise, her instruction was limited to
the acquisition of elegant accomplishments such as singing, dancing
and drawing. Henrietta apparently excelled at these pursuits, and also
developed a passion for amateur theatricals. Nevertheless, she would
live to regret that serious study had been so completely neglected. In
her splendid isolation at St Germain there was nothing to hinder the
development of a blinkered pride in her religion and nationality, a

sentiment which quite obscured any recollection that her father had been a religious sceptic, and her mother the scion of a Florentine banking family made good.

Henrietta's closest companion in her early years was her brother Gaston, just a year older. Her lifelong attachment to this worthless creature did a great deal more credit to her loyalty than to her judgement. In her own character there were early signs of both wilfulness and charm. 'I pray you excuse me if you saw my little sulky fit which held me this morning,' runs her first surviving letter, to Madame de Montglat. 'I cannot be right all of a sudden; but I will do all I can to content you; meantime, I beg you will no longer be angry with me, who am and will be all my life, Mamangat, Your loving friend Henrietta.' The affectionate tone of this note, with its endearing use of the nickname Mamangat, leaves a benign impression of Madame de Montglat's rule. Even so, court etiquette was strictly maintained, not least on occasion of the rare and forbidding visits of Madame de Medici. The starchy atmosphere which Henrietta's mother promoted – in contrast to her dead father's preference for easy informality – perhaps helped to induce in the child a tendency to judge by style and appearance rather than by content and worth. Henrietta would always be something of a snob, to a degree surprising in one whose position set her so far above the social scramble.

Marie de Medici, so careless of her daughters' education, showed the keenest interest in securing them brilliant marriages. By 1613 she had succeeded in arranging a double marriage treaty with Spain, under which Henrietta's brother Louis XIII was betrothed to the Infanta Anne and her eldest sister Elizabeth, still only thirteen, to the future King Philip IV. The marriages took place in November 1615, and Henrietta accompanied the royal party down to Bordeaux where the two brides were exchanged. The event brought little joy either diplomatically or personally. Elizabeth, isolated in the dreary grandeur of the Spanish court, clung to the memory of her pretty little sister in France, asking for her portrait and sending clothes for her dolls, in the hope, as she wrote, that 'when you play you may remember me'.

Henrietta's other sister, Christine, was more fortunate. In 1612 James I of England had begun negotiations for her hand, offering first his eldest boy Henry, and then, when that promising prince

expired, blithely substituting his second son Charles. But the project
fizzled out, in part because the French considered Charles to be too
uncouth. Christine was still unmarried in 1617, when her mother
fell from power. Marie de Medici had antagonised every group
in the kingdom, not least by the favouritism she displayed to
the Italian adventurer Concino Concini. Under her auspices this
upstart became Marshal of France and the Marquis d'Ancre. But
success went to Concini's head, and he made the fatal mistake of
attempting to run Louis XIII's life. The young King, who up to
that time had seemed wholly content to allow his mother a free
hand while he concentrated on hunting, struck back savagely. In
April 1617 Concini was murdered in the Louvre, and his body
dismembered by the Parisian mob.

It was another sharp lesson for Henrietta in the hazards of politics,
and this time, aged seven, she would have been old enough to register
it. Her mother, the remote but formidable figure of her infancy, was
sent to live in exile at Blois. Marie de Medici asked if Henrietta
might accompany her, but this request was summarily refused.
Louis XIII's sudden burst of self-assertion, however, did nothing
to improve the system under which Henrietta was being educated.
Madame de Montglat, the governess, continued to preside over a
regime of vacuous frivolity, rendered the more pernicious by the
influence of her daughter Madame de Saint-Georges, who became
a close friend of Henrietta's. Madame de Saint-Georges was one
of those Frenchwomen for whom appearances are everything. At
least, though, the Queen Mother's eclipse enlarged her daughters'
matrimonial prospects. Christine married Prince Victor Amadeus of
Savoy in February 1619, while Louis XIII, for reasons of internal
French politics, encouraged a match between Henrietta and the
Comte de Soissons. 'Mamanga has told me all your little *amours*
with the Comte de Soissons,' wrote Elizabeth from Spain. But the
plan came to nought. De Soissons ruined his hopes by espousing the
cause of Marie de Medici against Louis XIII. Although the King was
soon afterwards reconciled with his mother he did not forgive the
Count's desertion.

So Henrietta lost her chance of a French husband, the only kind
of husband, perhaps, for which her upbringing had prepared her.
Marie de Medici, once more assuming a position at the centre of

affairs, was determined that her daughter should marry a king; and that now meant, *faute de mieux*, a king of England. Yet initial French feelers, made at the end of 1620, were not well received in London. James I had now set his heart on a Spanish match for Prince Charles. His son-in-law Frederick had been expelled from the Palatinate by the Habsburgs, and James hoped, more than a trifle optimistically, that the Spaniards might evacuate the territory for the honour of uniting the Infanta Maria to an English prince.

In February 1623, after the marriage negotiations with Spain had dragged on for a couple of years without any result, Prince Charles and the Duke of Buckingham set off on an extraordinary escapade to Madrid, apparently convinced that a romantic gesture would clinch the match which diplomacy only seemed to delay. On their way they passed incognito through Paris, where they adorned themselves with new wigs and proceeded, under the less than imaginative aliases 'John Smith' and 'Tom Brown', to the Louvre. There they saw both Louis XIII's queen and the thirteen-year-old Henrietta Maria dancing in a rehearsal for a court masque. It would be pleasant to record that Charles was instantly struck by his future wife: in fact he hardly seems to have noticed her. He found Anne of Austria, the Spanish Queen, 'the handsomest' of all the dancers, 'which', he told his father, 'hath wrought in me a great desire to see her sister' (the Infanta Maria).

In Madrid Charles, notwithstanding his willingness to agree to almost any terms to secure the marriage treaty, met with nothing more encouraging than polite prevarication. It took him five months to realise that he was being strung along to no purpose, but by the time he left Spain at the beginning of September he thought only of revenge for the humiliations which he had inflicted on himself. Although the Spanish marriage project was not officially abandoned until March 1624, neither the Prince nor the Duke of Buckingham, who was by this time in virtual control of English policy, had any intention that negotiations should succeed. Their sights were already set elsewhere. As early as the autumn of 1623 an English friar named Robert Grey, who had been in Madrid with the Prince, visited the French court on his way back to England in order to sound the prospects for an alliance based on the marriage of Prince Charles and Henrietta Maria.

The following February, Buckingham, eager to explore the ground further, sent Henry Rich, Lord Kensington, to Paris. 'M. Quinsinton', as Rich became known, was a handsome, charming and thoroughly worldly young man who immediately found himself at home in the French court. The acquisition of the beautiful and dangerous Duchesse de Chevreuse as a mistress only enhanced his enthusiasm for the French alliance, and he sent back glowing accounts of Henrietta to the Prince. 'She is a lady of as much loveliness and sweetness to deserve your affection as any woman under heaven can do,' Charles was informed. 'Her growth is very little short of her age, and her wisdom infinitely beyond it. I heard her, the other day, discourse with her mother and the ladies about her with extraordinary discretion and quickness.' Henrietta's dancing and singing were also commended in the most flattering terms, though when we learn that Rich left this paragon with the impression that Charles was 'the most complete young Prince and person in the world' the value of his compliments is somewhat diminished. Nevertheless, Rich was undeniably a success at the Louvre. He passed round a miniature of Charles to all and sundry until Henrietta overcame her girlish modesty so far as to ask for it to be brought to her. 'She opened the picture in such haste', Rich reported to Charles, 'as showed a true picture of her passion, blushing in the instant at her own guiltiness. She kept it an hour in her hands, and when she returned it, she gave it with many praises of your person.' So far, so good. But no doubt the English were right in deciding to send out the Earl of Carlisle to undertake the more serious negotiations. As for Rich, he was created the Earl of Holland as a reward for his labour of love.

Yet however well disposed the French court might be, there was naturally no idea of giving Henrietta away without striking a hard bargain. The Comte de Tillières, ambassador in London, issued warnings which, in the light of future events, did the greatest credit to his judgement. With his knowledge of the strong Puritan element in the English Parliament, he recognised both the need to protect an isolated Catholic queen, and the difficulty of doing so without securing general guarantees for the English Catholics. Although Tillières's reservations about the match led in June 1624 to his recall from London, the cautionary note which he had sounded did not go unheeded in Paris. There was a feeling that it did not behove the dignity of France to settle for much less than Charles had been prepared to concede to the Spaniards, which was a great deal.

Like the Spaniards, too, the French required a special dispensation from the Pope before they would send their Princess into the heretic island. They therefore expressed to His Holiness the hope that a French Catholic queen might once more lead England into the fold of the Church. (The reference was to Bertha, daughter of a sixth-century Frankish king, who had married the pagan King Ethelbert of Kent, and been instrumental in the conversion of England.) The English negotiators, by contrast, were given to understand that the demand for the toleration of Catholics in England was only put forward to placate the Pope. Out of respect for James I's difficulties with Parliament, it was agreed that the clauses of the treaty relating to the religious issue might be incorporated in a separate, and secret, document. Even so, the negotiations were regarded with considerable suspicion in England, despite the tremendous popular relief at the collapse of the Spanish marriage project. 'My heart goeth not with this match neither,' wrote the staunchly Protestant Francis Nethersole, 'and I find so many of the same pulse here, that I am sorry my noblest Lord [Carlisle] is employed in the business.'

Nor, from the English point of view, were negotiations made any easier by the emergence of Cardinal Richelieu at the head of Louis XIII's government in August 1624. The Cardinal could not be satisfied with any bargain until he had extracted precisely what he required. In consequence discussions proceeded according to the hallowed traditions of Anglo-French diplomacy. 'These perfidious monsters,' stormed the Earl of Carlisle of his French counterparts. To complicate matters further the Pope proved intransigent. Urban VIII was actually Henrietta's godfather, having been papal envoy in Paris at the time of her birth, and he did not underestimate the dangers to which her faith would be exposed. Rome made such difficulties that by March 1625 Richelieu was ready to concede, in flat contradiction of the previous French position, that the marriage should go ahead without papal permission. The dispensation arrived soon afterwards.

The death of James I on 27 March 1625 meant that Henrietta became Queen of England from the moment of her marriage. It was a proxy wedding that took place on 11 May. The English King showed no inclination to travel abroad to meet his bride, while the French were only too glad to be spared the cost of receiving him. The Duc de Chevreuse, the husband cuckolded by Rich, represented Charles at the nuptial mass in Notre Dame, from which the English delegation withdrew lest the religious susceptibilities of either country be offended. Nothing that pride could demand, or money supply, was lacking from the celebrations. Henrietta was magnificient in a gold and silver dress embroidered with fleurs-de-lis, her queenly status emphasised by a crown ringed with diamonds.

Yet the treaty that underlay this splendour was a travesty, for which the English King bore full responsibility. Under its terms, Henrietta was guaranteed the right to exercise her religion freely, to which end she would have a free chapel, open to English Catholics, wherever she chose to reside. That much, at least, might be accomplished: indeed a chapel at St James's, designed by Inigo Jones and the first classical church in England, had been begun in 1623 for the Spanish Infanta. Other clauses in the treaty, however, could only lead to controversy. Henrietta was to be in charge of the religious education of any children born to the marriage until their thirteenth year. She was to be allowed twenty-eight priests who might wear their religious habits at any time or place. Her household was to consist in the first instance entirely of French Catholics appointed by the French King, though future vacancies might be filled by English Catholics. Most impossible of all to deliver, the English Catholics were no longer to be troubled in the peaceful exercise of their religion. It was easy enough for Charles, on the very day of his proxy wedding, to issue orders to the judges and bishops that the execution of the penal laws against Catholics should be relaxed. What would happen, though, when he had to face the House of Commons again? The fact that Charles had been careful to keep Parliament prorogued while the treaty was being negotiated suggests that he knew the answer very well. On the most generous possible interpretation he was guilty of wilful self-delusion in signing the articles; on any objective judgement, of simple bad faith.

Not only was Henrietta delivered into England under conditions that were most unlikely to be upheld: on the French side she was given dangerously inflated notions about the role which she might fulfil. The night before her proxy wedding she spent in a convent being drilled in her duty to act as protector to the English Catholics, a message which was re-emphasised in letters from the Pope and her mother. 'Do not forget', ran the letter drafted in Marie de Medici's name, 'that you are the daughter of the Church and that this is the highest position you can possibly hold . . . be unto them [the English Catholics] an Esther, who had the grace of God to be the defender and deliverer of His people from her husband Ahasueres . . . Do not forget them, my daughter; God has sent you into that country for their sake; for it is His people who have suffered for so many years.' This was a heavy burden for an intellectually and emotionally immature fifteen-year-old girl to assume. Henrietta wrote to both the Pope and her brother Louis XIII to show that she understood her Catholic duty. No doubt she imagined herself destined for the outer regions of heathenism.

That impression would not have been effaced by Father de Bérulle, who accompanied her to England as her confessor, or by the Bishop of Mende, who led the cohort of twenty-eight priests allowed by the treaty. De Bérulle was a saintly Oratorian of stern and narrow piety who did not dissemble his horror of heretics, and who meant at all costs to keep Henrietta clear of their infection. The Bishop of Mende, on the other hand, was Richelieu's nephew, a sophisticated and witty young nobleman who rejoiced in the name of Daniel de la Motte du Plessis d'Houdancourt. With three *particules* he could scarcely avoid despising the English. Since no one troubled to explain to him what he was quite incapable of divining himself, that the rude islanders were at that period the leaders of European civilisation in intellectual, literary and musical achievement, his illusions of superiority were perfectly secure. Henrietta, unfortunately, adored him.

As though to minimise the risk of contamination from the natives, the new Queen travelled to her kingdom with a suite of 106 persons. Besides the priests and the ladies-in-waiting (among them the insidious Madame de Saint-Georges), her household included a chamberlain, eleven equerries, twelve pages, ushers and *valets de la chambre*, an apothecary, six couriers, three coachmen, an *argentier*, ten chambermaids, and a whole battery of servants connected with the table. In addition there were unofficial hangers-on like the Duchesse de Chevreuse who came to England to indulge her passion for Rich and brought her husband along to share the experience. This odd combination in Henrietta's entourage of high-minded Roman Catholic ecclesiastics who were dedicated to the battle with heresy and fashionable Frenchwomen who could hardly be brought to acknowledge the existence of a world beyond Paris did not promise well for the new Queen's relations with either her husband or her subjects.

And indeed the first year of the marriage appears as a kind of extended parody of the misunderstandings and prejudices that eternally plague attempts at Anglo-French harmony. Henrietta arrived at Dover on Sunday 12 June 1625, one of those rainy English summer evenings that are liable to depress even the most sanguine spirits. Charles I, who had been at Dover some days before but who had retired to Canterbury when Henrietta failed to materialise, was not there to greet her. In no time at all the French contingent was complaining. Dover Castle, where they were lodged, was gloomy; the furniture was threadbare; the food execrable. It all seemed a very long way from the Louvre and Fontainebleau. Charles arrived early the next morning, and although he covered his wife with enthusiastic kisses on their first meeting he was stiff, awkward and difficult with her attendants. The man was impossibly dressed, the French quickly decided; besides, he stammered and looked so glum. The English, for their part, concluded with equal rapidity that they were entirely unimpressed by the airs and graces of their visitors. The French women, reported one observer, 'were a poor lot, not one worth the looking after, save herself [Henrietta] and the Duchess of Chevreuse, who though she be fair, yet paints foully'.

Though Henrietta declared at her first meeting with Charles that she was ready to be used and commanded as her husband might wish, it immediately became evident that this was a pretty prepared speech rather than a serious declaration of intent. When Charles, himself no more than five foot four inches, gauchely looked down at her feet as though checking out whether her diminutive stature had been increased by high-heeled shoes, Henrietta bridled. 'Sir,' she told Charles, 'I stand upon mine own feet. I have no helps by art. Thus high am I, neither higher nor lower.' And that very afternoon when the King and Queen departed for Canterbury, there was a sharp dispute between them about Madame de Saint-Georges, who arrogantly assumed a place in the royal coach. Charles indignantly ordered her out, but Henrietta argued so heatedly for her friend that he was forced, seething, to give way in order to avoid a public scene. That night at Canterbury he personally barred all seven bolts in the matrimonial chamber. It was observed, on the following morning, that the King seemed uncharacteristically merry. Henrietta, by contrast, was plunged into melancholy and despair.

Charles's good humour proved short-lived, for the marriage speedily degenerated into an interminable succession of wrangle and counter-wrangle. The King and Buckingham believed, with reason enough, that Henrietta's French entourage were poisoning her mind against all things English. Buckingham took a particular dislike to the Bishop of Mende. The feeling was heartily reciprocated, for the Bishop's encounters with the islanders had only enhanced his prejudice against them. 'I have always considered the English less reasonable than the Swiss,' he wrote after his return to France, 'and at the same time less faithful, while I think they are just as vainglorious as the Spaniards, without possessing anything of their real merit . . . It would need a very definite command to induce me to live there again.'

Perhaps the Bishop would have formed a higher estimate of his hosts if he had condescended to learn a word of English; and certainly Henrietta would have been better served if he had not insisted upon the exclusive use of French in her household. Not until 1641 did the Queen trust herself to write a letter in English. When Buckingham suggested, within three weeks of her arrival, that three English women should be added to her household the Bishop of Mende reacted with horror at the idea of this 'Huguenot' influence. Father de Bérulle was equally ungracious. Though the moral tone set by Charles was positively prudish compared to that in the Louvre, Henrietta's confessor never modified his belief that Protestant courts were the haunts of the Devil. His only comment, when Charles gave Henrietta a painting of the Nativity, was that the subject was older than the religion of its donor.

The Queen's main secular companion was the Duchesse de Chevreuse, a woman described by the Cardinal de Retz, who should have known, as acknowledging 'no other duty but that of pleasing her lover'. With no one to check Henrietta's blind French arrogance, it is not surprising that she often behaved like a spoilt and petulant child. Equally understandably, Charles felt hurt and angry that, while the Queen was lively and full of fun with her French ladies, she invariably sulked in the presence of the English. Whereas the Bishop of Mende could stroll into her apartments at any time, he, her husband, was often refused entry on the dubious grounds that she was ill. By the end of July, less than two months after Henrietta's arrival, the royal couple, chased out of London by the plague, were to be found living in separate country residences. While Charles established himself at Beaulieu in order to go hunting in the New Forest, Henrietta stayed at Titchfield where she behaved with typical foolishness. Discovering that her hosts were holding an Anglican service in the house without her prior permission, she walked back and forth through the heretic congregation, laughing and talking loudly to her French ladies, with her dogs yapping at her heels. Thus in her youthful stupidity did she contrive to lay the foundations of an unpopularity that would not pass in her maturity.

Yet Henrietta's behaviour was not wicked, merely the aggressive-defensive reaction of a fifteen-year-old girl who had been taught to consider herself in an intolerable position and discovered little evidence to the contrary. The pity of it was that she might have been much loved if only she had possessed the confidence or been given the encouragement to break out of her tight French circle. With her short stature, prominent teeth and long nose Henrietta was never a beauty, but she was blessed to the highest degree with the ability to make those whom she wished to please forget the fact. Englishmen who spoke French and saw her at ease among her own people were invariably captivated. Sir Toby Matthew, a Catholic convert, who had acted as her interpreter in France, thought her 'a most sweet, lovely creature', full of wit, and sitting already on 'the very skirts of womanhood'. James Howell, another accomplished linguist, who observed Henrietta on her journey from Dover to London, was equally struck, comparing her favourably with the Spanish Infanta, whom he had seen in Madrid. 'This daughter of France', he considered, 'is of a more lovely and lasting Complexion, a dark Brown, she hath eyes that sparkle like stars and on her Physiognomy she may be said to be a mirrour of perfection.' Even the Puritan Simon D'Ewes, who watched her at dinner in Whitehall, found her 'deportment amongst her women . . . so sweet and humble, and her speech and looks to her other servants so mild and gracious, as I could not abstain from divers deep-fetched sighs that she wanted the knowledge of the true religion.'

Sweetness and humility were less in evidence when Henrietta's eye lit upon her subjects. Joseph Mead, a Cambridge don, saw her in the same circumstances as D'Ewes, but in quite another mood. 'The Queen, however little of stature, is of a spirit and vigour of more than ordinary,' he recorded in July 1625. 'With one frown, divers of us being at Whitehall to see her at dinner, and the room somewhat overheated with the fire, she drove us out of the chamber. I suppose none but a queen could have cast such a scowl.'

Henrietta probably had a great deal more on her mind than an overheated chamber. If she preferred to live in the midst of a sneering French cabal that was at least partly because she found so little to tempt her therefrom. The faults on the English side were quite as grievous as those on the French. She had not been in the country for a month before Parliament began to grumble about the toleration being accorded to Roman Catholics, and early in August Charles, in flat contradiction of his promise in the marriage treaty, gave orders for the enforcement of the penal laws against them. It was a cruel blow to Henrietta's idea of herself as a delivering angel sent among the faithful oppressed, and no doubt Charles's perfidy was much dwelt upon in the comments of the Bishop of Mende.

Yet Henrietta would have forgiven her husband, and understood his need to conciliate Parliament, if she had been in love with him. The root of her problems was that Charles appeared to her to be so very unlovable. He entirely lacked the light easy touch that might have instantly annihilated the barriers between them. There was something strained and unnatural about him, as with so many who live by the will. The key to his character, perhaps, was that he had been brought up in the shadow of his infinitely more glamorous and talented elder brother Prince Henry. Across the endeavours of the adult man there always lay the ghost of the ill-favoured child. Charles addressed himself to kingship with gritted teeth, rather as, with immense determination, he had turned himself from a physically weedy boy into a reckless and dashing horseman. It was admirable, but it was never quite convincing.

The remote dignity which Charles cultivated obscured, but did not

obliterate, his underlying sense of inadequacy. He needed to reduce
the chaos of events to a system that he could understand and control.
For that reason he loved ceremonial and made his court the most
formal in Europe, while his own habits were as regular as clockwork.
When events failed to conform to his shaping, he preferred to ignore
them. It is difficult, however, to ignore a discontented wife. Charles's
marriage left him baffled and frustrated. He was quite incapable of
finding the easy way to Henrietta's heart – that of relaxing his
guard, admitting his errors, and trusting in a humanity which may
be common even between an Englishman and a Frenchwoman. His
manners were always stiff, and no doubt the fiasco with the Spanish
Infanta had done nothing to increase his confidence with women. The
more provocatively his wife behaved, the more pompous, humourless
and unapproachable he became.

Worst of all, from Henrietta's point of view, Charles was wholly
dependent emotionally upon the Duke of Buckingham. The achievements of this creature never began to match his magnificent style,
but Charles had eyes only for the brilliant image. There was nothing
sexual in his devotion; nor, though, was there place for a second icon
in his proud and lonely heart. Buckingham, in any case, meant to take
no chances of having his position undermined by a royal love-match.
Henrietta came to believe that he had deliberately fomented trouble
between Charles and herself. Certainly the Duke took unpardonable
liberties with Henrietta, accusing her to her face of behaving '*en
petite demoiselle et non pas en reine*'. The impertinence was almost
more than a daughter of Henri IV could comprehend. Buckingham's
cheek knew no bounds: he even set himself up as sexual counsellor.
Evidently Charles had discussed the most intimate details of his
marriage with his favourite, for the Duke told one of the Queen's
French ladies-in-waiting that Henrietta should conduct herself more
affectionately at night. Perhaps he also favoured the King with some
rough masculine advice, for Charles remarked to Henrietta that he
was sure that the Duke of Buckingham would never permit *his* wife
to behave in such a refractory manner.

By the autumn of 1625 Charles had convinced himself that
his marriage would never prosper until Henrietta had been separated from her entourage. Temperamentally he preferred trying
to abolish difficulties rather than addressing himself to the more

taxing process of resolving them. When Parliaments were awkward, he dissolved them; when the Queen's French suite threatened his domestic peace his instinctive reaction was that they must go. 'Seeing daily the maliciousness of the monsieurs, by making and fomenting discontentments in my wife,' he wrote to Buckingham on 20 November 1625, 'I could tarry no longer from advertising of you, that I mean to seek for no other ground to cashier my monsieurs.' Number One on the list, we need have no doubt, was the Bishop of Mende. Nevertheless, Charles hesitated to act without the imprimatur of his friend – 'I shall put nothing of this into operation until I hear from you,' he nervously added. Apparently Buckingham counselled caution, for a month or so later no action had been taken. 'As for news,' Charles wrote, 'my wife begins to mend her manners: I know not how long it will continue, for they say it is by advice; but the best of all is, they, the monsieurs, desire to return home; I will not say this is certain, for you know nothing that they say can be so.'

Alas, the *monsieurs* did not return home, nor did the mending of Henrietta's manners prove to be enduring. The royal couple proceeded with their bickering quite untrammelled by the dignity of their position. Charles, perhaps, showed the meaner spirit. At Christmas 1625, for instance, he suddenly cancelled a pastoral that Henrietta and her ladies had been rehearsing for months. Henrietta, on her side, merely had to obey the instructions of the Bishop of Mende if she wished to be unpleasant. No matter how earnestly Charles entreated her, she sternly refused to attend the coronation on 2 February 1626, on the grounds that a good Catholic girl could never be expected to imperil her soul by exposing it to the snares of Anglican ritual. The most that Henrietta would concede was to watch the procession from a window of the gatehouse at Whitehall. Here, on coronation day, she was observed 'frisking and dancing' with her French companions, a dreadful spectacle for an English crowd to witness. A few days later there was a particularly futile quarrel over where Henrietta should sit for the opening of Parliament. Charles had reserved her a position on the balcony of Buckingham's mother's house, but Henrietta, when the moment came, pleaded that, owing to the rain, she would prefer to watch the ceremony with the French from Whitehall Palace. Although she eventually capitulated to her husband's will, the incident rankled, and for some days the two of them were not on speaking terms. The argument degenerated into a squabble about whether it had, or had not, been raining on the day of the coronation. Again Henrietta was the one who gave way – 'if you believe it to be so, I will do the same' – so that shortly afterwards the Venetian ambassador was able to send home the happy news that the King and Queen were once more sleeping together.

To add to the tension, relations between England and France were in sharp decline from the end of 1625. First, the English fleet returning from an ill-fated expedition to Cadiz attempted inglorious amends for its failure by seizing French ships in the Channel. Then in February 1626 an armed fray developed outside the French ambassador's residence in the Strand after Charles had alerted his officers to take the names of all English subjects attending Mass there. By this point the atmosphere was deteriorating to the point where pretty well anything that Henrietta did was subject to adverse comment. And of course the more she was criticised, the more determinedly she clung to her religion as the only security she knew. Her subjects judged that her observance of Lent that year was too severe. It was as well that they did not see the letter which she wrote in April to the Pope, in which she pledged herself again to do all that she could for the English Catholics.

Her influence upon her husband, however, appeared to be absolutely minimal, even on secular matters. One night that summer, in bed with Charles, she handed him a list of officers she wanted appointed to administer some estates she was being given by way of a marriage portion. Charles had only to see that the list included some of her French retinue to refuse the request, 'whereupon', as he told Buckingham, 'she fell in a great passionate discourse . . . which when I offered to answer she would not so much as hear me'. In the absence of any proper agreement about her allowance, Henrietta's debts steadily mounted, until she was obliged to borrow from her own servants. Charles was as parsimonious with sympathy as with money. When Henrietta suffered from such an agonising toothache that she was reduced to writhing on the floor he took no interest beyond admonishing her for her lack of control. Meanwhile the row about her household dragged on without any resolution. There was one notable passage of arms when Henrietta insisted that she was only claiming the same rights as her mother-in-law, Anne of Denmark, had enjoyed. That, retorted Charles, had nothing to do with the case: his mother was quite a different woman. Yes indeed, rejoined Henrietta aflame with her Bourbon pride, there was certainly every difference between the daughter of a king of Denmark and the daughter of a king of France.

Such conflicts sealed the fate of the *monsieurs*. When, in June 1626, Henrietta (or so it was alleged) walked to Tyburn and publicly prayed there for the executed Catholic martyrs, Charles eagerly seized his chance. He believed, or professed to believe, that her French advisers had been responsible for a deliberately planned insult to English religious sensibilities, and decided that the moment for action had arrived. A report had been received from France earlier in the year that Richelieu was too preoccupied with other affairs to pursue a quarrel with England. Now, therefore, an ambassador was sent to Paris to give notice of the King's intention to expel Henrietta's suite. Perhaps it was imagined that Louis XIII's expulsion of his own queen's Spanish retinue might inhibit the French capacity for moral outrage. At all events, Charles did not pull any punches. Early in August he asked Henrietta to come and see him privately. Henrietta demurred, claiming that she had the toothache. Charles, accompanied by the entire Privy Council, thereupon proceeded to her chamber where the French attendants were once more discovered to be 'unreverently cavorting and dancing'. The women were abruptly dismissed, and their mistress no less abruptly informed that her entire household, swollen by hangers-on to perhaps four hundred people, was to be sent back to France.

After a moment's stunned, incredulous silence, Henrietta reacted hysterically. According to Richelieu's *Mémoires* she threw herself on the floor, seized Charles's knees, kissed his feet, implored his pardon for having offended him, and recalled the promises he had made in the marriage treaty, sworn on oaths that God would avenge – 'mais', the account tersely concludes, '*tout cela en vain*'. According to an English version, Henrietta rushed to the window in an attempt to shout to her departing attendants, broke several panes of glass, and clung so desperately to the bars that Charles had to exercise considerable force to tear her bleeding hands away. The Bishop of Mende, meanwhile, had been informed of what was happening and quickly arrived to protest at the insult to France. But Charles had

had enough of France, and still more of the Bishop of Mende. His only response was to order the Yeomen of the Guard to use force if necessary, so long as the Queen's compatriots were removed from Whitehall. The Frenchwomen, it is reported, 'howled and lamented as if they were going to an execution'.

The discarded French were temporarily lodged in Somerset House, whither Charles proceeded to explain his action. 'I have decided to possess my wife,' he told them, 'which was not allowed me when she was surrounded by you.' His listeners, however, were more concerned with securing payment of their inflated expenses than with the fate of their former mistress. Charles was all for giving them anything they wanted if he could thereby be rid of them. When, after a week, they were still in Somerset House, he could not contain his exasperation. 'I command you', he wrote to Buckingham, 'to send all of the French away tomorrow out of town. If you can, by fair means (but stick not long in disputing); otherwise force them away, driving them away like so many wild beasts until you have shipped them and so the Devil go with them.' As an afterthought he recommended the gift of some jewels, as being the argument most likely to impress Frenchwomen. Thus was his deliverance achieved, with £30,000 for their expenses and £20,000 for the jewels. Charles never grudged a penny of these sums.

As for poor Henrietta, she shut herself up in her room and refused either to eat or to sleep until she was permitted to retain at least some of her French servants. Charles remained determined to exclude her intimate friends like Madame de Saint-Georges, but he did relent to the extent of allowing her to keep one or two of her countrywomen who might exercise a less baleful influence. Likewise, two of her twenty-eight priests were reprieved, the Scotsman Robert Philip, who henceforward acted as her confessor, and a French Oratorian. To the Bishop of Mende Henrietta wrote in piteous style: 'I hide myself as much as I can in order to write to you. I am treated as a prisoner, so that I cannot speak to anyone, nor have I time to write my miseries nor to complain. Only, in the name of God, have pity on a poor prisoner in despair, and do something to relieve my sorrow. I am the most afflicted creature in the world. Speak to the Queen my mother about my miseries, and tell her my troubles. I say good-bye to you and to all my poor officers, and I charge my friend S. Georges, the Countess, and all my women and girls, that they do not forget me, and I will never forget them, and bring some remedy to my sorrow, or I die.'

The tragedies of existence are apt to appear extreme to teenagers, and certainly Henrietta had cause enough to believe herself in the middle of a dark night of the soul. Her marriage had been a failure on every count. England and France, instead of being brought closer, were more than ever divided. The English Catholics, to whom she had been supposed to act as guardian, were being persecuted with increasing venom. Her husband, besides being emotionally in Buckingham's grip, appeared to Henrietta to nurture an irrational phobia of all that she held most dear. No wonder rumours circulated that the Queen was preparing to return to France.

2

And yet, only a few days after the French had departed, the King and Queen were reported to be 'very jocund together' at Nonsuch Palace.

Such a dramatic change might seem to justify the crudest male chauvinist theory. Crack the whip, make the woman understand who is master, and watch how she responds – one has only to state the proposition to be damned for brutish insensibility. In this instance, however, it remains difficult to deny that the removal of Henrietta's French household was a turning-point in her marriage. She did not possess the kind of spirit that can cling to a grievance and mope indefinitely. Alone in England, no longer influenced by the sneers of her French entourage, she began out of sheer necessity to draw nearer to Charles, and in doing so she perhaps sensed beneath his taut exterior an emotional isolation no less affecting than her own. That is not to say that the rifts between them suddenly disappeared without a trace. A French ambassador who interviewed Henrietta in October 1626 found her still smouldering with fury over the treatment of her servants. Nevertheless, though the rows continued, their tone seemed diminuendo after the great drama of the household's expulsion.

Charles's high-handed measure generated much diplomatic froth, but no very alarming action. The Pope raved about the hideous consequences of having sent a good Catholic girl 'among the satellites of hell', while the Spanish and the French agreed that an armada was required to vindicate the stain upon the honour of the Church and France. When it came to the question of who was to pay for the engines of war, however, the Catholic powers presented a less united front. England and France finally stumbled quite independently into war at the end of 1626 for causes only partly concerned with the dismissal of the Queen's servants. Henrietta did her best first to preserve and subsequently to restore peace, though ironically the war served her very well, as it removed the Duke of Buckingham from the English scene for five months from June to November 1627. The Duke led an expedition to La Rochelle, and while he was away Charles and Henrietta became positively amorous. 'I cannot omit to tell you', the King wrote to the absent warrior in August, 'that my wife and I were never better together; she, upon this action of yours, showing herself so loving to me, by her discretion upon all occasions, that it makes us all wonder and esteem her.'

That summer Henrietta spent some time at Wellingborough in Northamptonshire, where the iron-carrying waters were supposed to encourage fertility. She returned for another visit in July 1628, by which time she was so far relaxed with Charles as to introduce a teasing note into her incessant demands for money. She wrote to him asking for £2 with which to relieve a destitute young Frenchwoman, and when Charles rather dimly enquired whom she had in mind, replied that it was herself. 'This piqued the King greatly,' reported the Venetian ambassador. Charles never did have much sense of humour: nevertheless, his irritation is understandable. He was desperately short of money himself, yet nothing ever seemed to staunch Henrietta's need for cash, whatever he gave her.

The mention of Charles's financial difficulties serves as a reminder that the first years of his marriage to Henrietta were passed in an atmosphere of political crisis that tended to obscure the possibility of domestic pleasures. The ascendancy of Buckingham involved a succession of diplomatic, military and political humiliations, but Charles appeared quite unable to break free from his evil genius. Indeed, the more conclusive the evidence of Buckingham's failure, the more desperately Charles clung to him amidst the resulting shambles. When the Duke returned in November 1627 from the disastrous La Rochelle expedition, Charles received him as though he were a conquering hero, blaming himself for not having provided adequate reinforcements, rather than the Duke for having organised the calamitous adventure. Parliament, to which Charles now found himself obliged to turn for money, was less forgiving. In an abject attempt to conciliate the House of Commons the King gave orders – once more in flagrant breach of the marriage treaty – that English Catholics attending the Queen's Chapel should be arrested. Henrietta, whether out of fear or impotence, or perhaps even because she had gained some inkling of her husband's difficulties, raised no recorded objection. It must have been gall and wormwood to her, however, that Charles was prepared to surrender to the prejudices of the Commons on the Catholic issue, while he would not contemplate the sacrifice that would have won him her favour, namely the removal of Buckingham from his counsels.

A crueller fate was reserved for the favourite. On 23 August 1628, in Portsmouth, the Duke of Buckingham was killed by an assassin's dagger. Charles was at his prayers when they brought him the news. With the icy self-command that he could display at moments of supreme personal crisis he motioned for the service to continue; and then, when it was finished, retired to his chamber, not to reappear for another two days. Henrietta, who was still at Wellingborough when she heard of Buckingham's death, at once divined that this time of acute vulnerability for Charles afforded her best, perhaps her last, chance of reaching into his deeply repressed nature. All her own grievances were forgotten as she hurried south to comfort Charles. No doubt, as Henry Percy wrote cynically to the Earl of Carlisle, the Queen's mourning for the Duke was rather 'out of discretion than out of a true sensation of his death. I need not tell you she is glad of it, for you must imagine as much.' Yet Percy expressed only the kind of half-truth that the worldly wise are apt to take for sophistication. If there was an element of calculation in Henrietta's actions – and since she went out of her way to be kind even to Buckingham's relations that would be hard to deny – it was the sort of calculation that is only open to the generous-hearted. A mean-minded or vindictive woman does not seek to make harmony out of matrimonial discord; nor do feminine wiles forge enduring bonds of devotion unless they are allied to a deeper capacity for love.

For the role which Henrietta played, that of the wife bringing comfort to her husband from afar, was transformed within a few weeks into the reality of dearest companion to his heart. World-weary courtiers were treated to the astonishing spectacle of the King and Queen suddenly falling in love after three years of squabbling. 'Every day', noted an observer, 'she concentrates in herself the favour and love that were previously divided between herself and the Duke.' There was, moreover, the same almost slavish quality in Charles's adoration of Henrietta that he had previously shown in his relations with Buckingham. The Duke and the Queen, after all, were the only two beings who ever succeeded in penetrating Charles's emotional reserve; and the very difficulty which the King experienced in making other contacts rendered him absolutely dependent on them both in turn. The sharp anguish of Buckingham's death receded, and Charles's defensive carapace closed over again to insulate the new passion, as once it had insulated the old, from any rival affection. Upon Henrietta the King poured forth his devotion; to the rest of the world he remained as he had always been: tight, rigid, secretive and overcontrolled. Henceforth the remote and gracious centre of his being belonged to his wife alone.

Henrietta recognised her good fortune. 'I am not only the happiest princess, but the happiest woman in the world,' she told the French ambassador, the Marquis de Châteauneuf. The most telling indication of her changed attitude was that she no longer seemed to care a jot whether or not she had a French entourage. She appeared more concerned, the French ambassador noted with disgust, with avoiding a matrimonial quarrel than with acquitting the honour of her native land. 'Every time she wants to speak [to Charles] he listens and replies: but as she does not apply herself and worries very little about things, and does not know how she must speak, it does little good and is regarded by the English ministers as of no importance . . . which I have told her several times.' Charles, to rub his triumph in, could not resist putting on a most uncharacteristic public display of connubial billing and cooing for the ambassador's benefit. 'You do not see that in Turin,' he remarked as he kissed his wife again and again (a hundred kisses per hour according to Châteauneuf's estimate), 'nor in Paris either.' Instead of becoming the subject of a prolonged dispute, as any self-respecting diplomat might have wished, the issue of the French household was quietly forgotten. Henrietta's religious needs were settled in April 1629 by the Treaty of Susa, which ended the war between England and France. The next year, in fulfilment of its terms, twelve Capuchin monks arrived in London to take the place of the Oratorians who had been expelled in 1626. Charles, after his experience of du Plessis d'Houdancourt, resolutely refused to accept another French bishop.

By 1631 Henrietta was professing a desire to be 'altogether independent of France'. The remark, it is true, sprang from a moment of exasperation at Richelieu's animosity towards her mother, on whose behalf she had been copiously if unsuccessfully intriguing with her brother Gaston; nevertheless, it expressed a sentiment that she could never have entertained for a second five years previously. Her existence became wholly centred on Charles. The attraction between them was very much that of opposites – her liveliness against his melancholy; her impetuousness against his reserve; her quick wit against his more ponderous deliberation; her superficiality against his gravity; her volubility against his hesitant stuttering; her laughing eye against his measured dignity. The bond, however, was absolute.

'The only dispute between us now', Charles wrote to Marie de Medici, 'is that of subduing one another by affection, each considering ourselves victorious in following the will of the other.' The least separation became hard to bear. When Henrietta went to take the waters at Tunbridge Wells in July 1629, while Charles hunted at Theobalds in Hertfordshire, they both travelled considerable distances to Oatlands, in Surrey, apparently for no other reason but to spend the night together. In the following month the King gave Henrietta Oatlands, along with Greenwich, Grantham, Boston and other manors. So attentive a husband might easily have been taken for granted, but Henrietta's devotion never waned. At the end of 1632, when Charles was struck down with smallpox, she attended him daily, in utter disregard of the risk to herself. Four years later she fainted from apprehension upon being told that there was a lunatic on the loose, threatening to kill Charles.

The royal romance, if not the waters of Wellingborough, proved rich in consequence. Henrietta's failure to give birth before 1628 might be ascribed to physical immaturity: if so, maturity came pat with the death of Buckingham. On 13 May 1629, nine months less ten days from the Duke's demise, the Queen was delivered of a son, who died after only a few hours. This sorrow, however, was soon anaesthetised by a succession of healthy children. For nearly half of the 1630s the Queen was pregnant. Her eldest surviving son, the future Charles II, was born on 29 May 1630; Mary on 4 November 1631; the future James II on 14 November 1633; Elizabeth on 19 December 1635; Anne on 17 March 1637; Katherine on 29 January 1639 (she died the same day); and Henry on 8 July 1640.

There is no mistaking the maternal pride lying beneath the candour with which Henrietta described Prince Charles in a letter to Madame de Saint-Georges. 'If my son knew how to talk I think he would send you his compliments. He is so fat and tall that he is taken for a year old, yet he is only four months: his teeth are already beginning to show. I will send you his portrait as soon as he is a little fairer, for at present he is so dark that I am ashamed of him.' A year later Henrietta was still, just as unconvincingly, professing herself ashamed – 'he is so ugly'; even so, 'I wish you could see my *cavalier*, he has no ordinary look about him. He is so serious in everything he does that I'm sure that he is far wiser than me.' Despite Henrietta's affection for Prince Charles, it would be groundlessly sentimental to imagine her sparing much time or attention for her children. Seventeenth-century queens did not concern themselves with the tedium of nurture. In this connection it is interesting that, though the Queen apparently sang her children snatches of French songs, none of them grew up able to speak their mother's native tongue with any proficiency. Like the King, who hung a superb Van Dyck portrait of the children above his breakfast table in Whitehall, where he could contemplate it in peace and quiet, Henrietta preferred the ideal to the reality of parenthood.

Indeed, the royal couple's entire life together during these halcyon years had the quality of an illusion. Charles dissolved Parliament in March 1629 and thereafter, for eleven years, ruled as an absolute monarch. The court, increasingly isolated from the workaday world of the rest of the country, became a kind of dream kingdom where Charles and Henrietta lived out their idyll at the expense of their temporarily impotent subjects. In all, it has been reckoned, the royal household employed between 1,800 and 2,600 people: together with the hangers-on and dependants the total would have come to about the same as the population of Exeter, the seventh or eighth largest community in the kingdom. Some £260,000, or two-fifths of the King's annual income, raised at the cost of vicious resentment, was absorbed by this leviathan.

Henrietta took naturally to the economics of fairyland. Even Charles was obliged to admit that she was a rotten housekeeper, the sort of woman who could never tolerate that her income should exceed her expenditure. It was not that her resources were consumed by one overriding passion. She had, for instance, no particular propensity towards building, that classic cause of royal bankruptcy. She tinkered here and there with her palaces; she built a chapel at Somerset House; and she finished the fine classical house that Inigo Jones had begun for Anne of Denmark at Greenwich. In this area she might well be praised for restraint, while the Greenwich house remains a monument of which any queen could be proud. No, it was not building that absorbed Henrietta's resources so much as her insatiable desire to fill every passing hour with amusement and delight.

This side of her character is evident in the letter which she wrote to Madame de Saint-Georges in 1631, from which the passage about her son's ugliness has already been quoted. 'Send me some sweet chamois gloves, a dozen pairs,' she went on, 'also, please, one of doeskin; a game of *jonchets* [spillikins], and one *de poule et de regnart*, and the rules of any species of game now in vogue. I assure you that if I do not write to you as often as I might, it is not that I have ceased to love you. I confess my idleness, and I am ashamed to say that I think I may be pregnant again.' To offset this queenly ennui Charles kept her well supplied with jewels, though such presents were more easily provided than paid for. Sir Thomas Roe, having bought some £2,500 worth of jewels for the King and waited in vain for reimbursement, optimistically wrote to Henrietta asking her to use her influence on his behalf. The only answer he received was that the Queen would be mentioning him in her prayers. That is the kind of tawdry fact which should be remembered when looking upon Van Dyck's remote and dignified images of the King and Queen. The Dutch painter, as propagandist for the court, was one man who did receive payment on the dot, and very handsome payment too.

In the closed, frivolous and slightly epicene atmosphere of the court, the search for distraction eagerly embraced the grotesque and the fantastic. Henrietta had a particular affection for a pet dwarf, Jeffrey Hudson, who first appeared in her life when he burst out of a pie placed before her at table, a present from the Duke of Buckingham. In 1630 Hudson was sent to France to bring back a midwife for the Queen, only to be captured by Flemish pirates. His disappearance left Henrietta so distraught that, as one cynic put it, there was 'more upset at court than if they had lost a fleet'. 'Strenuous Jeffrey' eventually returned safely to resume his character role, in which his fierce temper greatly assisted the quest for laughs. Less amusingly, he later, in France, shot a fellow courtier stone dead in what his opponent fondly imagined to be a mock duel, a tragedy which reveals the tensions that underlay his performance. To be fair to Henrietta, such freakish tastes were common enough at the time. The peculiar mixture of an unconsciously callous disregard for the misfortunes of others with a highly conscious sense of refinement is well caught in a visit which Charles and Henrietta made to Bedlam in 1636. They were, as a court witling put it, 'madly entertained' with the behaviour of the lunatics, until, alas, the foul language of some of the inmates caused them to retreat in shock and dismay.

The world of make-believe in which the royal romance flourished found its most perfect representation in the court masques. Charles and Henrietta both delighted in these entertainments, in which they took prominent parts. The masque, a bizarre amalgam of drama, music and dance, was the ultimate in exclusive art. Not only did the cast consist of courtiers of the highest rank: even the audience was carefully selected. 'No great lady shall be kept out, though she hath but mean apparel,' ordained the Lord Chamberlain, 'and no inferior lady shall be let in, but such as have extreme brave apparel, and better faces.' To a modern mind the masque – and there were twenty-five of them at court between 1625 and 1640 – appears in need of all the snob appeal that could be mustered. Though it would be dangerously philistine to dismiss out of hand these immensely costly spectacles when many of them were designed by Inigo Jones, and Ben Jonson frequently provided verses, the thought of performances lasting up to eight hours, featuring actors chosen by virtue of their social position, does chill the soul.

The masque, however, did not aim so much at entertainment as at the presentation of an idealised vision of Charles's rule. Typically, a philosopher-king would be shown bending his noble spirit to the service of his people's welfare, while the people bemoaned the unhappy fact that their short lives did not afford sufficient opportunity to sing the praises of so beloved a monarch. Real life, unfortunately, offered different perspectives. When, for instance, William Prynne presumed to issue a lengthy tome in which he attacked the use of woman actors (and Henrietta, by implication, among them) he was hauled before the Star Chamber court, fined £5,000, imprisoned for life and deprived of both ears in the pillory.

If the masques served any useful purpose at all it was to teach Henrietta some English, for she was compelled to memorise long parts. Whatever the fictions perpetrated at court, in the country resentment against Charles's rule was rife, alike among country gentlemen being milked by arbitary taxation and among puritans persecuted for beliefs that they held with no less conviction and considerably more moral energy than Henrietta brought to her Catholicism. These were formidable men with genuine grievances. Henrietta, though, could only see them as treacherous factions bent on feathering their own nests.

Inevitably, the Queen's own set attracted the same criticism. That does not mean that Henrietta turned her household into an exclusively Catholic cabal. Quite the contrary: in the early 1630s there were continual complaints from the papal envoy and other Catholic diplomats that the Queen 'allies herself to the Puritans'. The 'Puritans' in question were not, in fact, conspicious examples of Protestant rigour, Catholic ambassadors tending to be rather hazy about the various divisions of heresy. One such 'Puritan' was the Earl of Holland, the erstwhile Henry Rich, still in favour with Henrietta, still combining perfect courtesy with perfect mediocrity, never a figure to be depended upon in time of trial. Then there was the Percy family, for which Henrietta developed great affection, especially for Henry, with whom she shared a disastrous penchant for intrigue, and for his sister Lucy, Lady Carlisle, who became her best woman friend. Lady Carlisle was attractive, quick-witted, and poison. 'She chooses to know only the fortunate,' a contemporary noted, and Henrietta would live to learn the truth of that observation.

The fact was that the Queen never cared a fig for anyone's abilities, religion or behaviour, so long as they were aristocratic, charming, easygoing and amusing. Her indifference about the morals of those she liked applied even to sexual misdemeanours, concerning which Charles was particularly severe. It was not that Henrietta's own conduct was lax, like that of her sister Christine of Savoy. 'She has no sin, except those of omission,' her confessor reported to Rome. 'As to faith, or sin of the flesh, she is never tempted.' Even the malicious tittle-tattle of her enemies never really succeeded in making any scandal stick. Yet when Henry Jermyn, who had entered her household in 1628, and subsequently became her most trusted confidant, got Buckingham's niece with child, Henrietta stoutly supported him in his refusal to marry the girl. Charles, by contrast, reacted sharply, and insisted upon Jermyn being temporarily banned from court. The sinner soon returned, however, to find himself more than ever in the Queen's favour. Jermyn had little to recommend him apart from Henrietta's patronage. He set himself to amass a fortune at court with the same shameless voracity that he brought to the consumption of his daily dinner. Plump, sleek and self-satisfied, he repaid his benefactress with three decades of indifferent counsel.

The kind of company which the Queen preferred is well conveyed by a letter which Panzani, the papal agent at the English court, wrote in 1635 concerning his successor. The new man, Panzani advised, should be of noble bearing with a fine presence, rich enough to keep up a good table and household, of exemplary life though of no strait-laced piety, and not too close to the Jesuits. He must know French well, and be able to please the Queen, who liked scents, beautiful clothes and witty conversation. It would also be well that he should be accomplished in paying court to Henrietta's ladies-in-waiting, through whom much business was done at the English court. Such requirements, drawn up by a man bound by his position to be favourably disposed towards the Queen, indicate her essentially frivolous nature.

By corollary, Henrietta instinctively tended to dislike the solid and the worthy. In particular Richard Weston, the Lord Treasurer who struggled gamely with the impossible task of putting the King's finances in some kind of order, incurred her displeasure. Not merely did the man have no breeding: he actually presumed to cut down on the expenditure of the royal household. Weston died in 1635, ironically enough becoming a Catholic on his death-bed. His successor, William Juxon, was hardly any better liked by Henrietta; no more were any of the other ministers who sought to prop up Charles's government, men such as William Laud, the Archbishop of Canterbury, or Sir Francis Windebanke, Secretary of State. Administrative competence never sufficed in Henrietta's judgement to compensate for a humdrum background, least of all when allied to earnest endeavour. The greatest of all the King's ministers, Thomas Wentworth, who became Earl of Strafford in January 1640, came from a rather more respectable family, but he also was unpopular with the Queen in the mid-1630s.

Henrietta has frequently been charged, both by her contemporaries and by historians, with responsibility for Charles's more disastrous policies. Yet the King proved time and again that he was perfectly capable of making his own mistakes. Those who, like Clarendon, wrote of Henrietta's 'absolute power' over the King were often royalists who instinctively preferred to blame the foreign Queen rather than the revered master. On the other side, the puritan view of Henrietta was distorted by their acute hostility to the Roman Catholicism which they saw being openly practised at court. Yet it would seem that, at least before the late 1630s, the Queen had very little effect on affairs of state. She had prejudices not policies, and in the days of her content she lacked the persistence and the drive required to achieve her fitful aims.

That was just as well. As a good Bourbon Henrietta was viscerally anti-Spanish, and her association with the 'court puritans' in the early 1630s involved an attempt to bring the government into alliance with the French against the Habsburgs. It seems that she had no inkling of the deeper purposes which her allies harboured. The Earl of Holland, whose charms she relished so deeply, was hand-in-glove with a group of opposition peers. War against Spain, this group calculated, held the prospect of rich pickings from the Spanish American empire. Just as important: when the enemy fought back, the King would be forced to turn to Parliament for financial aid, thus ending the period of personal rule. Henrietta, all unknowing, had joined a conspiracy against her husband. Charles, however, had learnt to be cautious about foreign ventures as a consequence of the unlucky expeditions which Buckingham had organised. He flirted with the anti-Spanish policy, but never quite committed himself. The one consistent strand in his foreign policy remained his desire to restore his sister and brother-in-law to the throne which they had lost in the Palatinate, an ambition to which Henrietta was entirely indifferent.

Nothing more conclusively demonstrates the King's imperviousness to the Queen's influence than her complete failure to alter his religious views. It was simply beyond her power of imagining that the man she loved might be as firmly wedded to the Church of England as she herself was to Rome. There were, in fact, grounds for her misapprehension, because Charles showed evident sympathy for some aspects of Catholic practice. He was strongly attracted to the moral discipline of the confessional; he took a reverent interest in religious relics; and he saw the Inquisition as a powerful ally of absolute monarchy. In addition, his mother had been a Catholic, and though she failed to pass on her religion to her son, she did bring him up with a love of all things Italian, in particular of Italian art.

Hearing of this, Cardinal Barberini, the Pope's nephew, declared that he would 'not hesitate to rob Rome of her most valuable ornaments, if in exchange we might be so happy as to have the King of England's name amongst those princes who submit to the Apostolic See'. Masterpieces were dispatched to England from Rome by the crateload, a happy event for a monarch who was as great a connoisseur as has ever reigned. There is a touching description of the arrival of one such consignment in 1637, with Charles excitedly collecting together Henrietta, the Earls of Holland and Pembroke, and Inigo Jones to open the treasures, after which they competed with each other to guess the artist from the style. Rome sent papal envoys as well as papal treasures: Gregorio Panzani from 1634 to 1636, and George Con from 1636 to 1639. Charles got on very well with both men, particularly Con, who was amazed by the licence given to him. 'I have dealt on religion with the King in a manner', the envoy reported, 'that, if he were not such a good prince, I should rather have lost my head than gained his good graces.'

In the circumstances it was natural that Rome, and Henrietta, should have hoped for a conversion. Their optimism, however, was misplaced. Charles enjoyed his religious discussions with Con because he was entirely secure in his own position. Anglicanism perfectly reflected his mystical idea of himself as God-appointed head of the nation, and he never felt the least temptation to abandon it. He could and did regret that the Roman Catholic Church and Anglicanism were in schism: in December 1634 he even appointed a commission to investigate the possibilities of union between the two Churches. At heart, though, he knew that Archbishop Laud was right: 'if he [the King] wished to go to Rome, the Pope would not go a step to meet him.' Besides, Charles considered that he was already a Catholic, and that the appellation 'Roman' Catholic was a contradiction in terms. In his mind Rome had perverted to its own ends the purer doctrines of the Early Church. He had been shocked, when in Spain, to see how the people knelt to the Madonna while they only bowed to the crucifix. Now he noted with disapproval Henrietta's laxity about attending mass on time, and strove to inculcate a better discipline in her practice.

In truth, the Queen's Catholicism stemmed rather from the school of St Francis de Sales, who sought to reconcile devotion with the life of this world, than from the ascetic ideals of the New Testament. Rome expected too much of her if it looked for some kind of Catholic spiritual renaissance springing from her influence. Instead, Henrietta achieved a number of court conversions, which proved a mixed blessing for the Church. The sight of frivolous aristocratic women turning to Rome at the instance of Henrietta's well-bred Capuchins did little to inspire run-of-the-mill converts, though it certainly stirred up a great deal of puritan fury at the papist Queen and all her works. Even ordinary English Catholics, staid country gentlemen rather than court sycophants, regarded the Queen's circle as quite alien, and felt no gratification whatever at the accession to their faith of a poetaster like Walter Montagu, a particular favourite of Henrietta's. The Queen repaid their suspicion in kind, being especially incensed by the English Catholics' hope of support from Spain. 'They would think little of Heaven itself', she acidly remarked in 1637, 'unless they got it at the hands of Spain.'

Henrietta's bitterness was understandable, for she felt that she deserved their gratitude for the relaxation of the laws against the Catholics in the 1630s. It is, in fact, difficult to be certain how far she influenced Charles in this matter, since the King, though he rejected Roman Catholicism for himself, never shared the repulsion that so many of his subjects felt for that religion. If it cost him nothing, he was content that the Catholics should be physically unmolested; if political necessity required, he was equally prepared to persecute them. In the period of his personal rule political necessity did not, on the whole, require; and so the 1630s were celebrated as a time of 'sweet and agreeable peace' for the Romanists compared with what had gone before (still more, with what would come after). Yet the toleration which Catholics enjoyed was always limited and conditional. The more sanguinary sanctions were no longer applied, and Charles set several recusants free from prison 'at the instance of our dearest consort the Queen'. Nevertheless, there was a sense in which Clarendon was justified in his claim that 'the penal laws were never more rigidly executed' than during the time of Charles's personal rule. For although the Catholics escaped the rack and the scaffold in this period, they were made to pay dear for their freedom through being taxed at double rates.

Even at court, where the old faith was practised without hindrance, Henrietta was made sharply aware of the dangers of flaunting her religion. In December 1636 there were impressive ceremonies at the opening of the new Catholic chapel in Somerset House, but when, after three days, the stream of worshippers showed no sign of abating, Charles ordered the doors of the chapel to be closed. There was never any intention that the liberty of worship accorded to the Queen should serve as cover for Catholic proselytism. In 1637 the conversion of the fashionable Lady Newport, an event which shocked her husband considerably more than her persistent adultery, caused such a furore that Henrietta thought it necessary to make a show of scolding her Capuchins, publicly warning them not to meddle with other people's religion.

Henrietta's caution was a far remove from the wild hopes that had been entertained for the reconversion of England: from the worldly point of view, however, it was undoubtedly well advised. Beyond the court the papist Queen and all her works aroused the deepest suspicion and hostility. In puritan pulpits Henrietta was denounced as 'a daughter of Heth', while prayers were offered that 'her eye might be opened, that she might see Jesus Christ whom she hath pierced with her infidelity, superstition, and idolatry'. One especially zealous spirit claimed to have 'watched day and night for seven years to keep her Highness out of hell'. Clearly Henrietta would have done her co-religionists no favour by too open an espousal of their cause. She did not even dare to insist on the terms of her marriage treaty, whereby her children should be christened and educated as Catholics until the age of thirteen: all of them save the youngest were brought up as Anglicans. Behind the scenes, indeed, Henrietta battled fiercely against Archbishop Laud; and no doubt she deserved the jewelled cross that the Pope sent her in recognition of her services to the faith. The limited nature of her achievement, however, is reflected in the fact that so many Catholics, impoverished by fines during the 1630s, remained studiously neutral during the civil wars of the 1640s.

3

With the benefit of hindsight, the season of Charles's troubles may be seen to have begun with the attempt to impose the English Prayer Book upon the Scots in 1637. Here, most certainly, was a blunder of which Henrietta may be acquitted. Rather touchingly, Charles had brought her a copy of this prayer book in order to show her that the rituals prescribed were close to those of her own Church. He was wasting his time. In the Queen's mind Charles's Anglicanism and the Scots' Presbyterianism were hardly to be distinguished: they were both heresies and that was that. After the Scots had signed a National Covenant in March 1638, pledging themselves to defend their religion to the death, Henrietta pleaded with the King to withdraw the Prayer Book rather than risk a fight. It was the best advice she ever gave him. By June 1638, however, Charles had become adamant that the Scots must be confronted if his royal authority was to remain intact. 'I *will rather die* than yield to their *impertinent* and *damnable* demands,' he wrote with uncharacteristic emphasis to the Duke of Hamilton.

Although Henrietta had nothing to do with the origins of the Scottish war, the imminence of hostilities helped to precipitate a change in alliances at court in which she was deeply concerned. Between 1637 and 1640 a distinct *froideur* gradually began to creep into her relations with the Protestant aristocrats who had enjoyed her favour in the earlier part of the decade. The prospect of war with Spain, through which Henrietta had gained these unlikely friends, quickly receded in the face of the menace from the Scots, and those who had calculated upon some foreign imbroglio forcing Charles to call a Parliament now looked eagerly to his northern kingdom. The Crown, indeed, appeared completely isolated before the coming storm. Henrietta's hope of a French alliance proved a mirage. Richelieu was too shrewd to commit himself to such a feeble power as England had now become: besides, he had no time for Henrietta, who had constantly plotted against him with her mother and her brother, and whom he considered to be a fool.

The logic of these developments took time to work itself out. Henrietta, however, increasingly found herself at the head of a mainly Catholic set of courtiers, consisting of men like Walter Montagu and her secretary Sir John Winter, while Northumberland and Holland, her Protestant favourites of earlier years, eventually dropped away and ended up supporting Parliament in the Civil War. These changes unfortunately tended to narrow Henrietta's perspective; nor was the sudden reappearance in London of her old friend the Duchesse de Chevreuse in March 1638 any incentive to calm and measured judgement.

Worse still for the royal cause, Marie de Medici, having by this time exhausted her welcome throughout the continent, arrived in England in October 1638. Henrietta was delighted to see her mother again, and observers noted how she showed her excitement 'by the action of her hands'. After thirteen years in England she was still very much the Frenchwoman: *chic, petite, difficile* and *dévote*, as Carola Oman observed in her excellent biography. As for Marie de Medici, Charles, who had discouraged his mother-in-law from coming in the previous year, cannot have been a whit pleased to see her now. Marie de Medici's residence at St James's Palace, together with that of her six hundred attendants, cost him £36,000 a year that he could ill afford, although Her august Highness was well above treating this expense as a reason for being pleasant. Very foolishly Henrietta allowed herself to be drawn into her mother's and the Duchesse de Chevreuse's plots against Richelieu, without appearing to realise, or care, that hostility to the Cardinal had now become, in effect, hostility to France. The Queen was overheard using 'strong, violent persuasions to the King, such as must presently make us ill with France'. The time was not far off, however, when the Crown would need all the help from Richelieu that it could get.

On 29 January 1639 Henrietta gave birth to a daughter who died after a few hours, a depressing and inauspicious beginning to the year. At the end of March the King departed to fight the Scots. His army was an undisciplined rabble formed out of the trainbands of the northern counties, and appallingly led to boot. It is said that Henrietta had secured the appointment of the Earl of Holland, still in favour, as Master of the Horse, an office in which he covered himself with ridicule. The Queen was also fond of the Earl of Arundel, whom Charles made Commander-in-Chief, and of the Duke of Hamilton, who became Admiral of the Fleet. They were, indeed, just the sort of men the royal couple appreciated: beautifully mannered, connoisseurs of art, loyal, brave – and perfectly ignorant of the rudiments of military or naval affairs. The consequence was predictable: in June the King was compelled to sign a humiliating truce. Henrietta, meanwhile, had added to her unpopularity, and fed puritan suspicions of the Crown, by organising a collection of money from English Catholics. By June some £10,000 had been raised, though many Catholics seemed wary of tying their fortunes too closely to a monarchy that appeared already on the verge of collapse.

At court there were no prognostications of doom. On 5 December 1639 Charles told the Privy Council that he meant to summon a Parliament for the following April, yet in the interim the King and Queen continued to live as though the bases of absolutism were eternally guaranteed. To cheer Henrietta up, for she was pregnant again, Charles spent over £16,000 buying her Wimbledon Manor. For her part Henrietta arranged an extravagant masque for 29 January 1640. The King played Philogenes triumphing over discord, while Henrietta, dressed as an Amazon, descended from the heavens in order to inspire him to further acts of virtue. All the great figures at court took part: Howards, Russells, Lennoxes and Herberts – 'a company of worse faces was never assembled than the Queen had got together', the Earl of Northumberland sourly observed.

Henrietta showed an equal lack of flair in the political arena. She still distrusted Strafford, on whose formidable abilities the King's

future now depended. It was, according to Clarendon, 'by the open
and visible power of the queen' and with the aim of balancing
Strafford's power, that Sir Henry Vane, a court time-server, was made
Secretary of State. Strafford vigorously resisted this appointment
of a man whom he despised, and found himself the target of
Henrietta's 'declared and unseasonable displeasure' for his pains.
Events, unfortunately, proved him correct. When Parliament met in
April 1640, Vane's mismanagement of the Commons, after Strafford
had brilliantly dominated the Lords, helped to wreck the King's hopes
of receiving subsidies. Following this failure, Vane, supported by
Henrietta, could only counsel that the assembly be dissolved. Thus,
after only twenty-two days, ended the Short Parliament. Vane's
loyalty lasted a little longer, until Charles had dismissed him from
all offices, but by the end of 1641 he had gone over to Parliament's
side. Too late, in May 1640, Henrietta realised that she had misjudged
Strafford. He now appeared to her what he had seemed all along
to impartial observers, 'the most capable and faithful of the king's
servants'. But she was still the same Henrietta, unable to discover
the moral qualities of that iron figure without also noting that he
had 'the finest hands of any man in the world'.

After the failure of the Short Parliament popular fury fell upon
the Queen, whose part in securing the dissolution was widely
suspected. Someone scratched a message on the window of Charles's
antechamber in Whitehall Palace: 'God save the King. God confound
the Queen with all her offspring.' Yet Henrietta, albeit in the
last stages of pregnancy (she gave birth to Prince Henry on 8
July), was all energy and determination. No longer did she advise
Charles to conciliate the Scots: rather, she was eager that they
should be taught a lesson. She herself would help to provide the
wherewithal. An appeal went off to the Pope, explaining her plight
and soliciting aid. Rome had perhaps grown a little disenchanted
with Henrietta, who in preceding years had exasperated officials
by the pertinacity with which she sued for first George Con and
then Walter Montagu to be made Cardinals. Montagu was regarded
as a particularly unsuitable choice. Now in reply to Henrietta's
pleas the Pope was apparently obliging, in reality wholly unhelpful.
Of course he would give her money: she could have eight thousand men as well, always provided that Charles declared himself

a Catholic. Of that, as Henrietta well knew, there was no chance whatsoever.

Charles's second attempt to subdue the Scots, in the summer of 1640, proved even more catastrophic than his first. His army was really non-existent as an effective fighting force, so that when the Scots marched into England and occupied Newcastle, he had no choice but to buy them off with a subsidy of £850 per day. That in turn meant that he would have to call another Parliament to find the money. Yet, though it was obvious that the King's personal government was breaking down, there was no attempt to trim policy to the coming storm. Charles's desire to please Henrietta led him, in celebration of Prince Henry's birth, to order the release of all Catholics held in captivity. By September puritan outrage had reached such a dangerous pitch that the Secretary of State advised that the papal agent should leave the country and the Queen's Capuchins be sent out of London for their safety.

The Long Parliament, which met on 3 November 1640, would, over the next year, systematically dismantle the entire system of government whereby Charles had carried on his personal rule. The initial fury of the Commons, however, fell less on Charles than on Henrietta. To protect her, Charles had given out that it was on her advice that he was calling Parliament, but no one was fooled by this transparent ploy. As the opposition could not at first quite steel itself to attack the King directly, it chose as scapegoat a less intimidating target, the detested papist Queen. Through *her* influence, it was alleged, the Catholics had been protected; through *her* intermediacy the Crown had been in collusion with the Pope. Everything pointed, in puritan eyes, to a 'grand conspiracy of the Pope and his Jesuited Instruments'; and since it was not possible, in seventeenth-century England, to have a Catholic plot without gunpowder, Parliament ordered all Catholic houses to be searched for explosives. A committee was set up to investigate why the penal laws against recusants had not been properly enforced. Windebanke, the Secretary of State, convicted of having issued pardons to Catholics, fled the country to escape the wrath of the Commons. Henrietta herself was bitterly criticised for her attempts to raise money from the Catholics. On 22 November a mob gathered outside the Queen's Chapel and assaulted the worshippers coming away from mass.

Charles, forced to bow before the storm, issued a proclamation ordering convicted papists to withdraw ten miles from London within fifteen days under pain of death. In January 1641 another edict ordered all Catholic priests to leave the country within three months. In the face of this persecution Henrietta veered wildly between defiance, surrender and policy, grasping desperately at one expedient after another. 'I am ready to obey the King,' she announced in one of her bolder moods, 'but not to obey four hundred of his subjects.' An attempt by Parliament to secure the dismissal of all her Catholic servants was bravely resisted. At other times, though, she contemplated flight, or dreamt of an alliance with France. On 5 February 1641, fearful because her favourites Montagu and Digby were under questioning by the Commons, she attempted conciliation, promising to send the papal agent home and to limit the number of Catholics attending her chapel. But whichever way she turned, nothing ever diminished the implacable hatred of her enemies. Even the Fates now seemed malign: in the midst of all the papist-hunting madness her three-year-old daughter Anne died.

In January 1641, after all hope of help from Richelieu had been abandoned, Charles entered into an alliance with Holland, betrothing his daughter Mary to the Prince of Orange's son. Henrietta's snobbery was ineradicable, even *in extremis*, and it was only with ostentatious difficulty that she managed to reconcile herself to the marriage of her daughter, '*la fille d'une fille de France*', with a Dutch princeling. When the fourteen-year-old bridegroom arrived in England on 19 April 1641 Henrietta was unable to unbend so far as to give him a conventional kiss.

Meanwhile the parliamentary opposition, led by John Pym, had determined upon the judicial murder of the Earl of Strafford, whom they had identified as the one man capable of defeating their aims. Henrietta went to Westminster Hall with the King to watch the trial, in which Strafford defended himself with such skill that by 10 April the case against him had patently failed. Undeterred, the opposition bloodhounds brought forward a Bill of Attainder, which simply *declared* that Strafford was guilty of treason and should therefore be executed. Years later, Henrietta would recall how she had arranged secret meetings at the dead of night with parliamentary leaders – perhaps her 'puritan' cronies of the 1630s – in order to persuade them to vote against the bill. If so, her efforts were in vain. The bill passed the Commons on 21 April, and Pym ruthlessly used the London mob to cow the House of Lords into submission.

To make assurance doubly sure he also released details of a plot to free Strafford which had been hatched in the Queen's circle during March. Henrietta had unquestionably been privy to this scheme, which involved seizing London with the remnants of the forces that had been marshalled against the Scots. A far-fetched idea at the best of times, it had been hopelessly bungled in execution. Nevertheless, its disclosure helped to convince the doubters that Parliament could never be secure while Strafford lived. No doubt the Attainder Bill would have passed in any case, but after their Lordships had been regaled with the horrors of the plot to spring Strafford from the Tower, the majority was an overwhelming 49 to 11.

Would Charles give his assent to the Attainder Bill? He had expressly assured Strafford that he was safe: 'Upon the word of a king you shall not suffer in life, honour, or fortune. Your constant, faithful friend Charles R.' His courage might indeed have been proof against any danger to himself from the mob that now surrounded Whitehall, howling for blood. There was, after all, a guard of two thousand men posted around the palace, and Charles never gave any sign of being a physical coward. But the presence of Henrietta, as well as that of the children at St James's, undermined his powers of resistance. To the outside world the Queen was still capable of bravado. When Parliament warned the royal couple not to attempt flight, she replied loftily that a daughter of Henri IV did not know how to flee. The long slow hours of suspense, however, brought a cumulative tension that might have broken the staunchest spirit.

At this critical juncture, moreover, Henrietta was without spiritual counsel. Her Capuchins had scattered to houses of safety; Rossetti, the papal agent (still in England), durst not unbar the doors of his house for six days; and Father Philip, her confessor, did not possess the weight and authority required to stiffen her will. Exactly what passed between the King and Queen will never be known: it would not be stretching credulity, however, to imagine that Henrietta became hysterical, intensifying the pressure on Charles. At any rate, on 9 May he signed the Bill of Attainder and sent Strafford to the scaffold, a decision which haunted him for the rest of his life. 'An unjust sentence that I suffered to take effect', he recalled when he too came face to face with death, 'is punished now by an unjust sentence on me.' Just before Strafford died Charles sent him word – small comfort indeed – that he would gladly have defied the Attainder if the King's life alone had been at risk.

During the weeks after his betrayal of Strafford Charles, it seemed, hardly cared what he signed. On the very day that he assented to the Bill of Attainder he also put his hand to a bill which undermined the whole basis of royal rule by establishing that Parliament could only be dissolved with its own permission. Thereafter he signed bills that effectively made unparliamentary taxation illegal and destroyed the system of prerogative and ecclesiastical courts through which the Crown had enforced its justice. Charles allowed these measures because he was already plotting a coup by which they might be reversed. To that end he travelled to Edinburgh in August 1641, hoping that, by making concessions to the Scots, he might acquire from them the military means to overawe Parliament.

Henrietta, meanwhile, had tried to leave the country. In July she told Parliament that, for reasons of health, she intended to take the waters in France. Popular rumour immediately put it about that she meant to join Jermyn, who in the scurrilous gossip of the streets was held to be her lover. Flight, however, proved more difficult to accomplish than Henrietta had imagined. Richelieu sent a stark refusal to receive her in France, while Parliament showed itself singularly unimpressed by her desire to take large quantities of jewels and plate on her supposedly convalescent mission. The Queen's departure at this time, the Commons decreed, would not be opportune: they themselves would undertake to see that whatsoever Her Majesty's health required was provided in this country. 'I give many thanks to both Houses of Parliament', Henrietta crisply returned, 'for their great Care of my Health, and their Affection to me; hoping I shall see the Effect of it.'

So while Charles was away in Scotland Henrietta was left alone at Oatlands for three months. Her isolation had become extreme. The Duchesse de Chevreuse, fairest of fair-weather friends, had left England in May 1640. 'Happy we shall be', the Earl of Northumberland mordantly remarked on her going, 'if a greater loss do never befall this country.' Rossetti, the papal agent, who had stuck bravely at his post in the face of considerable personal risk, finally departed in June. Marie de Medici, whose allowance had perforce been stopped by Charles in February, took leave of her youngest daughter for the last time in August, *en route* for Cologne. With Charles away there was no one to whom Henrietta could turn. The Earl of Holland, now an open enemy, came to Oatlands by the direction of Parliament in order to remove Prince Charles to Richmond, where he could be educated beyond the compass of any papist taint. Henrietta, who feared that some attempt might be made to seize her own person, sent the rest of her children away to another country house. Even communicating with the King by letter presented difficulties. 'I am so ill provided with persons I dare trust,' she wrote to the King's secretary, 'that at this instant I have no person that I dare send. Pray do what you can to help me, if little Will Murray cannot go, to send this letter.' Alas, even little Will Murray would turn out to be suspect.

'I swear to you', Henrietta wrote to her sister Christine on 8 August, 'that I am almost mad with the sudden change in my fortunes. From the highest pitch of contentment I am fallen into every kind of misery which affects not only me but others. The sufferings of the poor Catholics and of others who are the servants of my lord the king touch me as sensibly as can any personal sorrow.' 'You have had troubles enough,' she told Christine, 'but at least you were able to do something to escape them; we have to sit with our arms folded, quite unable to help ourselves.'

Henrietta's concern for the Catholics was well founded. After Strafford's death Charles gave up any attempt to stay the anti-papal fury. Whereas in January 1641 he had stoutly defended a priest called Goodman from execution, in June he made no effort to intervene to save some other Jesuits from the scaffold. In September his secretary counselled the dismissal of Henrietta's Capuchins before Parliament itself did the deed. 'I know not what to say,' Charles nervously replied, 'if it be not to advertise my wife of the Parliament's intentions concerning her Capuchins, and so first to hear what she will say.' The Catholic plight became still more acute when news of a widespread rebellion in Ireland reached London at the beginning of November. Wild rumours circulated that three hundred thousand

Protestants had been massacred, and there seemed every disposition to ensure a reciprocal atrocity of equal proportions. Popular outrage fell particularly upon Henrietta. It was alleged that her secretary had been in contact with the leader of the rebels and that an Irish Catholic army was standing by to invade Lancashire. People spoke of 'the Queen's rebellion'. Henrietta's confessor was hauled before the Commons and imprisoned when he refused to take the oath upon the King James Bible. Some members demanded that the Queen herself should subscribe to a declaration asserting her 'detestation of the execrable and pernicious Catholic conspiracy'.

In the circumstances it must have been a relief for Henrietta to be reunited with Charles on 24 November: she travelled to Theobalds in Hertfordshire in order to meet him on his return from Scotland. The collapse of their fortunes had made them more than ever dependent on each other, and enhanced Henrietta's influence. Parliament had secured the dismissal of all the ministers owing personal loyalty to Charles, and the administration of affairs was now in the hands of men who, if not all outright enemies of the King, were far from being submissive friends. Henrietta had become the only available confidant to whom Charles could reveal his determination to escape from the parliamentary vice. Whatever the Queen's limitations, she rarely lacked either force or decisiveness, and these qualities exerted an almost hypnotic appeal over the King in the baffling new world which had suddenly come into being. When in Scotland he had given instructions that any difficulties should be referred to the Queen, 'for she knows my mind fully'. She not only knew it; by this time she was helping to form it.

Unfortunately, though, Henrietta did not have it within her to weigh a situation accurately and give cool dispassionate advice. A level head and sound judgement are always necessary in politics, and never more so than at the end of 1641 when, for the first time since Parliament had met, there seemed to be some chance of Charles regaining the initiative. The more moderate spirits in the Commons were beginning to take fright at the lengths to which Pym was driving the revolution. The Grand Remonstrance, a document which rehearsed the wrongs endured by the nation under Charles's rule and made further suggestions for reform, passed by only eleven votes after debates that threatened to end in fisticuffs or worse. Here (one sees with hindsight) was the moment for the King to stand forth as a figure around whom the more conservative elements in the Commons could rally against the hotheads. With the appointment of the moderates Falkland and Colepeper respectively as Secretary of State and Chancellor of the Exchequer at the beginning of 1642, it seemed that Charles might be preparing to occupy the middle ground.

Seventeenth-century kings, however, were not to be converted upon the instant into nineteenth-century constitutional monarchs. Charles might twist, turn, lie and prevaricate in search of support, but he was never able to make concessions in the one place where, above all others, they were needed – his own mind. Henrietta's influence over him became supreme because she shared this ultimate intransigence. Unfortunately, though, when under threat her nature instinctively reacted with aggression. The tedious subtleties of parliamentary management were no more within her ken than the ability to distinguish between varieties of heresy. She saw only that the Commons had set themselves against the Crown, and must therefore be broken.

At the beginning of 1642, therefore, at the precise moment when Charles ought to have been doing everything in his power to appear conciliatory, he made the catastrophic error, with Henrietta breathing hotly down his neck, of trying to arrest Pym and four other leading opponents in the Commons. Pym, indeed, worried about his declining authority, had been deliberately attempting to provoke some rash act, though he can hardly have hoped for quite such a blunder. After the Grand Remonstrance he had dropped heavy hints that the Commons were about to move on to the impeachment of the Queen. According to Clarendon, Lady Carlisle was responsible for suggesting this tactic. This old friend of Henrietta's, 'who exactly knew her nature, passions, and infirmities', had now become the mistress of Pym. She knew that there was no more likely way of goading Charles to folly than to threaten his wife.

The plan to arrest the five members is said to have originated with George Digby, who was just the man to catch Henrietta's attention – aristocratic, dashing, brilliant, cosmopolitan (he spoke French and several other languages perfectly), and ever ready with some hare-brained scheme which would, as he promised, transform the situation in a trice. How dull in comparison appeared the cautious counsels of the moderate royalists. 'Go, poltroon,' Henrietta is supposed to have laughingly apostrophised Charles as he departed for the Commons to seize the five members on 4 January 1642, 'pull the ears of these rogues, or never see me again.'

Worse, Henrietta let Lady Carlisle into the secret of the impending coup, information no doubt swiftly passed on to Pym. Charles himself, though, in his usual bungling fashion, also gave the game away. The day before the attempted arrest the five members had been indicted in the Commons, though foolishly allowed to remain free. That evening Charles further advertised that some bold stroke was in the offing by forbidding the Lord Mayor to send the London militia to guard Parliament. The following morning the King's bodyguard was seen opening boxes of ammunition. No gaffe of Henrietta's, therefore, was required to persuade the five members to make themselves scarce. They deliberately lured Charles on by ostentatiously appearing in the Commons, but, by the time that the King arrived at the House to arrest them, they had fled. Instead of dramatically asserting himself, as Henrietta had intended, Charles could only make a humiliating retreat from the chamber.

Having thus exposed the depth of their hostility to the Commons, the King and Queen became once more the hate-figures of the London mob. Crowds paraded before Whitehall Palace with clubs, waving placards which extolled the virtues of 'liberty'. As at the time of Strafford's Attainder, Charles began to worry about the threat to Henrietta, 'of whose person', the Earl of Warwick observed, 'he was always more chary than of his business'. He sent orders to Portsmouth, ordering a ship to be held ready, presumably to take the Queen to France. And then on 10 January, suddenly and without warning, the royal family slipped out of London. Whether or not this move was dictated by Charles's concern for Henrietta, it proved to be another fatal error. The financial and commercial centre of the kingdom was left in the hands of their enemies. The King would not see Whitehall until he returned to die there seven years later; Henrietta would not enter the capital for nineteen years.

Hampton Court, their first port of call after their flight, was so ill prepared for their coming that the entire royal family was obliged to spend the night on a single bed. Two days later they removed to Windsor. With the King and Parliament now both making preparations for war, it was decided that Henrietta would be better out of the country. A letter addressed to her by Digby, explaining that the Prince of Orange would provide help, had been intercepted by Parliament, a mishap which produced a fresh outburst of fury against the treasonous Queen. Fortunately an excuse for her departure was at hand. She would accompany her daughter Mary (still only ten) to The Hague, where the Prince of Orange was anxiously awaiting his child bride. (If Henrietta felt any compunction about leaving her other children the fact went unrecorded.) Charles went with Henrietta and Mary to Dover, the journey being arranged 'in such post-haste', as an outraged courtier reported, 'that I never heard the like for persons of such dignity'. Henrietta did not forget, however, to take with her many of the crown jewels as well as all the personal jewellery belonging to her and Charles. She needed them to raise troops and arms for the royal cause.

The King and Queen spent a week (16–23 February) at Dover waiting for a passage. On 19 February, as if to justify Henrietta's flight, Parliament presented the King with a declaration of grievances deploring the Queen's intervention in his affairs and advising that all Catholics should be removed from employment about her person. The malice of Charles's and Henrietta's enemies, however, only strengthened the bond between them. Henrietta's departure from Dover, a fugitive with her daughter, attended by a mere handful of courtiers, made an affecting contrast with her arrival seventeen years before as a young girl steeped in the pride of France. 'His Majesty', the Venetian ambassador reported when she finally embarked, "accompanied his wife as far as the shore, and did not know how to tear himself away from her, conversing with her in sweet discourse and affectionate embraces, nor could they restrain their tears, moving all those who were present.' As Henrietta's ship made out to sea Charles rode along the cliffs to keep her in view as long as possible, waving his hat in farewell while the Queen responded from the ship's railing. The scene would have made a perfect tear-jerking ending to the royal romance. The measure of their suffering, however, had not yet been accomplished.

4

Although the Prince of Orange had pressed for his daughter-in-law Princess Mary to be sent over for education in Holland, he must have been less than enraptured that her mother should have arrived as well. The welcome he extended at The Hague was polite but by no means fulsome. Charles's sister Elizabeth of Bohemia, who was in Holland, also regarded Henrietta with some coolness for she considered her a disastrous influence upon her brother. 'I find by all the queen's and her people's conversation', Elizabeth wrote of her sister-in-law, 'that they do not desire an agreement between His Majesty and his Parliament, but that all be done by force, and rail abominably at the Parliament. I hear all and say nothing.' Elizabeth's nine-year-old daughter Sophia, who would live until 1714 and only miss becoming Queen of England in her own right by seven weeks, provides another interesting glimpse of Henrietta. Having previously only known her aunt from Van Dyck portraits she was astonished to discover 'a small woman raised upon her chair, with long skinny arms, and teeth like defence works projecting from her mouth'. After a while, though, Henrietta's charm worked its magic. 'She did me the honour', Sophia recounted in her memoirs, 'to say that she thought me rather like Mlle her daughter. So pleased was I, that from that time forwards I considered her quite handsome.'

Henrietta soon left The Hague for Breda. She loathed the Dutch, and they were not much better pleased with her. It was hardly to be expected that the light-minded Catholic queen should hit it off with dour Calvinist republicans. The Dutch, she realised with a mixture of incredulity, outrage and amusement, just did not understand what it meant to be a queen, and showed little disposition to rectify their ignorance. They would subject her to long stares and then walk away without saying a word; or even sit down in her presence without removing their hats. Nevertheless, Henrietta worked hard to gather money for the royal cause, swallowing her Bourbon pride in order to haggle with hard-faced Dutch merchants whose sympathies were entirely with Parliament. They knew how much the money was needed, she wrote to Charles in May, so 'you may judge . . . how they keep their foot on our throat'. The ordeal of parting with jewels was severe. 'You cannot imagine how pretty your pearls were', Charles was informed in the same letter, 'when they were taken out of their gold settings and made into a chain.' Through such sacrifices she succeeded in raising handsome sums; and she borrowed some more. Unfortunately, though, very little of the ammunition and supplies which she sent to England reached its destination. Nothing daunted, Henrietta tried desperately, though again unsuccessfully, to patch together a foreign alliance – with the Dutch, with France, with Denmark, with anyone who might be able to help her knight in distress. When Richelieu died in November 1642, Henrietta immediately solicited aid from his successor, Cardinal Mazarin.

Above all, she wanted to return to England to be with Charles. The King, however, had lost control of the Navy. Parliamentary vessels were patrolling the Channel, and, as Henrietta complained, she had as little influence over the winds as her husband did over Parliament. Even getting reliable news from England was difficult enough. Rumours of disasters abounded: the King had been killed, the Prince of Wales had been taken prisoner, a great battle had been lost. The uncertainty must have been torture for Henrietta. There was a story that she had donned a disguise and gone all alone to a bookshop in order to enquire for news, only to have her incognito betrayed by her extreme agitation. Her feelings found relief in a series of letters to Charles (*'Mon cher coeur'*, they always began) that afford a valuable insight into both her character and her relations with her husband. The sheer volume of the correspondence is remarkable in one who found letter-writing a struggle and who in addition had to render all her messages into cypher. Hysteria, however, lent her energy. She did not trust Charles an inch as a strategist or a politician, and she eagerly assumed the wifely duty of chastising, scolding and bullying him into effectiveness.

Her first concern was that he should seize the port of Hull, with its valuable ammunition stores. 'Rumour has it that you are returning to London,' she wrote to him soon after her arrival in Holland. 'I do not believe it and hope that you are more constant in your resolution, for you have already learnt to your cost that want of perseverance has been your ruin.' Nothing, however, was ever so inconstant as Henrietta's confidence in her husband. Having declared in one sentence her faith in Charles's determination to occupy Hull, she proceeded in the next to parade her doubts. 'Assuredly you will

never change: if that is the case good-bye for ever; I must bethink
me of my plan to enter a convent.' This threat of the convent, and
her imminent self-immuring therein should Charles fail to follow
her instructions, would be a recurring theme in Henrietta's letters.
Or perhaps she would be forced to take still more dramatic steps.
'If you go back on your word,' she stormed, 'there is only death for
me.' She had left England, she told him, because she apprehended
that his fears for her might undermine his resolve, but since he now
continued as irresolute as ever she might just as well be with him
at York: 'my journey is rendered ridiculous by what you do.'

Surprisingly, when Charles did fail to secure Hull, Henrietta let him
off comparatively lightly. 'You have demonstrated your weakness;
now is the time to demonstrate your justice . . . Courage! I have
never had so much. It is a good omen.' Concerning the governor of
the town, who had defected to Parliament, she was less forgiving: 'I
would have flung the rascal over the walls, or he should have done the
same thing to me.' In the long term, however, misfortune redoubled
Henrietta's hectoring propensities. According to Clarendon she had
extracted a promise from Charles, before she left England, that
he would 'receive no person into any favour or trust, who had
disserved him, without her privity and consent.' Now the Queen
convinced herself that the King was on the point of selling out both
his friends and his principles. In her imagination she and her tiny
circle in Holland – Jermyn and Digby to the fore – were the only
true upholders of the royalist faith.

Nothing could have been more unfair. Not only was Charles, in
England, bearing the heat and the burden of the day; his mind was set
like rock against compromise. 'I have set my rest on the Justice of my
cause,' he declared after the inconclusive battle of Edgehill in October
1642, 'being resolved that no Extremity or Misfortune shall make me
yield. For either I will be a Glorious King or a patient Martyr.' It was
very much the latter role that appears in his relations with his wife.
Henrietta's carping turned to white fury when, rightly or wrongly,
she came to believe that the King's followers were criticising her for
having achieved so little in Holland. 'If everyone had done their duty
as I have, you would not be reduced to the condition you are now
in,' she shot back. To these importunate adjurations Charles never
offered anything but abject replies. He wrote to her of his loneliness

and failing health, insisting always on how much he missed her. Amidst his own difficulties and sufferings, he continually extended sympathy and sorrow for *her* afflictions. 'I think it not the least of my misfortunes', he told her in February 1643, 'that for my sake you have seen so much hazard.' Clarendon, in his *History*, complains that Charles 'saw with her eyes, and determined by her judgement; and did not only pay her this adoration, but desired that all men should know that he was swayed by her: which was not good for either of them'.

This dog-like devotion is usually interpreted as the psychological quirk of a man stretched upon the rack and searching desperately for an authoritative and reassuring hand. But there was more to it than that. Henrietta scolded, but her lively, spontaneous letters – spontaneous in spite of the cypher – also show her as both loving and lovable. 'Forgive me if I have said anything in my letters a little passionate,' she wrote. 'It is the affection I have for you which makes me do it, and my care for your honour.' The prickings of Bourbon pride excluded the possibility of concession: 'to die of a consumption of royalty is a death which I could not endure, having found by experience the malady to be insupportable.' She longed to be with him again, 'in spite of all the wicked people who wish to separate us'. 'The news of you that I am waiting for will be life or death to me, for if it should happen that I cannot join you, that would be my death: I cannot live without you.' The likelihood of Henrietta's imminent demise lost force through repetition; nevertheless, one feels, her sentiments were sincere. 'This country', she complained in more down-to-earth style, 'is too trying to the patience of persons who, like me, have none.' Part of the trouble was that, having sent off the money she had raised, she found herself penniless. 'Adieu, *mon cher coeur*,' one letter pointedly ends, 'I am going to take my supper, and as it has cost money I must not let it be spoiled.' The same impish wit appears in another of her epistolary farewells, parodying the Puritan preachers of London: 'I'll go pray for the man of sin that has married the popish brat of France.'

Even when, early in February 1643, Henrietta did finally succeed in getting away from Holland, misfortune still dogged her. Throughout her life it seemed that she only had to board a ship to set the tempests howling: 'Maman's weather', her children called it. On this occasion the elements exceeded themselves: for eleven days and eleven nights Henrietta's little fleet was blown helplessly about the North Sea. Two of the ships, laden with military supplies, went down. In the appalling conditions the most basic sanitation was impossible, so that after the voyage everyone's clothing had to be burnt. Yet Henrietta rose magnificently above the danger and indignities. Tied to her berth, she derived much entertainment from the sometimes startling last confessions of her terrified Catholic attendants. 'Comfort yourselves, *mes chères*,' she cheered them, 'Queens of England are never drowned.' This prediction has proved correct. Nevertheless, she told Charles after landing safely back in Holland, 'I did not think to see you again. My sole regret in dying was that in this accident your enemies might find comfort and your friends the reverse.'

The frightening experience did not prevent Henrietta from re-embarking almost immediately. This time, for once, her voyage was calm, though there was still the danger from the parliamentary navy. Charles's opponents knew that nothing would be more likely to bring him to terms than the capture of his wife. Henrietta's ships, however, managed to avoid an encounter by feinting north towards Newcastle, before actually landing at Bridlington Bay in Yorkshire. The enemy, however, soon caught up with its quarry. Henrietta landed safely and settled down for the night in a cottage on the quayside, only to be awakened in the early hours of the morning by the sound of cannon balls crashing around her, 'of which you may believe', as she wrote to Charles later that day, 'that I did not like the sound'. The Queen beat a hasty retreat inland, though, according to her own rather vainglorious account, when she insisted on returning to her cottage to rescue a pet dog a man was blown to pieces only twenty paces from her. The succeeding couple of hours she spent in a ditch – in Yorkshire, in February, at 5 a.m., in her nightclothes – until the Dutch admiral Van Tromp arrived, '*un peu tard*', Henrietta thought, to scatter the attacking vessels. Two cannon balls, it was discovered, had penetrated the cottage where she had lain.

The Queen had been bombarded, a parliamentary pamphleteer cynically observed, 'for the king's Own Good'. But Henrietta, judging by her excited description of the event, thoroughly enjoyed the episode, at least in retrospect. Her arrival in England, with military equipment for Charles's cause, gave her a prestige in which she rejoiced. She did not suffer either, like some of the more sensitive royalists, from any feeling of revulsion at the idea of civil conflict. On the contrary, this was war, and she was a daughter of Henri IV. There would be time for scruples and displays of honour when the battle had been won. Staying with the Strickland family at Boynton Hall on the way to York, Henrietta coolly possessed herself of the magnificent silver which the family had been rash enough to bring out in her honour. The times demanded such sacrifices, she explained, leaving a portrait of herself in recompense. Surprisingly, General Fairfax, the commander of the parliamentary forces in the area, wrote to Henrietta asking if he might have the privilege of acting as her escort, an offer which was wisely ignored. Henrietta was in the highest spirits, even teasing Charles about reports of him which she had picked up on her arrival. 'You pass for a dangerous creature,' she mocked, 'but I am entirely yours.'

In the event, though, another five months passed before she saw her husband. Charles was in Oxford, and Parliament's forces lay between them. From March to June 1643 Henrietta was obliged to remain in York, while the King bent his military policy to the great end of trying to effect a reunion. During this period the royal forces in the north enjoyed some success, which did nothing to moderate Henrietta's aggressive instincts. She cut a dashing figure with the troops, and volunteers flocked to her standard. In addition, she became fast friends with William Cavendish, Earl of Newcastle, the royal commander in the north, an able man of great wealth and influence who might have done even better if he could have managed to rise before noon on a regular basis. Constant coaxing was required to dissuade him from resigning his post. Most of the supplies that Henrietta had intended for Charles were given to Newcastle's army, in which she took a proprietorial pride. She revelled in discussions about strategy, and some sharp differences of opinion with Charles developed. Henrietta wanted to subdue the entire north, and champed at her inactivity in York; Charles needed both men and supplies for his own use. As invariably occurred when Henrietta was crossed, the convent made a reappearance in her letters. 'When I see you,' she wrote to Charles, 'you will say that I am a good little girl, and very patient, but I declare to you that being patient is killing me, and were it not for love of you, I would, with the greatest truth, rather put myself into a convent than live in this manner.'

For a short time Henrietta almost seemed to encourage Newcastle to defy Charles's authority. 'You are not the only one who has been chid,' she told her general, 'I have had my share of it, but that does not affect me when I have reason on my side.' She had again got it into her head, again mistakenly, that Charles was intent on making some compromise settlement. 'If you make peace and disband your army,' she stormed at her unfortunate spouse, 'I am absolutely resolved to go into France, not being willing to fall again into the hands of these people, being well assured that if power remains with them, it will not be well for me in England.' A month later, ironically enough, Parliament sent a deputation to Henrietta urging her to mediate with her husband for peace. The unsurprising failure of this mission led to a backlash against the Queen which showed that her wariness was fully justified. Troops in London seized her Capuchin priests and smashed up her chapel. Then in June the Commons formally impeached her on a charge of high treason.

Assured of the malice of her enemies, Henrietta did manage to grasp that those who do not hang together are all too likely to hang separately. Only a fortnight after threatening Charles with her departure to France she was exerting her charm to mend the breach. 'All my actions and thoughts have been for you,' she told him. 'Therefore, if that be any fault let me confess it; since you think it, I recognise and confess it, and hope for absolution.' She also sought to bring Newcastle back into line. 'Let us not mind our passions,' she wrote to him on 10 May, 'and let us reflect that for a small offence we may ruin all. I give you no advice which I have not taken myself, having subdued my vexation upon the march of the army for the public good . . .'

Such time as Henrietta was able to spare from the strategy of war she devoted to diplomacy, eagerly offering Denmark the Orkney and Shetland islands in return for military assistance. She also still nursed hopes of help from France. Neither of these negotiations achieved anything, nor did anything constructive emerge from her meeting with Montrose, who arrived in York to plead for money and troops with which to subdue Scotland. Henrietta instinctively liked Montrose, and perhaps, left to herself, she would

have trusted him. Charles, however, preferred more cautious counsels.

By May Henrietta's optimism about the military situation in the
north was beginning to evaporate. 'This army is called the Queen's
army,' she complained, 'but I have little power over it, and I assure
you that if I had, all would go on better than it does.' To the
south, however, the position had improved sufficiently for Charles
to command her to come to Oxford immediately, bringing as many
men as she could. The King, indeed, intended that Newcastle also
should join him, but Henrietta's on-the-spot strategical analysis did
not in this instance permit obedience. She herself, though, left York
early in June, and as soon as she was on the road her morale soared.
Years later she retained romantic and immodest memories of this
journey. 'The queen', she recalled, 'was always on horseback, living
with her soldiers without any feminine refinement, as one might
imagine Alexander living with his troops. She used to eat quite
informally in the open air, treating them like brothers. For their
part they loved her beyond compare.' A letter that she sent to Charles
from Newark, on the way south, captures her euphoric mood. She
explained that she was bringing him three thousand foot, thirty
companies of horse and dragoons, six pieces of cannon and two
mortars. Jermyn was in command while, as she wrote, '*Sa Majesté
généralissime, et extresmement diligente*, brought up the rear with
a hundred and fifty wagons of baggage to govern in case of battle.'
She was obviously having a whale of a time.

Military necessity requiring a somewhat circuitous route, Henrietta
passed through Stratford-on-Avon, where, tradition has it, she stayed
with Shakespeare's daughter at New Place. On 13 July, at the foot of
Edgehill, where battle had been joined the previous autumn, she at
last met Charles again, after nearly seventeen months. It is reported
that, skittish as ever, Henrietta refused to see her husband in private
until he promised to make Henry Jermyn a peer. Here was food
for the gossip-mongers, who were forever speculating upon some
impropriety in the Queen's relations with her chief adviser. Charles,
however, granted the request without demur. For the moment, fortune
shone upon the royal pair. On the very day of their reunion Prince
Rupert scattered a parliamentary detachment at nearby Adwalton
Moor, and in Wiltshire there was substantial victory at the battle

of Roundway Down. Then at the end of the month Rupert took Bristol. The King and Queen had some reason to believe that the tide had turned.

Oxford accorded them a triumphant welcome. The King was living in Christ Church, and Henrietta installed herself nearby in the Warden's lodgings at Merton. (The Warden himself, having espoused the cause of Parliament, had long since departed.) There was a private way between the two colleges so that Charles could visit his wife without attracting public attention. At Merton the magnificent chapel once more echoed to the sounds of the mass, a circumstance which, transferred on the wing of rumour to London, became an assurance that papistry was pullulating on every Oxford street. Henrietta's Anglican ladies-in-waiting resorted for their devotions to Trinity where they appeared in the chapel 'half-dressed, like angels'.

The vision was captivating but also disastrously flawed. For though the soldiers had ousted the university dons, importing their coarse brutalities into the slumbrous haunts of Academe, Oxford never convinced as an army headquarters. About the royal court there hung that same air of unreality that had pervaded Whitehall in the 1630s. The King and Queen might be seen walking with their spaniels through the golden quadrangles; pastoral plays were performed in college gardens; portrait painters pursued their flattering trade; the women of the court minced and simpered as though the most pressing business of the hour was the prosecution of intrigue. It was not that Charles and Henrietta actively promoted frivolities: rather, that frivolities were an inalienable part of the world over which they had presided before the war. The Cavaliers might be as determined and true as Henrietta herself, but the times demanded a harsher and sterner ethos than any which she or Charles could inspire. Already in East Anglia Cromwell was forging a mighty military instrument through the Puritan imperatives of discipline and prayer.

The royalist cause, moreover, suffered from divided counsels, with the King never able to impose a single, consistent view. Henrietta, when she arrived in Oxford, wanted to follow up the recently gained successes with an immediate attack on London. Whether she was right or wrong – and in this instance she may well have been right – she always knew her own mind, that first prerequisite for military leadership which Charles so notably lacked. But in Oxford she soon discovered to her mortification that new counsellors had risen to prominence in her absence. There was, for instance, Sir Edward Hyde (later Lord Clarendon), a moderate, pragmatic man of rare ability, steadfast principle and peculiarly English common sense — or, as Henrietta saw him, a vain and pompous proser, running to fat and wholly lacking in the courtly graces which she valued so highly. Another, very different, influence was Charles's nephew Prince Rupert, whose reputation, based on his dash and fire as a cavalry leader, stood at its zenith in the middle of 1643. He might be thought just the type to capture Henrietta's admiration, but somehow she never liked or trusted him. Perhaps he was too arrogant to trouble himself with gaining her good opinion. Anyway, Henrietta felt the gravest misgivings when, early in August, Rupert persuaded the King to undertake the siege of Gloucester; and events were to prove her justified.

At the same time the Queen was involved in another policy dispute, though her role in the matter is not altogether clear. The Earl of Holland, her courtier friend of earlier years, had opted for Parliament when the war broke out, but after the royalist victories in the summer of 1643, this unblushing opportunist appeared in Oxford to make his submission to the King. Sir Edward Hyde advocated that the returning prodigal should be treated with honour in order to encourage further defections, but the King was distant and unforgiving. Henrietta is often assumed to have been responsible for Charles's recalcitrance, though it is also reported that Holland's charms very soon began to win her round. Perhaps in her heart she had always been ready, notwithstanding her fulminations against traitors, to forgive her former favourite, for Jermyn, who never crossed his patroness, had argued Holland's case from the first. In any case the discussion soon proved academic, for Holland, disappointed with the welcome accorded him, returned to the parliamentary fold in London, where he complained that there had been too much papistry in Oxford for a patriot of his type to stomach.

In truth, after the first thrill of reunion with Charles, Henrietta's life in Oxford proved to be a sad anticlimax compared with the excitements of her journey thither. She still carried on her negotiations with France, but the best that can be said about them is that they attracted less odium than Charles's efforts to bring troops over from

Ireland. For the rest, Henrietta whiled away her time writing mildly flirtatious letters to the Earl of Newcastle, in nostalgic tribute to the bond she had formed with him in the north. At the beginning of August the King asked her to pass on to the Earl his orders to march into East Anglia. 'I answered him', Henrietta informed her former comrade, 'that you were a better judge than he of that, and that I should not do it. The truth is that they envy your army.' With Charles temporarily away from Oxford, Henrietta professed herself fearful of a siege. 'I must flatter you', she told Newcastle, 'so that, if the King does not come to the rescue, you will.' After the battle of Newbury – 'a very great victory' according to Henrietta; in reality an inconclusive slaughter – she took credit for the part played by the men from 'our army of the North'. Even so, the Solemn League and Covenant which Parliament signed on 22 September, and which brought the Scots into the war against the King, carried a message of doom into Cavalier Oxford. 'I am fed up,' Henrietta wrote, 'not with being beaten but with hearing people talk about being beaten.'

Soon, though, even her own naturally confident spirit began to droop. By the end of October 1643 she realised that she was pregnant again. (She was, after all, still only thirty-five.) This discovery, combined with the approaching threat from the Scots in the north, for the first time undermined her enthusiasm for the war. 'No one could be in a more miserable state than I,' she wrote to her sister Christine in February 1644, 'being pregnant and not knowing where to go for safety, there being no stronghold in the country and all being nothing but battle.' Talk of a truce no longer aroused her scorn and contumely: 'the fact is', she told Newcastle, 'the king's army here needs it'. The tone in which she wrote to her former general became rather sharper, to the extent of stinging him to protest. 'Remember what I told you at York,' she riposted with a flash of her old coquetry, 'I only scold my friends, never those for whom I care nothing.'

Charles, desperate on Henrietta's behalf amidst all his other worries, ordered Prince Rupert to break off his campaign in the north in order to escort her to Chester, only to change his mind a day or so later. As the Queen's health suddenly appeared in sharp decline she would go south-west to Bath to take the waters. Henrietta left Oxford on 17 April. Charles accompanied her as far as Abingdon, where they parted – for ever as it turned out. This time, though, there is no poignant account of their leave-taking as with their farewell at Dover in 1642. No doubt they imagined that they would see each other again soon enough. Ignorance of the future, indeed, was the only blessing still vouchsafed to them. Before Charles, as he rode back to Oxford, lay defeat, captivity, trial and execution; before Henrietta, as her coach jolted southwards, years of poverty, struggle, humiliation and heartbreak.

The troubles of the moment, however, more than sufficed. Henrietta's pregnancy was giving her pains that made the journey a torture; and Bath, when she arrived there, proved to be no longer the amiable little spa that she remembered, but a war-famished outpost ravaged by disease. Henrietta feared capture above all things, and Parliament's forces were menacingly close. Deciding to press on into the royalist heartland of the south-west, she reached Exeter on 3 May. From thence she sent Charles such an alarming volley of bulletins about her health – 'the time has come for me to think of another world' – that the King took fright and sent to his doctor in London: 'Mayerne, for the love of me,' he wrote, 'go to my wife.' Mayerne, although over seventy, duly proceeded to Exeter. His methods were certainly direct. 'I think I shall go mad,' the Queen bemoaned in her distress. 'There is no occasion to fear it, Madame,' the imperturbable doctor replied, 'you are mad already.'

On 16 June Henrietta gave birth to a daughter, Henriette-Anne, the future Minette, but still her condition seemed to worsen. On 28 June she sent Charles a list of her symptoms that lacked nothing in comprehensiveness. She told of 'a seizure of paralysis in the legs and all over the body'; of bowels and stomach that 'seemed to weigh more than a hundred pounds'; of 'the same weight' that pressed upon her back; of a heart 'so tightly constricted that I seem to suffocate'; of an arm 'without any feeling'; of knees and legs 'colder than ice'. 'I am sometimes like a mad woman, scarcely able to stir and quite doubled up.' As if that were not enough, 'the disease has risen to my head, and I can no longer see with one eye'. Modern medicine diagnoses puerperal sepsis, but it is difficult to avoid the conclusion that Dr Mayerne's blunt opinion also had something to it. '*La plus malheureuse créature de monde*,' Henrietta signed herself, 'who cannot write any more.' Of their new daughter she made no mention. It was a ghastly letter for Charles to receive at a time when he was overwhelmed by military catastrophe. For on 2 July, at Marston Moor, Cromwell destroyed royal power in the north.

Meanwhile the Earl of Essex, in command of the parliamentary army in the south, appeared bent on capturing the Queen. When her sanguine request that he should grant her safe passage through his lines was curtly refused, Henrietta knew that she must move on, whatever her condition. In that disastrous letter of 28 June, she also explained that she was making for Falmouth and thence, she hoped, for France. 'I am showing you by this last action', she wrote with some complacency, 'that nothing weighs with me so much as your preservation . . . for your affairs, as they now stand, would be prejudiced if you came to help me. I know that your love for me will make you hazard all to do so, which is why I also hazard something, my unhappy life, which is worth little enough except as you value it.'

Ironically enough, Charles did come to the south-west and achieved his most notable triumph of the war by so doing, for he trapped Essex's army at Lostwithiel. But by the time the King reached Exeter in late July, Henrietta had long been gone. She took several companions with her, including the inevitable Jermyn, her pet dwarf Jeffrey Hudson, and several spaniels; her infant daughter, however, was left behind entrusted to the care of one of her ladies-in-waiting. The seriousness of Henrietta's condition, however, cannot be doubted. 'Here is the woefullest spectacle my eyes yet looked on,' wrote a Cornish gentleman who saw her just before embarcation, 'the most worn and weak pitiful creature in the world, the poor queen shifting for an hour's life longer.' Even after she put to sea on 10 July she came close to destruction. Her ship was chased by a parliamentary squadron which opened fire and scored a hit before a storm – 'Maman's weather' again – scattered the pursuers. Henrietta, by her own account, behaved with the utmost courage, giving orders that the ship should be blown up before she should be taken prisoner. Her enemies, for their part, boasted that she had enjoyed 'no other courtesy from England but cannon balls to convey her to France'.

5

The desperately ill refugee who struggled ashore at Le Conquet near Brest instantly became, once established as the daughter of Henri IV, the honoured guest of France. A queen reduced to the lowliest level of misery and distress is always an affecting spectacle, and the natural flow of sympathy towards Henrietta acquired an added momentum from the knowledge that it was England, the hereditary enemy, which had brought this daughter of France so low. The Queen Regent, Anne of Austria, allotted her sister-in-law a pension of thirty thousand *livres* a month; better still, from the point of view of posterity, she also temporarily allotted her as companion and lady-in-waiting Madame de Motteville, to whose ready pen we owe some vivid glimpses of the Queen of England in her native France.

At first Henrietta made her invalid way to Bourbon l'Archambault, a lovely town in the peaceful heart of France, where the thermal springs were credited with special healing qualities. 'I begin to hope that I shall not die,' she wrote encouragingly to Charles in September 1644. At this stage she still thought confidently in terms of returning to England the following spring. She was, she told her husband, very well treated in France, but there was always one essential lacking. 'I have there [i.e. in England] what I have not here, which is *you*, without which I can never be happy.'

By November she had recovered sufficiently to go to Paris, accompanied by her brother Gaston whom she had not seen since they had been so close as children. Anne of Austria's bounty did not abate: Henrietta was given an apartment in the Louvre, while St Germain, where she had spent such happy days as a girl, was set aside for her use in the summer. About her there soon gathered a little coterie of Cavaliers, who displayed that bent for squabbling invariably found among political exiles who are supposed to be serving the same cause. There was the inevitable Jermyn, '*son favori*', as Madame de Motteville dubbed him without any hint of disapproval save for his lack of brain-power; there was Wilmot, a dismissed royal general who threatened to fight a duel with George Digby in 1647; Prince Rupert, who arrived in the middle of 1646; the Earl of Newcastle, who had left England after Marston Moor but who found himself copiously forgiven by Henrietta for his military failure; and a shifty assemblage of gentry many of whose families had known better days under the Tudors – Careys, Denhams, Crofts, Killigrews and Berkeleys. It was a motley collection, and when Montrose, the noblest of the royalists, came to see Henrietta in the spring of 1647, he was shocked by the prevailing atmosphere, to the extent of refusing to allow his niece to serve as lady-in-waiting to Henrietta. 'There is neither Scots man nor woman welcome that way,' he explained, 'neither would any honour or virtue, chiefly a woman, suffer themselves to live in so lewd and worthless a place.'

The truth was that Henrietta, for all her sorrows, possessed naturally high spirits that soon began to bubble again in her native land. 'Her temperament inclined her to gaiety', Madame de Motteville reports, 'and even amid her tears, if it occurred to her to say something amusing, she would stem them to divert the company.' Equally, while no one could ever doubt the strength of her opinions, she advanced them with 'a charm and raillery which belied any signs of *hauteur*'. As always she worked tirelessly on Charles's behalf; as always, too, she failed in all that she undertook. She insisted on placing hopes in Mazarin, though the Cardinal was more than content to see England reduced to impotence by internal divisions. Charles was quite rightly sceptical about gaining any help from that source, for he knew that Mazarin was also in correspondence with the Speaker of the House of Commons. No failure, however, was ever humiliating enough to dash Henrietta's promiscuous enthusiasm for negotiations. She sought money from Venice, soldiers from the Duke of Lorraine, an invasion from Ireland, intervention from the Pope. (Rome by now had grown definitely tired of Henrietta's solicitations, and complained that she was surrounded by Protestants.) When earthly aid failed, Henrietta even tried to get Father Robert d'Aubrissel, the founder of Fontevrault, canonised, in the hope that he might manage some heavenly addition to the good offices he had performed for English kings during his life.

At the same time Henrietta also applied herself with renewed vigour to the wifely duty of keeping her husband up to the mark. Incredibly, at the beginning of 1645 both the King and Queen remained confident about the outcome of the war. Charles nevertheless found it necessary, for appearance's sake, to enter into discussions with the Presbyterian majority in the Commons, whose aim was to reform the Church of England by abolishing bishops and establishing elected councils in their place. Henrietta was outraged by these negotiations. 'For the love of God,' she wrote in January 1645, 'don't trust these people.' On no account, she scolded, should Charles allow control of the militia to slip from his hands; nor should he ever abandon those who had served him, 'as well the bishops as the poor Catholics'. Charles assured Henrietta that he had not the remotest intention of submitting to unfavourable terms, and pleaded with her to show more consideration. 'Believe me,' he told her in April 1645, 'thy kindness is as necessary to comfort my heart as this assistance is for my affairs.'

By the end of 1645, however, after the conclusive defeat at Naseby on 14 June, not even the King or the Queen could avoid recognising that their cause was in ruins. Charles's tactics in this situation were to make a play of seeking a settlement in order to gain time. His hope, not an ill-founded one, was that the various factions ranged against him – the Commons, the Army, and the Scots – would fall out, thus creating a situation which he could exploit. There was one matter, though, on which he declared himself unwilling to waver, even in temporising negotiations. He would not betray the Church of England.

To stick on *that* point was quite incomprehensible to Henrietta. As the crisis confronting the King deepened, she who for so long had chided him not to yield an inch of ground became the pragmatist, prepared in the last analysis to cede whatever was necessary in order to save the throne. After twenty years of marriage she still did not understand the depth of her husband's religious commitment. Her concern of the previous year that he should not sacrifice the Anglican bishops was now quite forgotten. 'Presbytery, or something worse, will be forced upon you, whether you will or not,' she told him. 'Come, the question in short is, whether you will choose to be a King of Presbytery, or no King; and yet Presbytery or perfect Independency be.' Without dispute this was sound and sensible advice, but perhaps it would have come better from someone who had not spent the previous five years animadverting hysterically against any suspicion of a settlement. In any case, her counsel fell on deaf ears. Charles not only saw the Church of England as ultimately 'the only firm foundation' of his power; he was also deeply attached to Anglican devotions. 'With what patience', he demanded of Henrietta, 'wouldest thou give ear to him who should persuade thee, for worldly respects, to leave the communion of the Roman church for any other? Indeed, sweetheart, this is my case; for, suppose my concession in this should prove but temporary, it may palliate tho' not excuse my sin.'

From May 1646 to January 1647 Charles was at Newcastle, to all intents and purposes a prisoner in the hands of the Scots, who rubbed in his helplessness by administering daily lectures on the merits of Presbyterianism. 'I never knew what it was to be so barbarously baited before', Charles complained to Henrietta in June 1646, '. . . there never was a man so alone as I.' He had already begun to let drop phrases which hinted that he expected to die for his principles. The memory of how he had betrayed Strafford was constantly on his mind, and he acted now as though that sin could only be redeemed by his own suffering even unto death. He did weaken to some degree, offering on at least three occasions in 1646 and 1647 to adopt Presbyterianism for a limited period. Such concessions rather undermined his moral position *vis-à-vis* Henrietta, despite his insistence that Anglicanism should eventually be restored. Henrietta, however, only cared that what had been offered was too little, too late. 'You must begin again', she instructed in December 1646, 'or leave the work undone.'

As she began to realise that Charles was bent on self-destruction, her entreaties became more and more desperate. The poet Abraham Cowley, who acted as her secretary in Paris, complained that he was giving all his days and two or three nights a week to poring over cyphers. Many of Henrietta's letters from the period have been lost, but that they were hectoring and insensitive is evident from Charles's replies. 'The causeless stumblings and mistakings of my friends', he told her, had hurt him more than anything else since the rebellion began; 'yet whilst I was rightly understood by thee, I despised them all; but, since from whence my chiefest comfort comes, I am now most mistaken, it may easily be judged how my misfortunes are multiplied upon me'.

Apparently Henrietta resurrected the old threat of the convent. 'For

God's sake leave off threatening me with thy desire to meddle no more with business,' Charles pleaded in November 1646. '. . . [and] as thou lovest me give me so much comfort (and God know I have but little, and that little must come from thee) as to assure me that thou wilt think no more of any such thing, otherwise than to reject it.' In truth, he must have known by this time that Henrietta would never cease to 'meddle', and that it was equally unlikely she would take the veil. Often, when reading these letters, one receives the impression that King and Queen alike were in the grip of psychoses – his moral, hers hysterical – that quite prevented any effective communication between them. It is as though they were both performing elaborate dances to entirely different music. Yet just as they seem to have missed each other completely and for ever, they produce expressions of affection that melt the heart. 'Above all,' Charles concluded one letter to Henrietta, 'thou must make my acknowledgements to the queen of England (for none else can do it), it being her love that maintains my life, her kindness that upholds my courage, which makes me eternally hers.'

The threat to the King made it all the more essential to the royalists that the Prince of Wales should be secure from capture. Charles sent him into the West Country in 1645; and in the following spring the Prince, forced back by Parliament's armies into the very extremity of England, escaped first to the Scilly Isles and then to Jersey. Both the King and Henrietta were determined that he should immediately proceed from there to join his mother in Paris. The Prince's advisers, Sir Edward Hyde to the fore, were strongly against this course. Hyde dared not openly say that he feared the Queen's influence, or that he mistrusted the circle with which she was surrounded, but, a true gallophobe, he made no bones about the dangers of the next King of England falling into the toils of Cardinal Mazarin. Already there were rumours, perhaps too easily believed in the Prince's entourage, that Jermyn intended to barter the island of Jersey to the French in return for military assistance and a French dukedom for himself.

Royal servants like Hyde, however, can hardly persist in disobedi-ence to the King, and Charles made it crystal-clear that the Prince should go to his mother, albeit with one proviso. 'Let the world see', he wrote, 'that the queen seeks not to alter his conscience.' The arrival of the heir to the throne in Paris created a problem of precedence of the kind that engages the French mind to its fullest extent. Henrietta, who took the matter quite as seriously as her hosts, somewhat ambitiously considered that her son should have precedence over Louis XIV himself. For two months, while the question was being debated, the French court neglected officially to receive the Prince at all, though it was eventually decreed that he merited a *fauteuil* of exactly the same shape, size and proportions as the King's.

Prince Charles spoke very little French, which suggests, as has been mentioned, that Henrietta had principally exercised maternal devotion at a distance: Charles, after all, was her favourite son. The French preferred the very far from amusing Duke of York, the second boy, on account of his greater gift for languages. Prince Charles, one of the courtiers noted, seemed *fort sérieux*, an opinion which may be thought to reflect nothing so much as the propensity of the French and English to misunderstand each other. Yet the Prince could appear *gauche* at this stage of his life, and one of the reasons Henrietta wanted him in Paris was to give him a bit of polish. She deplored, so Bishop Burnet recorded, her husband's lack of ease, 'and the stiff roughness that was in him, by which he disobliged very many, and did often prejudice his affairs very much'. Her sons, by contrast, should be educated to a 'wonderful civility'.

Henrietta's educative attentions also included the matter of finding a wife for Charles. Her preferred candidate for this role was Mademoiselle de Montpensier, 'La Grande Mademoiselle', the immensely rich, immensely self-satisfied and moderately attractive daughter of her brother Gaston. There was nothing subtle about Henrietta's match-making techniques, as the intended victim herself recorded. 'The Queen of England would have liked to persuade me that the Prince was in love with me; that he talked of it incessantly; that, had she not prevented it, he would have come to my apartment at all hours; that he found me entirely to his taste, and was in despair at the Empress's death, being extremely apprehensive that they would marry me to the Emperor.' Alas, La Grande Mademoiselle was far from being deceived by these sledgehammer maternal hints. 'I knew', she drily observed, 'that I should not make great account of what I was told on behalf of a man who could say nothing for himself.'

These comic interludes in Paris, for all that Henrietta was very far from being amused, made a strange counterpoint to the tragedy moving inexorably towards its climax in England. Henrietta, in spite of her urgent pleas to Charles, could still at times be remarkably obtuse about how grave his situation was becoming. 'I conjure you', she wrote to him in November 1646, 'that, 'till the Scots shall declare that they will not protect you, you do not think of making any escape from England. They are startled here at the naming of it; and in so doing you would destroy all our hopes in the general peace, which [Cardinal Mazarin] assures me is like to be made very suddenly.' However much Henrietta enjoyed playing the great diplomat, this was invidious counsel to deliver from the security of the Louvre. Charles quite rightly ignored it, though his attempt to escape from Newcastle in a Dutch ship on Christmas Day 1646 was hopelessly botched. Early in the New Year, the Scots, despairing of an agreement, sold the King to Parliament in return for £400,000 in arrears of pay. Parliament, however, refused to pay off its own forces, with the result that, in June 1647, the royal prisoner was unceremoniously seized by the Army leaders.

Charles was well treated by his new captors, and the senior officers, with Cromwell to the fore, risked their own positions by offering the King terms far more generous than the Army rank and file would have approved. There would be religious toleration for all save the dreadful papists; use of the Anglican Prayer Book would be permitted, though not enforced; and the bishops, while shorn of their authority, would not actually be abolished. On the debit side a reformed Parliament would be intimately concerned with all aspects of government; nevertheless, it was proposed that 'His Majesty's Person, his Queen, and Royal issue, may be restored to a condition of safety, honour and freedom in this nation, without diminution of their personal rights.' Charles should have jumped at such a settlement, as Henrietta immediately realised. She sent Sir John Berkeley over from Paris to persuade the King to accept the terms. But the King still prevaricated, following his old policy of playing for time. On this occasion, though, he knew not the force with which he dealt. After the negotiations failed a terrible resolution began to form in Cromwell's powerful will. Had not the Lord time after time witnessed in battle against this deceitful monarch?

In 1648 the outbreak of the Second Civil War, as a consequence of Charles's foolishly opportunistic treaty with the Scots, enabled the Lord and Cromwell (His appointed servant) to do some more witnessing. Many more men were slaughtered in battle, and Cromwell's puritan soldiery began to speak with ominous intent of 'Charles Stuart, that man of blood'. Charles himself was quite untouched by such slurs. As he saw the matter – as Henrietta had formerly seen it – he had been merely carrying out his God-given duty in striving to protect the royal prerogative that had been entrusted to his care. So Charles and Cromwell faced each other: two men to whom the Lord had spoken so exceedingly clear, albeit to such contradictory effect. In spite of the King's political deviousness, the ultimate depth of his convictions, and the eloquent courage with which he maintained them in adversity, lent his last weeks a sublime nobility. By a series of deliberate steps, taken alone amidst his enemies, he prepared to die for his idea of kingship.

With that sustained Calvary Henrietta had little or nothing to do. As long as she had believed that Charles would win the war, no one had been fiercer in persuading the King not to compromise his principles. But she was, after all, the daughter of the Huguenot Henri IV, the man who concluded that Paris was worth a mass. She was not drawn to martyrdom by temperament, least of all to martyrdom on behalf of the Anglican Church. Thus in the last months of Charles's life Henrietta's influence over him waned. Perhaps indeed it had never been as dominant as had once appeared, for Charles showed himself as obstinate without her encouragement as he had ever been with it. What he had looked for from Henrietta was emotional, not political, support.

In any case, Henrietta inevitably lost touch with currents that were flowing in England under the surface of events. After 1647 it is difficult to know how many of the letters which the King and Queen wrote to each other reached their destination. Charles in captivity, first at Hampton Court and then in the Isle of Wight, took to burning incoming letters and stopped making copies of his own. He still hoped that Henrietta would send a French ship to Southampton to enable him to escape to France, but communications between them were tenuous. There was 'no greater service' to be done for the Crown, he told a messenger, 'but to get a letter conveyed to my wife for me, and to take care that I may have the answer returned.'

Thus isolated, Charles, who had not seen Henrietta for four years and who already felt himself to be living in the shadow of the scaffold, allowed himself in 1648 an *amitié amoureuse* – and with a married woman at that. Jane Whorwood, ungallantly described in a parliamentary report as 'a tall well-fashioned and well-languaged gentlewoman, with a round Visage and pock holes in her face', first met Charles in 1647, when she was thirty-two. Within a year the King, who had always been known for his dignity and distance, was addressing her as 'Sweet Jane Whorwood' and signing himself 'your most loving Charles'. It all seemed light-hearted enough, with Charles calling himself 'her best Platonic Lover or Servant', and teasing her through an intermediary that 'her Platonic Way doth much spoil the taste of my mind'. Such trivialities signify nothing by the modern measurement of love. They were, however, an extraordinary departure for Charles, and important enough for him to beg Jane in August 1648 not to leave the Isle of Wight. Though Henrietta would not have appreciated the fact, her husband's delight in Jane Whorwood was one of several instances which showed how, under the pressure of suffering, he was losing that 'stiff roughness' she so much deplored in his day-to-day relations.

Henrietta's own life at this time presented its problems. During the Second Civil War she felt that she had to allow the Prince of Wales to go to Calais, where he would be ready to cross the Channel in support of his father. The Prince had been fretting on the maternal leash in Paris, being wholly dependent upon her for money; he longed to win his spurs in action. Henrietta had tried to raise cash and supplies, but really there was little she could do beyond dispatching her last jewels to be pawned in Amsterdam. Every penny she possessed had long since been devoted to the cause, whether sent into England or distributed among the seedy band of expatriates who made up her own entourage. It was noted with disgust, though not by Henrietta, that whereas most English royalists in Paris wondered where the next meal was coming from, the egregious Jermyn was still contriving to salt away the cash. Henrietta herself, whether for religious or for financial reasons, went to live in a Carmelite convent in the summer of 1648. When visited there by Madame de Motteville she showed her a small gold cup, which she claimed to be the last valuable object remaining to her.

The way she was treated in France, indeed, exemplified the melancholy maxim that in the world of the courtier sympathy evoked on a regular basis soon turns to contempt. More serious to Henrietta than the sneers of the *bon ton*, however, was the fact that Anne of Austria could no longer pay her allowance. From mid-1648 the Regent's government was under severe threat in a prolonged crisis that culminated in the two insurrections known as the *Fronde parlementaire* (January 1649) and the *Fronde princière* (1650–52). In this crisis Henrietta unblushingly approached Anne of Austria as an apostle of peace and compromise: the troubles in England, she warned, had started from far less combustible material. Anne, however, went her own way; and as a result of the ensuing broils Henrietta was not paid her pension for six months. The popular leader Paul de Gondi, later Cardinal de Retz, made political capital out of her impoverishment when he visited her in the Louvre around the turn of the New Year 1648–49. Outside in Paris the mob raged in a manner that must have put Henrietta in mind of earlier days at Whitehall; inside the freezing palace Gondi found the Queen of England in her daughter Henriette-Anne's room. She was there, she explained, because the little girl was unable to get out of bed for want of a fire. 'You will do me the justice to believe', Gondi grandiloquently pronounced, 'that the Princess of England did not keep her bed the following day for lack of a faggot.' Shortly afterwards he was responsible for the Parlement de Paris granting Henrietta forty thousand *livres*.

It is difficult to be certain when Henrietta finally grasped what Charles had been hinting at for years, that the peril in which he stood was mortal. 'We know not but this may be the last time we may speak to you or the world publicly,' the King wrote to the Prince of Wales on 29 November 1648. His line of communication to Henrietta, however, seems to have been completely cut off; or, if any letters reached her, they have not survived. On her side Henrietta had managed to convey two letters for Charles to a Major Bosvile, who had previously contrived to get messages through to the royal prisoner. The Major lived up to his reputation by bribing a servant to conceal these letters in the King's close-stool, but unfortunately they were discovered before Charles could read them.

By the end of 1648, Henrietta would have heard that the Army had purged Parliament of moderates in order to proceed to the trial and execution of the King. Her reaction was a hopeless, despairing act of loyalty and courage. She wrote to both the Speaker of the House of Commons and to General Fairfax, begging them for a safe conduct so that she could join her husband in his extremity. There was no reply: both letters were set aside and remained unopened until the end of her son's reign, in 1683. All through that bitterly cold January of 1649, therefore, while the King faced down his judges with heroic disdain, Henrietta could only wait in ignorant terror and foreboding.

In England, Charles, however caught up in the elevation of martyrdom, did not forget what his queen had been to him. 'A principal point in your honour', he instructed in his last letter to the Prince of Wales, 'will consist in your deferring all respect, love, and protection to your mother, my wife, who hath many ways deserved well of me, and chiefly of this, that having been a means to bless me with so many hopeful children . . . she hath been content with incomparable magnanimity and patience to suffer both for and with me and you.' We know that Charles sent Henrietta at least two messages, one by a page called Henry Seymour, the other on the day before he died by his daughter Elizabeth. 'He bid me tell my mother', the Princess recalled, 'that his thoughts had never strayed from her, and that his love should be the same to the last.'

It is to be hoped that Henrietta never heard that Charles had also recommended their daughter a book against the snares of popery. For here was the kernel of the Queen's tragedy, the awful truth to which she could never really reconcile herself: her adored husband sacrificed himself for what, to her every instinct, was abominable heresy. Charles in his last days found ever greater security in the Church of England. 'I tell you I have tried it,' he wrote in that last letter to his son, 'and, after much search and many disputes, hath concluded it to be the best in the world, not only in the community, as a Christian, but also in the special notion, as reformed, keeping the middle way between the pomp of superstitious tyranny, and the meanness of fantastic anarchy.' So on 30 January 1649 the Anglican martyr went to what he called his 'second marriage day', forgiving all his foes, but insisting even upon the scaffold that 'a subject and a sovereign are clean different things', until the fall of the headsman's axe swept his argument into eternity.

For another nine days Henrietta knew nothing of what had happened. Once, indeed, a rumour reached her – or was it wishful thinking? – that Charles had been led out to execution, and that the London mob had risen to save their King. Miracles being readily conceivable where information is scarce and the mind is desperate, Henrietta kept the flame of hope flickering a while longer. Uncertainty, though, extended itself to almost unbearable lengths. Perhaps the Fronde had interrupted communications between Paris and the outside world; perhaps no one dared to approach her with the appalling truth. Finally, on 8 February, she sent a messenger to the French court at St Germain to ask for news. When she complained at the messenger's tardiness in returning, Jermyn, who had evidently heard the worst, took it upon himself to point out that if the report had been good the man would certainly have come back by this time. The hint sufficed for Henrietta's quick mind: a moment later she knew that she was a widow. She did not, as might have been expected, instantly give way to wild hysterics. Far more alarming, that most voluble of women sat on for hours staring dumbly into space, lost in a stupor of grief. Night came on, but still she did not move. Only when the Duchesse de Vendôme, one of her closest friends, knelt down and kissed her hand did she burst into a paroxysm of tears.

6

The truth, Henrietta kept repeating when Madame de Motteville visited her two days later, if only Charles had known the truth, he would never have been lost. But what truth? One might imagine that she was referring to the Catholic faith, but in fact it was the lessons of politics, too lately learnt, which now obsessed her. Let the Queen Regent of France be warned, she told Madame de Motteville, never to provoke her subjects unless she possessed the power to quell them. As for herself, having lost a king, a husband, a friend whom she could never sufficiently mourn, she was condemned to suffer for the rest of her days.

Madame de Motteville assures us that henceforth Henrietta did, indeed, 'wear perpetual mourning on her person and in her heart'. By this version, the widow of the martyr, purged by unhappiness of any further concern with this world, addressed herself to securing her salvation in the next. So, certainly, the story *ought* to have ended; so Henrietta liked to see herself. But the old Adam is not to be instantly annihilated. Honesty compelled Madame de Motteville to add a rider to her portrait of the inconsolable queen. Henrietta *did* mourn, 'at least so far as she was capable, for by nature her mind had more gaiety than gravity'. La Grande Mademoiselle, who was rather less given to charitable judgements, put the matter more frankly. She found Henrietta 'not so deeply affected as she should have been considering that the king her husband had loved her so deeply and treated her so *divinement bien*'.

It was one thing for Henrietta to declare that she could never live without Charles, quite another to fulfil this dismal prophecy. No one, as Jane Austen tartly observed, ever died of a broken heart; and French women have often shown a particular talent for surviving the sorrows of widowhood. Henrietta lived on; and for all the genuineness of her grief, for all the sincerity of her devotions, she appeared very much the same person as before. That was natural enough: very few people, thank heaven, can sustain mourning at full intensity over a period of twenty years. Yet the extension of Henrietta's life for so long after Charles's death did rob her of tragic status. Consider her beside Marie-Antoinette, with whom she had several points in common. Marie-Antoinette was also a light-minded, pleasure-loving woman, arguably less responsible than Henrietta for her husband's fate. Marie-Antoinette, though, was punished out of all proportion to her crimes. The sufferings of her last years appal and stun the reader into sympathy, while her end on the guillotine preserves her for ever in the role of hapless victim. But had she escaped after the execution of her husband, and resumed a life of frivolity at the Austrian court, what then? Very likely she would stand forth like Henrietta as a woman who had endured much, and learnt little.

Henrietta, though she retired to her favourite convent in the

Faubourg St-Jacques for a few weeks after Charles's death, emerged to exhibit the same misguided ardour in the cause of restoring Charles II to his throne as she had formerly shown in the affairs of Charles I. An imperious letter was dispatched to the new King in Holland, summoning him immediately to Paris and ordering him on no account to appoint any member to his Privy Council without prior consultation with his mother. That was the manner in which Henrietta had acted toward Charles I, and that was the way in which she meant to continue. Charles II, however, was a very different proposition from his father, at once much cleverer and far more ruthless. Henrietta, to her consternation, found that her instructions were simply ignored. It was June before Charles II reached Paris, and, having got there, 'he did as good as desire her', as Clarendon recorded, 'not to trouble herself in his affairs'.

Clarendon, though still, until 1660, mere Sir Edward Hyde, established himself from the very beginning of Charles II's reign as his principal counsellor. Upright, able, solid and pompous, exactly the kind of man Henrietta disliked, his policy for restoring the King was essentially to wait upon events. He tried to avoid rash commitments, and to exploit opportunities as they arrived. Henrietta, as ever, was full of schemes, principally, in 1649, that Charles should regain his throne with the help of the Catholic Irish. Hyde rightly believed that no policy could be better calculated to ruin the King in England. He saw Henrietta, Jermyn and the rest of her English entourage at the Louvre as a disastrous, contriving, ignorant, thick-headed crew, who could no more be trusted to form a reliable judgement than to keep a secret. Under this influence Charles adopted a polite but distant attitude towards his mother. 'Finding her passions strong,' Clarendon wrote, 'he frequently retired from her with some abruptness, and seemed not to desire to be so much in her company as expected.' Henrietta did her best to disguise what was happening, perhaps even from herself. 'My son lives with me in the greatest affection possible,' she crowed to her sister Christine. But Charles's affection was increasingly tempered with irritation. It did not help, either, that Henrietta both controlled the purse strings and made him know it. After less than three months at the French court the King decamped to Jersey, where he possessed some independent income.

Henrietta still looked to her niece, Mademoiselle de Montpensier, for the solution to Charles's financial problems. She could not resist, however, scoring off the woman who had considered herself too good for her son. Knowing that La Grande Mademoiselle had been disappointed in her ambition of marrying the Austrian Emperor, she wrote to her with sweet malice when the Emperor was once more widowed, suggesting that there might be a better chance second time round. Having delivered this shaft, however, Henrietta reverted to her shameless attempts to persuade her niece to marry Charles, solicitations which she continued throughout the 1650s without any gains in either subtlety or effect.

With Henrietta the failure of one scheme inevitably led to the hatching of another. Cromwell's campaign in Ireland (1649–50) having crushed any hope of a restoration from that quarter, she simply turned her hopes to Scotland. Charles, though, stunned her by the cool hypocrisy with which he accepted Presbyterianism in order to gain Scottish help. Henrietta had formerly berated Charles I for his inflexible hostility towards the Presbyterians; now she complained that Charles II had betrayed the principles for which her husband had died. Never again, she told him, would she act as his political adviser. Charles may have found this threat less than daunting; in any case, after he had been overwhelmed by Cromwell at the battle of Worcester (3 September 1651), it hardly seemed that he would require any more advice. Misfortune dogged the family at every turn. Henrietta's daughter Elizabeth had died in England in September 1650, and her son-in-law the Prince of Orange in the following November. Now, after Worcester, Henrietta waited in suspense for six weeks, expecting every day to be told of Charles II's capture and execution. When, at last, she heard that he had landed in France, she rushed to Rouen to meet him. No wonder that in Paris that winter she was reported to be 'constantly, wonderfully merry'.

All the same, while Charles had been in Scotland Henrietta had to some degree, and very much in her own fashion, satisfied her oft-repeated desire to withdraw from the world. The Order of the Visitation was a society after her heart, founded by St Francis de Sales for women of gentle birth and good education who did not, in the Catholic phrase, feel themselves called to any extraordinary austerities. Madame de Motteville introduced

Henrietta to the Order's Paris house, where the nuns were especially well connected; and it was soon decided that the widowed Queen's charitable impulses should be diverted to the establishment of a sister foundation.

Henrietta, of course, was entirely without means for such a project, being dependent on Anne of Austria's pension and such additional benefactions as the French nobility from time to time bestowed upon her. But she was not the kind of woman to be daunted by lack of funds. Under her persuasion the Queen Regent extended her bounty to allow Henrietta to acquire a large ruined mansion at Chaillot, then on the outskirts of Paris, today the site of the Trocadéro. There were many difficulties, legal and practical, to overcome before the property was secured and twelve suitable nuns installed, but Henrietta's energy and enthusiasm overcame all obstacles. The enterprise also evoked her talent for interior decoration, so that when the nuns first arrived at the restored property, they were appalled, notwithstanding their relatively easy rule, at the luxury in which they were expected to live. This difficulty was solved by Henrietta taking all the best rooms in the front of the house, while the nuns were relegated to the rear quarters. The arrangement worked so well that Henrietta sometimes attended to her devotions in the convent for as long as three consecutive months.

Charles, too, was sometimes to be seen at Chaillot, waiting on his mother with a silent respect that masked his intense boredom and dissatisfaction. The time he spent in Paris between 1652 and 1654 was the very lowest point in his life: by 1653 he was positively ill with depression. Although the French court gave him a small pension after February 1652, it only spasmodically paid, and then 'so far forth as the Queen of England desired, and not otherwise'. Henrietta, alas, did not always desire: at times even the meals that Charles ate at her table were charged against his allowance. This enforced dependence did not pass unnoticed. Sir Edward Nicholas, a friend of Hyde's and another of Henrietta's *bêtes noires*, reported from The Hague that numerous royalists were now giving up the struggle and returning to England, 'as having little hopes left to them, seeing they hear his Majesty intends to make use of the Louvre counsels'. His Majesty in fact intended no such thing; he simply lacked the means to go elsewhere.

In Henrietta's defence, in 1652 her own pension was still jeopardised by the continuing troubles of the Fronde, by now a power struggle in which her brother Gaston and her niece La Grande Mademoiselle were among the leaders of the anti-court faction. Henrietta's attempts to mediate between the *frondeurs* and the court achieved nothing save unpopularity with the Paris mob. She was terrified that events in France were going in the same direction as in England, but no one would listen to her. Again her efforts to advise Anne of Austria were not appreciated. Did she wish to be Queen of France as well as Queen of England? the Regent tartly enquired. 'I am nothing,' Henrietta returned with dignity, 'but you, do you be something.' 'I see myself on the eve of dying of hunger,' she wrote a trifle melodramatically to her sister Christine, 'and know not so much as where to look for safety.' Her fears proved unjustified, both for France and for herself. In the autumn of 1652 Louis XIV entered Paris in triumph, and a happy by-product of the royal victory was the resumption of Henrietta's pension. The only permanent effect of the Fronde in her life was that, since Louis XIV thenceforward lived at the well-fortified Louvre, she had to move out into the Palais Royal.

Yet despite the Queen Regent's kindness, and despite the consolations of Chaillot, Henrietta at this period constantly showed herself to be thoroughly difficult. She was, after all, a woman in her mid-forties. Not only did she attempt to dominate Charles by twitching the purse strings; in 1650 she had also quarrelled violently with her second son, James Duke of York, who, no less than Charles, disliked the quality of the Englishmen with whom she surrounded herself. It seems that Henrietta continually deprecated James to her toadies, eventually goading the infuriated youth to flounce off to Brussels, though not before he had accused his mother of loving Henry Jermyn more than her own children. It was a telling shot. Ever since Charles I's death rumour had flown about Paris that Henrietta not merely loved, but had actually married the favourite. The story was much too good to need any proof, though it seems in the highest degree unlikely that Henrietta, always so acutely conscious of breeding, could have stifled her Bourbon pride sufficiently to contemplate a match with the second son of an English knight. Jermyn did not even look distinguished; he would live to be derided by Andrew Marvell for his 'drayman's shoulders' and 'butcher's mien'.

Family affairs deteriorated still further in 1654. That summer Charles's sojourn in France finally ended. French sentiment might be with the Stuarts; French interest could not but reckon that Oliver Cromwell was a dangerous man to offend. Already in 1652 diplomatic relations with Cromwell's government had been resumed, an event described by Henrietta as 'the last death-blow, which I never expected to receive from France'. Now the two countries actually concluded a treaty against the Dutch, a treaty under which Cromwell insisted that France should no longer harbour the Stuart King. Charles suddenly found himself offered full payment of his French pension on condition that he left the country within ten days. Such terms, of course, delighted him.

Henrietta, having been baulked in her attempts to dominate her first two sons, now turned her attention to the third. Henry Duke of Gloucester was in many ways her most promising child, full of spirit and courage. Charles I, on the day before his execution, had been much pleased by the nine-year-old Henry's reply to his injunction never to accept the throne so long as Charles and James were alive. 'I will be torn in pieces first,' the boy assured him. After his father's death he remained a prisoner in England, until in 1652 Cromwell decided his presence was more trouble than it was worth, and gave permission for the boy to be sent abroad. Thus Henry came to Paris. Charles II was content for him to remain there under his mother's care, on the express condition that no attempt should be made to wean him from his Anglican faith. The King had been prepared, reluctantly, to allow his sister Henriette-Anne to be a Catholic, for she was to all intents and purposes a Frenchwoman, but he rightly calculated that if he countenanced the conversion of an English prince of the blood he could say farewell to any hopes of his restoration.

Yet no sooner was Charles out of France than Henrietta began her campaign to make Henry Catholic. She could not even claim to be acting within the terms of her marriage treaty, for that document only gave her rights over her children's religion up to the age of thirteen – and Henry was fifteen in 1654. More damning still was the manner in which she pursued her aim. Henry, she told Charles, had 'too many acquaintances among the idle little boys of Paris, so I am sending him to Pointoise with the Abbé Montagu, where he will have more quiet to mind his book'. The Abbé Montagu, in fact, was the insinuating genius behind the enterprise, being none other than that same Walter Montagu who had begun his career as a *littérateur* at Charles I's court. Having converted in 1631, he owed his present position to Henrietta and burnt with convert zeal to repay the debt. At Pointoise every pressure of argument and moral blackmail was brought to bear on Henry, but the boy, though he found himself unable to refute the Abbé in logic, deeply resented what he regarded as this 'mean and disingenuous action'. He wrote to Cologne to complain to his brother Charles, who urged him in the strongest terms to stand firm and sent the Marquis of Ormonde to the rescue.

He also sent a stinging rebuke to his mother. 'I cannot expect your Majesty does either believe or wish my return to England,' he wrote, pointing out that her attempts to convert Henry were in direct contradiction to the last wishes of Charles I, 'whose memory I doubt not will work upon you'. The memory did not work upon her in the least. After Ormonde had brought Henry back from Pointoise to Paris, Henrietta announced her intention of sending the Prince to a Jesuit college. When Henry refused to go, she exploded in fury. She told him that she never wanted to see him again, ordered that both he and his belongings should instantly be removed from her house, and forbade all English persons in Paris to offer him lodgings. The Prince tried to waylay his mother to ask for a parting blessing as she drove back to Chaillot, but Henrietta turned away and would not speak to him. When Henry returned to the Palais Royal he discovered that his horses had been turned out of the stables, his sheets stripped, and orders left that he should not be fed. Ormonde had to pawn his Garter and jewel in order to spirit the Prince away from Paris. Henrietta never saw her youngest son again.

No doubt Charles's scathing indictment was correct: his mother *had* lost hope that he would ever be restored to his throne. The English episode in her life had now been translated into a distant idyll, an invocation against the humiliations of her French existence. 'I was the happiest and most fortunate of queens,' she gushed at Madame de Motteville, 'for not only had I every pleasure the heart could desire; I had a husband who adored me.' England, she informed the incredulous French courtiers, was a beautiful country, full of brave, generous and good-humoured people: the Civil War had been the work of merely a few 'desperate and infatuated persons'. These encomia were particularly directed at La Grande Mademoiselle in order to impress her with what she might be missing in declining to marry Charles. But her niece now had a withering reply to Henrietta's over-eager match-making. 'Since he [Charles] does not live on good terms with your Majesty,' she asked, 'why is it to be believed that he should do so with me?' The barb cruelly exposed the present reality that underlay Henrietta's prattle about the glorious past. She, a daughter of Henri IV, was now forsaken and impotent, a poor relation living on her family's charity. Henrietta, who knew so well the lore of courts, would not have been deceived, however brave her façade, about what her situation implied. Louis XIV, to give him his due, was always respectful; not so his brother, the preposterous 'Monsieur', who resented the English claims of precedence. 'Why should these people, to whom we give bread, pass before us?' he demanded. 'Why do they not take themselves elsewhere?'

So it is not necessary to credit Henrietta with any extraordinary devotion in order to understand why she often liked to escape from the court to the consolations of Chaillot. 'All that I can now contribute is my prayers,' she wrote to Charles in 1655. The observation was intended as a complaint rather than a mellow resignation to the will of God. Her thoughts were still very much with this world. England might appear to her to be a lost cause, but there was always the dream of pulling off the one great matrimonial coup that would restore her fortunes at a stroke. Louis XIV was eighteen in 1656; and Henrietta was the mother of two available daughters.

The elder one, Mary, the widowed Princess of Orange, appeared, at twenty-five, rather too old to have any chance of landing the prize. Still, for one reason or another, she came to Paris in 1656 to visit her mother, having first mortgaged herself to the hilt to buy jewels suitable for the occasion. Henrietta complained that her daughter really ought to be more careful with her money, though she was unable to resist the brag that in her heyday she herself had possessed rather more of such baubles. Certainly no one accused her of extravagance any more: such was her reputation for economy with her children that Mary, probably forewarned by Charles, brought her own firewood and candles with her. Still, Henrietta enjoyed organising parties for her daughter at the Palais Royal, although, if she had ever indulged any hope of Mary catching the King's eye, she was disappointed. Louis never so much as spoke to his cousin, La Grande Mademoiselle reported with satisfaction.

Henrietta's main hope of capturing Louis lay with her youngest daughter Henriette-Anne, still only twelve in 1656. Though not a beauty, Henriette was an engaging child whom the world, and most encouragingly Anne of Austria, found easy to love. Unluckily, though, Anne's enthusiasm for the girl produced the opposite effect in Louis. On being forced by his mother to dance with Henriette the King remarked, at the august age of seventeen, that he did not care for little girls. Worse followed for Henrietta. In 1658 it looked as though Louis was about to marry a daughter of her sister Christine of Savoy, a prospect that tested family affection almost beyond endurance. Happily, at the end of 1659 Cardinal Mazarin concluded a peace with Spain under which the Infanta Maria Teresa was betrothed to Louis XIV. This diplomatic volte-face transferred the burden of maternal agony on to Christine, who was reported to be knocking her head against the wall in her disappointment.

Henrietta, however, enjoyed few satisfactions in the late 1650s. Even Chaillot, for all the edification which pious Catholic writers have drawn from her residence therein, did not altogether fulfil her needs. In 1652 Louise de la Fayette, a woman who had founded her reputation upon the admirable precept of resisting the advances of Louis XIII, became Mother Superior, a change which led to the imposition of a rather stricter regime than Henrietta might have wished. It was intimated that the former Queen of England should no longer, perhaps, receive friends in her private apartments. Henrietta gracefully acceded to the austerities of the new order, but she eventually began to look for an alternative, more secular retreat, sufficiently removed from Paris to escape the malice of the court, yet near enough not to deter potential visitors. In 1657 she found what she was looking for in the old château at Colombes, seven miles to the north-west of the capital. As with Chaillot, the financial difficulties of which she complained to her children suddenly disappeared, which is to say that the long-suffering Anne of Austria once again stumped up the necessary funds. Henrietta evidently felt uneasy about the debt to her sister-in-law since that summer she took the extraordinary step of applying to Cromwell through Cardinal Mazarin for the payment of the dower due to her as a former Queen of England. The Protector, needless to say, was not impressed. Basing his argument on Henrietta's refusal as a young girl to attend the coronation service, he simply returned that she had never been recognised as a Queen of England.

Cromwell's death in September 1658 naturally occasioned much rejoicing in Henrietta's circle, though she herself no longer nursed any hopes. 'I see no great advantage likely to result from it,' she told Madame de Motteville, and for once her political diagnosis appeared correct. The Protector's son Richard took over the reins in England without any break. Charles, meanwhile, had in 1657 further undermined Henrietta's relations with the French court by making an agreement with Spain, still, then, at war with France. As a result, in 1658 her other two sons, James and Henry, had fought with distinction, albeit unsuccessfully, against the Anglo-French alliance.

The situation only emphasised how alien the Stuarts had become from English affairs. The hope of a restoration had never seemed more unlikely than when Charles visited Henrietta at Colombes in December 1659, the first time that he had seen her for more than five years. Charles's arrival was marked by his heartily embracing a lady-in-waiting, whom, he claimed, he had mistaken for his sister Henriette-Anne. Nevertheless, mother and son, it was reported, 'found entire satisfaction with each other', with Charles managing to listen politely as Henrietta expounded her latest schemes for raising armies. The realities of the Stuart position, however, were exposed by the arrival of a note from Mazarin ordering him to leave France as soon as possible. Charles went on to Brussels, but before he left he set the seal on the reunion by promising to create Jermyn the Earl of St Albans. It was a gesture which pleased his mother, and hardly seemed any more to matter one way or another in the English context.

7

Then in 1660, suddenly, and in a manner fortunately beyond Henrietta's interference, came triumph. On 1 May the House of Commons passed a resolution asking Charles to return to England, without any conditions attached. This extraordinary reversal of fortune was a complete vindication of Sir Edward Hyde's passive tactics, since it occurred as an internal, strictly English, decision. The propertied classes had come to the hard-headed conclusion that, with Cromwell's strong hand removed, their best hope of peace and security against the threat of social revolution lay in the King's return, and in the disbandment of the Army. To Henrietta, however, who had never understood English affairs, and who had thought always in terms of foreign armies imposing the King by force on a reluctant people, the Restoration could only be explained as a miracle. The hand of God, she wrote to Charles soon after his arrival in England, could be 'perceptibly traced' in what had happened. Rather touchingly, though, she remembered at this point whom she was addressing. 'I will finish my sermon for fear of wearying you,' she added.

Neither on Henrietta's side, nor, it would appear, on Charles's, was there any irresistible desire that she should proceed immediately to England. Charles doubtless felt that the morrow of his Restoration was hardly the moment to introduce a figure so closely identified with the bad old days of Stuart rule. Henrietta, for her part, basked in the sudden eagerness of the French court to pay her homage. Her satisfactions included putting La Grande Mademoiselle in her place, which she deemed to be decidedly inferior to her own. Strangely, though, Henrietta professed herself more anxious than ever that her niece should marry her son. Perhaps this apparent generosity was merely a refinement of her triumph, for at the same time she was toying with the notion of matching Charles with Hortense de Mancini, Cardinal Mazarin's niece. At all events, La Grande Mademoiselle could not summon up the gall to accept in Charles's prosperity the marriage she had so strenuously refused in the period of his adversity. Nor indeed would Charles have been willing. Such considerations, however, were scarcely relevant: Henrietta had come into her own again. Her letters to Christine resumed with a vengeance, lest her sister should miss any detail of her resurgence. Besides, she had a new remedy to prescribe for Christine: 'Tea, a certain leaf which comes from India.' It was 'the best cure in the world for colds'.

Foremost among those who discovered a new respect for the Stuarts was Monsieur, Louis XIV's brother. Formerly he had complained bitterly about his English relations; now, urged on by his mother, he began to contemplate marrying his cousin Henriette-Anne. This was the principal reason that Henrietta chose to remain in France: her sharp eye discerned the main chance, and her quick mind determined to seize it. Her hopes were speedily gratified: by the end of August Monsieur had asked Henriette-Anne to marry him. Henrietta spoke of having to gain Charles II's consent to the match, but her meaning was only that she would have to take Henriette to England in order to negotiate a suitable dowry. She was, of course, beside herself with joy. Her hitherto despised daughter would be the third woman in France after Anne of Austria and the Queen; she would become the mistress of St Cloud, the occupant of magnificent apartments at the Tuileries and Fontainebleau, the chatelaine of Villers-Cotterets and Montargis. That was *un bon mariage* as Henrietta understood the term, Catholic piety be damned. The fact that Monsieur was an outrageously flaunting homosexual who loved dressing up in women's clothes – *'un enfant vicieux; une fausse femme; quelque chose de faible, d'inquiétant, et de nuisible'* – troubled her not for an instant.

What *did* upset her, most dreadfully, was the news that her son James, the Duke of York, had become matrimonially entangled, by dint of a pre-marital conception, with the talented daughter of a highly distinguished Englishman. The girl was Anne Hyde; her father – and this really hurt – Henrietta's old enemy Sir Edward Hyde. The Stuart snobbery about this man, who had undergone great sacrifices to serve them, and to whom they owed so much, is not attractive. Henry Duke of Gloucester, with whom Henrietta had quarrelled, was still sufficiently his mother's son to find the family's association with a man of business intolerable. He could never see Anne Hyde, he remarked, without being reminded of her father's green bag. This proved to be one of Henry's last witticisms, for he was suddenly carried off with smallpox in September 1660, just after James had secretly married Anne.

Henry's death occupied rather less space in Henrietta's letters than her outrage at the humiliation James had brought upon the family. The scandal relegated even Henriette-Anne's marriage to second place in her mind, and brought her to England at the end of October 1660 in militant humour. 'I go', she wrote to Christine, 'to marry the King my son [Henrietta was now eager to promote Charles's marriage with Catherine of Braganza], and also to try to unmarry the other.' James himself was now looking for a way out of his predicament, falsely and dishonourably pretending to believe various cronies who came forward with accusations that there were others with equal claim to the privilege of having fathered Anne's child. This was just a ruse: James knew perfectly well that Anne had only yielded to him after receiving a promise that they would marry. Henrietta, however, was more than willing to believe the worst when it suited her so well to do so. 'A girl who will abandon herself to a prince will abandon herself to another,' she somewhat unconvincingly argued.

So Henrietta came once more to Dover, to that grim fortress of a castle where the fates thrice brought her at important turning-points of her life. On this occasion all four of her surviving children were with her. James had escorted her from France, receiving many a maternal scolding *en route*; Charles had come down from London to greet her; Henriette-Anne travelled with her mother; and Mary, the Princess of Orange, had arrived in England on the plea that further residence in Holland would be quite unendurable. Henrietta showed as little disposition to accommodate local sensibilities on this triumphant return as she had done in 1625: the Abbé Montagu being in her retinue, High Mass was ostentatiously celebrated wherever the party stopped on the way to London. On the other hand the Queen Mother made a deliberately low-key entry into the capital, possibly because of fears that the cheers of the citizens could not be guaranteed, perhaps because Henrietta herself deemed celebrations inappropriate for the widow of the martyr.

It must, indeed, have been harrowing to find herself once more lodged at Whitehall, even sometimes to eat in the banqueting hall from which her husband had gone so bravely to his death. Henrietta never, apparently, went to Windsor to pay her respects to Charles I's grave: there are things too painful to contemplate. Inevitably, though, she experienced moments of depression at being once more in apartments that suggested at every turn happiness for ever gone; depressed, too, to see so many of Charles I's pictures gone from the walls – sold by the Commonwealth for a song. The memory of Cromwell was still fresh in Whitehall, no less because his head mouldered on a pole set atop Westminster Hall.

Yet Henrietta was never the person to sustain a depression. Though Pepys, who saw her dining in her presence-chamber at Whitehall on 22 November, judged her 'a very little plain old woman, and nothing more in her presence in any respect nor garb than any ordinary woman', it is clear that she still retained her capacity to delight those prepared to be pleased. 'Her Majesty charms all who see her,' wrote her compatriot (though Huguenot) the Countess of Derby. 'She has constantly received visitors since she came, without having kept her room.'

No effort at all, however, was made to charm Anne Hyde, her new daughter-in-law, who had given birth to a son on 22 October, just seven weeks after her marriage. It mattered not to Henrietta that Charles II, sensibly making the best of a bad job, now welcomed Anne as 'a woman of great wit and excellent parts'; it mattered not either that James's friends now confessed that the accusations which they had brought against her had been complete fabrications. Henrietta was obdurate. 'If that woman enters Whitehall at one door, I go out at another,' she pronounced. At this point a genuine tragedy supervened on this farrago of vanity and pride. Henrietta's daughter Mary, like Prince Henry three months previously, developed smallpox, and died on Christmas Eve. It was not, however, any chastened awareness of the mutability of human affairs that finally induced Henrietta to abandon her campaign against Anne, but a communication from France. Cardinal Mazarin let it be known that there would be no welcome in her native land if she left England on bad terms with the King and his ministers. On New Year's Day, therefore, in the banqueting hall at Whitehall, Henrietta was seen to raise the Duchess from her kneeling posture, kiss her, and lead her to the table. She even became godmother to Anne's boy.

Still more remarkable, she managed a moderately cordial interview with Anne's father. Here, however, there were other factors at play. Lord Hyde, as he had now become (in 1661 he would be the Earl of Clarendon), was, for all his lack of breeding, in charge of Charles II's government; and the Queen Mother did not scruple to inform him that, in return for her condescension, she would expect 'all the offices . . . which her kindness should deserve'. This was a good deal more than an empty phrase. Henriette-Anne's dowry had been satisfactorily settled, but – doubtless the root of Cardinal Mazarin's concern – there were still uncertainties about Henrietta's own pension. Parliament had voted her a handsome £30,000 a year, on top of which she was to receive a further £30,000 a year from the King's bounty. The parliamentary grant, however, had been made conditional upon her remaining in England. Since she returned to France in January 1661, after a stay of only two months, in order to set the seal on Henriette's marriage, the Chancellor's friendship might be useful. 'The King says she will return soon,' reported Lady Derby, 'but I doubt it.'

Yet after Henrietta had safely launched Henriette-Anne on her miserable marriage in March 1661, time hung heavy on her hands. When Charles II, having wedded Catherine of Braganza in May 1662, pressed his mother to come and see his bride (also, he must have hoped, to cheer her up) Henrietta readily acceded. She had always strongly supported the marriage, for Europe did not possess a more Catholic princess than Catherine. It was unfortunate, then, that when Henrietta returned to England at the end of July 1662 she should have brought with her the beautiful Frances Stuart, a girl who would so fire Charles II's lust that within a few years he would seriously be contemplating divorce on her account. Another member of her train whom Henrietta would perhaps have done better, in the light of subsequent events, to leave behind in France was an illegitimate son of Charles. This boy then went under the name of Crofts: very soon, albeit against Henrietta's advice, the King would make him the Duke of Monmouth.

Henrietta professed delight with every aspect of her second post-Restoration visit to England. 'Never was a king so absolute as is my son,' she reported to Christine, with more satisfaction than accuracy. Now that she had at last learnt not to interfere with Charles's political schemes, her relations with him regained much

of their early warmth, and not just on her side. 'The truth is, never
any children had so good a mother as we have,' Charles wrote to
Henriette-Anne in September 1662, 'and you and I shall never have
any disputes but only who loves her the best, and in that I will never
yield to you.' As for Catherine of Braganza, Henrietta from the very
first did all she could to set the unhappy Queen at ease. 'I should
never have come to England', she told her, 'but for the pleasure of
seeing you, to love you as a daughter, and to serve you as a queen.'
She pronounced Catherine to be 'a saint . . . altogether *dévote*',
and even discovered, in a letter to Christine, that the King and
Queen 'love each other exceedingly', a consummation that escaped
all other observers. Perhaps she offered Catherine some good worldly
advice, namely that her rival Barbara Castlemaine would have to be
tolerated if the Queen was to live on terms with Charles. Certainly
Henrietta accepted Castlemaine's presence with that of the Queen, as
witnessed by Pepys on 7 September 1662. Her morality was always
selective.

Henrietta once more occupied her old residence of Somerset House.
Since the building was full of Cromwellian mementos (the Protector's
corpse had lain in state in Henrietta's bedchamber) and had fallen
into disrepair, she eagerly undertook the task of restoration, most
especially of the chapel. In February 1664 Pepys was reporting
that she had run into debt, though he admitted that the results
were 'mighty magnificent'. Catholics once more began to flock to
mass at Somerset House, and this at a time when a proclamation of
1663 had ordered all Jesuits and priests to leave the kingdom. But
Henrietta, who had first come to England with dreams of reclaiming
the country to the faith, no longer meddled in such matters: as long
as her chapel was open, she appeared content.

There was time, too, for secular pleasures. The fickle courtiers, observing what Henrietta refused to acknowledge, that Queen
Catherine was despised by the King, preferred to resort to the
Queen Mother. Henrietta was always good company, and a new
generation loved to hear her rattle on about the old days. 'If I
had known the temper of the English some years past, as well as
I know it today,' she told them, 'I had never been obliged to quit
this house.'

She stayed in England almost three years. In the end it was climate that defeated her, together perhaps with the first signs of the Great Plague of 1665. She had grown very thin and had a consumptive cough which, she believed, only the waters of Bourbon could cure. Before leaving for France at the end of June she obtained Charles's promise that her chapel at Somerset House would not be closed in her absence. Her Capuchin monks were charged to remain at their posts for the benefit of English Catholics: she hoped, she told them, to be back amongst them before long.

But she never did return. The story of her last four years is quickly told. She lived a retired life, spending her winters in Paris and her summers at Colombes, interspersed with regular visits to Chaillot. She gave thanks, she said, for two things: for having been born a Christian, and for having been '*La Reine Malheureuse*'. These edifying sentiments, however, should not be taken to signify complete detachment from earthly concerns. Relations between England and France invariably presenting difficulties, Henrietta felt herself called to mediate. In August 1665 Louis XIV came to Colombes for a long and private discussion with his aunt about English affairs; and when war broke out between the two countries in the following year, the French King was solemnly warned that she would not be able to pray for his success. After 1666, though, it began to appear that Charles II, against all the prejudices of his subjects, was contemplating an alliance with France. Colombes became a centre for secret negotiations, always a delight for Henrietta. Letters between the English and French Kings were exchanged under the cover of her private correspondence, while Jermyn, tortured by gout, laboured between Paris and London with urgent messages.

Only once was Henrietta's pleasure in her son darkened, when Charles, at the end of 1668, ventured to suggest that in view of his financial difficulties her pension should be cut by a quarter. One might think that £45,000 a year was still a comfortable sum in all conscience, but the prospect of having to live on such a pittance abruptly roused Henrietta from her devotions. The proposal, she wrote to Charles, 'has surprised me to a degree that it is very difficult to express to you . . . I feel sure that when you have reflected you will not wish to render the rest of my days, which will be short, unfortunate . . . What touches me especially is that people see your economies extend to your mother, and that for the want of 20,000 jacobuses she may be in the greatest inconvenience. It is difficult to be persuaded that this sum ruins you.'

Henrietta was justified, at least, in her belief that her days were numbered. Her health had long been poor, and from the spring of 1669 it was obvious that she was in terminal decline. She admitted to a terror of death, and spoke of retiring permanently to Chaillot in the autumn in order to prepare her soul for eternity. Yet the spirit of wilfulness that had been so evident in the child who had married Charles I never left her. Once it had been English heretics who aroused her suspicions; now it was French doctors with their cures for insomnia. The great Theodore Mayerne, she told them, had expressly warned her against just such drugs as they were prescribing. Louis XIV's medical experts, nettled, insisted on the efficacy of their treatment. Henrietta gave way, took the dose, and died that night (21 August). 'They gave her some pills to make her sleep', commented the still-unmarried Mademoiselle de Montpensier, 'which were so successful that she never woke again.'

Two months later, at Chaillot, Bossuet delivered himself of one of his most famous funeral orations. The performance, it must be said, was a great deal more remarkable for force and eloquence than for accuracy. The preacher discovered that the ills which had attended the kings of England sprung from their having abandoned the one true faith. As for Henrietta's virtues, they had no bounds. Madame de Motteville, in preparing biographical notes for Bossuet, had allowed herself a gentle criticism to the effect that Henrietta's conversation was so free that it was difficult to know who might be hurt next. The orator, however, solemnly discoursed upon Henrietta's appreciation of the value of silence and upon her aversion from any untruthful remark. One would like to think that there were some sniggers among the congregation at this portentous cant. For the high style is really quite inappropriate for Henrietta. Her impulsive and generous nature shone brightly in private life, whereas the majesty of a throne only set her very ordinary abilities in sharp relief. It is not difficult to understand why Charles I loved her; on English politics, however, her disastrous influence would only be exhausted with the flight of her son James II in 1688.

Henrietta's heart was interred at Chaillot, her body in St Denis. In death as in life she would be exposed to 'desperate and infatuated persons', for her bones were scattered into a common ditch by the vandals of the French Revolution. As for the immortal part of her, who would not echo the prayer of Madame de Motteville, that her virtues should be rewarded, her sins forgiven, and her soul enfolded in the mercy of God?

Catherine of Braganza

1638–1705

I

The union of Catherine of Braganza and Charles II presents one of the oldest and saddest tales in the world: that of the good, defenceless, unremarkable woman who marries a charming and powerful cad. She adores him, naturally; is abominably treated, of course. Suffering in proportion to her love, she fights desperately to assert herself, but her husband mercilessly humiliates her until her will is broken. Thereafter she resigns herself to his infidelities, at the cost of blighting the development of her own personality. Rather than parade her injuries, she prefers to discover extraordinary virtue in her errant husband's sporadic displays of loyalty. Last scene of all, the bereft widow looks back nostalgically on the blessings of her wonderful marriage. In short, Charles II reaped the rewards of a model husband while behaving like an arrant scoundrel. It is enough to make the practitioners of household virtue despair.

Or was Charles actually rather better than such a view of his marriage would suggest? Many have thought so. The 'Merry Monarch' not only got away with his sins during his life; in this world, at least, he has been abundantly forgiven after his death. The most proper and prudish people condone behaviour in this king that they would judge outrageous in any other. Harpies who delight to pounce on the slightest evidence of male iniquity find, in this one instance, cause for indulgence. Nor is it difficult to see why. On any superficial reckoning Charles II is the most attractive of all English monarchs – courageous, stylish, witty and intelligent at all times; kind-hearted and affectionate too, so long as his own pleasure was not at stake.

Moreover, his supporters might justly argue, it would be absurd to judge a seventeenth-century monarch by the standards of the Victorian middle class. The King's marriage was primarily an act of state. If he got on well with the Queen that was a bonus; if not, the most that could reasonably be expected of him was to keep up appearances. Charles II was a highly sexed man – his grandfather, after all, had been Henri IV of France – with nothing of the puritan in his make-up. His mother's aim, albeit never achieved, had been to bring him up as socially polished in the French style: morals hardly entered into her system. Granted the temptations to which Charles was exposed, his unfaithfulness to Catherine cannot be a matter for either wonder or censure. The question remains, though, whether he behaved towards her in a manner that could be described as even half-way decent. Catherine herself, without doubt, would have answered with a resounding affirmative. That must be powerful evidence in Charles's favour, but it is not conclusive. The Queen tended to see the best in everyone. Her story would be better told without that debilitating constraint.

The proposal that Charles and Catherine should marry had first been mooted in 1645 when Charles was only fifteen and Catherine six. Five years previously Portugal had broken free of Spanish rule and Catherine's father, Dom João Duke of Braganza, the titular leader of the revolt, had been declared King. The real force behind Dom João's nationalism, ironically enough, was his Spanish wife Doña Luisa, daughter of the Duke of Medina Sidonia, who had commanded the Armada against England. The Portuguese triumph, however, was precarious, for Spain appeared far from resigned to the loss of its neighbouring kingdom. Portugal possessed a vast maritime empire in Brazil, Africa and the East, but it lacked sufficient resources at home to continue the struggle indefinitely and alone. The marriage proposal of 1645 was an early recognition that England might provide the necessary support.

The royalist defeat in the English Civil War, however, followed by the execution of the King and the establishment of the Common-wealth, put the projected match out of court for fifteen years. There was scant political advantage to be gained from marriage to a penniless exile such as Charles had now become. Yet the amity between Portugal and England remained. Cromwell, in return for various trade concessions, sent the beleaguered country a few regi-ments of horse and foot. King João died in 1656, but Queen Luisa never lost hope that Charles might one day return to his own. Even though, as the years slipped by, it became progressively more likely that the English King would pass his entire life in futile plotting and debauchery, no alternative match for Catherine was ever contemplated.

And so when, early in 1660, Charles's star suddenly began to shine brightly again, Portugal was the first foreign power to attempt to exploit the change in his fortune to advantage. Well before Charles had returned to England, the Portuguese ambassador in London was raising the possibility of the King's marriage to Catherine. The ambassador also advised that Charles should move his headquarters from Brussels in the Spanish Netherlands to Breda in the United Provinces, lest the Spaniards should attempt to hold him to ransom on the brink of his Restoration. The Portuguese, having seen their long-nurtured hopes flicker into life, were taking no chances. It was only a pity that they did not prevent Charles from falling into the toils of a beautiful young married woman called Barbara Palmer.

Portuguese enthusiasm for the match was enhanced by the peace concluded between France and Spain in 1660, under which the French undertook to give no support to the enemies of Spain. The marriage proposals which the Portuguese ambassador formally presented after Charles II's Restoration, therefore, were most attractively baited. First, the English were offered Tangier and Bombay. Tangier, Charles was somewhat optimistically informed, would enable its possessors 'to give the law to all the trade of the Mediterranean', while Bombay would provide the defensible base that the East India Company needed in order to develop its commerce in India with security. The Portuguese also held out the prospect of special trading privileges for the English in their eastern possessions. Such terms represented a tacit licence for the English to infiltrate an empire that the Portuguese were no longer able to hold. More germane to Charles's immediate needs, however, Catherine would also bring with her the huge dowry of two million *cruzados* (about £320,000), to be paid in sugar, Brazil-wood and cash.

Charles himself appeared favourably disposed to the marriage. His advisers, in so far as they were consulted, were neither eager nor hostile, though Clarendon permitted himself to wonder why His Majesty did not consider a Protestant princess. The King replied that he could not find one except among his own subjects, 'and among them he had seen no one that pleased him sufficiently for that purpose'. He specifically rejected any idea that he should marry the Princess of Orange, for he could never forget that her mother had scorned the suggestion when he had been an exile. Thus the negotiations with Portugal might have proceeded to a speedy conclusion had not the Spaniards been so determined to prevent the match. The Spanish ambassador expressed his deep concern that Charles should so far lower himself as to contemplate mixing his royal and ancient blood with the offspring of a rebel: such an error, moreover, would certainly lead to an expensive war with Spain. Besides which, had His Majesty not heard that the Portuguese Princess was sickly, ugly and deformed? Everyone in Spain and Portugal knew that she was incapable of bearing children. Why, therefore, did His Majesty not consider the beautiful and accomplished Princesses of Parma? If His Majesty's inclinations veered in that direction, the King of Spain would undertake to confer upon the chosen princess the same dowry that had been provided for the Infanta when she had married Louis XIV.

The calumnies against Catherine's person, if not the hollow threat of war, gave Charles pause for thought. The Earl of Bristol was dispatched to Italy to investigate the Princesses of Parma. He reported back that they were so unprepossessing that he had on first sight of them instantly abandoned any thought of negotiating a marriage with either. The Spanish ambassador, quite undismayed, changed his tack. In view of English prejudices against the one true faith it was perfectly obvious, he said, that Charles should marry a Protestant princess. His Most Catholic Majesty of Spain felt so strongly about this that he was prepared to pay the dowry of some suitable heretic – the Princess of Denmark, perhaps, or the daughter of the Elector of Saxony.

Meanwhile French influence had been working in Catherine's favour. Henrietta Maria, Charles's mother, arrived in England in the autumn of 1660 and ardently supported the Portuguese match. Not only was she genuinely concerned on her own account that her son should marry a Catholic; she had also been well briefed by Louis XIV. The French King recognised that the peace which he had recently concluded with Spain had left Portugal dangerously exposed. Though he himself had undertaken to remain neutral, that did not prevent him from doing all he could to thwart the Spaniards by promoting the Anglo-Portuguese alliance. An agent was sent to England to explain that Louis himself had thought seriously about marrying the Portuguese Princess, so impressed had he been by the most reliable reports of her attractions and attainments. Alas, 'for the better perfecting of the peace with Spain', he had been compelled to renounce this paragon, but he generously conveyed his hope that Charles would not forego the privilege of such a wife. In case there was any question of Charles being too straitened to afford the reinforcements demanded by Portugal, Louis sent £50,000 to ease the difficulty. Two months later, in April 1651, Clarendon blandly suggested that the French should lend a further £50,000, but on this occasion it was made clear that no more funds would be forthcoming until the marriage with Catherine had definitely been agreed.

Fortunately the Portuguese had by this time contrived to produce a portrait of Catherine that appeared to give the lie to the more alarming rumours about her looks. Looking at Dirk Stoop's picture of the Princess, Charles saw a neat, *petite* figure, with a hideous hair-style admittedly – a semi-circular lock was plastered across her forehead and great mats hung down the sides of her head – but also with beautifully set dark eyes that stared intriguingly out of a girlish face. 'This person cannot be unhandsome,' the King pronounced. For the second time he laid the Portuguese marriage project before Clarendon, on this occasion as a *fait accompli*.

Clarendon, however, once more pressed the advantages of a Protestant wife, and mentioned the large number of German princesses available. 'Odds fish,' replied the King, 'they are all foggy, and I cannot like any one of them for a wife.' It was typical of Charles to pass off a deep prejudice with a light remark. The religious issue was more important to him than he cared to admit. That exceedingly shrewd observer Lord Halifax wrote in his *Character of King Charles II* that, during the King's exile, 'a general creed, and no very long one, [had been] the utmost religion of one whose age and inclination could not well spare any thoughts that did not tend to his pleasures'. Yet Halifax also noted Charles's revulsion from 'the ill-bred familiarity of Scotch divines', to which he had been exposed in 1650, and which had prejudiced him irremediably against the extremer forms of Protestantism. As for the Church of England, Charles was not the man to remain indifferent to the sneers of sophisticated Frenchmen at the pitiful figure cut by the little band of impoverished Anglican divines in the Faubourg St-Germain. By the time of the Restoration, Halifax believed, the King 'was as certainly a Roman Catholic as . . . he was a man of pleasure; both very consistent by visible experience'. Perhaps Halifax went too far, but there can be no doubt of the King's Catholic sympathies, whatever role he was obliged to act in public. And if he was set on a Catholic wife, Catherine appeared the best bet. Clarendon tried once more to discuss the rumours that the Portuguese Princess was barren, but Charles brushed them aside as malicious Spanish inventions.

By the beginning of May 1661, therefore, the marriage had been finally negotiated, and Charles collected his second £50,000 from Louis. Even at this early stage of his reign he showed an alarming enthusiasm for accepting gratuities from France. Catherine's dowry remained much as originally proposed, while Charles for his part agreed to use his good offices to secure peace between Portugal and the Dutch, to guarantee the defence of the Portuguese East Indies in the case of warfare, and to supply ten thousand troops for the defence of Portugal against Spain. He was in no doubt that he had gained a considerable political bargain. As for his queen, he told Parliament: 'if I should never marry until I could make such a choice against which there could be no foresight of any inconvenience that may ensue, you would live to see me an old bachelor.' It remained to be seen, however, what kind of wife he had gained.

The reports emanating from Thomas Maynard, the English ambassador in Portugal, could hardly have been more encouraging. 'There is no doubt his Majesty hath made both nations infinitely happy in this choice,' he wrote. 'She is a lady of incomparable virtue, of excellent parts, very beautiful, and of indifferent stature, being somewhat taller than the Queen, His Majesty's mother.' Catherine's virtue, at least, has never been in dispute. The Iberian peninsula had once been under Moorish control, and the manner in which the Portuguese guarded their women made it easy to recall the fact. As Maynard explained, Catherine had been 'bred hugely retired. She hath hardly been ten times out of the Palace in her life. In five years' time she was not out of doors, until she heard of his Majesty's intentions to make her Queen of England.' The news of her elevation had been celebrated by a visit to two saints' shrines in the city; 'and very shortly she intends to pay her devotion to some saints in the country.' It would be hard to imagine a preparation further removed from the seedy decadence of Charles II's court.

Perhaps Queen Luisa, if she thought about Catherine at all as a person rather than as a bargaining counter, reckoned that her daughter's purity and naivety offered the best hope of engaging the interest of a notorious voluptuary like Charles II. Catherine's education, if the word implies the transmission of any useful worldly knowledge or accomplishment, had been almost entirely neglected. She was twenty-three in November 1661, which was old for a seventeenth-century princess to be married, yet notwithstanding her mother's ambitions for her, she spoke hardly a word of English or French. She knew nothing of fashion or clothes, and she was wholly without the elegance or sophistication that passes for civilisation in the world of courts. But was she so entirely innocent? Where women live in purdah, the assumption must be that men are dangerous beasts. Catherine's own brother bore out this theory. King Alfonso was a murderous degenerate whose idea of fun was marauding round the streets with an armed band attacking and robbing his subjects – hence Queen Luisa's regency. Catherine had probably heard stories of women culled from Lisbon's sleaziest brothels being herded into the royal palace in order to gratify His Majesty's whims. Rumours from England were also rife at the Portuguese court, so that Catherine may also have divined something of her future husband's character. The one piece of information that Queen Luisa did impart to her daughter, with dire results, was that she should have nothing to do with Mrs Palmer.

2

The need to secure Tangier, and then the desire to spare Catherine a winter voyage, meant that she did not leave Portugal until late in April 1662. Charles II, after the marriage was arranged, must needs content himself with a letter to his bride – in 'the worst Spanish that ever was writ', as he told Clarendon. He looked for her coming, he told Catherine, with as deep a longing as he had felt to be among his own people when in exile: 'only the presence of Your Serenity is wanting to unite us under the protection of God, in the health and content I desire'. This tiresome epistolary chore completed, he turned again to the business of impregnating Mrs Palmer. 'The Lady', as Clarendon derisively called Barbara in his autobiography, had given birth in February 1661 to a daughter, whose paternity was contested between the King, Lord Chesterfield and her unfortunate husband, with the odds increasingly favouring Chesterfield as the child grew up to resemble him. In September Mrs Palmer conceived again, and this time no one but her spouse presumed to challenge the royal claim. Charles himself was sufficiently convinced of his achievement to create the wretched Palmer Earl of Castlemaine in February 1662, with the inheritance of the title limited to 'heirs of his body gotten on Barbara Palmer his now wife', 'the reason whereof', as Pepys noted, 'everyone knows'.

Lady Castlemaine's sex appeal must have been stupendous: the mere sight of her underclothes hung out to dry was enough to send Pepys, a connoisseur in these matters, into ecstasies. For all her allure, however, the Lady was a vicious and rapacious termagant, determined to milk the King for all she could get, and more than ready to treat him to her tantrums if she did not obtain it. Her viciousness was wholly unflawed. Not for her to stoop to subtlety or long-term calculation: indeed, there was a kind of translucent integrity about her grasping designs that might easily have proved self-defeating. All her actions showed her for what she was: a lovely, unblushing nineteen-carat bitch with a deadly instinct for the jugular. With any other monarch she could hardly have lasted beyond her first tantrum, but Charles, whether out of lust, laziness or lax good nature, usually found it convenient to give her what she wanted. Just now, fearing that the Portuguese match might put an end to her sway, Barbara wanted a great deal; and since the King could set her expenses against Catherine's forthcoming dowry, he was in a generous mood. Nevertheless, in the spring of 1662 the future cannot have appeared unclouded to Lady Castlemaine. The bloom of motherhood, so delightful in conventional circumstances, is apt to take something off from the charms of a mistress. Barbara must have known that she would have a fight on her hands with the imminent arrival of the Queen. Fighting, however, was her especial forte.

Meanwhile Catherine, in Portugal, remained free to indulge what-ever fantasy she wished about Charles. It was not remotely within her scheme of imagining that her husband might continue with any liaison after their marriage, whatever entanglements the poor man might have found himself ensnared in during his bachelor days. No doubt Charles's past enhanced his romantic appeal. In Catherine's mind he was the outcast wanderer who, after many adventures, had finally come into his rightful inheritance, as husband no less than as King. As a good Catholic girl she knew it was her duty to love her husband, and she never dreamt that the task might be difficult. 'My gratitude', she replied to Charles's letter, 'is too active to endure delay, the greatest torment which attends approaching felicity.' And in her case she meant what she wrote.

For a moment, however, the delay in their meeting threatened to become infinite. Queen Luisa, having lately had to expend funds in warding off a Spanish attack, suddenly discovered, when the moment came for handing over Catherine's dowry, that the cupboard was bare. She informed Lord Sandwich, who had arrived with the fleet to collect both Catherine and the treasure, that she could only pay half the sum required 'with which she hoped His Majesty would remain satisfied, and she faithfully promised to pay the rest within the year'. Sandwich, who had specific instructions that the King's marriage with Catherine was absolutely dependent on the Portuguese first fully performing their side of bargain, was placed in a hideous dilemma. In the end he gallantly informed the Portuguese that the Princess was far more valuable than her dowry. Nevertheless, the incident placed Catherine at a psychological disadvantage before she ever arrived in England. She appeared as the recipient of charity from a king who was always hard pressed for money, and who in moments of tension could scarcely be expected to forget that his wife had proved to be less than the gold-mine for which he had negotiated. In fact, the dowry was not fully paid until 1670.

Catherine travelled with a suite of over a hundred Portuguese attendants, though in view of the impression they made in England it might have been better if they had all been left behind. The contingent included, if Anthony Hamilton's *Memoirs of Count Gramont* is to be believed, six chaplains, four bakers, a Jewish perfumer, 'and an officer with no apparent duties who was known as The Queen's Barber'.

Presiding over the entourage were the Countesses of Penalva and Ponteval, two dowagers of an unbending hauteur and a ceremonial stiffness that never relaxed. Under their command were 'six frights who called themselves maids of honour, and another monster who passed herself off as governess to these rare beauties'. These less than beguiling guardians conceived it their duty to uphold the honour of Portugal by a rigid adherence to etiquette at all times. It was noted that when Catherine said goodbye to her mother – and they both must have known they were parting for ever – neither registered a flicker of emotion. When Catherine so far forgot herself as to run back along the deck for a last glimpse of her brothers, King Alfonso sternly reproved her.

The voyage was rough, and throughout its thirteen days Catherine never left her cabin. When the fleet at last arrived in English waters it was Charles's brother, James Duke of York, who was deputed to welcome the new Queen at Portsmouth on 14 May. The King himself, it appeared, was tied up with parliamentary business and could not get down to Portsmouth before 20 May, though he was not so busy as to be obliged to forego supper with Lady Castlemaine on every evening of this intervening period, including the night on which bonfires were lit to celebrate the Queen's arrival. 'There was no fire at her [Lady Castlemaine's] door,' Pepys recorded, 'though at all the rest of the doors almost in the street; which was much observed.' The King and his mistress amused themselves by weighing each other to see who was the heaviest, and the Lady, in her advanced state of pregnancy, carried the day.

Gossip soon put it about that Catherine insisted on wearing her Portuguese dresses, complete with the farthingale, a framework of hoops which plumped out the skirt to a vast girth that prohibited any close approach to the wearer. As this fashion had barely been seen in England since the beginning of the century, its reappearance caused much amusement, and confirmed the beau monde in its opinion that Portugal must be an extremely backward country. Yet, although Catherine's attendants appeared inalienably wedded to the farthingale, she herself took care to wear an English dress when receiving the Duke of York, and had only assumed her native attire in deference to the Duke's gallant request. When she landed at Portsmouth she immediately consulted Lady Suffolk, who had been appointed principal lady of her bedchamber, about which clothes would be most suitable for receiving the King.

Catherine made a favourable impression on everyone she met. The Earl of Sandwich, who might have been expected, from his Puritan background, to take a dim view of a papist queen, wrote enthusiastically to Clarendon. 'She is a princess of extraordinary goodness of disposition, very discreet and pious, and there are the most hopes that there ever was of her making the King and us all happy.' Lord Chesterfield, her Chamberlain, echoed these sentiments, with additional comments on her attractiveness: 'She is exactly shaped, and has lovely hands, excellent eyes, a good countenance, a pleasing voice, fine hair, and in a word is what an understanding man would wish in his wife.'

By the time that Charles finally reached Portsmouth in the early afternoon of 20 May, Catherine, feeling somewhat peaky, had taken to her bed. Nevertheless, the first brief meeting of the King and Queen, which took place in her chamber as soon as Charles had had time to change from his travelling clothes, seemed to be a success. 'Her face is not so exact as to be called a beauty,' the King reported to Clarendon early the next morning, 'though her eyes are excellent good, and not anything in her face that in the least degree can shock one. On the contrary, she hath as much agreeableness in her looks altogether as I ever saw, and if I have any skill in physiognomy, which I think I have, she must be as good a woman as ever was born; her conversation, as much as I can perceive, is very good, for she has wit enough, and a most agreeable voice; you would wonder to see how well we are acquainted already; in a word, I think myself very happy, for I am confident our two humours will agree very well together.'

Perhaps Charles exaggerated his felicity rather than admit any misgivings to a chancellor who had been lukewarm about the marriage. Sir John Reresby, who was in Portsmouth, received a different impression. 'It was very discernible', he wrote, 'that the King was not much enamoured of his bride . . . [who had] nothing visible about her capable to make the King forget his inclination to the Countess of Castlemaine.' Reresby's account is borne out by a note Lord Dartmouth made in his copy of Burnet's *History of My Own Time*. According to Dartmouth, Charles remarked of Catherine to a bystander that 'he thought they had brought him a bat, instead of a woman; but it was too late to find fault, and he must make the best he could of a bad matter'. Dartmouth went on to append his own unflattering description of Catherine. 'She was very short and broad, of a swarthy complexion, one of her fore teeth stood out, which held up her upper lip, [and she] had some very nauseous distempers, besides excessively proud and ill-humoured.'

Dartmouth's comments, however, should be treated with suspicion. First, it is most unlikely that Charles would have spoken so slightingly about the Queen to anyone: he may have been lacking in moral sense, but his pride would scarcely have allowed him to fail so conspiciously in *politesse*. Second, Dartmouth was not born until ten years after Catherine's arrival in England, and if his description of the Queen is accurate at all it applies to her later years rather than to her youth. All that can be gathered from contemporary accounts of Catherine when she first arrived in this country is that beauty lies in the eye of the beholder. Lord Chesterfield's favourable opinion has already been quoted. Lord Sandwich spoke of 'the most lovely and agreeable person of the Queen'. Sir John Williamson called her 'of person short, but lovely, fair, and black-eyed'. Sir John Reresby, on the other hand, found her 'very little, not handsome (though her face was indifferent)'. John Evelyn, while deeming the Portuguese attendants 'sufficiently unagreeable', considered the Queen better-looking than any of them – 'tho' low of stature prettily shaped, languishing and excellent eyes, her teeth wronging her mouth by sticking a little too far out; for the rest lovely enough'. Pepys, on 31 May 1662, wrote that 'all people say of her to be a very fine and handsome lady; and the King is pleased enough with her: which, I fear, will put Madam Castlemaine's nose out of joint.' Pepys saw Catherine for himself on 7 September of that year and judged that 'though she be not very charming, yet she hath a good, modest, and innocent look, which is pleasing'. In December 1662 he 'opposed mightily' his aunt's opinion that the Queen was handsome, only to record on 13 July 1663 that Catherine was 'mighty pretty'. Two days later he awarded his supreme accolade, 'sporting in my fancy with the Queen'. At the very least, then, the evidence suggests that Catherine presented Charles with no insupportable amatory burden, especially since, in Halifax's words, the King's disposition in these matters contained 'as little mixture of the seraphic part as ever man had'.

As Catherine felt better the morning after her first meeting with the King, the wedding was immediately fixed for that day. First, at Catherine's earnest request, there was a Catholic ceremony in her bedchamber. The Princess always remained true to the Portuguese ambassador's promise that 'she would be content to enjoy her own religion without concerning herself with what others professed'; even so, she was far too devout a Catholic to imagine that she could be married according to the Church of England. Naturally, this Catholic service was kept a secret: for the world at large the wedding in the Grand Hall of the King's House that afternoon was the only one that had taken place. 'I must tell you I think myself very happy, I was married the day before yesterday,' Charles wrote to his sister Henriette-Anne who could be relied upon to relish his irony. Henriette, or 'Minette' as he called her, was unhappily married to Louis XIV's homosexual brother the Duc d'Orléans ('Monsieur'). She was perhaps the only woman whom Charles ever really loved, and she returned his devotion with rather more sincerity than his mistresses did. Brother and sister had no secrets from each other. 'The fortune that follows our family is fallen upon me,' Charles told her in his world-weary roué vein, '*car Monsieur Le Cardinal m'a fermé la porte au nez*, and though I am not so furious as Monsieur was, but am content to let those pass over before I go to bed to my wife, yet I hope I shall entertain her at least better the first night than he did you.'

There are, indeed, no grounds for scepticism about Charles's abilities as a lover. Catherine fell passionately in love with her husband. Charles, too, initially seemed to be more than content. He possessed in full measure that essential requirement for a successful Don Juan, the ability to believe wholeheartedly in the emotion of the moment, no matter how insecurely it might be based. 'I cannot easily tell you how happy I think myself,' he wrote to Clarendon on 25 May, 'and I must be the worst man living (which I hope I am not) if I be not a good husband. I am confident never two humours were better fitted together than ours are.' It was left to the worldly-wise Lord Chesterfield to doubt whether the Queen's merit would suffice: 'if it should I suppose our court will require a new modelling, and then the profession of an honest man's friendship will signify more than it does now'.

The King and Queen remained in Portsmouth for some days, there being an insufficient number of carts to transport all the farthingales, without which, as Charles wrote resignedly to his sister, 'there is no stirring'. The Portuguese ladies-in-waiting also created difficulties by their refusal to sleep in any bed previously defiled by male occupancy. Nevertheless, by 29 May Charles and Catherine had reached Hampton Court, where the King proposed to spend the summer. For a while everything continued to go well, with Charles going out of his way to be attentive and to lay on entertainments for his queen. Early in June, however, Catherine's happiness was placed in jeopardy by an event entirely beyond her control. Lady Castlemaine was delivered of her baby.

It had never been the Lady's plan to yield demurely to the Queen and fade gently out of sight. Aggression was the very core of her being. She had at first intended that her baby should be born at Hampton Court in the midst of the royal honeymoon. This plan proved incapable of fulfilment, but as soon as her boy had been christened on 18 June, with Charles as godfather, she hastened to her brother's house at Richmond in order to be as close as possible to the King. No further allurements were required: very soon Charles was visiting her every day. It was not so much that he was fed up with the Queen as that it never occurred to him for a moment that he should deny himself what he desired. He did not think, he once said, that God would make a man miserable for taking a little pleasure out of the way; and the idea that he himself might be making his wife miserable, if it intruded into his conscience at all, would have been swiftly dismissed as a facile and commonplace branch of ethics beneath the consideration of a king. Charles's main concern was to keep his throne, not to go on his travels again. Beyond that he acknowledged few constraints upon his behaviour. Fortunately he had been endowed with a pleasant, easygoing nature. It was not pleasant enough, however, to save Catherine.

There was perhaps another factor in his readiness to betray the Queen. Like most men of the world he was keenly sensitive to any hint of mockery. If his chaplains reproached him with immorality he would take the rebuke in good part: that was what these boring little fellows were paid for. But any suggestion that he was being laughed at by the sophisticated cut him to the quick. It was therefore a disaster for Catherine that the antics of her Portuguese attendants at Hampton Court attracted the sneers of their English counterparts. There is no missing the contempt in Clarendon's description of the Portuguese ladies – 'women for the most part old and ugly and proud, incapable of any conversation with persons of quality and liberal education' – and Clarendon was a noble nature compared with most of the courtiers who hung around Charles II. The Portuguese women, he went on, 'desired and indeed had conspired so far to possess the Queen themselves, that she should neither learn the English language, nor use their habit, nor depart from the manner and fashions of her own country in any particulars; "which resolution", they told her, "would be for the dignity of Portugal, and would quickly induce the English ladies to conform to Her Majesty's practice"'. Such delusions could only invite merriment. Then there were the Queen's musicians, whose curious warbling attempts to master the Italian style attracted much derision. Moreover the length and intensity of Catherine's devotions could not but make the court butterflies recoil. In no time the Portuguese had become a laughing-stock.

Lady Castlemaine, if she had been simply a woman of easy virtue rather than a dedicated exponent of vice, might have rested content with confirming the fascination which she exercised over the King. There is no evidence that Catherine knew the cause of Charles's sudden enthusiasm for going to Richmond, and even if she had found out, the conventional proprieties might still have been observed. Lady Castlemaine's appetite, however, grew by what it fed on: she demanded not just victory but public acknowledgement of her power. She remembered that Charles had made some promise that she should be a lady of the bedchamber to the Queen and determined to hold him to it. Her ambition was easily accomplished, for the King was not inhibited by any conventional considerations of honour, and he may have imagined that Catherine knew nothing of his liaison. If so, he was quickly undeceived. When the list of suggested appointments was presented to the Queen she deftly scored out Lady Castlemaine's name and approved all the rest. 'The King was angry and the Queen discontented a whole day and night upon it,' Pepys recorded on 26 July, 'but the King hath promised to have nothing to do with her hereafter.'

With a breathtaking display of outraged virtue Charles wrote off to complain to his sister that someone had been poisoning the mind of the Queen, but for once Henriette gave him no comfort. 'You tell me that someone has spoken maliciously about a person near to the Queen your wife,' she mocked. 'Alas! How can such things possibly be said? I who know your innocence marvel at it. But jesting apart I pray you tell me how the Queen takes this. It is said here that she is grieved beyond measure, and to speak frankly I think it is with reason.' Catherine also received emotional support from the Queen Mother, whom she visited at Greenwich on 28 July. Henrietta Maria was the kind of Frenchwoman who considers adultery the inevitable concomitant of an attractive husband, but she was so pleased to have a devout Catholic daughter-in-law that she treated Catherine with great kindness. Through her influence some improvement in relations between the King and Queen was detected on their return from Greenwich.

Evidently, the seemingly meek little Queen had more stuffing in her than anyone had hitherto realised. Yet this sudden flare of resentment between Charles and Catherine might have subsided without inflicting undue damage had the King not become conscious of whispers about the court that he was being governed by his wife. The King's grandfather, the great Henri IV, it was said, would never have allowed such a state of affairs; *he* had obliged *his* queen to treat his mistresses with respect. The imputation struck Charles at his weakest point, which may explain, though it can never excuse, the blackguardly course of behaviour on which he now embarked.

His initial gambit was to appear unheralded in his wife's chamber, brazenly leading Lady Castlemaine by the hand. Catherine, whose grasp of English was still minimal, did not catch the newcomer's name and at first talked to her with her usual shy friendliness. Whether some kind Portuguese attendant corrected her misapprehension, or whether she herself suddenly realised with whom she was dealing, Charles's tactic soon rebounded with terrible effect. Catherine had no sooner sat down, by Clarendon's account, 'but her colour changed, and tears gushed out of her eyes, and her nose bled, and she fainted; so that she was forthwith removed into another room, and all the company retired out of that where she was before.' Charles, who doubtless felt that royalty had no business to throw hysterics in public, 'looked upon it with wonderful indignation'. The court toadies, of course, shared his outrage. It was terrible that the King should be so put upon by his wife. In concert with these sycophants, Charles's will locked irrevocably into the determination that Lady Castlemaine *would* become a lady of the bedchamber to the Queen no matter what the consequences. An appointment that had originated as a whim of his mistress had now become a test of his marital authority.

For a while, though, Charles still seemed to believe that his charm would carry the day. 'The King used all the ways he could, by treating the Queen with all caresses, to dispose her to gratify him in this particular, as a matter wherein his honour was engaged.' He also promised, with his scoundrel sincerity, 'that he had not the least familiarity with her [Lady Castlemaine] since Her Majesty's arrival, nor would ever after be guilty of it again, but would live always with Her Majesty in all fidelity for conscience sake'. Catherine reacted, however, by unloosing further tempests of rage, which only confirmed the general opinion at court that the woman really was impossible. At this point the mask of the easygoing man of the world slipped from Charles, and he acted, as a contemporary observed, with the ferocity of a wild boar showing his tusks.

The unfortunate Clarendon, whom Catherine greatly respected, was instructed to use his influence and bring the Queen to heel. For the Chancellor there could have been no more ungrateful task. A man of rigid honour and principle, he had given up the best years of his life to exile in order to serve his idealised vision of monarchy, yet now that the long-cherished dream had been realised, he saw only a corrupt and decadent court, ruled by a king whose sense of duty rarely stretched beyond the gratification of his own desires. In particular Clarendon hated Lady Castlemaine, whose cause he was now called upon to plead. While others prostrated themselves before the all-powerful mistress, Clarendon had done everything possible to obstruct her rise, forbidding his wife to exchange so much as a word with her. Before he confronted Catherine, therefore, the Chancellor bravely tried to make Charles see the wickedness of 'laying such a command upon the Queen, which flesh and blood could not comply with'. Clarendon went on to remind the King how critical he had been of his cousin Louis XIV for exposing *his* queen to the insolence of his mistresses. Had not Charles called Louis's behaviour 'such a piece of ill-nature, that he could never be guilty of'?

Charles listened to his Chancellor's lecture politely enough, only taking issue when Clarendon suggested that a king's mistress dishonoured herself in the same degree as any other fallen woman. The King showed himself remarkably sensitive about the damage he had done to Lady Castlemaine's reputation, which he unblushingly claimed to have been 'fair and untainted till her friendship for him'. Lord Chesterfield, to name but one, would have been surprised to hear it. But Charles was now far gone in self-righteousness. He liked Lady Castlemaine's company, he said; he enjoyed her conversation, 'from which he would not be restrained, because he knew there was and should be all innocence in it'. In short, he was bent on having his way no matter what the cost to Catherine. 'I wish I may be unhappy in this world and the world to come if I fail in the least degree of what I have resolved,' he wrote to Clarendon about this time, 'which is of making my Lady Castlemaine of my wife's bedchamber, and whosoever I find use any endeavours to hinder this resolution of mine (except it be only myself) I will be his enemy to the last moment of my life.' The implication was clear enough: if Clarendon wanted to remain Chancellor he must use his best endeavours to crack Catherine's resolve.

The Chancellor's first attempt to raise the subject with the Queen led to such a torrent of tears that he was forced to withdraw. The next day, however, she was a little calmer. Clarendon tried to explain that her position was by no means as insupportable as she appeared to imagine. When Catherine, 'with some blushing and confusion and some tears', protested that 'she did not think that she should have found the King engaged in his affection to another lady', Clarendon explained that what the King had been before his marriage had nothing to do with her, and reiterated that 'all former appetites were expired'. Catherine seemed almost prepared to believe this, thanked the Chancellor for his pains, and asked him 'to help in returning her thanks to His Majesty, and in obtaining his pardon for any passion or peevishness she might have been guilty of'. So far, so good. But as soon as Clarendon moved on to the matter of making Lady Castlemaine a lady of her bedchamber, 'it raised all the rage and fury of yesterday, with fewer tears, the fire appearing in her eyes where the water was'. His Majesty's request, she stormed, 'could proceed from no other ground but his hatred of her person'. Rather than submit to it, she would take any boat that she could find back to Lisbon. Clarendon withdrew and reported back to Charles, wisely counselling delay in the pursuit of his intent.

The King, however, only had ears for those courtiers who told him to assert himself. That night, Clarendon reports, 'the fire flamed higher than ever: the King reproached the Queen with stubbornness and want of duty, and she him with tyranny and want of affection: he used threats and menaces, which he never intended to put into execution, and she talked loudly "how ill she was treated, and that she would return again to Portugal". Charles retorted, "that she should do well first to know whether her mother would receive her: and he would give her a fit opportunity to know that, by sending to their home all her Portuguese servants; and that he would forthwith give order for the discharge of them all, since they behaved so ill, for to them and their counsels he imputed all her perverseness."'

It is perhaps necessary, since Charles so effectively adopted the role of a reasonable man tried beyond endurance, to emphasise again that Catherine's 'perverseness' consisted in refusing to accept her husband's mistress as one of her ladies of the bedchamber. For this presumption the Queen was now subjected to the cruellest psychological pressure. The Portuguese attendants were duly expelled, save the Countess of Penalva 'who, by the infirmity of her eyes and other indisposition of health, scarce stirred out of her chamber', and a few inferior servants. The revenue officers were instructed to value the goods that had been brought to England as part of the Queen's dowry at strict market rates. The Portuguese ambassador, sickened by the sudden collapse of all his hopes for the marriage, retired to his London house. Catherine was left in almost total isolation, spending much time 'melancholic in her chamber in tears', while Charles ostentatiously enjoyed himself with 'the young and frolic people of either sex [who] talked loudly all that they thought the King would like and be pleased with'. So Charles passed his nights, 'and in the morning came to the Queen's chamber, for he never slept in any other place.'

Worst of all Catherine's humiliations, Lady Castlemaine 'came to the court, was lodged there, was every day in the Queen's presence, and the King in continual conference with her; whilst the Queen sat untaken notice of: and if Her Majesty rose at the indignity and retired into her chamber, it may be one or two attended her; but all the company remained in the room she left, and too often said those things aloud which nobody ought to have whispered.' Deliberately it was borne in upon Catherine that there was 'universal mirth in all company but in hers, and in all places but in her chamber; her own servants showing more respect and more diligence to the person of the lady, than towards their own mistress, who they found could do them less good.'

Clarendon continued to entreat her to give way, but the Queen remained immovably entrenched on the highest moral ground. She could not conceive, she said, 'how any body could, with a good conscience, consent to what she could not but suppose would be an occasion and opportunity of sin'. The influence of her Catholic confessors is surely evident here. There was a touching moment when Clarendon tried some flattery, declaring that it could not be within the power of any woman to deprive the Queen of the King's affection, if only she would exercise her charms. Catherine listened intently, 'sometimes seeming not displeased, but oftener by a smile declaring that she did not believe what he said.' Her resolve seemed unbreakable. The King might do what he pleased, she declared; she would never agree to accept Lady Castlemaine. Yet in other respects she showed a humble and contrite spirit that would surely have melted a generous heart. 'She acknowledged with tears', Clarendon wrote, ' "that she had been in too much passion, and said somewhat she ought not to have said, and for which she would willingly ask the King's pardon upon her knees; though his manner of treating her had wonderfully surprised her, and might be some excuse for more than ordinary commotion. That she prayed to God to give her patience, and hoped she should be no more transported with the like passion upon what provocation soever." '

But the stand that Catherine had made in her rage proved harder and harder to sustain as the full tide of her emotion receded. One may suspect too, though there is no evidence on this point, that the attitude of her Catholic confessors may have been modified as she found herself so completely ostracised. It is not quite clear exactly how long Catherine kept up her resistance – perhaps a month, perhaps longer. At some stage in the late summer or early autumn, however, without any warning whatsoever, she cracked. Such was her desperation that, from one day to the next, the pendulum swung full tilt. She did not just accept Lady Castlemaine; she 'let herself fall first to conversation and then to familiarity, and even in the same instant to a confidence with the lady; was merry with her in public, talked kindly to her, and in private used nobody more friendly'.

It was as though Catherine, having been forced against her better instincts to abandon all her hopes for the marriage, became possessed with an urge to humiliate herself completely. In her loneliness and desperation nothing seemed to matter any more save getting back on terms with her husband. The tragedy of Catherine's volte-face, however, was that it occurred too suddenly and too completely to carry conviction, and therefore failed in the very purpose for which it was intended. The courtiers had witnessed a woman driven to self-destruction; they chose to believe that a tiresome neurotic had been brought to heel. Even Clarendon, though he had previously done all he could to break Catherine's resistance, blandly concluded that she had surrendered on the brink of victory. Before, he had told Catherine that the King would never give way; afterwards, he gave it as his opinion that Charles, under his insouciant exterior, had been growing weary of the struggle, to the point that he was about to banish Lady Castlemaine from the court. The King, on this theory, had begun to respect Catherine's heroic virtue; now he could only despise her abject submission. The whole episode had ended by confirming his cynicism about women. Obviously, Catherine's tantrums had just been another female ploy, which he congratulated himself on having defeated.

One may have doubts about Charles's potential as a respecter of feminine virtue without necessarily believing that Clarendon was wholly wrong in his analysis. Pepys, Evelyn and Halifax all agree that the King's most fundamental characteristic was love of ease, and Catherine's intransigence had threatened to render his life far from easy. For that reason alone he might well have brought himself to dispense with Lady Castlemaine's services. As things were, though, it was the Queen's and not the mistress's power which was extinguished. Catherine's surrender destroyed her as a force to be reckoned with. For the rest of the reign she was doomed to be essentially a passive figure, sometimes admired for her goodness, more often (such is the way of courts) despised for her ineffectualness.

3

The value of Charles's undertaking to reform, once Catherine had accepted Lady Castlemaine, was all too soon apparent. The Queen was broken: her whims no longer merited consideration. Although Lady Castlemaine did not formally become a lady of the bedchamber until 1663, already in September 1662, as Clarendon wrote to the Duke of Ormonde, 'every body takes her to be of the bedchamber; for she is always there, and goes abroad in the coach. But the Queen tells me that the King promised her, on condition she would use her [Lady Castlemaine] as she doth others, that she should never live in court: yet lodgings, I hear, she hath. I hear of no back stairs.' Pepys, on 25 April 1663, reported 'that the Queen is much grieved of late at the King's neglecting her, he having not supped once with her this quarter of a year, and almost every night with my Lady Castlemaine'. The Lady now had a chamber in Whitehall next to the King's own; 'which I am sorry to hear, though I love her much'.

Thus the Queen was forced to live cheek-by-jowl with her rival, who attended her even in her chapel. (The Lady was beginning to feel that Roman Catholicism might be her kind of religion, notwithstanding that her husband belonged to that faith.) Catherine, as a reward for her capitulation, found the King affable enough, so long as she caused no trouble. On 7 September 1662 Pepys, taking advantage of the ramshackle informality of Whitehall, saw the royal family at ease in the Queen Mother's presence-chamber. Catherine and Henrietta Maria were both there; so, of course, was Lady Castlemaine. They were making much of James Crofts, the King's thirteen-year-old boy by Lucy Walters, when Charles came in. 'The King and Queen were very merry; and he would have made the Queen Mother believe that his Queen was with child, and said that she said so. And the young Queen answered, "You

1. An early thirteenth-century wall-painting discovered in 1964 in the chapel of Sainte Radegonde at Chinon, thought to represent Eleanor of Aquitaine (*left*) with her daughter-in-law Isabella of Angoulême.

2. Eleanor of Aquitaine's funeral effigy at Fontevrault.

3. Henrietta Maria presenting Charles I with a laurel wreath, by Daniel Mytens (c.1632). The head of Henrietta Maria is after, perhaps even by, Van Dyck. The symbolic pose reflects the artificial atmosphere in which the King and Queen lived at court.

4. Catherine of Braganza soon after her marriage,
by Samuel Cooper: '. . . not anything in her face that in the
least can shock one'.

5. Charles II at the end of his reign, by Edward Lutterel: '. . .
as little mixture of the seraphic part as ever man had'.

6. *above* Caroline of Brunswick as Princess of Wales, 1804, by Sir Thomas Lawrence.

7. *above opposite* Queen Caroline in 1820, at the time of her appearance in the House of Lords, by Sir George Hayter.

8. *below opposite* The silver wedding of the Duke and Duchess of Teck at White Lodge in Richmond Park, 12 June 1891. Princess May is standing with her three brothers, from left to right Prince Alexander ('Alge'), Prince Francis ('Frank') and Prince Adolphus ('Dolly').

9. Queen Mary in 1937, accoutred in the style
to which she had grown accustomed.

lie;" which was the first English word that I ever heard her say; which made the King good sport; and he would have taught her to say in English, "Confess and be hanged." ' After which happy family scene the King, the Queen, the mistress and the bastard son by another mistress all departed together in a single coach.

For Catherine, though, anything was preferable to her general habit of loneliness. Pepys saw her a week later, 'and some fine ladies with her; but, my troth, not many.' All too quickly the despised Queen became the natural resort of court frumps and bores. Even Lord Sandwich, who had been so smitten on her arrival in England, now spoke of her with brutal indifference. Her wit and patronage, he said, were not enough to sustain any man – 'and therefore he thinks it not his obligation to stand for her against his own interest'.

In the spring of 1663 the Queen showed one last flicker of fight when she protested vehemently against the King's decision to create his son Crofts the Duke of Monmouth. Charles compounded the insult by ordering the boy to put on his hat in the Queen's presence, in order to emphasise his royal status. To Catherine the gesture seemed like a public expression of the King's belief that she would never produce an heir, a particularly hurtful slight since her hopes of restoring her position depended so largely upon becoming a mother. Even in 1663 the pre-nuptial rumour of her barrenness was already gathering pace, to the point where the court gossips began to whisper that the King would put her away in favour of another wife.

Catherine's disappointment must have been rendered more bitter by the fecundity of Lady Castlemaine, who gave birth three times between 1663 and 1665. The Lady's pregnancies, however, at least had the merit of temporarily cooling Charles's devotion, especially when, as in 1663, he attributed the honour of paternity to another of her admirers. It was not in the King's soul to condescend to jealousy; nevertheless, in the middle of 1663, Lady Castlemaine very definitely lost favour. In consequence Catherine immediately began to look much better and happier – witness Pepys's enthusiasm for her in July 1663.

Unfortunately, though, the Queen was not the sole gainer by the Lady's fall from grace, for Charles's attention also turned to Lady Frances Stuart, whom Henrietta Maria had introduced among Catherine's women. This was naughty of the Queen Mother, who must have realised the likely consequences of placing '*la plus belle fille du monde*' under her son's nose. Nevertheless Catherine infinitely preferred '*La Belle Stuart*', who treated her with deference and respect, to Lady Castlemaine, who never troubled to disguise her insolent contempt. 'How can you sit so long a-dressing?' Castlemaine asked the Queen, implying that the disparities of nature could never be obliterated by the contrivances of art. 'I have so much reason to use patience,' returned Catherine with dignity, 'that I can very well bear with it.' With the Lady temporarily out of action, however, relations between the King and Queen blossomed. That summer they went to Tunbridge Wells and to Bath in the hope that the waters might enhance the Queen's fertility. Catherine's love for her husband was evident to all. The shy Portuguese girl who had been brought up in the strictest etiquette now rushed to greet the King with embraces whenever he came to her.

Charles was unmoved by such artless expressions of sentiment. As soon as Lady Castlemaine had been delivered of her impediment, she rushed to join the King and Queen at Oxford and experienced no difficulty in restoring herself to favour. Back in London Charles once more supped with her every night. Catherine's disappointment, after so short a respite, must have been intense. In October she fell seriously ill. The doctors spoke of 'spotted fever', which one would imagine to be chicken-pox or measles, had not the symptoms been so grave. For days she lay helpless in her room, while attendants milled around her fussing about her will, doctors applied pigeons to her feet, and priests encircled her shaven head with a cap full of relics. These ministrations might have killed her if Charles had not insisted upon her room being cleared.

Even then Catherine continued to decline, and extreme unction was administered. The will to struggle against death appeared to be entirely lacking. She begged Charles that her body should be sent back to Portugal for burial, and made him promise not to abandon the Portuguese alliance to which her life had been sacrificed. For the rest, she said, she quit life without regret, save that of leaving him. According to the Gramont memoirs she also spoke of her husband's future: 'Not possessing sufficient charms to merit his tenderness, she had at least the consolation in dying to give place to a consort who might be more worthy of it, and to whom heaven, perhaps, might grant a blessing that had been refused to her.' Charles, Lord Arlington wrote to the Duke of Buckingham, was 'very much afflicted', as well he might have been. His sensibility, however, did not prevent him from supping regularly with Lady Castlemaine throughout the Queen's illness, or from being much in the company of Lady Frances Stuart, 'with whom', the French ambassador reported on October 22, 'he is very much in love'. Still, it is clear that Charles did support Catherine at this time. 'He conjured her to live for his sake,' as Anthony Hamilton put it, 'without supposing that she would take him at his word.'

Oddly enough, though, it was after the fever had left her that Catherine's mind began to ramble. Her delusions made it heart-breakingly clear what trauma had been oppressing her. When Charles visited her she told him that she had just been delivered without any pain or sickness of a 'very ugly boy'. 'No,' said the King to humour her, 'it is a very pretty boy.' 'Nay,' she replied, 'if it be like you it is a fine boy indeed, and I would be very well pleased with it.' The scene might belong to a Shakespearean tragedy. A day or so later Catherine imagined that she had three children and that one of them, a little girl, resembled Charles. At other times her remarks smacked of the sharpness of the Fool. 'You need not scratch your head,' she told her doctor, 'there is hair little enough already in the place.' The Queen's attendants feared that she might permanently lose her wits, but after four or five days Catherine was once more able to confront the appalling reality of her situation. 'My wife is now out of all danger,' Charles remembered to tell his sister on 2 November, after he had dilated upon the latest gossip from the French court. She had, however, 'talked idly' for a while.

The prospect of Catherine's death had temporarily elevated her into a figure of some consequence, and the French ambassador reported fevered speculation at court about who her successor might be. With her recovery, however, the Queen again appeared to courtiers as hardly worth the trouble of attention. Only one man, Edward Montagu, her Master of the Horse, concerned himself with her welfare. Charles would tease him for his romantic devotion to Catherine, asking him how his mistress did. The King's jocularity, however, knew limits, for in May 1664 Montagu was summarily sacked. Pepys thought that the reason for his dismissal was 'pride, and most of all his affecting to seem great with the Queen'. Montagu never let anyone else near Catherine. The court wags put it about that the real cause of his dismissal was that he had presumed to squeeze the Queen's hand and that Catherine had asked her husband what this gesture could possibly mean.

It has become so much the fashion to treat the court of Charles II as roguishly amusing that some corrective may be required if the reader is to appreciate what Catherine had to endure. She lived in a poisoned atmosphere, where the transitory satisfactions of vice left an enduring stench of corruption. The King's cynicism about virtue was so profound that he was perfectly indifferent as to the kind of people who surrounded him. Anthony Wood, the antiquary, was a well known misanthrope, but his description of the revolting physical habits of the courtiers when they came to Oxford during the plague of 1665 aptly sets off the moral contagion surrounding Charles II. 'Though they were neat and gay in their apparel, yet they were very nasty and beastly, leaving at their departure their excrements in every corner, in chimneys, studies, coalhouses, cellars. Rude, rough, whoremongers; vain, empty, careless.' Or consider what Thomas Povey, who was a member of the Queen's Council, told Pepys about the courts: 'if there be a hell it is here. No faith, no love, nor any agreement between man and wife, nor friends.' Pepys generally thought Povey a fool, but not on this matter. On 26 April 1667 he ran into John Evelyn, and the two diarists passed two hours together anatomising the awfulness of the times: 'nothing but wickedness, and wicked men and women command the King . . . it is not in his nature to gainsay any thing that relates to his pleasures'.

Inevitably, in this ambiance, Catherine's religion was dismissed as bigotry. Even Charles, who was attracted to Catholicism, expressed amazement at his wife's devotion when he wrote to Minette asking her to send Catherine 'some images to put in prayer books'. 'I assure you it will be a great present to her, and she will look upon them often, for she is not only content to say the great office in the breviary every day, but likewise that of Our Lady too, and this besides going to chapel.' Yet Catherine was not above making doomed and rather sad attempts to join in the more innocent amusements of the court. Charles being an excellent dancer, she too must learn to dance, though the attempt only emphasised the defects of her stubby, short-legged figure. It was said that she 'liked mightily to have her feet seen'. And not just her feet. We read of the Queen 'exposing her breast and shoulders without even the glaze of the lightest gauze, and her tucker, instead of standing upon her bosom was, with licentious boldness, turned down and lay upon her stays'. No one could complain she had remained a slave to Portuguese styles of dressing; at the same time, though, she was hardly likely, by such means, to menace the sway of Lady Castlemaine and Frances Stuart. Her influence on the fashionable world was confined to the introduction into England of fans from India and, perhaps, to the popularisation of tea-drinking. She also greatly enjoyed card games, once pulling off a coup at odds of 1,000 to 1 at faro. Pepys greatly disapproved of Catherine's habit of playing cards on Sundays, a sin which has always seemed more heinous to Protestants than to Catholics.

The Queen, then, was certainly not a killjoy. Yet to the extent that she allowed herself to be drawn into the entertainments of the court, she only fostered the general impression that she was a cypher. Being without the necessary strength of personality to impress herself on her environment, her status ultimately depended on the lead given by the King; and everyone could see that Charles, for all his superficial politeness, was fundamentally indifferent. Every night he would make a parade of escorting Catherine to her chamber; every night he would immediately return to the more stimulating embraces of his mistresses. The world took its cue from such behaviour, even down to Goodman, the actor, who once kept Catherine waiting for a performance until Lady Castlemaine, whose favours he shared with the King, was properly settled in her place.

Yet from 1663 Frances Stuart, cleverly alternating the arts of allurement with the coquetry of virtue, was steadily gaining on Lady Castlemaine, to the point where Barbara finally turned papist in her efforts to regain Charles's esteem. Whether Catherine welcomed this new recruit to her faith may be doubted: even her sweet nature may have descended to cynicism when a special oratory was provided in the Lady's Whitehall apartments in order to facilitate her devotions. Lady Castlemaine, however, discovered to her disappointment that the rewards of religion are not to be gathered in this world. Pepys's court informer told him in January 1664 that the King 'do doat upon Mrs. Stewart only; and that to the leaving of all business in the world, and to the open slighting of the Queene; that he values not who sees him or stands by him while he dallies with her openly'. Even sadder for Catherine, Pepys reported on 8 February 1664 'that the good Queen will of herself stop before she goes sometimes into her dressing-room, till she knows whether the King be there, for fear he should be, as she hath sometimes taken him, with Mrs Stewart'.

Moreover, while the King continued to lavish jewels and money on both his past and intended future mistresses, Catherine was kept short of funds. Charles was not mean, but his low estimate of human nature left him convinced that if anyone wanted anything they would ask for it. That was Lady Castlemaine's technique, and even at this doubtful point in her fortunes she both asked for, and was given, a great deal. In February 1664, for instance, one of her hangers-on, Lord FitzHarding, received two leases that actually belonged to the Queen, worth £20,000. Catherine, being too well bred to ask for anything, suffered accordingly. When she was setting out to go to Tunbridge Wells in 1663 it was discovered that the Treasury had paid her not the £40,000 that was due in her first year, but a mere £4,000. If, by the end of the reign, Catherine acquired a reputation for being tight-fisted, that was a natural reaction to the exigencies of these early years. By nature she never had extravagant tastes. In June 1664 Pepys was shown her bedchamber, 'where she had nothing but some pretty pious pictures, and books of devotion'. The comparison with the gaudy luxury of the mistresses' apartments afforded material for many a pious reflection upon the ways of the wicked world.

Still, by the spring of 1666 Lady Castlemaine's stock had fallen so low that Charles was prepared to support even Catherine against her. There was some minor passage of arms between the two women about Charles's nocturnal peregrinations. Catherine boldly hazarded to Lady Castlemaine that the King took cold by staying so long with her, to which the Lady retorted that 'he left her house betimes, and must stay with some one else'. In view of Charles's obsession with Frances Stuart this explanation was very likely correct. It certainly touched a raw spot with the King, who happened to overhear. He berated the Lady as 'a bold impertinent woman', and bid her be gone from the court. Evidently he had ceased to be quite so worried about Barbara's reputation. His own reputation, however, remained a cause of concern. When the Lady resorted to blackmail, threatening to publish his letters to her, he quickly rescinded his sentence and allowed her to stay at court, with the same profit as before.

It seemed that Catherine would never be rid of Lady Castlemaine. That summer, when she again went with the King to Tunbridge Wells, she made matters still worse for herself by inviting players down from London in a kindly attempt to please him. She succeeded beyond her intention: Moll Davies and Nell Gwyn were among the actors. The days when Charles was content with one mistress at a time were nearly at an end.

In this respect the events of 1667 proved crucial. Charles's unabated (and still unsatisfied) passion for Frances Stuart had heightened the rumours that he was contemplating a divorce from Catherine. More and more insistently the whispers went abroad that the King and Queen's marriage ceremony had been invalid. News of the first, Catholic, wedding leaked out, much to the disgust of true-blooded Englishmen, while the second service was also deemed suspect because Catherine had failed to give the proper responses. (The fact that she could hardly speak a word of English at the time was conveniently forgotten.) There is no evidence that Charles inspired or lent an ear to such gossiping: at the same time, though, there could be no denying that Catherine's continuing failure to produce an heir created succession problems. Some believed that Catherine had conceived in 1666, but Charles held that this was 'a false conception'.

Then, at the beginning of 1667, the King's mind was wonderfully concentrated by the realisation that the Duke of Richmond, whose wife had died that January, was attempting immediate consolation by suing for the hand of Frances Stuart. Charles immediately offered to create Frances a duchess in her own right, and even went so far as to hint that he might dispense with the services of Lady Castlemaine. At the same time he consulted the Archbishop of Canterbury on the vexed theological question whether, in the event of both husband and wife consenting, and one of them being unable to produce children, the Church of England might possibly sanction a divorce. It really seemed that he might be planning to set Catherine aside in favour of Frances Stuart.

According to the less than reliable *Memoirs of Count Gramont* it was Lady Castlemaine who saved the situation for the Queen. She conducted the King to Frances Stuart's apartment where the siren who had so scrupulously guarded her virtue against royal attack was discovered *in flagrante* with the Duke of Richmond. This was one of those moments when Charles's languid sense of style somehow deserted him. The Duke, in fear of his life, made the speediest possible exit, while Frances, after putting up a commendable display of outrage at having her privacy disturbed, threw herself on the mercies of the Queen. She had been a foolish and wicked girl, she confessed with many tears, driven on by vanity and love of admiration. Kind, tender-hearted Catherine comforted the poor innocent and extended her protection until, in March, Frances eloped from court and married the Duke of Richmond.

Charles, furious, persuaded himself that the Archbishop had blabbed of the divorce proposal to Clarendon, and that Clarendon had then promoted the Richmond marriage in order to frustrate any possibility that Frances Stuart might become Queen. From this time, in the judgement of several well-informed contemporaries, Charles was bent on destroying the Chancellor. As it happened the opportunity soon come to hand, for the complications in the King's love-life coincided with a severe political crisis. In June the Dutch fleet inflicted the worst humiliation in English naval history, when they sailed into the Medway and destroyed English ships that had been laid up for want of funds. Though the revenues that had been allotted to Charles at the Restoration were insufficient, popular fury was also correct in its belief that the monies lavished upon Lady Castlemaine would at least have helped to keep the Navy up to the mark. For a few weeks the monarchy and the whole edifice of government appeared to be tottering. In the event, however, it was Clarendon, not the King, who became the scapegoat. Charles threw his old servant to the wolves without compunction. Inexcusably, he also forewarned Lady Castlemaine of his dismissal, so that the Lady was at her window in Whitehall to exult over her fallen enemy's final departure from the palace. Clarendon looked contemptuously up at the Lady's laughing and triumphant face. 'Pray remember', he told her, 'that, if you live, you will grow old.'

The fall of Clarendon brought no comfort to Catherine. The

world falsely charged that the minister had deliberately planned the Portuguese match in the knowledge that Catherine was barren, so that his own daughter, married to the Duke of York, might become the mother of monarchs. This was a travesty of the truth, as Charles could have testified, had he been so moved. Nevertheless, Catherine was popularly perceived as Clarendon's creature, so that the mob which jeered at the Chancellor invariably included the Queen in its ignorant imprecations. More seriously for Catherine, the Cabal, as the group of ministers upon whom Charles now relied was known, contained two of her established enemies – the Duke of Buckingham, who had long connived at projects for her replacement, and Lord Arlington, who had allied himself to Lady Castlemaine.

Yet in the spring of 1666 the machinations of the Queen's ill-wishers were temporarily confounded when she became quite indubitably pregnant. Charles's attention at this time, however, was chiefly taken up with the Duchess of Richmond's – that is, with the former Frances Stuart's – smallpox. 'I must confess,' the royal sentimentalist wrote to his sister on 7 May 1668, 'this last affliction made me pardon all that is past, and cannot hinder myself from wishing her very well'. After which the King moved on to matters of less importance: 'my wife miscarried this morning'. He was, he said, 'troubled at it, yet I am glad that tis evident she was with child, which I will not deny to you till now I did fear she was not capable of. The physicians do intend to put her into a course of physic which they are confident will make her hold faster next time.'

In the summer Catherine generously played her part in the rehabilitation of the Duchess of Richmond by appointing her a lady of her bedchamber without any demur. The King was unable to restrain himself, when drunk, from informing Richmond that his wife had proved a good deal more complaisant after her marriage than she had ever been before. Such distractions, however, never hindered Charles in the due performance of his matrimonial duties. In May 1669 he told his sister, with a wealth of gynaecological detail, that he was sanguine about another pregnancy. Once more, though, disappointment quickly followed. On 7 June the King added a short tailpiece to a lengthy letter to Minette on political matters: 'I have no more to add but to tell you my wife after all our hopes has miscarried again without any visible accident. The physicians are divided whether it were a false conception or a good one, and so good night for tis very late.' Thenceforward Charles never seriously believed that Catherine could produce an heir.

As a consequence of this second failure, stories that the King and Queen would be divorced were soon rife again. Rumour had it that the Duke of Buckingham, 'that vile man', had offered to kidnap Catherine and send her to a colony where she would be well cared for, but never heard of again. Another, more likely scheme, with which Charles may have been involved, was that Catherine should become a nun, whereupon Parliament would pass a divorce. But Catherine, for all her religiosity, steadfastly refused to admit to any vocation beyond that of wife. In February 1670 it was noticed that the King appeared to be taking a particular interest in the bill to grant Lord Roos a divorce. Charles attended the House of Lords regularly throughout the debate, remarking that the proceedings were better than any play. The Queen was not so amused, and wept bitterly 'day and night' at the suggestion put forward by the Bishop of Chester that 'immundicity of the womb' constituted grounds for divorce.

Charles himself is supposed to have remarked about this time that he did not see why, if a man could be divorced for impotence, a woman should not be put away for barrenness. He continued, moreover, to use his influence in favour of Lord Roos, so that when the peer's divorce was confirmed gossip predicted a royal initiative. Bab May, one of Charles's closest cronies, actually undertook to bring forward a bill in the Commons to divorce him from the Queen, but three days before the motion was to be debated the King instructed him to proceed no further in the matter. Whether his conscience finally kicked up against the proposal, whether he baulked at the political risk of antagonising his brother James by casting his succession into doubt, or whether he feared that a substitute queen might prove less conveniently complaisant than Catherine, the King abandoned the notion of a divorce. And of course, having made up his mind, Charles did not intend to lose any moral credit that might attach to his decision. It would be a wicked thing, he said, to make a poor lady miserable, only because she was his wife, and had no children by him, which was no fault of hers.

Perhaps, indeed, the King had only countenanced the talk of

divorce in order to distract attention from his foreign policy. For at this period he was engaged through his sister Henriette-Anne in fiendishly subtle and dangerous negotiations for a treaty with France. This is no place to enter into the details of his diplomacy, beyond noting his instinctive respect for Louis XIV's Catholic absolutism. Charles recognised that, without help from abroad, power in England was bound ultimately to pass to Parliament. Rather than accept this he was prepared to betray previous treaties and reduce England's role in international affairs to that of a pensionary of France. Catherine, who never meddled in politics unless her beloved Portugal was concerned, had nothing whatever to do with Charles's plans, though she did accompany him down to Dover where the final discussions about the French alliance took place. Probably she never knew of the undertaking Charles gave Louis, to declare himself a Catholic when he judged the moment to be ripe, nor of Louis's reciprocal promise to provide two million crowns for putting down any rebellion that might break out after the English King's conversion was announced. Whether or not Charles seriously intended to carry out his promise, it is easy to see why this section of the treaty, signed on 1 June 1670, was kept secret.

At Dover Catherine met Charles's sister Henriette-Anne, who described her as a 'very good woman, not handsome, but so kind and excellent it was impossible not to love her'. This was potentially valuable support, for, as the French ambassador noted, Henriette 'had much more power over the King her brother than any other person in the world'. Charles's love for his sister, however, did not prevent him from being powerfully struck by one of her ladies-in-waiting, 'the baby-faced Bretonne', Louise de Kéroualle. When Henriette sought to present him with a parting gift from her jewel-case, he boldly declared that the only jewel of hers that he coveted was Louise. His sister refused to countenance this request, perhaps out of respect for Catherine, perhaps because she had promised to return the girl to her parents.

There the matter might have ended but for the tragedy of Henriette's sudden death a few days after her return to France. The blow left Charles prostrate with grief, perhaps the only time in his life, apart from the day that he heard of his father's execution, that he was mastered by emotions of tenderness. In both England and France, however, cool heads remembered the King's attraction to Louise and pondered the diplomatic advantages of installing a French mistress in Whitehall. Charles being the last man on earth to resist a scheme of this nature, Louise returned to England in the autumn of 1670. Still more significantly, she was appointed lady of the bedchamber to the long-suffering Catherine.

Louise's arrival at court was well timed. Lady Castlemaine had at last been successfully paid off with the grant of the title of Duchess of Cleveland, together with huge amounts of land and cash. She retired first to Cleveland House in St James's, and subsequently to Paris, where she occasionally interrupted her love-life to complain about the morals of the younger generation. By October 1671 Louise de Kéroualle, Madame Carwell as the English called her, was firmly established as *maîtresse en titre*. Louis XIV, *le roi très chrétien*, sent his congratulations. As for Charles, he indulged in some mock ceremonial at which, as Evelyn put it, 'the Fair Lady Whore was bedded . . . and the stocking flung, after the manner of a married bride'.

For Catherine, the years that followed were as bleak as this contemptuous gesture might imply. Louise, behind her sweet smile and superficial respect, turned out to be as avaricious as Lady Castlemaine. Worse, she had a talent for interior decoration. At Whitehall she eventually took over twenty-four rooms and fifteen garrets, which apartments 'she twice or thrice rebuilt to satisfy her prodigal and expensive pleasures'. Evelyn described her rooms as having 'ten times the richness and the glory of the Queen's'. Poor Catherine always recoiled from luxury. Evelyn despaired of her in 1671 when, together with the King, he tried to interest her in a carving by Grinling Gibbons. Catherine seemed at first to share Charles's enthusiasm, but alas, when the King had gone, 'a French peddling woman, one Mad. de Boord . . . began to find fault with several things in the work, which she understood no more than an ass or a monkey, so as in a kind of indignation, I caused the person who brought it to carry it back to the chamber, finding the Queen so much governed by an ignorant French woman'.

Madame Carwell gave birth to a son in 1672, an achievement acknowledged in the following year by her elevation to Duchess of Portsmouth. Like many another mistress, Louise began to dream dreams: the French ambassador recorded her delight in talking of the Queen's ailments 'as if they were mortal'. Her only real rival, it appeared, was Nell Gwyn, who proved adept at undercutting French airs of refinement with her earthy plebeian wit. Once when the mob, mistaking her for Louise, began to jeer, Nell knew exactly how to handle the situation. 'Good people, be civil,' she cried, 'I am the *Protestant* whore.'

Catherine, though, shrank away from the all-powerful French favourite. Happily, she now possessed the means of escape. Henrietta Maria's death in 1668 both increased the Queen's income and made her the mistress of Somerset House. Thither, in the mid 1670s, Catherine increasingly retired, grateful to escape from the sleazy atmosphere of Whitehall to a residence where she could divide her days between devotion and card games. The King and Queen were still seen together on public occasions, but as far as their private relations were concerned the marriage to all intents and purposes no longer existed. Nothing suited Charles better than that Catherine should live out her days in insignificant isolation.

4

Fate, however, willed otherwise. For some time the course of events had been evolving in ways destined to make Catherine the innocent victim of public hostility. Two main factors were involved. First, although the crypto-Catholic policies embodied in the Dover treaty remained a secret, well-founded suspicions about Charles's intentions multiplied during the 1670s. In particular the Earl of Shaftesbury, a political operator as brilliant and unscrupulous as Charles himself, divined the King's enthusiasm for a Catholic absolutism on the French model, and ruthlessly manipulated the mob's detestation of popery to foil this intent. Shaftesbury's machinations spelt danger to Catherine. Already in 1667 English Catholics had been forbidden to attend her chapel. Now, as the papist menace became an article of faith amongst politicians, the Queen found herself in an increasingly vulnerable position. In 1673 a committee of the Lords was appointed to draw up a bill 'that no Romish priest do attend Her Majesty but such as are subjects of the King of Portugal'.

The second factor that threatened Catherine's peaceful seclusion in Somerset House was that the doubts about Charles's aims and ambitions were compounded by absolute certainty about those of his brother James, the Duke of York. James became a Catholic in 1672, shortly after the death of his first wife; and in the following year he set the seal on his conversion by marrying Mary Beatrice of Modena, a princess who had intended to become a nun before accepting at the Pope's behest the more meritorious sacrifice of marrying into the English royal family. For Catherine the arrival of another princess of her faith, albeit twenty years younger, must have been a welcome event; and she treated the newcomer with a kindness all the more conspicious in the prevailing atmosphere of Protestant bigotry. Unfortunately, though, the two devout ladies soon began to wrangle about rights of access to the Catholic chapel at St James's, so that they never became close friends.

Politically, moreover, Mary of Modena's presence, incorporating as it did the prospect of a Catholic succession stretching indefinitely into the future, put Catherine in an exposed position. The possibility of her divorce was no longer an option toyed with by a king eager to marry his mistress. It now became the tactic of a parliamentary faction determined that Charles should produce children in order to guarantee the Protestant succession. In these new circumstances Charles, who possessed a keen sense of the royal prerogative, felt bound to resist divorce. Thus, when in 1673, a member of the House of Commons proclaimed that there could be no security for the Church of England without a Protestant queen, and proposed bribing the King £500,000 to put away Catherine in favour of such a replacement, Charles put on a fine display of indignation. If his conscience allowed him to divorce Catherine, he told Lord Shaftesbury, it would equally allow him to murder her.

Charles had hoped, in the wake of the Secret Treaty of Dover, to carry a policy of religious toleration by appealing to the Catholics and dissenters in the country over the heads of the Anglican majority in the House of Commons. To this end, in 1672 he used his prerogative to suspend the penal laws against non-conformity. The fury and suspicion that this policy provoked, however, convinced him that his desire to help the Catholics was impracticable. In 1673 the Commons forced him to acquiesce in the Test Act, which denied civil and military office to all who refused to communicate in the Church of England. A new period of persecuting Anglicanism ensued, which Charles reluctantly accepted as the necessary price of gaining Commons majorities. His opponents were rather frustrated than appeased by the King's change of policy. For four years they strove to find means to destroy the solid block of parliamentary votes which the government commanded in the Commons. And when their chance came in 1678 with the 'Popish Plot', they fastened upon it with intemperate zeal born of long frustration.

The conspiracy was described unanimously by both Houses of Parliament as 'a damnable and hellish Plot contrived and carried on by Popish recusants, for the assassinating and murdering the King, and for subverting the Government and rooting out and destroying the Protestant religion'. In fact there was no such plot, merely a tissue of falsehoods concocted by brazen villains. After eighteen years of Charles's government, however, people were prepared to believe any accusation of duplicity, no matter how far-fetched; and Lord Shaftesbury skilfully exploited mob credulity to make matters as difficult as possible for the King. From the very beginning the prime target of the plot-mongers was Catherine, as though her enemies, having failed to rid themselves of her obstructive presence by divorce, were now determined to send her to the block for high treason. The very first accusations, made in August 1678, included statements that Sir George Wakeman, Catherine's highly respectable physician, had been paid by the Jesuits to poison the King. In October a Mrs Elliott sought an audience with Charles in order to apprise him that Titus Oates, the arch-fiend fabricator of the plot, 'wished to lay secret information against the Queen, tending to implicate her in the plot'. 'I will never suffer an innocent lady to be oppressed,' Charles coldly replied.

Very soon afterwards, however, the King had lost control of events. None knew better than Charles that the wild accusations of Oates threatened to stumble across truths that might sweep him from his throne. After all, there *had* been a real popish plot set down in the Secret Treaty of Dover. The King's initial tactic, therefore, was to discourage further investigation by treating the charges as beneath his notice: to this end he spent much time at Newmarket and Windsor, being studiously unconcerned. Oates, however, with his instinct for trouble, had named Coleman, a former secretary on the Duke of York's staff, among those involved in the conspiracy, and in this instance he had struck upon the real article. When Coleman's papers were searched a highly compromising correspondence with Louis XIV's confessor was discovered, in which plans for the overthrow of Protestantism in England had been freely rehearsed.

And then, on 17 October, Sir Edmundberry Godfrey, the magistrate with whom Oates had lodged his accusations, was found murdered. Public hysteria reached fever pitch. The plot-mongers, correctly judging that national credulity had now passed well beyond the restraints of reason, stepped up their campaign against the Queen. Early in November a crook named William Bedloe testified that Sir Edmundberry Godfrey had been stifled by two Jesuits in Somerset House, where Catherine lived, and that the body had then been removed by two of her servants. As for Oates, he had become a popular hero. The King needs must entertain him at a private dinner, and listen gravely while the rogue solemnly insisted that the Queen had sworn to 'revenge the violation of her bed' by commissioning his murder. Charles had seen through Oates from the beginning, and at an early interview had succeeded in exposing him as a liar, but in the prevailing mood truth had become superfluous.

Later in November Oates and Bedloe repeated their accusations before Parliament, complete now with melodramatic accounts of overheard conversations which, they claimed, had earlier slipped their memory. Bedloe, happening to find himself in the chapel at Somerset House, had listened while two French priests, some Jesuits and a Catholic lord had earnestly sought to persuade Catherine of the necessity of assassinating the King. The Queen, so Bedloe claimed, had burst into tears at this suggestion, but after further argument from the French priests had reluctantly given her consent. Oates rendered similar testimony to that of Bedloe, amplified by his flair for drama. 'I, Titus Oates,' he declared at the bar of the House of Commons, 'do accuse Queen Catherine of conspiring the King's death and contriving how to compass it.' In the face of such panache no one seemed to care when he was shown to be completely ignorant of the geography of Somerset House, where he too claimed to have heard the Queen descanting on the injuries she had suffered as a wife.

It seems incredible that such a farrago of nonsense should have found credence not only with the mob, but also with solemn lawyers. Yet once more good fortune assisted the perjurers. A Roman Catholic silversmith named Prance, who worked at Somerset House, was arrested and cast into an icy cell in Newgate, where he received an anonymous visitor who told him what to say if he wanted to save his life. Subsequently Prance declared that an Irish priest had commissioned him to murder Sir Edmundberry Godfrey. Three other men, two of them servants at Somerset House, had assisted him in this task. Two days later Prance recanted this story, but a further session in the Newgate cell persuaded him to recant his recantation. The Queen's servants whom he had named were hanged for murder in February 1679, though they protested their innocence to the last.

Catherine herself was in the gravest danger, and her peril would have been even worse had she not been stoutly supported by the King. She had, indeed, no other defender. The politicians were either hostile to her by policy or uninvolved through cowardice; the mob hissed and jeered her whenever she ventured into the streets. In public she avoided any display of emotion; in private she wept bitterly at her fate. The Popish Plot had not only revived all the old talk about a divorce in favour of a Protestant queen: this time the shadow of the scaffold hung over Catherine. Charles may therefore be accorded all the credit that belongs to a husband who refuses to make a judicial sacrifice of his wife. The Queen was a weak woman, he somewhat patronisingly told Dr Burnet, 'but was not capable of a wicked thing; and considering his faultiness towards her in other respects, he thought it a horrid thing to abandon her. He said he looked on falsehood and cruelty as the greatest crimes in the sight of God.' It was a pity, then, that he had treated Catherine with falsehood and cruelty for sixteen years.

As to his motives for supporting her, they may not have been quite so pure and unalloyed as he liked to make out. Aside from his protective feelings for Catherine, it was utterly repugnant to his conception of the royal prerogative that political agitators should be allowed to interfere with the succession. Moreover, he knew all too well that his own fortunes were tied up with Catherine's. The Queen employed as her secretary a Catholic called Richard Bellings who had been heavily involved in the negotiations for the Secret Treaty of Dover; indeed, he had been one of the four English signatories thereto. Luckily Bellings was a great deal more discreet than Coleman, the Duke of York's secretary, but Charles simply could not afford to risk the chance of having this agent unmasked. He always showed uneasiness about any investigations of the Queen's household. By extending his protection to Catherine, he acted to prevent the kind of free-ranging enquiry into her affairs by which he, far more than she, would stand condemned.

A further consideration that may have carried some weight in persuading Charles not to desert the Queen was the attitude of the Portuguese. Dom Pedro, Catherine's younger brother who had ousted the degenerate Alfonso from power in 1667 (though he did not claim the throne until Alfonso's death in 1683), kept closely in touch with events in England and rallied to the defence of his sister. The Portuguese were furious at the treatment meted out to their Princess, and the hotheads wished to end all commerce with England. Catherine wrote regularly to Dom Pedro, who sent a special ambassador to assist and comfort her in her troubles.

As the furore of the Popish Plot mounted, therefore, Charles made a public show of his confidence in Catherine by ordering her to return to her old apartments in Whitehall Palace, where the gates had to be locked against the papist-hunting mob. The Queen's birthday on 25 November, a moment when the accusations against her were at their most outrageous, was marked by determinedly gay celebrations. Catherine was pathetically grateful for this sudden revival of Charles's attention and wrote to her brother that the King's support was the one thing that bore her up. Even so, the essential sadness of her position had not really changed. The best way she knew of showing her gratitude to Charles was to include the Duchess of Portsmouth among the nine Catholic women allowed her when Parliament acted to limit the number of papists in the royal household.

In the final analysis, it was Catherine's own character, as much as the King's protection, which saved her. When the initial shock of Oates's accusations had receded it was obvious to all who had any knowledge of the Queen that the charges against her were ridiculous. She herself helped to allay suspicions by allowing the search of Somerset House without any demur and by assuring the Commons of her desire to co-operate in finding the truth. As

Charles wrote tactfully to her brother of the investigation, those who 'took but time to deliberate and to consider how the Queen hath lived, found motives to reject the complaint, and instead of favouring the accusation the time was only spent in magnifying of her virtues'. It was noticeable that when, at the end of November 1678, the House of Commons sent an address to the King urging him to remove the Queen and all papists from the court, only eleven votes in the Lords, where many members actually knew Catherine, supported the measure.

The opposition in effect acknowledged the weakness of the case against the Queen by turning their attention, at the beginning of 1679, to an alternative tactic, that of excluding the Catholic Duke of York from the succession. The possibility that the King might recognise the Duke of Monmouth as his successor was touted. Rumours proliferated that there was a black box which contained evidence of Charles's marriage to Monmouth's mother, Lucy Walter, so that in March 1679 the King was compelled to issue a written declaration that he had espoused none but Catherine. (The story would not die, however, and next year the King resorted to the public prints to make a second denial.) Yet Shaftesbury's attempts to exclude James from the throne, which would occupy the next eighteen months, did not mean that Catherine was out of danger. Innocence was an unreliable defence for Catholics to rely on in the England of 1679, as was shown by the conviction and execution of five Jesuits that June. A few days later the Privy Council resolved 'that it would be best for the Queen to stand her trial', and only the King demurred. 'I believe you will very soon see the Queen fallen upon, with intent to take her life,' wrote the Duke of York on 9 July.

The blow, however, was averted later that month when Wakeman, the Queen's doctor, was acquitted of having attempted to poison the King. The verdict was the first serious setback that Oates had encountered, and could not have been more timely for Catherine, since a conviction must have led to her own trial. The opposition was so outraged at the respect accorded to the evidence that Shaftesbury declared the judge to be unfit for his office. It was a moment for the King and Queen to savour. The Queen, the Countess of Sunderland acidly recorded, 'is now a mistress, the passion her spouse has for her is so great'.

The point of Lady Sunderland's sarcasm was that, notwithstanding the superficial rapport between husband and wife, the Duchess of Portsmouth was still firmly ensconced in Charles's affections. Lady Sunderland detested Louise de Kéroualle, whose fascination had bewitched her own husband, though she might have found some security in the way that the King continued to monopolise the charms of his French mistress. All this time when, by some accounts, Charles had been behaving so gallantly towards the Queen, Louise retained her position. In August 1679 Charles fell seriously ill, and though he took Catherine to Newmarket in September, his convalescence there included regular visits to the Duchess of Portsmouth after supper. Yet Louise, scarcely less than Catherine, had plenty of cause for anxiety from the madness of the times. At the end of 1678 she had been obliged to dismiss all her Catholic servants. More alarmingly, in June 1680 the Earl of Shaftesbury stood before the grand jury of the county of Middlesex and demanded that she be indicted as a common prostitute. As the Duchess of Portsmouth was liable to find herself put in the stocks for this offence, she understandably took a considerable degree of fright. All things considered, she judged, it would be better to join the Exclusionist cause. After all, if the Duke of Monmouth could be brought forward as a potential king, why not her own son, who had been created Duke of Richmond in 1675?

The strange thing was, however, that even after the Duchess of Portsmouth had gone over to the opposition, she did not seem to forfeit the King's affection to any appreciable extent. Perhaps Charles had by now grown so cynical that he cared not where a woman's heart might lie provided she put her body at his disposal. Alternatively, perhaps he had deliberately set her on to be a spy in the Exclusionists' camp. It is also possible that he was never so firm against the exclusion of James as he liked to pretend. Later he would admit to the French ambassador that he might have accepted Exclusion if the terms had been right, and conceivably his mistress's task in associating with the opposition was to try to negotiate those terms. Charles's thoughts were so opaque that it is always difficult to be sure about his motives and purposes. 'The King,' Shaftesbury considered, 'who if he had been so happy as to have been born a private gentleman, had certainly passed for a man of good parts, excellent breeding and well natured, hath now, being a Prince, brought his affairs to that pass, that there is not a person in the world, at home or abroad, that does rely upon him, or put any confidence in his word of friendship.' It meant nothing, then, that Charles declared himself against Exclusion: everyone believed that he would give way if he had to. 'He would sacrifice a hundred brothers rather than hazard his crown' was the common consensus. Equally, no matter how often Charles spoke of his loyalty to the Queen, the opposition held that he could be induced to sacrifice one defenceless wife.

Indeed, in January 1680 Charles was brazenly discussing with Shaftesbury the possibility that he would divorce and remarry a Protestant if Exclusion was dropped. No doubt he was just stringing Shaftesbury along, but inevitably such tactics served to keep the divorce issue alive. The last hope of indicting the Queen for treason disappeared when one of her accusers, Bedloe, admitted on his death-bed in August 1680 that she had been quite innocent of any design to murder the King. But the divorce proposal cropped up again after the failure of the second Exclusion Bill in November 1680, when Shaftesbury once more urged that the King should put Catherine aside in favour of a child-bearing Protestant queen. This time Charles, in a stronger position politically, flatly refused to consider the idea. Indeed he went so far as to demonstrate his resolve by taking an after-dinner nap in Catherine's room, instead of following his usual route to the Duchess of Portsmouth's chamber. That this move was sufficiently unusual to be interpreted as a ringing declaration of loyalty is a telling comment on the state of the royal marriage.

Catherine, in her goodness, felt only for her husband. 'His troubles give me more anxiety than my own,' she wrote to her brother. Her own troubles, though, were by no means over. In November and December 1680 she attended the trial of the Earl of Stafford, an elderly Catholic peer falsely accused of plotting against the King's life, and listened mutely while attempts were made to incriminate her in the imagined design. The trial symbolised the rottenness of English government at this period. A harmless old man was sentenced to be judicially murdered, and the King, who knew perfectly well that he was innocent, did not dare to interfere for fear of stirring up the hornet's nest still further. Such was the pass to which Charles's reputed political brilliance had brought him. The Duchess of Portsmouth, meanwhile, sat in her private box bestowing smiles and sweetmeats upon her new-found friends among the opposition.

There was a certain grim appropriateness, too, about the proceedings of the Oxford Parliament, as a result of which, in March 1681, Charles triumphed over his enemies – if it could be called a triumph to gain independence from Parliament by accepting subsidies from France. Apart from the continued agitation for the exclusion of James from the throne, the principal matter before the Oxford Parliament was the problem of financing the English garrison at Tangier, which, it will be recalled, had been part of Catherine's dowry. The opposition tried to make supplies for Tangier conditional on the King's acceptance of Exclusion, but Charles resisted the bargain. Having negotiated his subsidy from Louis XIV, he dissolved Parliament, so that in August 1683, Tangier, on which such hopes had rested, was abandoned.

Catherine had accompanied Charles to the Oxford Parliament, 'pretending', according to one observer, 'she can be nowhere safe but where the King is present to protect her'. The Duchess of Portsmouth and Nell Gwyn felt the same way, for they too were in Oxford to profit from Charles's protection. 'My dear Life,' Charles wrote to the Duchess, 'I will come tomorrow either to dinner or immediately after, but certainly I shall not mind the Queen when you are in the case. I am yours.' The note is undated, but it might just as well have been written at this period as at any other. Contrary to what is sometimes stated, Louise was very far from being out of favour: indeed the Secret Service accounts show that she received no less than £136,000 in 1681, enough to have kept the Tangier garrison for nearly two years. In 1683 the French ambassador reported that the besotted King did not scruple to caress his mistress in public.

It was all reminiscent of the way he had behaved towards Frances Stuart sixteen years before. Catherine had long since learnt to forgive her husband; and now, as the terrors of the Popish Plot receded, she once more slunk back into the shadows. Any physical attraction that she might once have possessed had vanished. She held no interest for Charles, however much he might declare his admiration for her virtue, or mask his indifference in the cloak of *politesse*. An incident in May 1684 showed how tautly stretched her nerves were. 'The Queen being at dinner, the Duchess of Portsmouth came to wait on her, which was not usual, and put the Queen into that disorder that tears came into her eyes, whilst the other laughed and turned it into a jest.' Nevertheless, after 1681 Catherine did possess a psychological lifeline previously denied to her, to which, in her loneliness and isolation, she clung with a kind of desperate credulity. Her husband had stood by her in her moment of peril, and her appreciation would never be exhausted.

5

To each his own reality. Catherine's vision of her husband as hero hardly accorded with what John Evelyn saw at court on 1 February 1685, the last Sunday of Charles's life. Evelyn, like Pepys, was an earnest Sabbatarian. 'I can never forget the inexpressible luxury and profaneness, gaming and all dissoluteness, and as it were total forgetfulness of God (it being Sunday evening) which . . . I was witness of, the King sitting and toying with his concubines, Portsmouth, Cleveland, and Mazarin, &c. a French boy singing love songs.' No Catherine, be it noted. 'Six days after', Evelyn recorded not without satisfaction, 'was all in the dust.'

And yet, how rarely any moral judgements do justice to the bewildering complexity of human nature. As Evelyn himself wrote of Charles, 'he was a prince of many virtues, and many great imperfections'. The king who had lived with such heedless self-indulgence died with courage, wit and style, sustained over five days from his initial seizure while doctors tortured him with red-hot irons, cantharides (to promote blisters) and cupping glasses. He regarded their efforts with the polite scepticism with which he invariably approached medicine, and apologised for being so long a-dying. Very different was the reaction of the women in his life. The Duchess of Portsmouth swooned and began to pack her jewels. Nelly set up a caterwauling and had to be led out, only to 'lay roaring behind the door'. But it was the much wronged Catherine who was the most completely prostrated, to such an extent that she had to be carried back to her apartments.

From the moment of Charles's collapse Catherine had but one aim in view. 'My sister,' she told Mary of Modena, the Duchess of York, 'I beseech you to tell the Duke that he, who knows as well as I do the King's convictions about the Catholic religion, should do what he can to take advantage of any opportunity that offers.' The Duke, when given the message, replied, 'I know, and I am thinking of nothing else.' Yet he found himself in a delicate position. Supposing that the King should recover, what damage might be wrought by any premature summoning of a Catholic priest? James was not a man to let his brother die a Protestant, but nor did he wish to submit him to the political embarrassment of living as a Catholic. Ironically enough, it was not Catherine but the Duchess of Portsmouth, acting through the French ambassador, who finally persuaded the Duke to act. Even then it was decided not to compromise the Queen by using one of her Portuguese priests, who in any case spoke no English. The discovery of Father Huddleston in her room, just as messengers were departing to fetch an Italian priest from the house of the Venetian ambassador, appears to have been fortuitous. It was indeed the happiest of accidents, for Huddleston had helped to save Charles's life when he had been in flight from Cromwell after the Battle of Worcester in 1651. 'Sir, this good man once saved your life,' the Duke of York told Charles, 'he now comes to save your soul.'

'Open the curtains, that I may see the light of day,' Charles instructed his attendants on his last morning. No death was ever more edifying than the end of this hard-bitten roué. Catherine went to see him just before the end, but had to retire again almost immediately, so great was her distress. From her own apartment she sent a message asking his pardon if she had ever offended him. 'Alas! poor woman,' murmured her husband. 'She beg my pardon! I beg hers with all my heart.' With all his debauchery, callousness, duplicity and cynicism, Charles never wholly succeeded in destroying his innate good nature. His manner of dying momentarily makes Catherine's adoration seem not merely understandable, but just. Whereas in Charles's lifetime her love had appeared as a pathetic act of self-deception, after his death her reverence for him, which grew as forgetfulness purged from memory the grosser details of their married life, seems almost natural.

Catherine was only forty-six when her husband died, and had twenty more years to live. For some while it seemed that, having been forced to play the martyr for twenty-three years of her married life, she had lost her appetite for any other role. Her letters in the period following Charles's death show her as self-obsessed, hypochondriachal and, above all, dreary. Reading them, one begins to suspect that lack of humour, as much as lack of beauty, had kept her apart from her husband. For all his faults Charles had always relished life to the full. In contrast, from the newly widowed Catherine there issued little save grievance and complaint.

It was only natural, of course, that she should want to return to Portugal. As a result of her years of misery in England her native land had assumed the guise of a lost paradise. The new King, James II, was extremely kind to her, but she had not long moved back into Somerset House before she began sending a stream of letters to her brother Dom Pedro, the King of Portugal, begging that she might be allowed to return home. In Portugal, as she well knew, this was hardly a decision which a woman might make on her own account. Dom Pedro, however, seemed less than enthusiastic about the prospect of seeing his sister again. The more he prevaricated, the more alarming became Catherine's bulletins on her health. 'I again remind you', she wrote on 2 May 1687, 'that my indispositions are so violent and severe that they do not allow of delays, nor does the great injury I do myself by living here diminish them . . . If my illness allowed I could dictate further, but breath is wanting to me.' Under this kind of pressure, Dom Pedro eventually agreed; and only then, apparently for the first time, did Catherine inform James II of her impending departure. James was understandably nettled, and declared that 'the affection she had won by all her goodness and affability was greatly diminished'. Still, he went down to Chatham to choose the ship on which she should sail, only to discover that, at the last moment, Catherine had changed her mind and decided to stay in England. Her health, she said, would not allow her to undertake the journey, a plea which by this time was greeted with some scepticism.

More likely, Catherine remained in England because she had involved herself in a potentially lucrative dispute with her Treasurer Lord Clarendon, son of the Chancellor who had tried to guide her in the first weeks of her marriage. Evidently the younger Clarendon had not stinted himself in the exercise of his duties, for although his salary was only £50 a year Catherine claimed that he had appropriated £36,000 that was rightfully hers. No doubt she prosecuted her suit with all the more vigour because she carried among her nostalgic memories of Portugal a sharp awareness that her brother was a singularly impoverished monarch and that she would require means of her own if she was to escape a servile dependence. She did indeed manage to recover considerable sums from Clarendon, though King James professed himself ashamed of his sister-in-law's resorting to the law courts. She was, he said, a hard woman to deal with.

James did not hesitate, however, to ask the Dowager Queen to witness the birth of his child on 10 June 1688, a duty she shared with Frances Stuart, now the Dowager Duchess of Richmond. Frances had now become 'very devout in her way', just as the Duchess of Portsmouth, when she retired to France, became 'very converted and penitent', using some of her ill-gotten gains to found a hospital for nuns. Charles II had a way of garnering penitents for the Church. Even the Duchess of Cleveland, the former Barbara Palmer Lady Castlemaine, attempted piety in her old age, bestowing £1,000 upon a Paris convent which agreed to take one of her illegitimate daughters. She might have done better to take the veil herself. Instead, in 1706, at the age of sixty-five, she married Major-General 'Beau' Feilding, who beat her soundly until she made the fortunate discovery that he already possessed another wife. The Lady then retired to Chiswick where dropsy 'swelled her to a monstrous bulk' in 1709 before her death. Clarendon's malediction – 'Pray remember that, if you live, you will grow old' – had been fulfilled.

Yet to judge from Catherine's last years in England the life of virtue afforded no greater security for contentment than the pursuit of vice. Political events moved sharply against her. The birth of a son to James, promising as it did a potentially continuous line of Catholic monarchs, proved to be the crucial event which determined the opposition to throw in its lot with William of Orange. James was removed from the throne with scarcely a struggle. It is interesting though that when, after failing to escape, he returned to London to make one last desperate attempt to save his throne, he found time to go and see Catherine at Somerset House. What passed between them is unknown. Perhaps he wanted to urge her to use her voice to rally support; perhaps he warned her of the evil fate in store for Catholics, and begged her not to confer legitimacy on the new regime by remaining in London. But although flight with James could have been the beginning of an escape to Portugal, Catherine apparently never contemplated it.

The 'Glorious Revolution', so often hailed as the dawn of religious toleration in England, notably failed to achieve anything of the kind for Roman Catholics. The laity was effectively excluded from English political life for a century and more; priests were liable to be hung, drawn and quartered if they presumed so far as celebrating mass. Such penalties were not always enforced because William III, though raised as a Calvinist, was fundamentally indifferent to religion. Queen Mary, however, was virulently anti-Catholic. The difference in outlook between the King and Queen was evident in their treatment of Catherine: William was frigidly polite, Mary aggressively hostile. Very early in their reign Catherine again determined to leave England as soon as possible, her resolution being finally formed, according to one source, by an attempt on the part of the House of Commons to limit the number of her servants. This time Dom Pedro, horrified by the persecution of Catholics, strongly supported her desire to return to Portugal. Unfortunately, though, his outrage did not extend to providing a ship for his sister, while, on the English side, William was initially too preoccupied to concern himself with the Dowager Queen's transport problems.

Sensibly, in the circumstances, Catherine showed no disposition to become a martyr for her faith. 'No one can do anything until things have run their course,' she told her brother about the persecution. She rendered the best service that she could have done to her co-religionists by giving as little offence as possible to the new regime. English politics did not concern her. 'I do not give the news from this place in this letter that I may not be a newsmonger,' she grandly declared, only to spoil the effect by adding, 'and because I do not know it.' Some of her time she spent in Islington, in what she described as 'a very small house hardly sufficient for a workman'. If so, the choice was hers, for William did not greatly reduce her income. As she lived in almost complete retirement she grew richer and richer, so much so that she later sounded the Earl of Devonshire about the purchase of Chatsworth. In fact, Islington, for all her complaints about her accommodation, was ideal, isolated from the politics of Whitehall, yet near enough to Somerset House to allow her to attend mass at her chapel on Sundays and feast days. This chapel was perhaps the only place in the kingdom where Catholics could worship without danger from the law. People came from a hundred miles and more.

So when William, on the eve of his departure to confront James in Ireland, ordered Catherine to leave Somerset House on account of the 'great meetings and caballings' that were carried on against his government there, she stood up for herself with determination. The charge of intriguing was too far-fetched to require rebuttal: as Catherine pointed out, she was only in England at all because the King refused to provide ships for her departure. King William quickly retreated and permitted her to stay at Somerset House. Probably the attack had stemmed from Queen Mary in any case. While her husband was away Mary launched another offensive against Catherine, accusing her of having forbidden the prayers prescribed for William's success in Ireland at the Savoy chapel, where the Protestants in her household worshipped. This time the Queen was foiled by Catherine's Chamberlain, who accepted all the blame. She did, however, manage to take petty revenge by closing the chapel at Somerset House when Catherine removed temporarily to Windsor. Catherine wrote angrily to her brother that despite all her troubles in England this was the first time her chapel had been shut, even for a single day. But then formerly she had had her wonderful husband to protect her.

Such incidents only increased her determination to be away. After nearly thirty years in England she was still to all intents a foreigner. Even her grasp of the language remained elementary. She wrote to her brother from 'Somerthouse', and called the Earl of Nottingham the 'earl of Nothimgāo'. But desperation for once lent some force to her style. All she got from King William, she complained, was compliments – and 'compliments will not carry me to Portugal'. 'If it were in my power, I would risk crossing the Pyrenees in the depth of winter, or embarking in ships full of spotted and malignant fevers, even were they certain to encounter the enemy.'

Dom Pedro was again informed that her health compelled her to curtail her letters. Even the events of Europe had no interest for her save as instruments of her great desire. When the Dauphiness of France died, Catherine eagerly suggested the Infanta of Portugal as a substitute – and the escort from Portugal might serve for her own return.

At last, in January 1692, William agreed to provide ships to conduct her, not to Portugal, but across the Channel to Dieppe. The long penance was over. She arranged for £10,000 a year to keep a full household at Somerset House after her departure, and, extraordinarily, settled £2,000 a year on the Duke of St Albans, Charles II's son by Nell Gwyn. On 30 March she looked upon the Thames for the last time, as her coach and entourage rolled across London Bridge *en route* for Dover.

It is a dangerous thing to achieve one's heart's desire, but as Catherine had never given way to bitterness in the face of hostility and neglect, so in her last few years she was able to relish a kinder fortune without vanity or world-weariness. No sooner had she crossed the Channel than she entered a new world in which she commanded respect and admiration for all the sufferings she had endured. Louis XIV, whom Charles had taught her to regard as the *beau idéal* of Catholic monarchs, earnestly solicited her to go to Versailles as an honoured guest. Catherine, however, continued on her quiet way, preferring to restrict her contacts with greatness to a brief visit to the exiled Jacobite court at St Germain. Thereafter she was content to continue at a modest rate of progress, making the most of her opportunity to sample the glories of France and wondering at the generous hospitality with which she was received. 'The King of France and all the kingdom are extraordinary towards me,' she wrote in amazement to her brother. Not until November did she reach Bayonne, just to the north of the Pyrenees.

Her homecoming was triumphant. Everywhere she found herself fêted, and with justice, as the heroine who had sacrificed her own life for the sake of the English alliance that had helped to save Portugal from Spain. How sweet the cheers of her own people must have sounded after the hissings and hootings that had greeted her in Whitehall. Nothing remained for her now, it seemed, but to enjoy a peaceful and honoured retirement.

Only occasional glimpses of Catherine survive from these last years. She became fast friends with Dom Pedro's wife, Queen Sofia, who stood by her when she refused to obey the King's injunction to adapt her clothes in conformity with the extreme conservatism of Portuguese taste. She travelled around the country more than her brother deemed suitable for the weaker sex, at one time eager to revisit her birthplace at the Villa Viçosa, ninety miles to the east of Lisbon, at another searching for the ideal place in which to build a palace for herself. Finally she settled for Bemposta, just outside Lisbon, and ordered the arms of England to be cut into the stone above her front door. For Catherine managed to transmute even her past into a source of delight. She retained the clearest memories, she told the English ambassador in 1693, of the love and kindness the English nation had for her: 'if they had any faults she forgave them all'. She even expressed great affection for Queen Mary. When the exiled King James died in 1701, she ordered her household in Somerset House to wear black for a year; nevertheless, during that same year she received 'with great pain' news of the death of King William, 'whose person and virtues I always greatly esteemed'. At the same time she rejoiced that James II's daughter Anne had become the Queen of that kingdom 'in which for so many years I knew the greatest happiness'. The Portuguese understandably became a little sceptical of Catherine's enthusiasm for all things connected with her former kingdom, not least when she recommended to Queen Sofia, who had just suffered a miscarriage, the English system of managing childbirth.

And then, at the very end of her life, Catherine suddenly found herself once more in the limelight, fulfilling a quite unlooked-for role. Such was her reputation in Portugal that she was appointed Regent when Dom Pedro fell seriously ill in 1704. In this post the woman who had been considered beneath the notice of Whitehall wits acquitted herself with distinction. 'She usually hath a resolution strong enough to make her orders obeyed,' reported the English ambassador, and insubordinate officials discovered the truth of this judgement. Despite her reverence for Louis XIV Catherine had no hesitation in rallying resistance to the French King's attempts to dominate Spain through his grandson Philip V. Her presence at the head of the Portuguese state had a symbolic appropriateness, for the alliance with England which her marriage had forged was being reconstituted for a joint attack on Spain. The sixty-six-year-old Regent worked hard to make the English and Dutch disgorge the necessary subsidies, and under her surprisingly energetic and forceful leadership the Portuguese achieved some striking successes.

The late emergence of an efficient and practical woman of affairs from beneath the carapace of the devout and humble queen suggests that England might have known a very different Catherine if her personality had not been crushed by a husband unable to return her love. No one could blame her if, in the circumstances of her early marriage, she had abandoned Charles. Nevertheless, her surrender, for all that it brought immediate relief from persecution, made her thenceforth a cypher in the eyes of the King and his subjects. Her potential was nipped in the bud and she was condemned to a life of thwarted possibilities. Yet when, on the last day of 1705, death finally stretched out its hand to take her, more speedily and more mercifully than it had lighted upon her husband, Catherine's final thoughts returned to the country where her life had been laid waste. She had been misunderstood, she insisted; she had never tried to promote her religion against the terms of the marriage treaty; and she had resisted French influence in England as stoutly as she had resisted it at Dom Pedro's court. So she protested her innocence in her last earthly moments; so, no doubt, she would continue to plead in the courts of heaven. It is pleasant to imagine, though, that the affable, amused and perhaps at last (for all things are possible with God) seraphic spirit of Charles might be on hand to suggest that perhaps, *sub specie aeternitatis*, these things do not really matter.

Caroline of Brunswick

1768–1821

I

For sleazy sensationalism nothing in the history of the English royal family, not even the Abdication, has ever approached the marriage of George IV and Caroline of Brunswick. Honour and virtue have no part in this story: the impression is rather of two frightful people endeavouring, with considerable success, to render each other's lives miserable. Caroline even managed to forfeit the sympathy that naturally attaches to the wife of a man like George IV. 'Fate cast her in the role of a tragic heroine,' wrote Max Beerbohm, 'but she preferred to play the role in tights.'

Nevertheless, there was a ruggedness and a directness about Caroline which contrasts favourably with her husband's well-bred perfidy. She was good-humoured where he was only witty. She relished the kind of jokes that undermine the solemn pretensions of royalty whereas he frequently took refuge in self-regarding pomposity. She retained her spirits in adversity; he invariably responded to the buffets of fortune with copious outpourings of self-pity. Above all, Caroline gave the distinct impression of possessing a heart. 'Oh mine God,' she would say in her peculiar fractured English, 'I could be the slave of the man I love.' While it cannot be denied that she became somewhat over-anxious to prove this point, her daughter, at least, was in no doubt where the first stone should be cast. 'My mother was wicked,' Princess Charlotte would say, 'but she would not have turned so wicked had my father not been much more wicked still.'

Yet in this century George IV, whether as Prince of Wales, Regent or King, has found his advocates. The campaign of denigration against him, we are told, was largely the work of political opponents. Today Londoners remember him with gratitude for the imaginative development of Regent Street and Regent's Park; aesthetes praise his patronage, which brought the nation so many fine works of art;

and biographers extol the last monarch with any claim to intellectual distinction. It has even become possible, in emulation of the court sycophants of his own time, to refer to the perfection and fascination of his manners without being suspected of irony. *Autres temps, autres moeurs*: while this prince lived, and for a hundred years afterwards, there was a fairly general consensus, stretching from his father the King to the lowliest Grub Street hack, that he was rotten to the core, whatever his superficial charms. When the Prince was only fifteen his tutor was asked to give an assessment. 'I can hardly tell,' the man replied, 'he will either be the most polished gentleman or the most accomplished blackguard in Europe; perhaps both.' It was a prescient judgement.

For however unjust nineteenth-century historians may have been in undervaluing George IV's intellectual and artistic gifts, it is surely equally perverse to turn a blind eye to his moral failings. Emotionally he was not just immature: he was a delinquent. One might say that he behaved like a spoilt child, save that there was nothing childish about his desires. Excess was the guiding principle of his career. He conducted himself as though self-control represented some kind of betrayal of his princely rank. He was always hopelessly in debt, and very often, pending requital, eternally in love. The object of his devotion would be showered with letters, presents and promises – and ruthlessly abandoned as soon as his passion had been sated.

It has sometimes been urged in George IV's defence that he had to wait many long years – until he was fifty-seven – before ascending the throne, and that his life as Prince had been blighted by the ruin of his greatest passion, that for Mrs Fitzherbert. His relations with Caroline, according to this argument, were doomed in advance by his previous experience of this most delightful of women. Yet his connection with Mrs Fitzherbert exhibits all the usual malignant symptoms of the Prince's emotional entanglements, albeit extended over a longer period and at a higher pitch of intensity. There is the same hysterical ardour in pursuit, and the same cold-hearted betrayal when the transports of love are exhausted.

The Prince had fallen headlong in love with Mrs Fitzherbert in 1784 when he was twenty-two and she was twenty-eight. She was not especially beautiful, but she represented just the kind of older woman – bosomy, elegant, matronly (Mrs Fitzherbert had twice been widowed) and reassuring – that he was coming to regard as the ultimate in feminine allure. Unlike other women favoured with his attention, Mrs Fitzherbert was almost universally admired for the grace and goodness of her character. The hitch, from the Prince's point of view, was that she was a devout Roman Catholic. She could not bring herself to become his mistress, while he, owing to the Protestant succession, would forfeit the throne if he married her. This impasse wonderfully encouraged the Prince's tendency to dramatics. He would kill himself, he declared, if he could not have her; nay, he would even forswear his inheritance. Mrs Fitzherbert, more than a little alarmed, prepared to take flight to the continent, but before she could get abroad anxious courtiers arrived at her house with the news that the Prince had stabbed himself.

Here was a quandary for the woman of virtue. Cynical observers reckoned that the Prince's attempt on his life had probably consisted of removing his bandage after being bled by his doctors, but Mrs Fitzherbert, oddly impressed by his assurance that 'nothing could induce him to live unless she promised to become his wife', allowed herself to receive a ring. Soon afterwards, protesting that a promise exacted under such conditions must be invalid, she escaped to the continent. The Prince, forbidden by his father to follow her abroad, unleashed a heavy epistolary bombardment of his '*beloved wife*'. The by-now routine suicide threats multiplied, interspersed with some literal tearing of the hair and much wild talk about abandoning his claim to the crown in order to emigrate to America. (Pending these extreme measures he found consolation with a Lady Barfylde.) In the event, after about a year, Mrs Fitzherbert with great reluctance yielded to his entreaties. 'I know I injure him,' she said, 'and perhaps forever destroy my own tranquillity.' On the latter point, at least, she was correct. Nevertheless, she returned to England at the end of 1785 and married the Prince. It was a secret wedding, which naturally meant that rumours of the event flew around society.

Mrs Fitzherbert fulfilled her difficult role of publicly unacknowledged wife with great tact and discretion, while in private the Prince discovered that the joys of requited love receded with less than their usual alacrity. By its very nature, though, his position was equivocal. He gave his closest political ally Charles James Fox to understand that he was still a bachelor, with the result that

Fox, claiming 'direct authority', strenuously denied in the House of Commons that any marriage had taken place. Mrs Fitzherbert managed to forgive the Prince for having in this way publicly branded her as his mistress, but thenceforward their relations became fractious. She did not love him, the Prince complained, as he loved her; and by the 1790s the poor man was assuaging his disappointment with a succession of mistresses, culminating in a rather more serious liaison with Lady Jersey. This female was a notable example of that peculiarly English phenomenon, the accomplished and enthusiastic seductress sprung from an ecclesiastical background. Her father, indeed, had been a bishop. By the time that the Prince fell under her spell she had become not merely a mother of nine but a grandmother to boot. For this Lothario, it seemed, ripeness was all.

Lady Jersey doubtless calculated that nothing could be more fatal to Mrs Fitzherbert's sway than the Prince's contracting another marriage, and equally that nothing was more likely to sustain her own influence than that the Prince should have an unattractive wife. As luck would have it, the idea of matrimony, this time the official variety, was beginning to float into the royal mind. Previously, the Prince had shown himself sublimely indifferent to dynastic considerations: he could never, he protested, submit to a loveless coupling, and surely his brother Frederick would look after the tiresome business of begetting heirs. But though Frederick married in 1792 neither he nor any other of the royal brothers seemed able to produce legitimate children.

The Prince imagined that, if he married for his country, Parliament would recompense him for his sacrifice by vastly increasing his income. By 1794 his debts were soaring over the half-million mark, money which had been spent, as one of his critics had remarked, on 'the mere gratification of caprice, luxury and appetite'. A large part went into the magnificent reconstruction of Carlton House. In this instance, unfortunately, the Prince denied posterity the privilege of delighting in his aesthetic taste, for when he became King and moved into Buckingham House he ordered that Carlton House should be demolished. Only the columns of the front portico survived, to grace the National Gallery. In 1794, however, the Prince was so desperate for funds with which to complete Carlton House that he steeled himself, with Lady Jersey's encouragement, to face the prospect of marrying a foreign princess.

His prior matrimonial entanglement might have been deemed some obstacle to this plan, but the Prince knew that Mrs Fitzherbert could be relied upon to be discreet under any provocation. And after all, the ceremony he had gone through with a Roman Catholic would hardly bear open scrutiny. On the morning of 22 June 1794 the Prince sent the customary letter of devotion to his 'dear love', declaring himself 'ever thine'; in the afternoon he dispatched another missive informing her that he would never enter her house again. 'Lady Jersey's influence', Mrs Fitzherbert endorsed the letter.

The needs of the Protestant succession made it almost inevitable that the Prince's bride would have to be German. As to the precise identity of his second wife, the Prince, having confronted his fate, put on a front of petulant indifference: he thought 'one damned German Frau as good as another'. In fact, there were at that time but two suitable candidates, Princess Louise of Mecklenberg-Strelitz, and Princess Caroline of Brunswick. Both were cousins of the Prince, the former being a niece of his mother and the latter of his father. King George and Queen Charlotte naturally took the parts of their respective relations, but the Prince, it seems, only considered Caroline of Brunswick. He felt it unfitting that he should shed his lustre over a tinpot principality like Mecklenberg-Strelitz. The Duke of Brunswick, on the other hand, was a distinguished soldier renowned throughout Europe, while his family was closely connected with the ruling houses of Russia, Austria and Prussia. Such considerations were all-important with the Prince.

Had he troubled to enquire, however, he would have gathered some alarming intelligence about the Brunswick family. Of Caroline's brothers, only the youngest, Frederick William, showed signs of normality. The eldest, 'fat and greasy as a barrel of oil', expired before he was thirty; the second was an imbecile; the third almost blind. There had also been a sister, Charlotte Augusta, married to the Prince of Württemberg. Charlotte had disappeared mysteriously in Russia, whither her husband had been posted on military duties. Rumour, sedulously propagated by Caroline, whispered that she had become involved with one of Catherine the Great's former lovers, by whom she had produced a child, an event that failed to amuse the Empress. Charlotte was banished to some remote castle on the Baltic, and shortly afterwards reported to be dead.

Caroline herself gave early indications of an absorbing interest in sex. Queen Charlotte, consort of George III, had warned her brother off any idea of marrying the younger Brunswick Princess with some choice items of family gossip: 'They say that her passions are so strong that the Duke himself said that she was not to be allowed even to go from one room to another without her governess and that, when she dances, this lady is obliged to follow her for the whole of the dance to prevent her from making an exhibition of herself by indecent conversations with men.' Oddly enough, though, Queen Charlotte does not seem to have pressed this information upon either her husband or her son. George III continued to cling to the comforting notion that Caroline's 'amiable qualities' would divert the Prince towards 'domestic felicity' and away from 'objects certainly not so pleasing to the nation'. The King was delighted with the match, for the Duchess of Brunswick was his favourite sister.

The Prince's brother Frederick Duke of York, who had been in Brunswick and met Caroline, also determined on positive thinking. 'She is a very fine girl . . . and a very proper match for you,' he wrote to his brother. But as Frederick himself had at one time been marked down as Caroline's husband, his letter might be interpreted as words of encouragement from a reprieved to a condemned man. Other sources spoke darkly of a 'stain' upon Caroline's character. Perhaps she had been detected in some liaison; she was, after all, twenty-six when the English match was first mooted. More likely, though, her reputation suffered simply from her penchant for shocking her audience. When she was sixteen, for instance, she responded to her mother's refusal to let her go to a ball by pretending to be in labour. Princesses are just not supposed to behave like that. It had to be admitted, though, that the combination of a lively mind with a total lack of tact rendered Caroline's conversation fascinatingly unpredictable. Asked by her tutor to define space and time, she replied instantly that space was to be found in Madame X's mouth, and time in her face. Caroline could never stand bores, and to do her justice she was rarely boring herself. With all her unconventionality, however, she took a strictly conventional view of her family's history. A Brunswicker, she proudly maintained, did not know the meaning of the word fear. The rest of her life would be dedicated to proving the truth of that adage.

In November 1794 the smooth and experienced diplomat James

Harris, Lord Malmesbury, arrived in Brunswick to negotiate the marriage, and set down his impressions of Caroline in his diary rather as one might assess an exhibit in a cattle show. 'Pretty face – not expressive of softness – her figure not graceful – fine eyes – good hand – tolerable teeth, but going – fair hair and light eyebrows, good bust – short, with what the French call "*des épaules impertinentes*". *Vastly happy with her future expectations*.' Later that evening Malmesbury danced with his new specimen, pronouncing her 'very amiable and pleasant'.

Gradually, however, it became apparent that there was considerable misgiving at the Brunswick court about the kind of figure that Caroline might cut in England. '*Elle n'est pas bête*,' the Duke confided in Malmesbury, 'but she has no judgement. She has been strictly brought up, *and it was necessary*.' The point was driven home by the Duke's mistress, Madame von Hertzberg, who began her conversation with Malmesbury, not altogether promisingly, by dismissing the idea that Caroline was actually 'depraved'. Nevertheless, she *was* exceedingly indiscreet, like her mother, who always thought out loud – if, Madame von Hertzberg felt obliged to add, she thought at all. Worse, Caroline was vain, and although not without spirit (Madame von Hertzberg wanted to be fair), her lack of depth made her peculiarly susceptible to flattery. She should therefore live a retired life when she first arrived in England, and be kept at all times on the tightest possible leash: it was just as vital that she should be frightened of the Prince as that she should love him. The Princess would have to be governed by fear, '*par la terreur même*'.

Malmesbury himself found abundant cause for concern as he got to know Caroline better. 'She has no *fonds*,' he recorded on 16 December, 'no fixed character, a light and flighty mind, but meaning well and well-disposed, and my eternal theme to her is, *to think before she speaks, to recollect herself*. She says she wishes to be *loved* by the people; this, I assure her, can only be obtained by making herself respected and *rare* – that the sentiment of being *loved* by the people is a mistaken one.' And, next day, 'Princess Caroline talks very much – quite at her ease – too much so.' Particularly upsetting to the fastidious Malmesbury (he was a Wykehamist) was the arch manner in which Caroline developed the notion that her aunt, an abbess, harboured a *tendresse* for him. The Princess, indeed, seemed anxious to discuss sex at any opportunity. 'I am determined not to be jealous,' she vouchsafed, 'I know the Prince is *léger*, and am prepared on this point.' More disturbing was her eagerness to speculate on the possibility that she herself might become involved in liaisons. Malmesbury decided that the moment had come to speak in no uncertain terms. He told her that it was high treason, punishable with death, to make love to the Princess of Wales, and that she herself would be liable to the same penalty if she countenanced any advances. 'This startled her,' he recorded.

Malmesbury would later be blamed for not warning the Prince about Caroline's eccentricities. In his defence he claimed that his brief was merely to arrange the marriage, not to assess its suitability. It is quite clear, though, that along with glaring faults he saw a great deal of good in the Princess. He liked her. She showed herself remarkably submissive to his constant lectures, even begging him to continue as her mentor in England. Unlike her parents she was naturally generous, even if she lacked the imagination to seek out or even discern genuine cases of need. In sum, Malmesbury decided, she possessed 'some natural but no acquired morality, and no strong innate notions of its value or necessity; warm feelings and nothing to counterbalance them; great good humour and much good nature – no appearance of caprice – rather quick and *vive*, but not a grain of rancour . . . In short, the Princess in the hands of a steady and sensible man would probably turn out well, but where it is likely she will find faults perfectly analogous to her own, she will fail.' No one knew better than Malmesbury how far the Prince fell short of being 'steady and sensible', for he had been a confidant during some of the early dramas with Mrs Fitzherbert. It would have been invidious, though, to warn the Prince against Caroline when he believed that the Prince's own failings constituted at least an equal threat to the marriage.

Besides, Caroline seemed so eager to learn and to do well that Malmesbury may have allowed himself to hope for the best, notwithstanding his charge's obvious eccentricity. The marriage treaty was signed on 3 December, but due to the danger from French troops in the Low Countries the journey to England had to be undertaken with great circumspection. There were many tedious delays in north Germany, rendered all the more trying by the extreme cold. Caroline, glad to be out of Brunswick, remained cheerful, though she was beginning to worry about what might be in store for her. 'She expresses uneasiness about the Prince,' Malmesbury recorded on 23 January 1795; 'talked of his being *unlike*, quite opposite to the King and Queen in his *ideas and habits*; that he had contracted them from the *vuide* in his situation; that she was made to fill this up; she would domesticate him – give him a relish for all the private and home virtues; that he would then be happier than ever; that the nation expected this at her hands; that *I knew* she was capable of doing, and that she would do it.'

Brave words, on which Malmesbury preferred not to comment, save by re-emphasising the necessity for proper conduct. By the end of January 1795, however, the seasoned diplomat was beginning to feel some confidence about his charge. It was true, as he wrote to the Duke of Portland, that she had been brought up in a situation quite dissimilar to that which she was about to fill. In Brunswick her position had been 'a subordinate one, and of great restraint, and where her mind had not fair play; where it could never act for itself, where it was governed severely not guided gently'. The court ladies, never imagining that they were dealing with a future queen, had been on terms of gossiping familiarity with her, very far removed from the kind of distant respect which she would be accorded in England. Nevertheless, 'since we have left Brunswick, the manner in which she has conducted herself towards those who have come to pay their court to her, has been the most becoming possible'. Clearly Caroline was not unteachable, given a sympathetic instructor. Prince Ernest of Mecklenberg-Strelitz wrote to the Prince on 21 January that she was winning all hearts '*par sa politesse et affabilité*'.

Encouraged by these signs of progress, Malmesbury steeled himself in February to tackle one particular source of unpleasantness which he scented in the Princess. 'Argument with the Princess about her toilette. She piques herself on dressing quick; I disapprove this. She maintains her point; I however desire Madame Busche to explain to her that the Prince is very delicate, and that he expects a long and very careful *toilette de propreté*, of which she has no idea. On the contrary, she neglects it sadly, and is offensive from this neglect.' Even this advice did not antagonise Caroline:

she appeared next day, Malmesbury observed, 'well washed *all over*'.

Another fortnight, and her mentor ventured further into this dangerous territory. 'I endeavoured, as far as was possible for a *man*, to inculcate the necessity of great and nice attention to every part of the dress, as well to what was hid, as to what was seen. (I knew she wore coarse petticoats, coarse shifts, and thread stockings, and these were never well washed, or changed, often enough.)' Again, this frank talking does not seem to have been in the least resented. When the party finally embarked from Stade on 28 March Malmesbury noted with admiration that it would be 'impossible to be more cheerful, more *accommodante*, more everything that is pleasant, than the Princess – no difficulty, no childish fears – all good humour'. The sailors were delighted with her. And Mrs Harcourt, an effusive lady-in-waiting, was 'sure the Prince will love her. She is so affectionate . . . her desire to please is so very engaging . . . she is all openness of heart, and has not a shadow of pride.' When someone remarked on her evident happiness, Caroline professed that it could hardly be otherwise. 'Am I not going to be married to the finest and most handsome prince in the world, and to live in the most desirable country in Europe?'

Reality brought a cruel awakening. The Prince had originally intended to sail in a yacht to meet the battleship carrying Caroline at the mouth of the Thames. Lady Jersey, however, who had been appointed a lady-in-waiting to the Princess (shades of Lady Castlemaine), feared a rough sea. This whim the Prince accepted as conclusive, not only against the nautical expedition, but also, apparently, against his taking part in any welcome at all. When, therefore, Caroline disembarked at Gravesend at eight o'clock in the morning on Easter Day, 5 April, and proceeded up the Thames in a royal yacht to Greenwich, she found no one appointed to greet her. A party of four courtiers had been dispatched from Carlton House, but as their number included Lady Jersey they had been obliged to delay departure for more than an hour while her ladyship put the finishing touches to her *toilette*. While Caroline waited at Greenwich she was awkwardly entertained by the Governor of the naval hospital. 'Mein Gott,' she exclaimed on seeing the inmates, 'have all the English only one arm and one leg?'

The royal coaches arrived, and Lady Jersey had hardly been introduced before she began to make further trouble. Caroline's dress,
she decreed, was quite unsuitable, though Mrs Harcourt had taken
great pains about it. Malmesbury, astonished that Caroline should
be thus addressed, sharply reprimanded Lady Jersey for her manner.
The Countess, however, was unstoppable. She had brought with her
a white satin dress which she insisted that Caroline should wear;
and perhaps it was not coincidence that this garment showed off the
Princess's dumpy figure to the worst possible advantage. At least
Caroline insisted on sticking to her own beaver hat, rejecting her
tormentor's thoughtful offer of a white satin turban with feathers in
it. Lady Jersey next announced that she should sit at Caroline's side in
the coach, as she could not bear facing backwards, but Malmesbury
again intervened, this time with effect. 'I told [her] that, as she
must have known that riding backward in coach disagreed with
her, she ought never to have accepted the situation of Lady of the
Bedchamber.'

As the coaches returned to London so much later than had been
expected, there were very few people lining the route, and still less
applause. By the time Caroline reached St James's, about half-past
two, she had every cause to be bristling. And now she was to be
subjected to a more decisive humiliation. Malmesbury's description
of her meeting with the Prince has become a classic of anecdotal
history. 'I, according to the established etiquette, introduced (no-one
else being in the room) the Princess Caroline to him. She very
properly, in consequence of my saying to her it was the right mode
of proceeding, attempted to kneel to him. He raised her (gracefully
enough), and embraced her, said barely one word, turned round,
retired to a distant part of the apartment, and calling me to him,
said, "Harris, I am not well; pray get me a glass of brandy." I said,
"Sir, had you not better have a glass of water?" – upon which he,
much out of humour, said, with an oath, "*No*; I will go directly to
the Queen," and away he went.'

It is usually assumed that Caroline's appearance was frightful
enough to make the Prince's appalling behaviour understandable, if
not forgivable. Yet even when the effect of the white satin dress is
taken into account his recoil from her seems absurdly exaggerated.
Malmesbury had found Caroline perfectly acceptable-looking, and

Horace Walpole reported that 'everybody speaks of her face as most pleasing though with too much rouge' (she may simply have been high-coloured). The newspapers, perhaps less reliably, lavished encomia upon her attractions. '[She has] teeth as white as ivory,' rhapsodised the *London Chronicle*, 'a beautiful hand and arm, and may certainly be deemed a very pretty woman.' It is not necessary to go that far in order to appreciate that the Prince's first reaction, which in any case would have been inexcusable even if Caroline had been the ugliest woman in the world, was not so much a reflection on her looks, as a typically petulant outburst from an indulged and dissipated wastrel fretful at being obliged for once to follow another principle than his own gratification.

But Caroline was not the woman to lie down under such treatment. Instinctively, like a true Brunswicker, she counter-attacked. '*Mon Dieu!*' she observed to Malmesbury as soon as he rejoined her, '*est-ce que le Prince est toujours comme cela? Je le trouve très gros, et nullement aussi beau que son portrait.*' As the Prince was more than seventeen stone it was difficult for Malmesbury to rebut this criticism, which, he could see, Caroline was disposed to augment. Luckily the King sent for him at that moment, but later, at dinner, Caroline was still at her aggressive worst, quite unmindful of all the advice she had received in the preceding weeks. Malmesbury recorded his disappointment at her behaviour: 'it was flippant, rattling, affecting raillery and wit, and throwing out coarse vulgar hints about Lady Jersey, who was present, and though mute, *le diable n'en perdait rien.*' Caroline did not miss much either. 'The first moment I saw my *futur* and Lady Jersey together, I knew how it all was,' she later observed.

Understandable though her loss of control was after all she had been through that day, it cost her dear. The Prince, who had truly behaved like a blackguard, appeared as the fine gentleman disgusted by the gross conduct of the woman he was to marry. Having been handed such an advantage he did not intend to throw it away through any generosity of spirit. Besides, under the pressure of Caroline's arrival, his thoughts returned with longing to the woman whom he had so ruthlessly abandoned. The day before the wedding he indulged himself to the extent of riding down to Mrs Fitzherbert's house at Richmond, but no sign came from within. That night he asked his brother William to tell Mrs Fitzherbert that she was the only woman he would ever love.

It was as well that the wedding, on 8 April, was not a great public occasion. 'There is no doubt', said one witness, 'but it was a *compulsory* marriage.' The Prince prepared for the event by drinking himself into a stupor, so that the Duke of Bedford was obliged to hold him upright throughout the service. The Prince 'looked like death and full of confusion', reported another onlooker, 'as if he wished to hide himself from the looks of the whole world' – not an inappropriate reaction in one about to commit bigamy. Observers noted that when the Archbishop of Canterbury asked whether there were any lawful impediments to the marriage he paused and fixed a penetrating gaze on the bridegroom. The Archbishop also laid particular emphasis on the phrases dealing with the obligation of matrimonial fidelity. At such moments the Prince found support by 'perpetually looking at his favourite Lady Jersey'. Notwithstanding this never-failing source of comfort, he was in tears for much of the ceremony. The only person, indeed, who appeared thoroughly cheerful was Caroline, who passed the time 'smiling and nodding to everyone'. This, of course, was taken as further proof of the woman's irremediable vulgarity. After the service the Prince could hardly bring himself to address a word to his bride, nor did he become any less drunk. According to Caroline's later reminiscences he 'passed the greatest part of his bridal-night under the grate, where he fell, and where I left him'.

2

In the face of this disaster Caroline did her best to keep up appearances, while the Prince continued to advertise his unhappiness. On the morrow of the wedding she appeared '*very well*'; he went for a solitary drive. Again, a few days later at Windsor, she 'looked happy', a state of affairs that the Prince soon contrived to remedy. From Windsor the royal couple went for some species of honeymoon at Kempshott Park, near Andover, where there was no other female guest save Lady Jersey, and where the Prince had invited some of his less reputable male cronies. If Caroline's later reminiscences are to be believed, these gallants daily drank themselves into oblivion and snored away their nights upon sofas without giving themselves the trouble of taking off their boots.

For a while, though, Caroline's determination to put a brave face on things allowed outsiders to hope that she and the Prince might, like so many ill-assorted couples, establish a *modus vivendi*. The Prince's sister Elizabeth told him in May that Caroline had spoken of her happiness. 'I flatter myself', Elizabeth concluded, 'that you will have her turn out a very comfortable little wife.' That was a misjudgement of Caroline's potential; nevertheless, in the first months of her marriage she lacked for nothing in loyalty and good will. The Duke of Brunswick wrote to the Prince in July that her letters had been full of gratitude for his solicitude. And even the Prince himself, after he had taken Caroline down to Brighton in June, was able to write to his mother about her without any expression of disdain. 'She is extremely delighted with this place which seems to agree with her most perfectly as she is in the best of health and spirits possible, excepting at moments a little degree of sickness which is the necessary attendant upon her situation.'

For, extraordinarily, Caroline was pregnant. 'I no more believed it dan any ting for long time,' she would recall in later life. The fact, however, was undeniable, and received with delight by the rest of the royal family, even by Queen Charlotte who, Caroline would complain, had been against her from the very beginning. Actually suspicion between the two women was mutual. Caroline's mother had always disliked her sister-in-law and passed on the prejudice to her daughter. Queen Charlotte, for her part, had certainly acted less than tactfully in conniving at the appointment of her favourite, Lady Jersey, as lady-in-waiting to Caroline. Yet for a while in the summer of 1795 the prospect of a grandchild temporarily turned the Queen into a model mother-in-law. She sent presents to Caroline, worried about her health, fussed about linen, and agonised over wet-nurses in quite the manner prescribed. As for King George III, he was always disposed to be a staunch supporter of Caroline, if only because his son, whom he detested, so obviously disliked her.

The Prince's initial reaction to his wife only hardened with the passage of time. Caroline's attempts to ingratiate herself with him proved disastrously inept. On one occasion, hearing that he admired a fine head of hair, she ostentatiously unloosed her locks in his presence. The experiment was not a success: 'I only wish you could have seen the poor man's face,' she laughed many years later. Her galumphing Germanic humour grated horribly upon a man who prided himself on his sophistication and wit. He did not like her shoes: 'well then', she told him, 'make me another pair and bring them to me'. It was enough to make even a real gentleman's heart sink. Nor, we may be sure, was the Prince vastly amused by Caroline's description of Mrs Fitzherbert as 'fat, fair, forty'.

Such incidents only intensified his frigid, unyielding hostility, so that after a few weeks even Caroline's constitutional cheerfulness began to waver. In July 1795 a Miss Holroyd retailed a sad account of the Princess at Brighton. 'She, poor Creature, is, I am afraid, a most unhappy Woman; her lively spirits, which she brought over with her, are all gone, and they say the melancholy and anxiety in her countenance is [*sic*] quite affecting.' In September the Prince departed for a few days to join his mother and sisters at Weymouth where, it seems, he strove to disabuse them of any idea that his marriage might be satisfactory. After his return to Brighton there was no attempt whatever to disguise his feelings from his family. '*Quand* [*sic*] *à nous*,' he wrote to his mother, 'we go on tolerably well . . . *aussi méchante aussi médisante* [scandal-mongering] *aussi menteuse que jamais*.'

On 7 January 1796, nine calendar months less a day after the wedding, Caroline was delivered of what the Prince described as 'an *immense girl*'. How typical of his wife, his phrasing seems to suggest, to have produced a female monster. At least, though, having provided the country with an heir, he could claim to have done his duty in the matrimonial lists. 'After I lay in,' Caroline later recalled, 'I received a message, through Lord Cholmondeley, to tell me I never was to have de great honour of inhabiting de same room wid my husband again.' The experience of fatherhood, indeed, produced a cataclysmic effect upon the Prince. He seemed normal enough on 9 January, when, the solicitous husband, he wrote to his mother explaining that he had ordered Caroline to be kept quiet; next day, however, prophesying his imminent demise, he made a will in which he left all that he possessed to '*my Maria Fitzherbert who is my wife in the eyes of God, & who is & ever will be such in mine*'. 'To her who is called

the Princess of Wales' the Prince bequeathed 'one shilling', though
he generously forgave her 'the falsehood and treachery of her conduct
towards me'. Her jewels, 'having been bought with my own money',
were to be given to their daughter Charlotte. The child, moreover,
should be removed from her mother. 'The convincing and repeated
proofs I have received of her [Caroline's] entire want of judgement
and feeling, make it incumbent upon me . . . to prevent by all means
possible the child's falling into such bad hands as hers.' The will
therefore entrusted responsibility for Princess Charlotte's upbringing
to the King and Queen.

As the Prince decided after all to live, this extraordinary document
remained a dead letter. Nevertheless, there was nothing false about
his determination to live apart from Caroline. 'I had rather see toads
and vipers crawling over my victuals', he declared, 'than sit at the
same table with her.' His feelings were exacerbated by the failure
of Parliament to grant him the large increase in income that he
had expected when he agreed to the marriage. The fact that he
had suffered in vain enhanced his determination to make Caroline
pay. It was not enough to set up two separate establishments within
Carlton House. The Prince began to persecute his wife in a manner
that convinced a shrewd judge like Lord Melbourne, who had no time
for Caroline, that he was mad. He allowed no one to see her without
his express permission, and even limited her visits to their daughter
to one short period every day. 'The Prince uses her unpardonably,'
Charles Abbot noted in his journal. 'She drives always alone, sees
no company but old people put on her list . . . goes nowhere but
airings in Hyde Park.'

'I do not know how I shall be able to bear the loneliness,' Caroline
wrote to a friend in Germany. 'The Queen seldom visits me, and my
sisters-in-law show me the same sympathy . . . The Countess [of
Jersey] is still here. I hate her and I know she feels the same towards
me. My husband is wholly given up to her, so you can easily imagine
the rest.' The Prince even took back a pair of bracelets that had been
part of Caroline's wedding jewels and bestowed them on Lady Jersey,
who gloried to wear them in the presence of the spurned wife. The
pampered mistress was forever running to the Prince and the Queen
with tales of the Princess's *faux pas*. She achieved a particularly rotten
triumph when she obtained some letters that Caroline had written

to Germany. Discovering several sour references to the royal family, Lady Jersey did not hesitate to communicate them to the Queen, who featured as 'de old Begum' in Caroline's folklore.

Finally, in April 1796, Caroline began to strike back. *L'animal est vicieux: il se défend.* The Prince had opted for warfare and over the next quarter-century he would get more than he bargained for. Yet Caroline's first target was Lady Jersey; she gave no indication of wanting to precipitate a final break with her husband. At the same time her opening salvo, notwithstanding the somewhat ungrammatical French in which it appeared, gave warning that she might be a formidable antagonist. 'As I see only too well, my dear Prince, that it would cost you too much to dine with me, I think you are not in a position to exact the same sacrifice from me, to dine alone with a person [Lady Jersey] whom I can neither like nor esteem, and who is your mistress.'

As there was no effective means of replying to this sally in logic, beyond pointing out that Caroline had seven other ladies-in-waiting with whom she might dine, the Prince resorted to the kind of pompous expostulation at which he excelled. His wife had once more offended against the canons of good taste. Her slanders upon Lady Jersey, '*my mistress as you* indecorously term her', were 'unwise, groundless and most injurious'. (He could hardly say that they were untrue when Lady Jersey's bed was now made up in his dressing-room at Brighton.) The Prince also reacted sharply to Caroline's suggestion that he should 'be as generous as your nation is, and keep your word as every good Englishman, since such is the character of the nation'. Such phrases were all too obviously intended for publication. It came to the Prince with sickening horror that his wife might appeal against his authority to public opinion. Such a course, he nervously warned, would be fatal.

Caroline, in reply, expressed herself as 'very unhappy that you have interpreted my letter so badly: it came from a deeply troubled heart'. She apologised graciously for having referred to Lady Jersey as his 'mistress': the word 'was at the end of my pen without thinking'. Equally, she was sorry for any offence which she had given at 'Breyten'. There was no question, of course, of her making any appeal to the English people. Indeed – and how Caroline

must have relished the irony of associating her detested mother-in-law
with her cause – she had always admired the way that Queen Charlotte had remained aloof from any suggestion of political intrigue.

The Prince could not resist returning that Caroline might also
seek to emulate the Queen in promoting her husband's comfort,
adding mysteriously that 'delicacy keeps me quiet on some peculiar points which even to yourself I never can insinuate'. Caroline
blithely ignored this reference to her uncleanliness. If *she* ought
to imitate the Queen's example, she told the Prince, then surely
he might profit from following 'the steady behaviour of the King
towards the Queen'. At this point the Prince informed his Chamberlain Lord Cholmondeley that he was 'tired to death of this silly
altercation'; rather than continue it, he asked Lady Cholmondeley
to tackle his wife 'woman to woman' on the matter to which he
had obscurely alluded in his last letter. Lady Cholmondeley was
also to explain the indelicacy of any public discussion of these
affairs. The Prince had yet to learn that Caroline could never be
deterred by any threat, least of all by the prospect of public embarrassment.

A higher estimate of her abilities might also have enabled him to
detect the danger in her seemingly innocent request that, to avoid
misunderstandings, he should set down in writing his scheme for
their future relations. The Prince hastened to comply in his best
huffing-and-puffing style:

> Madam,
>   As Lord Cholmondeley informs me that you wish I would
> define, in writing, the terms upon which we are to live, I shall
> endeavour to explain myself on that head with as much clearness
> and with as much propriety as the nature of the subject will
> admit. Our inclinations are not in our power, nor should either
> of us be held answerable to the other because nature has not
> made us suitable to each other. Tranquil and comfortable society
> is, however, in our power; let our intercourse, therefore, be
> restricted to that, and I will distinctly subscribe to the condition
> which you required through Lord Cholmondeley, that even in
> the event of any accident happening to my daughter, which I trust
> Providence in its mercy will avert, I shall not infringe the terms
> of the restriction by proposing, at any period, a connection of a
> more particular nature. I shall now finally close this disagreeable

correspondence, trusting that as we have completely explained ourselves to each other, the rest of our lives will be passed in uninterrupted tranquillity.

I am, Madam, with great truth, very sincerely yours,
George P

The immense self-satisfaction evident in this letter was speedily dissipated by Caroline's riposte, in which she stated that, having no other protector but the King, she was forwarding to George III an account of their differences, together with the relevant correspondence. The Prince, who knew that his father would treat his disgust for Caroline as just another symptom of his perennial self-indulgence, scurried down to Windsor to plead his case with the Queen. Whereas previously he seems to have thought in terms of keeping Caroline permanently immured as a prisoner in Carlton House while maintaining the public fiction of the marriage, he now began to hope for a complete separation. His fury against his wife fed on the knowledge that popular opinion was rallying to her as rumours of marital disharmony began to leak out of Carlton House. This was not, as he liked to believe, because Caroline courted the mob, nor was it because the mob spontaneously admired her. The man in the street was completely indifferent to the fate of a German princess; experience had most profoundly convinced him, however, that the Prince was a rotter. What more effective way to signal this awareness than by cheering the abhorred consort? When Caroline appeared at the opera on 28 May the entire house rose to applaud her. Surely, she gleefully remarked, she would be guillotined for such a demonstration.

Three days later the Prince submitted a request for a 'final separation' to the King. The emergence of Caroline as a popular heroine, in contrast to the hoots of derision that invariably greeted his own person, was more than his fevered emotions could stand. He was deeply concerned, also, to hear that his wife had been to see the King: 'I suppose', he complained, 'she has made the best of her own story and told her lies as usual.' In a series of deranged letters to his 'dearest, dearest, dearest mother' he poured out his psychotic loathing for the woman who had presumed to question his authority. 'Never for God's sake', he pleaded, 'propose to me to humiliate myself before the vilest wretch that this world was ever curs'd with, who I cannot feel more disgust for for her personal nastiness than I do for her entire want of all principle. She is a very monster of iniquity.' She was, in addition, '*a fiend*', the most 'unprincipled and unfeeling person of her sex', to whose 'wickedness', 'falsity' and 'designs' he could discern no end. If his own death could make amends he would 'glory in the sacrifice'. Alas, though, more was required. 'If the King does not manage to throw some stigma, & one very strong mark of disapprobation upon the Princess, this worthless wretch will prove the ruin of him, of you, of me, of every one of us. The King must be resolute & firm, or everything is at an end. Let him recall to his mind the want of firmness of Louis 16. This is the only opportunity for him to stem the torrent.' And more, much more.

With such a son, it is ironical that George III, stricken by porphyria, has gone down to history as the mad King. The good old man's reply to the Prince's request for a separation is a model of solid sense, and says all that needs to be said about the breakdown of the marriage. He pointed out that the Prince's marriage was by definition 'a public act, wherein the Kingdom is concerned'. The public being, as the King put it, 'certainly not prejudiced in your favour', the Prince would be wise to preserve appearances. He recognised that Caroline had not always behaved well, 'but if you had attempted to guide her, she might have avoided those errors that her uncommon want of experience and perhaps some defects of temper may have given rise to . . . I once more call on you to . . . have the command of yourself that shall . . . by degrees render your home more respectable and at the same time less unpleasant . . . In the contrary line of conduct nothing but evils appear.'

The King also took Caroline's part against Lady Jersey. In June 1796, under pressure, and with no grace at all, Lady Jersey resigned as lady-in-waiting. Caroline, having achieved the object for which she had fought, immediately extended an olive branch to her husband. Certainly, in seeking reconciliation, she was acting under instructions from the King, whom she could not afford to antagonise; nevertheless the warmth, humility and generosity of her letter are striking. She longed, she wrote on 25 June, finally to put an end to a misunderstanding which, on her side, no longer existed. 'If you do me the honour of seeking my company in the future, I will do all I can to make it agreeable. If I have displeased you in the past, be good enough to forgive me, and be assured that my gratitude will only cease with my life.' And how did the elegantly mannered Prince reply to this peace offering? 'Madam, I have had the honor of receiving your letter this day & propose having the pleasure of being at Carlton House some time in the course of Monday.' When he saw Caroline on that day he cut the interview short with the chilling politeness of the perfectly bred before departing to spend the rest of the day with Lady Jersey.

It would be wrong to idealise Caroline just because she was so shamefully treated. She was never a spotless victim. She continued to be wildly indiscreet, and specialised in gossip about sexual peccadilloes of other members of the royal family. To the courtier class, taking its cue from the Prince, she appeared as an outrageous and vulgar hoyden spreading embarrassment and dismay in the natural haunts of smoothness and civility. And indeed she would have taxed the forbearance of the most long-suffering husband. The Prince was particularly alarmed by her interest in Catherine the Great, and concluded from her taste for mannish clothes that she was modelling herself upon the Russian Empress. By the summer of 1796 he was far from being alone in questioning his wife's sanity.

Yet when all Caroline's failings have been admitted, the extremity of the Prince's abhorrence can only be adequately explained in terms of his own deficiencies. Of course he could not be expected to love to order, but nor was he obliged to act with such cruelty. Caroline was disastrously unfitted, alike by upbringing and by temperament, for the role which she had to fill, but she was neither malign, stupid or unreformable. She desperately wanted to do well, and it is difficult to discover, in the first two years of the marriage, that she committed any acts that put her entirely beyond the pale. She would always have been eccentric, but, treated with sympathy, she might have been passed off as a perfectly acceptable, even a well scrubbed, princess. If a sleek diplomat like Malmesbury could obtain results in these matters, what might a husband have achieved with a few scraps of kindness?

But the Prince of Wales, chagrined by his father's refusal to sanction a formal separation, merely intensified his campaign of petty persecution. He spent much of his time out of London, enjoying country delights with Lady Jersey, but when Caroline asked in October 1796 if she might spend two or three days away from Carlton House he professed himself hurt 'in the most sensible way possible' by the proposal. Although he based his outright refusal on his duty to uphold royal etiquette, the real cause was his terror that Caroline would use the opportunities of travel to whip up public support. The Princess had, indeed, been developing her populist instincts. During the celebrations that followed Fox's victory in the Westminster election of June 1796 she was very noticeably on view with her baby at a window of Carlton House. Later, she drove through the crowds in order, as the Prince supposed, 'to get herself applauded'. Once more, Caroline's apparent surrender to 'the worst of parties at the moment, the democratick', struck the royal nerves at their rawest point. Even when Caroline asked that their daughter's governess, the admirably competent Miss Hayman, should be allowed to help with her accounts, the Prince indignantly refused. Miss Hayman's attendance upon the child 'must be such as will entirely preclude every other occupation'. *His* concern for their child, he explained, sprang from genuine affection, and was not indulged 'for the sake of worldly applause'.

The Prince made no objections at all, though, when in August 1797 Caroline took a house in Charlton, Blackheath. At first she probably intended no permanent removal, for she remonstrated fiercely when the Prince removed furniture from her rooms at Carlton House. Yet before very long it appeared that, for practical purposes, the separation would be enduring. In December 1797 another row blew up over the Prince's continued insistence that his wife should see no one without his approval. Caroline appealed to the King against this ruling, another sign that she was developing claws, but in this instance George III upheld the Prince. Furious, the Princess demanded an interview with her husband, 'alone'. The Prince agreed, though he cautiously insisted that Lord Cholmondeley should also attend. The Chamberlain's presence did not inhibit Caroline. She rounded on the Prince, complaining that she had been treated in a manner befitting neither his wife, nor the mother of his children, nor the Princess of Wales: 'I give you notice here and now that I have nothing more to say to you and that I no longer regard myself as subject to your orders or your rules.' 'Is that all you wish to tell me, Madam?' the Prince icily demanded. Receiving an affirmative reply, he bowed and withdrew. This exchange, as it proved, ended all pretence that they were living together. Thenceforward it was tacitly accepted that Caroline might see whom she wished so long as she continued to reside at Blackheath.

'Oh! how happy I was,' she later recalled of her departure from Carlton House. 'Everybody blamed me, but I never repented me of dis step. Oh! mine God, what I have suffered! Luckily, I had a spirit, or I never should have outlived it.' This spirit, however, proved to be a decidedly mixed blessing.

3

Caroline seemed to know how a wronged princess, forced out of her husband's palace, *ought* to conduct herself. Dignified retirement in the face of intolerable provocation was clearly the line to aim for, and with part of her personality she strove gamely to play the role. She studied drawing. She sang, played the piano and took up the harp. She grew vegetables. She made lampshades out of dried flowers and learnt techniques for imitating marble. The unpretentious house at Charlton was well suited to such occupations; and even Montague House, on Blackheath, whither she moved in 1801, was 'a modest mansion, not so large as that of a petty German baron'. Conditions must have been cramped, for the Princess of Wales was obliged to keep a considerable household. If there was discomfort, however, Caroline never complained.

In May 1796, while still living in Carlton House, she had loftily informed the Prince that her unfortunate situation afforded the opportunity to give an example of patience and resignation under every trial. In the same letter, and in the same elevated strain, she had alluded to the gratitude she felt towards the husband who had provided her with the position and the means 'to indulge in the free exercise of a virtue dear to my heart – I mean charity'. Good works featured largely in the scheme of Caroline's life at Blackheath. Her particular field of interest, for obvious reasons, was orphaned children. Her own daughter Charlotte was being brought up away from her in Carlton House, under the care of governesses. The separation was not total, for the little Princess was taken to

Blackheath regularly, and in the summer lived in a house there. Inevitably, in these circumstances, Caroline's feelings for her daughter were fitful, but they were also intense. The meetings between mother and daughter came to be occasions dreaded by Charlotte's governesses, who owed their jobs to the Prince and dutifully considered that the little girl was over-excited by her mother's passion for romping about on the floor. Caroline, for her part, observed with satisfaction that Charlotte evidently preferred to be with her.

These sadly limited encounters, however, stimulated her maternal instincts without really satisfying them. She began to adopt local orphans and foundlings whom she placed in the care of local foster-mothers, with instructions that they should frequently be brought to see her. 'I have nine children,' she would boast, and sometimes her house did seem to resemble a nursery. A German visitor was impressed with the 'lively, jocose and truly maternal manner' in which Caroline talked to these infants, and he noted how she embraced one child with a particularly revolting open sore. The stuffier natives thought it odd, some even considered it disgusting, that the Princess of Wales should conduct herself in this way. Caroline herself was quite unperturbed. 'It is my only amusement, and [they are] the only creatures to which I can really attach myself – as I hate dogs and birds – and every body must love something in the world. I think my taste is the most natural and whoever may find fault with it may do it or not.'

Yet this protestation of Caroline's was more than a trifle disingenuous. If orphan children had indeed been her sole amusement, there could have been no grounds for complaint. She had not looked forward to becoming Princess of Wales, though, because she had dreamt of a lonely and virtuous existence away from the world's temptations. Her charitable impulses and her seemly hobbies helped to fill the time, but they never struck deep roots in her; nothing ever did with Caroline. She might toy with the part of long-suffering, self-effacing victim of her husband's malignity, but she could never sustain the role with any consistency. She was bored, and she wanted to have some fun. As a conventional princess she had disastrously failed to please her husband: perhaps as an unconventional one she might succeed in pleasing herself.

So the fashionable world was invited down to Blackheath, and, notwithstanding some grumbles about the distance, the fashionable world appeared for the most part only too delighted to accept. 'She has a system of seeing all remarkable persons,' one of those favoured complacently observed. Caroline, however, submitted her guests to entertainments very far removed from the discreet civilities that passed for entertainment at Carlton House. A fevered and rumbustious jollity pervaded her parties. The guests would have to act out French proverbs, or perhaps Caroline would make them link hands and charge through all the rooms in the house. Informality was the keynote: the hostess would sit on the floor and talk scandal, or, better still, she would make scandal. Men who caught her fancy would be taken off for long sessions alone with her in a private room while the other guests wondered, as of course they were intended to wonder, what on earth was going on.

That is a question which no one has ever been able to answer with any certainty. It is quite possible that Caroline's actual conduct was considerably more innocent than she liked to convey, and that her chief joy consisted in shocking the solemn and censorious. She was, after all, a woman who drank decanters of cold tea in order to give the impression that she was an alcoholic. The important thing for such temperaments is to be the centre of attention, no matter how scandalous: they are less concerned with action than with effect. 'Nobody can improve me in morality,' Caroline declared, 'I have a system quite my own.' That at least was beyond dispute, but exactly what her system permitted remains a mystery. The case for the prosecution might point to Caroline's peculiar prejudice against having ladies-in-waiting sleep in Montague House. Those women were appointed by the Prince, and perhaps she feared that all-too-accurate tales might be carried back to their employer. The defence might reply that the Princess would surely not have behaved so outrageously in public if she had had anything serious to hide in private. Or did she perhaps deliberately publicise her flirtations in order to revenge herself on the Prince and expunge the sexual humiliation of her marriage?

Perhaps Caroline was, as she liked to claim, 'a little devil in petticoats' (not so little, actually); perhaps she was merely a compulsive exhibitionist. Those who encourage the world to think the worst, however, generally find it only too happy to oblige. Society was soon ablaze with gossip about the goings-on at Montague House. William Pitt Lennox, who was only a little boy at the time, recalled 'the thousand and one Blackheath tales. They rivalled in popularity those of the Arabian Nights.' Several well known figures – Thomas Lawrence, George Canning, the Hon. Henry Hood, the Duke of Cumberland, even Walter Scott – were confidently reported to be her lovers. In each case the evidence is either tenuous or non-existent; and the very number of names brought forward rather diminishes confidence in each individual slander. Caroline's arch, teasing manner with men created smoke where there may in fact have been very little fire. It amused her, for instance, to tell Lord Sackville that 'she was very much *afraid* of him, for she was sure he did not approve of her dissipation'. And when Walter Scott hesitated to follow her down a dark corridor, she mischievously berated the poet for his fears: 'Ah! false and faint-hearted troubadour, you will not trust yourself with me for fear of your neck.'

Such conversation was deemed lively or coarse according to taste. One of Caroline's favourite topics, after she had left Carlton House, was the sexual inadequacy of the Prince of Wales. 'There was nothing of *any sort* she did not seem disposed to relate,' reported a stunned Lord Minto in 1798. 'It appears that they lived together two or three weeks at first, but not at all afterwards as man and wife . . . If I can spell her hums and haws, I take it that the ground of his antipathy was his own *incapacity*, and the distaste which a man feels for a woman who *knows* his defects and humiliations.' The Prince's other women, it is only fair to remark, complained of no such deficiency. But Caroline, naturally enough, had come to hate him. When the Prince asked her to return to Carlton House in December 1798 she flatly refused, correctly sensing that this seeming attempt at reconciliation had been forced on him by his political friends, who had become anxious about the depth of unpopularity he had incurred by his treatment of his wife. Yet for all her disdain for the Prince, Caroline insisted on the rights due to her as Princess. She would appear at Drawing-Room receptions, where the Prince was obliged to expend much effort in failing to notice her.

Nevertheless, there was, at the beginning of the new century, something of a truce between Caroline and her husband. The Prince had made a second attempt, at the end of 1797, to obtain a final separation, but he had no chance of success so long as a Tory government, obedient to the King's wishes, was in power. His mind therefore turned to ways of ameliorating his situation. Lady Jersey, to her considerable surprise and her still greater annoyance, was summarily dismissed; and Mrs Fitzherbert once again pursued with the usual patent mix of suicide threats interlaced with protestations of eternal devotion. Her determination to resist was rock-like, until the Prince hit on the happy idea of threatening to reveal their marriage to the King, which would have meant ruin for them both. Mrs Fitzherbert decided to consult the Pope, who duly decreed that she should return to her husband, a decision which confirmed the Prince in his belief that Roman Catholicism was 'the only religion for a gentleman'. Caroline, it must be said, was less impressed, acidly telling a friend of the Prince's that she hoped her husband would not feel *her* any impediment to the reconciliation he so desired.

In fact Mrs Fitzherbert, with less than perfect logic in the light of the Pope's pronouncement, insisted on living with the Prince 'as brother and sister'; nevertheless, her bargain was gratefully accepted. The succeeding years were probably the happiest in the Prince's life. Just occasionally he felt himself obliged to chastise Caroline, even, with quite breathtaking hypocrisy, to lecture her on extravagance, a rebuke which Caroline received 'with great good humour'. She had indeed been spending money on Montague House, by all accounts to disastrous effect. The house was 'all glitter and glare and trick . . . tinsel and trumpery' according to one visitor, 'altogether like a bad dream . . . the dining-room, *à la Gothique*, very pretty, but the rest of the house in abominable taste'. In response to the Prince's complaints she made some economies in her staff, but she continued to spend far in excess of her annual income of £17,000. For the most part the Prince was not inclined to bully her so long as she kept entirely out of his life, did not cause him any trouble, and accepted her situation without complaint. He heard the stories about the wild happenings at Montague House and was content to ignore them. Even when, in the autumn of 1801, and again in 1802 and 1804, the Prince received reports that the Princess had been delivered of a child, he did not trouble to have the matter investigated.

The relative calm of this period, however, was constantly undermined by the King. In 1801 George III suffered another bout of madness and, although he appeared to recover within a few weeks, his behaviour remained erratic, with a further bad attack in 1804. His condition caused a sharp deterioration in his relations with Queen Charlotte, who, terrified, took to bolting her bedroom door against him. Perhaps as a corollary of this marital breakdown, the King began to display more interest in Caroline. Early one morning in April 1801 he suddenly took it into his head, without telling anyone, to ride over to Blackheath to see his daughter-in-law. Caroline, who was in bed when he arrived, later professed herself terrified by his wild appearance, though she was shrewd enough to treat him with the deepest respect. The King assured her that he had been thinking about her during his recent illness and that she would in future find great kindness from all his family, with the exception, he was sorry to say, of one. Thereafter he made a habit of going to Montague House on Thursdays, riding back late in the evening over the country to Kew. Caroline liked to pretend that on one occasion he had made violent advances upon her, and that she had only escaped by her skill in slipping off a backless sofa. This story may well have been another instance of her readiness to embroider in the cause of self-dramatisation. She did, though, undoubtedly succeed in impressing the King with a firm sense of her inviolable virtue. Either he had not heard, or deliberately set aside, the more unsavoury rumours that emanated from Montague House. 'That kindness which I could not but feel you entitled to on coming into this country', he wrote to Caroline in November 1801, 'is still more deserved by the propriety of your conduct in a very difficult situation.'

The King's insistence upon Caroline's virtue must have been galling to the Prince, but hardly so alarming as his growing interest in his granddaughter. The Princess Charlotte was an enchanting child, whose joyful passage through childhood gave out sad hints of what her mother might have been. For in so many ways she resembled Caroline – in her quirky individuality, her boundless good nature, her quick, shrewd, unintellectual mind, and her headstrong passionate nature. In contrast to her mother, though, her affections were not entombed in egocentricity, her enthusiasm remained untouched by coarse, cynical disillusion, and her wilfulness stopped short of folly and madness. It was difficult not to love Charlotte. Even the Prince occasionally, very occasionally, forgot his dignity so far as to pet his daughter, only to veer off sharply into cold disregard, as if she reminded him of something that he did not care to recall.

George III, labouring under no such inhibitions, simply adored the child: 'there never was so perfect a little creature', he considered. In 1804 he concocted a scheme under which Charlotte should be brought up under his care at Windsor. At first the Prince went along with this plan, unaware that his father intended Caroline also to be involved. George III arranged to meet Caroline at Kew – 'because at Windsor he knew the Queen and Princesses would be rude to her'. 'I trust', he wrote, 'I shall communicate that to you which may render your situation much more happy than you have yet been in this country, but not more so than your exemplary conduct deserves.' It seems that he wanted Caroline to live with Charlotte. So at least the Prince imagined when he heard of the Kew meeting. The consent that he had so easily given to Charlotte's education at Windsor was now withheld, and long negotiations ensued. The conclusion, reached at the end of 1805, was that Charlotte should live at Warwick House, next to Carlton House, when the Prince was in London, and at Windsor for the rest of the time. Caroline might see her regularly, but only, it was emphasised, as a visitor.

The dispute about Charlotte's education reminded the Prince that his wife could still be a nuisance. And so when in November 1805 another scandalous account of Caroline came to his notice, he was naturally inclined both to credulity and to action. It was alleged that in 1802 the Princess of Wales had given birth to a boy, who was now being brought up in Montague House under the name of William Austin. The provenance of this gossip, had the Prince been disposed to think about it, might have warranted caution. For the charge had been brought against Caroline by a certain Lady Douglas, wife of Sir John Douglas, Lieutenant-Colonel (retired) in the Marines. Since 1801 the Douglases had rented a house in Blackheath, and Lady Douglas had suffered the acute anguish of being taken up and swiftly dropped by the Princess of Wales.

In 1802, the period to which her accusations related, Lady Douglas had conceived herself a most intimate friend of Caroline's, so intimate that she had been favoured, as she related, with many confidences relating to the imminence and the accomplishment of the Princess's *accouchement*. Her Ladyship's discretion in the face of these extra-ordinary revelations had at first been model: for three years, she said, not even her husband had been allowed to share the alarming secret. By the end of 1803, though, there had been unmistakable signs that Caroline's favour for Lady Douglas had transmuted into something that seemed distressingly like distaste. Worse, when in September 1805 the Princess was appointed Ranger of Greenwich Park – another sign of the King's favour – she set about using her position to secure the eviction of the Douglases from their comfortable Blackheath property. The unhappy tenants gave Caroline to understand that 'if Her Royal Highness did not act with great discretion' in this matter, she might have cause to regret it. But Caroline was not to be deterred by blackmail. On 9 November her right to evict was confirmed. Two days later the Prince of Wales received Lady Douglas's extraordinary intelligence and began to solicit advice on how he ought to proceed.

An unofficial enquiry was immediately set into motion, the results of which, delivered the following May, were sufficiently encouraging to persuade the Prince to press the matter further. For three whole years, he told his friends, he had forborne to interfere with his wife: if only Caroline had maintained a *show* of decent feeling, he would have tried to protect her. Duty, though, now compelled him to take another course. As it happened, duty was marvellously assisted in January 1806 by the arrival of the Whigs (including Charles James Fox) in office, carrying with them the promise that, if something could be proved against Caroline, he might finally be rid of his matrimonial burden. Such was the origin of the official enquiry into Catherine's conduct known as the 'Delicate Investigation'.

The report lacked for nothing in sensationalism. Lady Douglas represented the Princess as a woman with whom 'no human being could live . . . excepting her servants for her wages'. She was 'a person without education or talents, and without any desire of improving herself'. In support of this contention Lady Douglas cited Caroline's comments upon other members of the royal family. The impartial reader may consider that these excerpts, however lacking in taste and discretion, show a conversationalist of very considerable talents. The Prince of Wales, for instance, 'lives in eternal hot water and delights in it. If he can but have his slippers under an old dowager's table and sit there scribbling notes that's his whole delight . . . [I] ought to have been the man and *he the woman to wear the petticoats* . . . he understands how a show should be made or a coat cut, or a dinner dressed and would make an excellent tailor, or showmaker or hairdresser but nothing else.' Regarding the Prince's brothers she could trace in the Duke of Cumberland's features some family likeness to herself, 'but for all the rest they were very ill-made, and had plum pudding faces, which she could not bear'. The Duke of Kent 'had the manners of a Prince, but was a disagreeable man, and not to be trusted'. His Royal Highness the Duke of Cambridge 'looked exactly like a sergeant, and so vulgar with his ears full of powder'.

Lady Douglas, needless to say, had been infinitely shocked by these aspersions, yet what outraged her still more (if such a thing were possible) was the Princess's loose regard for the sanctity of the marriage vow. 'I wonder you can be satisfied only with Sir John,' Caroline was represented as telling her new friend, adding that for herself 'she got a bedfellow whenever she could; that nothing could be more wholesome'. Nothing, either, could have been more convenient than her room: 'it stands at the head of a staircase which leads into the Park, and I have bolts inside, and have a bedfellow whenever I like'. As for the Prince, he was perfectly complaisant: 'I go where I like, I spend what I please, and His Royal Highness pays for all . . . I am better off than my sister, who was heartily beat every day. How much happier am I than the Duchess of York! She and the Duke hate each other, and yet they will be two hypocrites, and live together – that I would never do.'

It is tempting to discern, under this crazy rattling talk, the sad wail of sexual frustration, yet some of the Montague House servants whom the commissioners interviewed apparently believed that the Princess had absolutely no grounds for complaint upon that score. Robert Bidgood, a page, deposed that he had seen Caroline kissing Captain Manby, a naval officer – 'a very close kiss'. William Cole, another page, considered that the Princess had been 'too familiar' with Mr Canning and Rear Admiral Sir Sidney Smith, the hero of the defence of Acre against Bonaparte in 1799. Thomas Roberts, a footman, a man of fewer words, simply declared that the Princess of Wales was 'very fond of fucking'. Yet the hard evidence against Caroline was either inconclusive or dependent on lengthy chains of hearsay. Thus one of the Douglases' servants relayed below-the-stairs gossip picked up from Montague House about the huge breakfasts consumed in the Princess's bedroom: 'and what extraordinary things she sent for, for a lady to eat in bed – meat, chicken, tongue, etc'. Likewise, Bidgood told how his wife 'had lately told him, that Fanny Lloyd had told her, that Mary Wilson had told Lloyd' that she (Wilson) had found the Princess and Sir Sidney 'in such an indecent situation that she immediately left the room, and was so shocked that she fainted away at the door'. It hardly encouraged confidence, either, that both Bidgood and Cole had previously been many years in the Prince's service.

Lady Douglas's principal charge, that Caroline had had a son, quite failed to stand up to investigation. William Austin, the boy in question, had, it was conclusively shown, been born to Sophia Austin in a hospital on 11 July 1802. His father was an out-of-work docker at Deptford, and the boy was simply one of the several poor children that Caroline had helped. Lady Douglas was utterly discredited. The interesting question, though, is whether she had simply made up her story out of spite against the Princess, or whether she had in fact faithfully reported what Caroline had told her in 1802. On the whole, the latter explanation appears the more likely. Surely Lady Douglas, however maliciously inclined towards the Princess, would not have dared to invent a series of outrageous lies which could so easily, as the event showed, be disproved.

To say that Caroline deliberately gave Lady Douglas to understand that she was with child when in fact she was not is tantamount to saying that Caroline was mad. Yet if one accepts the notion that she had, from the very beginning, ambivalent feelings about Lady Douglas, it does at least become possible to detect some method in her madness. Just possibly, Caroline was playing an elaborate and demented prank on a victim who was a highly suitable case for such treatment. Lady Douglas, a 'showy bold' woman of undeclared origins and dedicated social ambition, was extremely pretty and of by no means unspotted reputation. Caroline, notwithstanding the professions of virtue which Lady Douglas scattered through her evidence, believed her to be the mistress of Sir Sidney Smith. The admiral in fact lodged with the Douglases in Blackheath, so there was every opportunity for a *ménage à trois*. Whether or not this was in fact the case, the idea could have acted powerfully upon Caroline's sexually obsessed mind, and all the more emotively because she herself found Sir Sidney attractive. No doubt she resented Lady Douglas as any woman might resent a more beautiful and successful rival for a man's favour. In consequence she lashed out wildly. 'She told me that Sir Sidney Smith had often lain with her,' Lady Douglas reported. 'She believed all men liked a bedfellow, but Sir Sidney better than anyone else.'

If it is accepted that Caroline was in the grip of neurotic jealousy, much of her lunatic behaviour at Blackheath falls into a pattern. Her 'confessions' appear as part of a sustained and elaborate tease, a kind of shock campaign waged against Lady Douglas's false gentility. Caroline had begun by heaping over-elaborate praise on the rival's looks: 'Oh believe me,' she told Lady Douglas, 'you are quite beautiful, different from almost any English woman; your arms are fine beyond imagination, your bust is very good, and your eyes, Oh, I never saw such eyes . . .' Lady Douglas professed to be embarrassed by these compliments; she failed to detect the more sinister sub-text of resentment. Later Lady Douglas's own pregnancy sparked off Caroline's craziest tease, the pretence that she too was with child, together with the heavy implication that Sir Sidney Smith was the father in both cases. Once again the hint of mockery is discernible: 'I was sure you had found me out so I came to you,' Caroline began her 'confession' to Lady Douglas. 'Well, here we sit, like Mary and Elizabeth in the Bible,' she gaily remarked as she plonked herself down beside her on the sofa. Sometimes the note of derision seems unmistakable. 'That woman has such sharp eyes,' Caroline would tell others in the room, 'she finds me out in everything.'

Caroline insisted on attending Lady Douglas's lying-in, and then, a few months later, began to show off William Austin as *her* little boy. There was tragedy as well as comedy in the whole fantastic performance. Even in Lady Douglas's spiteful account it is impossible to miss, amidst Caroline's madness, the note of regret for the lost experience of motherhood. 'The Princess now took the child up, and I was entertained the whole morning by seeing it fed, and *every service of every kind performed for it by her Royal Highness the Princess of Wales.* Mrs Fitzgerald [a lady-in-waiting] aired the napkins, and the Princess put them on; and from this time the drawing-rooms at Montague House were literally in the style of a common nursery.' Mrs Fitzgerald, helplessly watching, tried to explain to Lady Douglas that William Austin had been brought into Montague House by a woman from Deptford, but Lady Douglas contemptuously dismissed this 'fable'. The joke, in fact, was getting out of hand; and when Caroline tired of teasing her rival, her hatred surfaced uncontrollably. Sir John Douglas received an anonymous letter with an obscene drawing of 'Sir Sidney doing Lady Douglas your amiable wife'. From this point events ran inexorably downhill to the Delicate Investigation.

So, at least, one possible interpretation of this strange affair might run. The task of the commissioners investigating Caroline's conduct, however, was not to speculate on motives, but to render judgement. In a sense this duty had been discharged when they acquitted the Princess of being the mother of William Austin. The servants' evidence, after all, was only unsubstantiated gossip and tittle-tattle. Perhaps the most damaging comment, in the final analysis, was the comparatively mild aspersion passed by a lady-in-waiting upon Caroline's behaviour towards Captain Manby. 'He was a person with whom she appeared to have greater pleasure in talking than to her ladies. She behaved to him only as any woman would who likes flirting. I should not have thought any married woman would have behaved properly who should have behaved as her Majesty did to Captain Manby.' At all events, the commissioners, while exculpating Caroline on the principal charge, felt obliged to add that there were other aspects of her behaviour 'such as must, especially considering her exalted rank and station, necessarily give rise to very unfavourable interpretations . . . the circumstances stated to have passed between her Royal Highness and Captain Manby, must be credited until they shall receive some decisive contradiction.'

The commissioners presented their report on 14 July 1806. For months Caroline had been under appalling strain, knowing that there was a hunt for evidence against her, but quite unaware of what might be discovered. Of course she protested her innocence, maintaining in a revealing phrase that she had 'never done anything, intentionally, which could have merited this cruel and illiberal treatment'. She kept up her courage to the world, insisting with her accustomed bravado that 'a Brunswick never has been conquered yet', but when she knew that the report had been submitted, and still heard nothing, she became ill with anxiety. In private she began to talk not of fighting like a Brunswicker, but of returning to Brunswick ('I do not feel', commented Lord Minto, 'that it would be so unwise a measure.'). It must have been particularly worrying that the King, to whom she always looked for support, had joined the conspiracy of silence. Finally, in answer to her repeated representations, she received a copy of the report wrapped casually in brown paper and without any seal, as if to emphasise her ostracism from royal circles.

Though Caroline was without friends she was not without allies. Her treatment was an obvious issue for out-of-office politicans to exploit. In 1806 it was the Tory followers of the recently deceased William Pitt who took up her case. Ironically, the rigorously high-principled evangelical Spencer Perceval stood forth as the foremost champion of the 'much-injured lady'. Perceval discovered that he greatly preferred the Princess, notwithstanding her 'exterior frivolity', to the 'professedly modest and apparently reserved of the sex in high life'. Romantic instincts suddenly surfaced in his arid legal mind. 'To the Tower or to the scaffold in such a cause,' this unlikely crusader cried. More to the point, he prepared, in the form of a letter to the King, an answer to the criticisms of Caroline made in the Delicate Investigation report. This 'letter' in fact ran to 156 printed pages and was a masterpiece of special pleading. Anyone reading it might be brought to share Perceval's own view of the charges against Caroline, that 'a greater farrago of gossiping trash and malignant accusation can hardly be conceived'.

Apparently, though, no one at Windsor was greatly impressed by Perceval's effort, neither the King nor the Prince, 'my Tyrant of glorious memory'. The lengthy epistle in the Princess's defence had been dated 28 September: nine weeks later there had still been no reply or acknowledgement. Perceval sadly recorded that the Princess was 'very much fallen away. She says she is quite sure it is intended that she should never be permitted to see the King again.' A letter expressing her dismay was dispatched to George III on 8 December, still without eliciting any reply. The Cabinet was unable to agree how the King should be advised to act. It was 28 January 1807 before George III finally wrote to Caroline informing her that he need not continue to decline receiving her.

Following the line of the commissioners' report, however, the King went on to convey his 'serious concern' about the Princess's conduct, together with his hope that her future behaviour would be unexceptionable.

Caroline, deciding to ignore the reprimand and accept the peace offering, eagerly wrote to suggest a date for her reception at court. She was informed that since the Prince had decided to put the evidence that had been collected into the hands of his lawyers, presumably with a view to obtaining the long-desired divorce, her attendance at court had better be postponed. Caroline, though, had begun to scent victory and countered in high-handed terms. 'The only remaining resource for the vindication of my character', she claimed, was the publication 'to the world' of all the proceedings relating to the Delicate Investigation. This was an astonishing threat to make, considering that the material to which Caroline referred included all the salacious charges against her. Nevertheless, she believed that the Prince's unpopularity would secure her against any unfavourable interpretation of her actions. Indeed, she was so confident that in this same letter she demanded that she should be restored to the use of her apartments at Carlton House, or, failing that, 'some apartment in another of the Royal Palaces'. This was 'indispensably necessary for my convenient reception at the Drawing-room'.

Caroline's threat to publish was about to be carried out – indeed 'The Book' of the Delicate Investigation proceedings was already in print – when the government fell and the Duke of Portland's administration took office, with Spencer Perceval as Chancellor of the Exchequer. Matters suddenly became wonderfully simple. 'The Book' was withdrawn, Caroline found herself asked to appear at court, and Kensington Palace was made available for her. On 4 June 1807 she duly appeared at a Drawing-Room. The ceremony cannot have afforded her much pleasure in itself. The Prince studiously talked to his sisters with his back to his wife, and when the Prince and Princess left they 'both looked contrary ways, like the print of the spread eagle'. All the same, Caroline had triumphed, in her fashion.

4

Victory, however, was of no avail. One might have thought, after the scares and humiliations of the Delicate Investigation, that Caroline would have learnt the need for propriety, or at least for discretion. But those who make a career out of being outrageous do not easily adapt to blameless routine. In 1807 Caroline visited Plymouth, with the formidable and highly critical Lady Hester Stanhope in her suite. Lady Hester had already been shocked by the indecent antics of a clockwork doll in Montague House: at Plymouth her indignation knew no bounds. 'Oh what an impudent woman was that Princess of Wales: she was a downright —. How the old sea captains used to colour up when she danced about, exposing herself like an opera girl, and then she gartered below the knee: – she was so low, so vulgar!' At Kensington, Caroline embarked on a new series of flirtations, with Lord Henry Fitzgerald, with the elderly lawyer Sir William Scott, with John Ward (future Earl of Dudley) and with William Henry Lyttleton.

Being admired by Caroline must have been a disconcerting experience, for her physical charms, never overwhelming, were now in terminal decline. Lady Charlotte Campbell, who became a lady-in-waiting in 1810, judged that in early youth Caroline had been a pretty woman, with 'fine light hair – very delicately formed features, and a fine complexion – quick, glancing, penetrating eyes, long cut and rather sunk in the head, which gave them much expression – and a remarkably delicately formed mouth. But her head was always too large for her body, and her neck too short; and, latterly, her whole figure was like a ball, and her countenance became hardened, and an expression of defiance and boldness took possession of it, that was very unpleasant.' The absence of neck, according to another source, was accentuated by wearing a variety of lace ruffs and frills, 'ill put on and some not looking too clean'. In addition, she was always reckoned to wear too much rouge.

Caroline used clothes for revelation rather than concealment. Her mountainous bust was frequently on display, and though the fashion was for low-cut dresses, Caroline always took the principle further than anyone else. One visitor to Kensington felt himself obliged to avert his eyes from the sight of the Princess of Wales 'very injudiciously attired, wrapped in a pink dressing gown'. Another vignette, taken at breakfast after an all-night party, presents Caroline 'in a gorgeous dress, which was looped to show her petticoat, covered with stars, with silver wings on her shoulders, sitting under a tree, with a pot of porter on her knee'. The difficulty is to find any account of Caroline being conventionally dressed. 'Such an exhibition!' wrote Mary Berry, who saw her at a ball in 1809. 'But that she did not feel at all for herself, one should have felt for her! Such an over-dressed, bare-bosomed, painted eye-browed figure one never saw! G. Robinson said she was the only true friend the Prince of Wales had, as she went about justifying his conduct.'

Despite such behaviour, Caroline was not ostracised by society in the years immediately following the Delicate Investigation. Indeed, one would have been more likely to meet a Cabinet minister at Kensington Palace than at Carlton House. The Princess's ally Spencer Perceval, now Chancellor of the Exchequer, continued to help her. He forwarded the repairs being made to Kensington Palace and settled her debts: she acted as godmother to his youngest son. Temperamentally, however, Caroline, like Byron, was 'born for opposition'. Perceval's appointment as Prime Minister in October 1809 was more than her loyalty could bear. He now appeared to her as 'a presumptuous, foolish lawyer', just as Lord Eldon was 'a vulgar bore', and the rest of the Cabinet 'drivellers'. As if that were not sufficient to damn her in the eyes of the government, she also pronounced – and the remark came to the Prime Minister's notice – that Perceval was entirely governed by 'that silly woman his wife', an observation which did not even have the merit of truth. By the end of 1809 Caroline was firmly committed to the Whig opposition and infuriating the government by actively canvassing against Lord Eldon in the contest for the Oxford University Chancellorship.

It was dangerous policy, as well as rank ingratitude, to desert the political friends who had served her so well. At the end of 1810 George III again went mad, and this time the doctors prophesied, correctly for once, that there was no hope of recovery. Henceforth, it was clear, the Prince of Wales, as Regent, would be the fount of honour and power; and the Prince would have nothing whatever to do with those who were received by his wife. (Caroline, by contrast, cheerfully declared herself rather partial to the Regent's friends.) Tory politicians, unexpectedly maintained in office by the Prince, saw no cause to be loyal to the woman who had spoken so scathingly of them. Suddenly Caroline found herself socially ostracised. There was one particularly sad dinner at Blackheath (Caroline kept on Montague House until the end of 1813) where the rows of unoccupied places testified that those whom Caroline invited no longer cared to accept, or even answer, her invitations. 'There is no more society for me in England,' the Princess reflected, adding with typical defiance that she was too proud to want those who had deserted her to return.

Nevertheless, the abandoned Princess might very shortly be Queen. In May 1811 George III was so ill that his life was daily despaired of. Inevitably, given her combative character, Caroline would fight for her queenly rights; no less certainly her husband would resist her claims. Clearly there was a first-rate constitutional crisis in the offing. For this reason Caroline became a magnet for ambitious radical politicians like Henry Brougham and Samuel Whitbread. Brougham in particular, a lawyer of the utmost brilliance and unscrupulousness, was a dangerously cynical ally. In public he professed outrage at the manner in which Caroline had been treated; in private he could be brutally frank about his motives in assisting her. The Princess, he said, was useful as 'a Constitutional means of making head against a revenue of 105 millions, and an army of half a million, and 800 millions of debt'. Caroline, for her part, was under no illusions about Brougham. 'His manner does not please her,' reported Lady Charlotte Campbell, a lady-in-waiting. 'They look at each other in a way that is very amusing to the bystander. The one thinks, "She *may* be useful to *me*"; and the other, "*He* is useful to me at present."'

Good lawyers invariably provoke bad feeling. While the nation concentrated its energies upon the final stages of the struggle against Napoleon, the Regent and his wife dedicated themselves to petty domestic squabbles. Caroline must have been encouraged by the Prince's unpopularity, which at this period reached depths that even he had never plumbed before. Leigh Hunt reflected the popular view when he savagely attacked a ridiculous panegyric which had referred to the Regent as 'an Adonis of Loveliness'. The truth, Hunt concluded, was that this Adonis in Loveliness *was a corpulent gentleman of fifty!* In short, that this delightful, blissful, wise, pleasurable, honoured, virtuous, true *and* immortal PRINCE *was a violator of his word, a libertine over head and ears in debt and disgrace, a despiser of domestic ties, the companion of gamblers and demireps, a man who has just closed half a century without one single claim on the gratitude of his country or the respect of posterity.*

Hunt spent two years in prison for thus failing, as he described it, to find the Regent slender and laudable, a punishment which aroused further outrage in the artistic and literary world.

In such circumstances the Prince would have been well advised to be cautious, but it was he who provoked the next stage in the matrimonial combat by seeking to restrict Caroline's access to Princess Charlotte. After the Delicate Investigation, Caroline had only been allowed to see her daughter once a week, rather than the two or three times previously permitted. Now it appeared that, during one of her visits to Kensington Palace, Charlotte, still only fifteen in 1811, had been left to converse with the atheist Sir William Drummond, who had spoken lightly of the Bible. 'I can assure Your Royal Highness there is nothing in it,' Sir William had told her, 'it is all allegory and nothing more.' The Prince, not hitherto noted for his devotion to religion, declared himself infinitely shocked, and Charlotte was thereafter forbidden to meet any society whatsoever at Kensington. Then in June 1812 the prohibition was further stiffened: Charlotte would henceforward not be allowed to visit her mother more often than once a fortnight.

Brougham and even the more moderate Lord Grey immediately scented an opportunity: the Prince's conduct, Grey thought, 'has given the Princess a great advantage, which it requires only common prudence on her part to turn to good account'. Yet the issue of how often Caroline and Charlotte saw each other was really an artificial one. Caroline, though she seized eagerly on the chance to attack the Prince, was too egocentric to care deeply or consistently about her daughter. Her letters, Charlotte complained, were 'the *shortest, driest* things in the world, & consist of five lines at the uttermost'. Moreover, though the Prince did not yet know it, Caroline had been guilty of an infinitely worse dereliction of parental duty than countenancing the sceptical conversation of Sir William

Drummond. In 1812 Charlotte had developed an adolescent crush for a Captain Hesse, whom she used to meet at Kensington. As she later remembered, she 'never could make out whether Captain Hesse was her lover or her mother's'. Caroline, however, had decided the point in favour of her daughter. One day she left Hesse and Charlotte alone together in her bedroom, and turned the key on them with the remark '*A present, je vous laisse, amusez-vous.*' Fortunately Captain Hesse restrained his brute male desire, but the episode hardly inspired confidence in Caroline's parental solicitude. And Charlotte on her side, though she was loyal to her mother and deeply suspicious of her father, found little joy (Captain Hesse apart) in her meetings with Caroline. She wrote of her 'duty' calling her to Kensington, and of 'a very disagreeable dinner at Blackheath'. She also, being a shrewd girl, expressed doubts about Brougham's motives in leading her mother on.

Caroline, in fact, hardly needed encouragement to make mischief. In August and September 1812 she boldly presented herself at Windsor and demanded to see her daughter. This was purely a publicity stunt, 'planned', as Princess Charlotte wrote, 'with the knowledge and consent of Mr Brougham and Mr Whitbread'. Caroline must have known that her demand would be refused. Indeed, after an earlier attempt to see the mad old King had been rebuffed, she had sworn never to go to Windsor again. 'The King is quite well, but he will not see you,' Queen Charlotte had told her, and 'smiled her abominable smile of derision'. The snub was now repeated in the case of her daughter, save that this time Caroline was not even allowed to see the Queen. When, nothing daunted, she returned to Windsor she was met by the Prime Minister Lord Liverpool, who handed over, at her request, a written letter forbidding a meeting with Charlotte. Clutching this valuable document (valuable, that is, for the purposes of publicity) Caroline returned to Kensington. It was such 'fun', she said, 'teazing and worrying' the Royal Family. Poor Charlotte, though, was left alone at Windsor to defend her mother's behaviour to her father. She stuck up for Caroline bravely, and subsequently gave a verbatim account of the interview to an eager audience at Kensington Palace. A few days later, to her horror, she saw everything she had said reported in the newspapers.

This, however, was but the beginning of Brougham's campaign. He now composed a letter to the Prince in which Caroline complained eloquently of the restraints upon her intercourse with her daughter and of 'the serious, and soon it may be irreparable, injury' which Charlotte was sustaining from her seclusion at Windsor. As essays in high-flown hypocrisy go it would be difficult to improve on this production, which ended with an expression of concern that Charlotte had not yet been confirmed, 'a circumstance in every way so distressing, both to my parental and religious feelings'. Brougham must have enjoyed penning that passage. Even so, he could not help being worried about Caroline's behaviour. 'It all stands excellently *if he has no case,*' he wrote to Whitbread shortly after dispatching the letter to the Prince on 14 January 1813. 'The difficulty you see is this – He may have a case and yet be very averse to produce it.'

At first the Regent simply refused to receive Caroline's letter, and even after the Prime Minister had read it to him he 'was not pleased to signify any commands upon it'. Brougham, disappointed at this failure to engage the enemy, decided to intensify the provocation. On 10 February he arranged for Caroline's letter to the Prince to be published in the *Morning Post*: and on 10 March the same newspaper began to reproduce extracts from the Delicate Investigation, presumably on the doubtful premise that they would provide further evidence of the Princess's unsullied purity. Caroline was in seventh heaven, basking in the publicity, intoxicated by the heady scent of battle. 'The Princess of Wales looked better than I ever saw her,' remarked a lady-in-waiting at this time. One might even be tempted to feel sorry for the Prince. The temptation should be resisted. In 1811, Mrs Fitzherbert, whose charms had once more worn thin, asked where her place was to be at a Carlton House banquet. 'Madam,' the Prince returned to the woman he had described as 'the Wife of my heart and soul', 'you have no place.' It was now Lady Hertford, 'a wonderful looking woman for her age' (fifty-one in 1811), who commanded his devotion.

Towards Caroline, who, unlike Mrs Fitzherbert, resolutely declined to fade gracefully away under his disdain, the Prince hardly knew how to act. His only riposte to Brougham's sallies was to place the documents from the Delicate Investigation, together with some later evidence, before the Privy Council, in the hope that it would produce an adverse verdict upon the Princess's morals. Meanwhile Charlotte was forbidden to see her mother under any circumstances. In the event, though, the Privy Council, in the way of committees, only produced a rather vague recommendation that the meetings between Caroline and Charlotte 'should continue to be subject to regulation and constraint', which in practice meant that Charlotte would have to get a separate permission each time that she wanted to see her mother. Brougham had succeeded in reinforcing Caroline's public image as a martyr to her husband's cruel whims. And the martyr scored a satisfying minor victory that summer when the Prince held a magnificent fête in Vauxhall Gardens to celebrate Wellington's victories in Spain. Caroline's decision to attend forced the host to boycott his own party, which did nothing for his temper.

These occasional emanations of malice, stimulating though they were for the moment, dismally failed to afford Caroline any deeper satisfaction. She believed passionately in the possibility of happiness – 'we must make up *vons* mind to enjoy de good, spite of de bad', she would say – but she was too intelligent to disguise from herself that she was leading an empty and meaningless existence. Increasingly she gave way to dark moods in which the rehearsal of her grievances and sufferings alternated interminably with maudlin philosophising. 'If anybody say to me at dis moment, "Will you pass your life over again or be killed?" I would choose death . . . sooner or later we must all die; but to live a life of wretchedness twice over – oh! mine God, no!' In more aggressive vein she would talk enthusiastically of those she would like to see dead, with the Prince naturally featuring at the head of the list. 'The only astonishing news I can offer you is, that the Regent is dangerously ill,' she wrote to a friend. 'Still I am not sanguine enough to flatter myself that the period to all my troubles and misfortunes is yet come. Yet one must hope for the best.' To bring that 'best' closer she took to sticking pins into wax effigies of the Prince. 'So long as dat man alives,' she would say in her peculiar mixture of Germanised English and fractured French, '*les choses vont de mal en pire* for me.'

And so they did. One of the occupational disadvantages of being a princess is that the world is not inclined to take one's troubles very seriously; and in Caroline's case this problem was exacerbated by behaviour which extinguished any dawning sympathy for her plight. It is all too easy to understand why Caroline was not loved. Whether it was misery that intensified her obsession with herself, or the other way about, she never really seemed to give a fig for anyone. There was an unattractive hardness about her, already noted in her attitude to Charlotte, whose situation she exploited without any care for her real interests. She showed the same indifference to her mother, who arrived as a refugee in England in July 1807, after her father had died of wounds sustained in battle against Napoleon. The old Duchess, like her brother King George III before his madness, was amiable enough in her eccentric way, but Caroline did not attempt to disguise the impatience, boredom and 'dullification' that she felt in her mother's company.

She was unable, though, to draw lasting satisfaction from anything. Her pleasures were always confined to the moment. Nevertheless the sparks of enjoyment did occasionally fly. The dereliction of the Tory politicians contributed mightily to the cheerfulness and conviviality of her dinner table, while the Regent's displeasure helped to lure into her circle men of learning, accomplishment and wit. Regular guests at Kensington included Sir William 'topographical' Gell, a classical expert with a pleasantly facetious sense of humour; M. G. Lewis, author of the celebrated Gothic novel *The Monk*; Keppel Craven, whose books on Italian travel would later have some success; and Richard Payne Knight, an artistic connoisseur and religious sceptic who had published an influential book on Taste, as well as (which may have appealed to Caroline rather more) a learned dissertation upon the worship of Priapus among the ancients.

Lord Byron also went two or three times to Kensington Palace 'to dine & dawdle away the Evening', having been introduced to the Princess in 1812 by his current inamorata Lady Oxford. Caroline piqued herself on her ability to manage the unpredictable poet. 'I always tell him there are two Byrons,' she wrote, 'and when I invite him, I say, "I ask the agreeable Lord, not the disagreeable one." He takes my *plaisanterie* all in good part, and I flatter myself I am rather a favourite with this great bard.' Byron rejected Lady Melbourne's teasing suggestion that the Princess took an unhealthy interest in him. 'I suppose at least that C is quiet,' he wrote, distinguishing the Princess from Lady Caroline Lamb, 'and I really think you pay me too great a Compliment – & her none – to imagine any doubts of our mutual decorum & discretion & all that.'

In such company Caroline was at her best. 'I never saw any person, not royal or royal, who understood so well how to perform the honours at their own table as the Princess,' wrote Lady Charlotte Campbell. 'She does it admirably and makes more of her guests than anyone else ever did.' And yet, the same observer noted in a more censorious mood, the kind of conversation in which the Princess most delighted was 'brilliant, evanescent, devoid of reflection – a sort of sparkling fire which only makes darkness visible – which moves the muscles of the face to laughter, but never dilates the heart with real joy'. No doubt Lady Charlotte had been rather out of things on that particular occasion, but she was perfectly right that Caroline's cheerful dinner-table rattle echoed hollow in the chasms of her soul. However jolly the evening's entertainment, the next morning would invariably find her plunged again in gloom and depression.

'I am like the Roman Empire, in a state of "decadence",' she wrote to a lady-in-waiting apropos of some physical ailment, but really it was her mental state that gave most cause for concern. She entirely lacked the inner resources that might have made her situation tolerable. No interest or hobby ever absorbed her for more than a moment. Her quirky idiosyncratic style made her a delightful letter-writer, but she was too lazy to develop this talent. She talked of writing a novel set in Greece: inevitably the project never materialised. The only work that she did produce, some short prose sketches of prominent contemporaries, has unfortunately disappeared. It was the same with her reading. She enjoyed scandalous historical memoirs but rarely bothered to do more than skim a book. 'From a quickness of perception, great tact, and an excellent memory, she catches the title of every work,' Lady Charlotte Campbell noted, 'and, having turned over the leaves, has a sort of smattering of the contents, which she *hashes* up with other people's opinions, and gives the whole *en réchauffé*, with a *faux brillant* which imposes on the many.'

Under the pressure of unhappiness Caroline's old need to shock intensified. 'The poor Princess is going headlong to her ruin,' wrote Lady Charlotte Campbell in 1813. 'Every day she becomes more imprudent in her conduct, more heedless of propriety, and the respect she owes to herself.' Whitbread bravely wrote to tell her to show less cleavage when she appeared in public. Caroline was not amused: 'she absolutely wept some tears of mortification of anger when she received this letter'. Though forty-four in 1812, she again began to delight in dropping elaborate hints designed to alarm her attendants with the possibility that she might be pregnant. Willikin (William Austin), she said, was getting too big: 'I must have a *little child*.' Further to encourage everyone's worst suspicions she shed her corsets.

She even appeared to have selected a young man for the role of father, manifesting an infatuation with a young Italian musician called Sapio. The entire Sapio family, father and mother as well as the especially favoured son, were given the run of Kensington Palace, and allowed to behave towards the Princess with a familiarity that verged on impudence. The elder Sapio had been music master to Marie-Antoinette, and found nothing daunting in Kensington Palace after the splendours of Versailles. Caroline's English attendants could hardly express the indignation they felt at seeing her 'let herself down so as to sing paeans to the fiddler's son'. Old Sapio was contemptuously nicknamed 'the ourang-outang'; the younger one 'Chanticleer'; and the family as a whole 'the Squallinis'. According to Lady Charlotte Campbell, Caroline's association with the Sapios was as unfortunate musically as morally. 'The old ourang-outang came to dinner, – more free and easy and detestable than ever . . . Then her Royal Highness sang – squall, squall! Why invite me?' In fact, Caroline was only too happy to be alone with the Sapios. To that end she took a cottage near them in Paddington, a sort of down-market Petit Trianon where she could play that favourite game of princesses in every age, pretending to be an ordinary person. Just how ordinarily she behaved with Chanticleer is unknown, although her conversation, as ever, was designed to make everyone fear the worst. 'To kill the Regent; then go abroad, with a court of her own making, of which the fiddler is to be king: this is her favourite plan,' reported Lady Charlotte Campbell.

Abroad! Increasingly Caroline dreamt of abandoning her prison-house of England, where her every attempt at pleasure seemed doomed to founder, in order to assuage her discontent in the more careless atmosphere of the Mediterranean world. At Blackheath, so she said, she had encountered two gypsies. 'They told me that I was a married woman, but that I should not be married long; and that my heart was a foreigner's, and that I should go abroad and there marry the man I loved, and be very rich and happy.' Such fantasies are common enough among women in their mid-forties – among men too for that matter. Caroline, however, differed from the general run in that she was desperate enough and courageous enough to translate them into action. While Europe had been torn apart by the Napoleonic wars her hopes necessarily rested in abeyance. But with the defeat and abdication of Napoleon in April 1814 all things became possible. Nothing but money was wanting.

At the beginning of 1814, in January, Caroline had sunk very low. Her state was perceptively described by her daughter Charlotte:

> The Pss. I find, feels *extremely* her situation, that is to say the *very few who will visit, who will come near her, & the numbers who now refuse, decline & keep out of her way. She has a great deal of pride & high spirit & feels mortified*, & fears she may be lower'd in people's eyes. She likes society, hates being shut out of it, & yet if she were to give parties people would then see *who she* is *reduced* to . . . From my own observations I should say she *was subdued*, & *was not*, because one moment she is in tears & another you see they are smothered in *indignant feelings*. The truth is I believe her to be both a *very unhappy* & a very *unfortunate* woman who has had great *errors*, great *faults*, but is really oppressed & cruelly used, not even to be treated with the common attentions fitted for her situation.

Now Caroline's ostracism would be made the more bitter by being paraded to the world. That summer the Allied leaders and sovereigns gathered in London to celebrate what all imagined was the final defeat of Napoleon. But in May, before they arrived, Caroline received a letter from Queen Charlotte informing her that, due to the Prince's 'fixed and unalterable determination not to meet the Princess of Wales either in public or private', she, the Queen, would be unable to receive her. This was a clear signal that Caroline would be excluded from all the peace celebrations. Brougham was delighted: here was another opportunity to air the Princess's grievances. 'I suppose no more signal blunder was ever committed,' he wrote excitedly of this latest snub. He drafted further letters on Caroline's behalf to the Queen and Regent, in which he insinuated that the Prince might as well behave less vindictively since he would eventually be forced to recognise his wife at his coronation. 'I suppose he will shake a little at this,' Brougham told Lord Grey. Caroline's spirits soared again at the whiff of grape-shot: she was 'vastly happy', recorded Lady Charlotte Lindsay on 31 May. Yet her excitement did not last long. As the impotence of her squibs, and the full extent of her social humiliation became clear, her morale plunged to new depths.

Every morsel of hope proved delusive. The Tsar, who thought the Regent 'a poor Prince', talked of going to Kensington, but in the end diplomatic pressure kept him and all the other dignitaries away. Even Caroline's own nephew, 'that little vile Prince of Wirtemberg' as Lady Charlotte Lindsay called him, refused to come. For Caroline there was no consolation save in continuing popular support, which profited her nothing and pleased her little. She was wildly cheered at the opera on 3 June. The Prince was also there, and 'turned pale' at her entrance, though this proved to be the last occasion on which he was exposed to the sight of his wife. Caroline, with a rare display of tact, refused to rise and make a curtsy to the audience. 'My dear,' she laughed, 'Punch's wife is nobody when Punch is present.' In truth she had already abandoned England in her mind. Brougham's petty exercises in point-scoring afforded no lasting solace. If she did not look forward to going abroad, she said on 8 June, she should die of despair. At the end of the month she heard that the government had granted her £50,000 a year, which seemed very like an invitation to carry out her plans to leave the country. Whitbread, however, who had no desire to see the Princess become a government pawn, urged her to write to the Speaker that she did not wish to become a burden on the nation, and would therefore accept only £35,000. This stratagem did not appeal to Caroline one bit, until Whitbread convinced her with the argument that £50,000 would oblige her to remain in this country whereas £35,000 would permit her to travel wherever she pleased for as long as she liked.

Just when everything seemed set for Caroline's departure, though, a sudden crisis intervened. At the end of 1813 her daughter Princess Charlotte had agreed, under intense pressure from the Regent, to become engaged to the Prince of Orange. Subsequently discovering, however, that she was obliged to turn her head away in disgust when her fiancé addressed her, and almost equally concerned that she might, after her marriage, find herself obliged to spend some time in Holland, she broke off the match on 16 June. This decision was assisted by the fact that she had fallen madly in love with the handsome, caddish Prince August of Prussia. The Regent, furious at the miscarriage of his plans, retaliated by dismissing Charlotte's servants, whom he suspected of having connived at Prince August's visits to their mistress. Charlotte, who had all her mother's spirit, responded by escaping from the close surveillance under which she was being kept, jumping into a hackney cab, and making for her mother's house, Connaught Place near Marble Arch. (Caroline had given up Montague House at the end of 1813, and taken Connaught Place as an alternative to the more formal Kensington Palace.)

Here, if ever, was a heaven-sent opportunity to embarrass the Prince. His own daughter had fled from persecution to the refuge offered by her ill-used mother. Yet Caroline showed no enthusiasm for exploiting the situation. She had some fun, admittedly, with Lord Chancellor Eldon and others sent to parley with her. These dignitaries were kept waiting interminably in her dining-room without anyone troubling to see them. Nevertheless, after Brougham had given his opinion that the Regent had full legal rights over his daughter and that Charlotte should therefore return to Warwick House, Caroline showed no stomach whatever for a fight.

Charlotte, however, remained obdurate, so that Brougham had to make a dramatic appeal to her. Taking the young Princess to the window and looking out at the dawn that was beginning to break, he expatiated upon the likely consequences of continuing to defy her father. 'Look there, Madam: in a few hours all the streets and the park, now empty, will be crowded with tens of thousands. I have only to take you to the window, and show you to the multitude, and tell them of your grievances, and they will all rise on your behalf.' 'And why should they not?' Charlotte demanded. 'The commotion', Brougham returned, 'would be excessive; Carlton House will be attacked – perhaps pulled down; the soldiers will be ordered out; blood will be shed; and if your Royal Highness were to live a hundred years, it never would be forgotten that your running away from your father's house was the cause of the mischief: and you may depend on it, such is the English people's horror of bloodshed, you never would get over it.'

The melodramatic appeal had its effect, and Princess Charlotte agreed to return home. Caroline's passivity, though, had been strangely out of character. One might have expected that the prospects which Brougham outlined – a rampaging mob, Carlton House in flames – would have impelled her to action. She had taken to mouthing democratic sentiments to keep her radical supporters in line, so that Brougham had written excitedly about the prospect '*of a popular Queen*'. Yet when her moment came, she showed no interest. Perhaps she was too intelligent to believe that a princess could prosper by encouraging anarchy. Or did her caution simply amount to an unwillingness to sacrifice all the hopes which she had built on her imminent travels?

Certainly Caroline's determination to be gone at this juncture overrode any regard for her daughter's welfare. Charlotte, having returned to Warwick House, was kept in semi-captivity, under the watchful eye of guardians whom she detested. The young Princess, who had always shown stout loyalty to her mother, often under extreme pressure, was flabbergasted by Caroline's desertion. To add insult to injury the Regent, vastly relieved, opined that his wife's decision to leave England was the wisest act of her life; he wished her well. Charlotte was allowed to go to Connaught Place to say goodbye, but the meeting only emphasised her mother's lack of feeling. 'What goes most to my heart . . . is the *indifferent* manner of taking leave of me . . . I feel so hurt at *that* being a *leave taking* (for God knows how long, or *what events* may occur before we meet again . . .).' They would never meet again.

Brougham, who had very different reasons for wanting Caroline to stay, did all he could to make her change her plans. On 30 July 1814 he sent her a strong letter intended to bring home the consequences of leaving England. 'Depend upon it, Madam, there are many persons who now begin to see a chance of divorcing your Royal Highness from the Prince . . . As long as you remain in this country I will answer for it that no plot can succeed against you. But if you are living abroad, and surrounded by the base spies and tools who will always be planted about you, ready to invent and to swear as they may be directed, who can pretend to say what may happen, especially after your absence shall have lessened the number and weakened the zeal of your friends?'

Caroline, though, had tired of obeying the dictates of Whitbread and Brougham, who only prolonged her fruitless struggles for their own purposes. Brougham's letter, sage and prescient though it was, produced no effect. Her only concession to her advisers was to keep on her apartment at Kensington as a token that one day she might return. On 9 August she set sail from Lancing for her new life. If the *Sussex Advertiser* is to be believed, her emotions on leaving were so overpowering that she fainted into the arms of her attendants as the English shore slipped away.

5

Caroline began her travels by returning home to Brunswick, but a fortnight in her native land sufficed to exhaust both the call of nostalgia and the fascination of her brother. Even while still in England she had expressed her intention of wintering in Naples, and now the receipt of a letter from the Prime Minister, in which he explained that it would be most impolitic to lend Murat's fragile Neapolitan regime the support of her presence, clinched her determination to proceed there immediately. She moved south with extraordinary energy, though not so fast as to inhibit her capacity for creating scandal wherever she went. It was as though she were seeking through her outrageous behaviour some sort of revenge for the nineteen years of misery and humiliation which she had endured. Her tiny entourage – Sir William Gell, the Hon. Keppel Craven, Lady Elizabeth Forbes, Lady Charlotte Lindsay, William Austin, Dr Holland and various servants – began to wonder how long they could continue, 'not so much from wrong doings as from ridiculous ones'.

At Baden, for instance, where the Grand Duke arranged a hunting party for her, she appeared on her horse with half a pumpkin on her head. Nothing, she explained to her astonished host, kept the head so cool and comfortable as a pumpkin. 'What was my horror', wrote a witness at a ball in Geneva, 'when I beheld the poor Princess enter, dressed *en Vénus,* or rather not dressed, further than the waist . . . If this is a commencement only of what she intends to perform in the South, she will indeed lose herself entirely.' While passing through Switzerland Caroline encountered Napoleon's wife Marie-Louise of Austria, whom she regaled with jokes in appalling taste about the absence of their respective husbands. Marie-Louise, accompanied by her one-eyed lover Count Neipperg, did not show much tact, either, in singing an air entitled 'L'Innamorata'. The two abandoned wives then joined forces for a duet. 'I wonder what Marie-Louise thought of the Princess's singing?' mused Sir William Gell. 'She must have been astonished.'

On 8 October Caroline reached Milan, where she passed eleven days sightseeing without, for once, fostering any major scandal. Perhaps this was because she was treated with full royal honours by the Austrian regime, while at the same time she also enjoyed great popularity with the Milanese, who looked for English assistance in casting off the Austrian yoke. Ironically, though, it was during this rare interval of comparative propriety that Caroline met the instrument of her ruin. She needed a new courier, and considered, reasonably enough, that it would be useful to have an Italian servant who could help with the arrangements for her life in Italy. The Marchese Ghisilieri, Chamberlain to the Austrian Emperor, was conveniently on hand to recommend one Bartolomeo Pergami.

No one has ever been able to throw much light upon the obscurity of Pergami's origins, although, like many a penniless adventurer, he gave out hints of fallen glory and respectable forebears. His grandfather, so the story went, had been a successful doctor, but, alas, his spendthrift father had decimated the family fortune. His mother, according to an Italian historian, Signor Clerici, 'belonged to a Cremascan family of some standing'. Of Pergami's own career little is known save that he had served in some humdrum capacity on the staff of General Pino, an Italian who had ardently embraced the Napoleonic cause. Apparently Pergami had been with Pino on the Russian campaign of 1812, though the story that he had acted as Napoleon's equerry in Moscow was surely a romantic embroidery. With the end of the war he found himself, as a committed but uninfluential supporter of the losing side, in a precarious situation. In the six months before Caroline's arrival in Milan he had, at the age of thirty, with a wife and daughter to support, been unemployed. All his life he had lived on his wits; now, having secured his appointment as Caroline's courier, he quickly spotted an opportunity for a more secure career. For the most important and least contested fact about Pergami was his intensely masculine physical presence. Tall, powerfully built and conveying an aura of insolent virility, he appeared to northern eyes as the quintessence of Italian machismo. Lady Charlotte Campbell, who caught up with Pergami at a later stage in Genoa, wrote of 'mustachios which reach from *here to London*'. Caroline was entranced.

The journey south continued. At Florence Caroline met an extraordinary survival from the past, the Countess of Albany, widow of Charles Edward Stuart, the Young Pretender. The old woman was not impressed with her visitor. '*La Princesse voyage pour justifier son Mari*,' she tartly commented. In Rome Caroline saw the Pope, attended a ball at which she scandalised the natives with another display of abandoned dancing in scanty dress, and dined with Lucien Bonaparte. She reached her destination, Naples, on 8 November.

At first everything went well: she was warmly welcomed both by Murat, then nearing the end of his reign as King Joachim, and by the English residents in the town. Among those who flocked to meet her was Lady Conyngham, who was destined to hold George IV in thrall for the last ten years of his life. But Caroline could never ride the tide of success without immediately plunging further into the abyss. Naples was in festival mood during her visit, which unfortunately gave opportunities for the usual displays of dishabille. Pergami shared and encouraged her delight in dressing up, or rather not dressing up. Under his influence, and with his aid, she appeared at one masquerade successively as a Turkish peasant, a Neapolitan peasant and the Genius of History. Her friends claimed in retrospect to find no fault with these costumes, but no one complained that she was overdressed. 'The Princess of Wales is playing all sorts of tricks all over Italy,' Lady Melbourne recounted in January 1815. 'They say of her "*Mon dieu, est-ce là la vertu opprimée dont nous avons tant entendu parler?*" ' Caroline herself saw things rather differently. '*Je mène la vie la plus tranquille du monde*,' she wrote from Naples on 9 January 1815.

The news of every outrage that she committed, as well as of many that she did not commit, was swiftly carried back to England on the wings of gossip; and the stories lost nothing in the telling. 'Everything, be assured, that in any way, decent or indecent, relates to the Princess, is known here,' warned a guest at Brocket Hall, where Lady Melbourne held court, as early as October 1814. Moreover, there were sources of information considerably more menacing to

Caroline than the inevitable purveyors of royal tittle-tattle. Brougham
had been perfectly right to warn that spies would dog her footsteps
wherever she went. The English government, acting on the Regent's
instructions, kept careful track of Caroline from the very beginning
of her continental travels.

Possibly, indeed, there was more than mere observation involved. It
has been suggested that the Marchese Ghisilieri was acting as an *agent
provocateur* when he thrust Pergami forward as a potential employee.
The principal espionage operation, however, was conducted through
the court of Hanover, more particularly through the Baron Freidrich
Ompteda, the Hanoverian envoy in Rome. Ompteda's orders were
'to locate himself as close as possible to the Princess with the object
of accumulating such evidence as can be brought up against her
in Court'. He met Caroline in Rome and followed her to Naples
where he appears to have succeeded in planting informants among
her servants. Caroline knew that she was under surveillance – '*Naples
est actuellement tout rempli d'espions*,' she wrote in January – but
she did not at this stage suspect Ompteda.

There was plenty for the spies to report. Though one should
be wary of accepting the testimony of those who knew perfectly
well what they were being paid to discover, in Naples Pergami
was swiftly elevated from the position of lowly servant to that
of principal organiser of Caroline's affairs. The execution of his
duties apparently necessitated a bedroom in close proximity to that
of the Princess. Perhaps as a result of these household arrangements,
Ompteda noted on 20 January that there had been a violent quarrel
between the Princess and her English suite. It is certainly true that
Keppel Craven and Lady Elizabeth Forbes left Caroline's service at
Naples, and Sir William Gell shortly afterwards. To be charitable,
this may have been simply because they did not want to commit
themselves to a long stay on the continent, or in Gell's case on the
grounds that he was suffering from gout, rather than because they
recoiled in disgust from the Princess's behaviour.

The festivities at Naples ceased abruptly on 5 March when the
news of Napoleon's escape from Elba arrived. King Joachim departed
with declarations of support for his old chief, and Caroline, who had
in any case by now decided that she detested Naples, also moved
northwards. By the time that she reached Civitavecchia, the port

for Rome, her English suite was reduced to Lord Frederick North and his sister Lady Charlotte Lindsay. The tiny party took ship for Leghorn, courtesy of the Royal Navy, in the frigate HMS *Clorinda*. In the course of this voyage Pergami sought out the ship's surgeon, to whom he recounted the hardships that he had suffered on the Russian campaign. 'In particular,' Dr O'Ryan recorded, 'he consulted me for pain and debility of back, loins and hips: he felt, as he expressed himself, as if those parts were frozen and rendered him perfectly indifferent to women, in short, that he lost all desire for the sex ever since his sufferings in the Russian campaign.' The mystery of Caroline grows deeper and deeper. Could it be that her relations with Pergami, which on the surface hardly appeared susceptible of misinterpretation, were in reality, like so much else in her life, an elaborate blind designed to make everyone think the worst? Or was Pergami, in his crude way, merely attempting to deflect the all too well justified suspicions of the *Clorinda*'s crew?

When, at the end of March, Caroline reached Genoa, the English ambassador fled in alarm. The French ambassador's daughter, however, remained to record her impression of the Princess of Wales with a typically Gallic attention to the improprieties of dress.

> There was a kind of phaeton constructed like a sea shell, covered with gilding and mother-of-pearl, coloured outside, lined with blue velvet and decorated with silver fringes; this was drawn by two very small piebald horses driven by a child who was dressed like an operatic cherub with spangles and flesh-coloured tights, and within it lounged a fat woman of fifty [almost forty-seven, in fact] years of age, short, plump, and high-coloured. She wore a pink hat with seven or eight pink feathers floating in the wind, a pink bodice cut very low, and a short white skirt which hardly came below her knees, showing two stout legs with pink top-boots. A pink sash which she was continually rearranging added the finishing touch.

The ubiquitous Ompteda was also in Genoa, a far more faithful shadow than Caroline's English attendants. Lady Charlotte Campbell had joined her at Genoa only to leave again after the Princess moved on to Milan in mid-May. She had daughters, she explained to her friends, and could not allow them to stay where there was such an example. For a time Caroline had no ladies-in-waiting. Pergami proved only too eager to supply the loss. His sister Countess Oldi became *dame d'honneur*; another sister, Faustina, was responsible for the linen; his brother Louis became an equerry; his cousin Bernardo received the grandiloquent title of Prefect of the Palace; and another cousin, Francesco, was put in charge of the accounts. Pergami's young daughter Victorine also came to live in the household, and was much petted by Caroline, whom she addressed as 'Mamma'. Her real mother, in fact, seems to have been the only member of the favourite family not to find a position with the Princess. The departure of Dr Holland in the course of a visit to Venice in July 1815 completed the dissolution of the attendants who had left England with Caroline.

At Genoa, however, Lieutenant Hownham, formerly one of the boys adopted by Caroline at Blackheath, had joined his benefactress. He took an instant dislike to Pergami who, he noted, was encouraging the Princess in both the worship of Napoleon and the loathing of England. Whereas previously Caroline had given the impression of contemplating a limited period on the continent, she now sounded another note. 'Tell Mr Brougham', she wrote to Lady Charlotte Lindsay in October 1815, 'that I will never return to England unless the Duke [the Prince] or the Grand Duke [King George III] should die or my daughter desperately want to see me.'

On her return from Venice in July Caroline bought a large villa, which she proceeded to make still larger, on the shores of Lake Como. The house was renamed Villa d'Este after the Guelph family of Este, from whom the Princess was descended. To the delight of the local inhabitants she constructed a road from the villa to the nearby village of Grumello; to the horror of the respectable, Pergami, now rejoicing in the rank of Chamberlain, took his place at the Princess's table, upon which he had but lately waited. The Baron Ompteda, needless to say, was on hand to observe these happenings, offering money to a servant if he would reveal exactly where Caroline slept and obtain keys to her apartment. Brougham, in London, wrote in December 1815 that 'the accounts of the Princess of Wales are worse and worse . . . My opinion is, that they will be afraid to touch her – at least until they have evidence of *English witnesses*; for no Italians would be believed.'

It might be thought that Caroline, having taken possession of her splendid new villa, would have appreciated a lengthy period of retreat. In November 1815, however, she set out on travels far more ambitious than anything she had previously attempted, nothing less than a Mediterranean tour that would end in the Holy Land. Perhaps her restlessness was unassuaged; perhaps she wanted to be away while the works on her house were completed; perhaps she needed to escape from the awkward problem of her ever-escalating expenses. She must also have realised that only in remote and distant parts could she achieve the privacy required to savour Pergami's charms to the full. At this stage she was still so far from recognising the real source of danger that she asked Ompteda to accompany her on her travels. The Baron declined on grounds of ill health, and in Caroline's absence continued his work of suborning the servants at the Villa d'Este.

It was a motley crew that set sail with the Princess from Genoa in HMS *Leviathan* under the incongruous salute of two lines of battleships. There were Pergami and his sister, William Austin, Hownham, one Michela Schiavini from Pergami's home town of Crema, a *maître d'hôtel* called Hyeronimus, and a Dr Mochetti. To Hownham's disgust, the first port of call was Elba, where the Princess slept two nights in Napoleon's house, carrying off a book and a billiard cue by way of souvenirs. There followed four months in Sicily during which Caroline demonstrated her ability to cope with the roughest conditions. In Syracuse she stayed in a miserable shack with bare walls and rats, 'thirty or forty of them in a troop'. At Catania she had her portrait painted for Pergami, choosing to pose as the repentant Magdalen, with 'her person very much exposed'. For once, though, Caroline herself was being subjected to embarrassment. The *Leviathan* having departed, the *Clorinda*, the ship on which she had sailed the previous year, was offered as a replacement; and the *Clorinda*'s captain drew the line at sitting at the same table as Pergami. In the end the Princess's party was compelled to hire a polacca, a type of Mediterranean merchant ship. The Chamberlain whom Captain Pechell had spurned, meanwhile, became the Baron del Franchino, by dint of Caroline's judicious purchase of a Sicilian estate.

On 1 April 1816 the polacca, after a door in the sleeping quarters had been nailed up with the apparent intent of securing discreet access between the Princess's and Pergami's cabins, left Sicily for a three-day (and exceedingly rough) voyage to Tunis. Caroline was delighted by the welcome accorded to her by the Bey; delighted also to discover that in the Bey's harem the women were especially prized for their fatness. The most favoured member, indeed, was 'so exceedingly fat as not to have been out of her room for several months'. This was encouraging, as was the number of presents that the Bey showered upon his guest. England, Caroline made clear, would not profit by his munificence. 'I shall certainly send them no antiquities, not even of my o[wn]self, good sound antiquite.' After a fortnight or so, notwithstanding the Bey's blandishments, she sailed off westwards across the Mediterranean to Malta, where she secured the appointment of Pergami as a Knight of Malta, and thence to Athens, which she reached on 8 May. She spent a few days indulging her undoubtedly genuine, if superficial, interest in antiquities; she also, more familiarly, attended two balls at which 'she dressed almost naked and danced with her servants'. Thence she continued to Constantinople (early June); to Ephesus, where she slept in a shed among (as it was recorded in ascending horror) 'horses, mules, Jews, Turks'; and onward via Cyprus to Acre, scene of Sir Sidney Smith's exploits, on 2 July.

There can be no doubt that Pergami, among his other virtues, was an efficient organiser. A few days sufficed to assemble the wherewithal for the journey southwards to Nazareth and Jerusalem. The party travelled by night on horseback, and though for the last hour or two of these nocturnal stints Caroline had to be propped up in her saddle by attendants, she never complained of any hardship. On 11 July, 668 years after the visit of Eleanor of Aquitaine, the Princess of Wales, with her accustomed sense of the fitness of things, entered Jerusalem riding on a donkey, Pergami as ever at her side. The symbolism was not lost on Caroline's chambermaid Mademoiselle Demont. The scene, she wrote, put her in mind of 'the Day of Palms, on which our Saviour made, in the same manner, his entry into Jerusalem. I imagined I beheld him, and inwardly made comparisons: for assuredly, if anyone can in any way resemble our great Saviour, it is this excellent Princess.' The tastes of the excellent Princess, however, remained eclectic. While in the Holy Land she acquired the services of an Arab dancer called Mahomet whose obscene gestures greatly amused her. Pergami collected another honour, being made Knight of the Order of the Holy Sepulchre. The Princess also created her own decoration, the Order of St Caroline, 'to recompense the faithful knights who have had the honour of accompanying her on her pilgrimage to the Holy Land'. The Baron del Franchino, needless to add, was appointed Grand Master.

Having investigated Bethlehem, aand discovered it to be 'a wretched habitation indeed', the party embarked from Jaffa on 19 July. Since the Governor of Jerusalem had presented Caroline with horses, in addition to which there were two donkeys (for Victorine) and two lion cubs on board, the return voyage was far from comfortable. Caroline and Pergami found the noise so disturbing that they preferred, both of them, to sleep under a tent, one tent, on deck. External drama was afforded by a threat from pirates, though Caroline appeared as immune to fear from this source as from all others. Nevertheless, by the time she landed in Italy, after many delays due to quarantine problems, she was completely exhausted. While disembarking she slipped, a mishap which called into question her forthcoming visit to the Pope. 'What will His Holiness say when he sees my black eyes?' she wondered. 'He will think I have been fighting.' By the end of September 1816, however, she was back at the Villa d'Este, and surely ready, at last, for a period of rest and calm.

'My palace is most *superbe*,' she pronounced with satisfaction after inspecting the works completed in her absence. The tranquil atmosphere which she must have desired, however, was not forthcoming. Almost immediately Baron Ompteda's machinations were discovered, whether through the loyalty of a someone he had attempted to bribe, or through the sharp vigilance of Pergami. The servants, Caroline triumphantly noted, '*all refused* to speak *ill of me* and even refused the money which [Ompteda] offered them very riskelly'. Ompteda was given a chilling reception when he appeared at the Villa d'Este: after being first ignored he was then presented with a huge key, supposedly to symbolise his office as a Hanoverian Chamberlain, actually in reference to his nefarious attempts to obtain a key to Caroline's chamber. To add to his troubles, the stalwart Hownham challenged him to a duel, while Caroline, in order to prevent the combat that she herself had inspired, prevailed upon the

Governor of Milan to ban him from the region. Ompteda attempted to save face by offering to fight in Mannheim, an invitation which, very sensibly, Hownham found himself unable to accept.

Yet the disappearance of Ompteda did not end the espionage, which continued under the auspices of a Peninsular War veteran called Colonel Browne. At the beginning of 1816 the Foreign Secretary, Lord Castlereagh, had stated precisely what objects were in view. The first aim was to procure sufficient evidence for ending the Regent's marriage. 'But', Castlereagh continued, 'there is another most important object short of Divorce, viz: – to accumulate such a Body of Evidence as may at any time enable the Prince to justify himself for refusing to receive the Princess in this country, or to admit her to any of those Honorary Distinctions, to which his Wife, if received into his Court and family, would be entitled.' Evidently Caroline would never be free from surveillance until she had surrendered her rights as prospective Queen.

Perhaps it was the realisation of this fact which, early in 1817, sent her once more on her travels, this time across the Alps into southern Germany. But however the places changed, the accounts of the Princess remained distressingly familiar. A German woman who saw her in Carlsruhe in March 1817 described 'an elderly, stout little old lady in a scarlet riding habit . . . With what loudness and unconstraint the scarlet amazon talked and laughed, whilst she boldly mounted her horse, so that her dress was lifted up high – very high – and the shocked people of Carlsruhe, who were assembled in great numbers, got a sight of flesh-coloured tights!' Caroline could not but notice that the official welcomes extended to her were becoming, under the Regent's instructions, less and less warm. In Vienna, where she arrived in April, there was no official welcome at all: the Emperor absolutely refused to receive her at court.

The sense of shadows closing in was enhanced by grave financial troubles. Ever since Caroline had left England she had spent money without any restraint. Her travelling expenses were colossal: for example, her first journey to Naples in 1814 had cost £10,000. Yet when she declared that 'Economy' was one of the motives for her peregrinations, she may have had a point. The stationary Caroline was even more extravagant than the moving Caroline. She had paid £7,500 for the Villa d'Este, £2,000 for the road that she constructed there, and £20,000 for building works and furniture. After her return from the Holy Land she had bought Pergami a villa in Milan, and two other houses in her own name. As the debts mounted she resorted to more and more dubious means of bridging the gap. In the spring of 1817 she stooped (or Pergami stooped) to criminal means to raise funds. A letter of credit for £2,500 was presented in Venice signed by Thomas Coutts, save that the signature appeared 'as like T.C.'s as it was like the great Moghul's'.

Caroline's Italian bankers, meanwhile, were refusing to surrender the jewels which she had deposited with them. There was but one solution: the Villa d'Este must go. In the summer of 1817 she succeeded in negotiating its sale to an Italian banker, reserving some rights for occasional residence. Henceforward, her main house would be the Villa Caprile, near Pesaro on the Adriatic coast. 'I am very happy here, in this wonderful climate,' she wrote soon after moving in. She looked forward to hearing news of her daughter Princess Charlotte, who had married Prince Leopold of Saxe-Coburg in the previous year. 'I shall now soon be a Grand Mother,' she enthused at the end of October 1817, 'and I trust to Haven [*sic*] that then all cabals against me will be at an *End*. I am a well established old lady and no more scandals can be created about poor me: besides the great world I have quite given up, and England I shall probably no more see.'

Caroline had heard very little from her daughter since going abroad. The conniving role she had played in the Captain Hesse affair had become known to the Regent at the end of 1814, giving him a fine opportunity for the display of moral outrage. Charlotte was directed to copy out the following: 'I promise upon my honor never to write from this moment directly or indirectly to [my mother], that all kind of communication shall cease, & that I will abstain from seeing her when she comes to England.' For a time Charlotte remained true to this undertaking, though she was allowed to send a letter to her mother when her uncle the Duke of Brunswick was killed at Waterloo.

After her engagement and marriage she may have written more regularly. Vague rumours of Caroline's scandalous life reached her. 'I am in despair of what you tell me about a courier,' she wrote to her friend Mercer Elphinstone at the end of 1815. 'Surely, surely

. . . there can *be nothing there*, a *low, common servant*.' Later, as it appeared that the first suspicions were all too justified, she changed her tune. 'I can only conceive my mother to be out of her mind, for no one in their common or right senses can have acted as she has done.' Later still she appeared to have become resigned. 'As to my mother taking a flight to Turkey, I should not wonder at it, as it is quite possible for her to do anything strange & out of the way.' It was only natural that Charlotte should occasionally give way to exasperation. 'As soon as I am Queen, I shall have my mother shut up, because she is mad,' Madame Lieven remembered her saying.

And then, suddenly, Charlotte was no more. She died on 5 November 1817 after giving birth to a stillborn child. The dreadful news came to Caroline fifteen days later, not as is sometimes alleged, through unofficial channels, but through a letter from Prince Leopold's Private Secretary delivered to her by the King's Messenger. There could have been no harsher blow. To die before one's children must be the wish of every parent, and more especially should one die before a child whom one has selfishly abandoned. Now that Charlotte was gone, Caroline did not fail to recognise her merits. 'England, that proud country, has lost everything in losing my ever beloved daughter,' she wrote, 'and I have not only to lament a darling of a Child, but my only truly warm and attached friend.' She had, in fact, lost a great deal more. Charlotte's death at once negated the value of what she had suffered in the past and undermined her hopes of future recompense.

Pergami found this an appropriate moment to preach economy: since it was not the custom to wear mourning in Italy, the Princess should not waste money putting her household in black. For once Caroline overruled her Chamberlain. Yet, being Caroline, she accoutred herself in what an observer called 'the *oddest mourning* I ever saw; a white gown, with bright lilac ribbons in a black crepe cap'. Outwardly, indeed, it very soon appeared that she had quite got over the calamity of her daughter's death. Even in the very moment when she first heard of the tragedy her remorseless egoism threw up a defensive barrier against grief. At least, she pronounced, Charlotte 'will never know all the torments her poor mother has suffered or will suffer'. The death of Charlotte, however, intensified Caroline's credo of despair, that this life is a meaningless bagatelle, unworthy of the least tribute to respectability and decorum. 'From henceforth', she determined in the wake of her loss, 'I will do just as I please. Since de English neither give me de great honour of being a Princesse de Galle [*sic*], I will be Caroline – a happy, merry soul.' In short, there would be no change of policy, save that the reckless bravado with which she lived this life was increasingly interspersed with a sense of higher expectations from the next. 'I may hope for some happiness in another world,' she wrote in 1818. 'I no longer look for it in this one.' So she lived on, a desperate, disappointed woman with nothing to lose, and a spirit that dared venture to the uttermost.

The great question, which everyone discussed and no one could resolve, was whether Caroline would be content to eke out the rest of her life in Italy, or whether, when George III finally died, she would return to England and demand to be recognised as Queen. For the moment she was given to discoursing on country delights. 'I only trust', she wrote to Sir William Gell in February 1818, 'that the few years I have still to live to pass *tranquille* in a quiet removed place. I have given up for ever the great world and nothing can or shall bring me back to it.' Sir William, who had christened Caroline 'Mrs Thompson', was never at all convinced by this line. 'I am told "we" are very happy,' he had reported from Italy. 'Mrs Thompson declares she is in paradise . . . At present, "we" completely despise England, and hate all its inhabitants; but we are apt to change our opinions, and I fancy when good King George the Third walks off, "we" shall choose to go and show ourselves as "*Queen*".'

That was the prospect that the Prince Regent dreaded above all others. He could become quite emotional on the subject, declaring his intention of 'unshackling myself from a woman who has for the last three and twenty years not alone been the bain & curse of my existence, but who now stands prominent in the eyes of the whole world characteriz'd by a flagrancy of abandonment unparalelled [*sic*] in the history of woman & stamped with disgrace and dishonour'. To further a divorce, in August 1818 he ordered a commission to proceed to Milan and gather evidence against Caroline, thus giving official recognition to the system of espionage that had prevailed ever since Caroline had left England. By the beginning of 1819 the

Prince believed that he possessed sufficient evidence to rid himself of his wife.

And what of Caroline's supporters? Brougham sent his brother James out to Pesaro in March 1819, to investigate Caroline's intentions and to estimate the strength of the evidence which had been collected against her. James doubted whether cast-off servants would prove reliable or convincing witnesses, but he harboured no illusions about the nature of Caroline's relations with Pergami. The villa had been bought in the Chamberlain's name, and he ran it as though he were the master. '*His* house and grounds, *his* plate, *his* ordering everything, he even buys her bonnets, this I saw, and all his family quartered upon her.' The sleeping arrangements also presented no mystery: 'they are to all appearances man and wife, never was anything so obvious. *His room* is close to hers, and his *bedroom* the only one in that part of the house.'

Yet, in stark contrast to other English reports, James Brougham declared Pergami to be 'a plain, straightforward *remarkably good sort of man* . . . people all like him'. Caroline also was extremely popular locally on account of her generosity and charities. She seemed perfectly content. The house resembled a cottage rather than a palace, though Caroline had added two large wings in order to accommodate a total establishment of some eighty people. 'She came here first for retirement and oeconomy [*sic*] to pay her debts, and now likes it here so much that she seems determined to live and die here.' She gave Brougham the impression that she was eager to strike some deal with the government, and even suggested that she would settle for the absurdly low lump sum of £100,000, less than three times her current income.

No doubt she meant what she said at the moment of speaking, just as later in the same year she meant it when she wrote that she was 'prepared for a Trial in Westminster Hall'. Any hint that the Regent was planning some kind of process against her instantly rekindled her fighting spirit. Brougham, meanwhile, was attempting, with questionable motives, to negotiate a settlement with the government. His interest in Caroline as a potential force in English politics had dwindled with the death of Princess Charlotte, and he may have calculated that, if he could prevent her coming back to England, a grateful administration would find some suitable reward.

At all events, acting on the basis of his brother's letter, but without troubling to inform his client (he later claimed that he did not want to commit her), he began in June 1819 to sound Carlton House on the possibilities of an agreement. The proposal was that Caroline would agree to stay out of the country and renounce her future title of Queen in return for a pension of £50,000 a year.

These negotiations, however, could hardly succeed without the consent of the principal person concerned. Brougham therefore proposed meeting Caroline in the south of France in the autumn of 1819. Caroline agreed, and proceeded to Lyons, to Aix and to Marseilles. But Brougham did not appear. His legal duties, he suddenly discovered, did not allow him to leave England. Perhaps he was afraid that, if he stood revealed as a government agent, Caroline would dismiss him; and he did not mean to be dismissed when her return to England, however unwise for herself, would afford unparalleled opportunities for her legal counsel. In private he now referred to his illustrious client as 'that old bore'. Caroline, on her side, was more than ever suspicious of him after his failure to come to the south of France.

The absence of a solid, disinterested adviser, with sufficient force of personality to command Caroline's obedience, was crucial at this point. On 10 February 1820 at Leghorn, where she had broken her journey back from France, she heard that she had become Queen of England, King George III having died on 29 January. Imperiously she demanded that one of His Majesty's ships should convey her back to England, but having made that gesture she seemed content to continue southwards to Rome, where she remained for some weeks.

Two slights, however, hardened her resolve to return. First, the Pope, acting under pressure from the heretic island, refused to grant her the honours normally accorded to a sovereign's consort. His Holiness, it was explained to Caroline, had received no official notification of her presence, and therefore 'does not know that the Queen of England is in Rome'. Secondly, Caroline heard that George IV, on the morrow of his accession, had ordered her name to be removed from the list of royalty to be prayed for in the Church of England liturgy. This gratuitous insult deeply affected the Queen, who henceforward dismissed the chances of reaching a satisfactory agreement with so vindictive an opponent. Either, she believed, she must stand forth as a vilely traduced woman, to whom all rights and privileges were owing, or she would be branded as a degraded slut with no claims on anyone. So long as there was the least imputation of guilt in any proposed settlement, how could she be sure that the terms would be honoured? Parliament would hardly rush to vote supplies to a proven adulteress. She knew her husband well enough: he would not scruple to turn her loose in Europe without either funds or royal status. No, she must either fight or risk humiliation. Given her reckless courage and her delight in a conflict, there could never be any doubt which she would choose.

Caroline knew that, as always, she might look for massive popular support. The Prince Regent's unpopularity had not instantaneously disappeared with his elevation to the throne. The government too was widely detested for its reactionary and repressive stance against manifestations of popular discontent. 1819 had been the year of the Peterloo Massacre in Manchester, when eleven workers were killed and over four hundred wounded by troops firing into a crowd. For five years the country had lived under a restrictive code. Magistrates searched houses at will, press freedom was curtailed, the Habeas Corpus Act was suspended. Caroline's return would at last offer radicals an opportunity of striking back, of uniting all the myriad strands of discontent into one great movement. 'A Queen's Party is forming,' wrote Anne Cobbett in February 1820. 'If she comes to England there will certainly be a row, many will espouse her cause out of mere *obstinacy* to the new King.' Alderman Wood, one of the leaders of radicalism in the City, and an active supporter of Caroline's since before she went abroad, had kept her informed of the powerful currents of opinion in her favour. He had his reward. In April 1820 Caroline wrote to tell him that she was returning to England, and asked him to join her at Calais. Wood, more anxious to please than Brougham, met her in Burgundy. With Pergami still in attendance the party moved northwards, reaching St Omer, just across the Channel, at the end of May.

'My mind is in a state that is *not to be* described,' wrote King George IV as the return of Caroline became imminent. 'How lucky', he remarked, 'that my daughter is dead. How much worse even this affair would have been for me if she had lived.' The Cabinet, trapped between the King's determination to be divorced and the gathering popular sympathy for Caroline, at last took serious alarm. Ministers were severely handicapped by their faith in Brougham, whose continued assurances that he would prevent Caroline from entering the country were still unaccompanied by any useful action. In April he had been sworn in as the Queen's Attorney-General, but when, in the same month, the government sought a settlement he once again failed to communicate the proposition to his client. The Duke of Wellington would later remark upon the error that the Cabinet had made in expecting so much from Brougham. 'It is the only mistake we have made,' he said, 'but it was a big mistake.'

Eventually, at the beginning of June, the Prime Minister positively ordered Brougham to hurry over to St Omer to attempt an eleventh-hour agreement. Since, however, the terms offered specifically stated that Caroline was not to be given the title of Queen 'or any title attached to the Royal Family of England', she contemptuously rejected them; and Brougham had no influence whatsoever in making her reconsider. That very day, 4 June, she left for Calais, where she chartered a boat and early the next morning set sail for England. Pergami did not accompany her, and if Caroline felt any regret at the parting she never showed it.

6

In England, after all, there were stimulants considerably more powerful than sated post-menopausal lust. From the moment that the Queen came ashore at Dover she was regaled with popular enthusiasm and devotion. 'Her blue eyes were shining with peculiar lustre,' reported an observer at Dover. The Brunswicker who knew no fear was going into battle. Alderman Wood's radical friends had whipped up the crowds in her support, and the acclamations multiplied as she approached the capital. In London the mob dragged her coach triumphantly through the streets. When the procession passed Carlton House, Wood rose to give three cheers and Caroline demonstrated her wifely loyalty by shouting 'Long live the King.' George IV had prudently retired to Windsor; his sentries no less prudently presented arms to his wildly fêted queen. Caroline stayed her first three days in London at Alderman Wood's house in South Audley Street, while her supporters gathered outside in their thousands to express their devotion, quite careless of her guilt or innocence. 'God save Queen Caroline', they cried, 'and her son, King Austin.' To be a supporter of the King, or a member of the government that was preparing to defend him, was to put both property and life at risk. Even the troops called out into the streets afforded no security. The windows of prominent Cabinet ministers were smashed, and the Duke of Wellington enjoyed another of his memorable encounters with the base *canaille*. Being approached by a gang of workmen armed with pickaxes and demanding that he should show his support for the Queen, he reacted with his usual aplomb. 'Well, gentlemen, since you will have it so, God save the Queen – and may all your wives be like her.'

The King was not by nature a brave man. Nevertheless, faced with the prospect of a reign blighted by the importunities of his consort, he showed an immovable resolution. The very day that Caroline arrived in London, he sent the evidence that the Milan Commission had collected against her down to the House of Commons, urging that it be given 'immediate and serious attention'. He had 'the fullest confidence . . . that the House . . . will adopt that course of proceeding, which the justice of the case, and the honour and dignity of his Majesty's crown, may require'. A commission of the House of Lords was appointed to investigate the documents, while attempts continued to find a compromise that would save the necessity of publicly indicting the Queen. On 9 June Caroline professed herself ready 'to consider any arrangement that can be suggested consistent with her dignity and honour'. It was too late now, though, to accept any settlement short of outright victory without appearing to be running away from the Milan Commission evidence. By 24 June it was clear that the negotiations had failed. On 4 July the Lords committee reported that the documents which they had examined provided evidence of 'conduct . . . of the most licentious character'. Next day, Lord Liverpool, the Prime Minister, announced in the House of Lords a Bill of Pains and Penalties under which Caroline would be declared guilty of adultery, deprived of the title of Queen and divorced from the King. Twenty-five years of sparring between husband and wife were over. The gloves were off for the decisive round.

The date for the second reading of the Bill, when the Queen's guilt would be debated, was fixed for 17 August. The delay gave time for scandal to ferment. Society buzzed with expectation and excitement, the unending flow of salacious gossip being thrillingly intermingled with prognostications of riot and revolution. There was no other subject of conversation but 'the great and frightful cause', and only the ultra-fashionable found it within themselves to be bored. 'An entire summer missed – and all for the mistress of Mr Pergami,' complained the clever and aristocratic Madame Lieven, wife of the Russian ambassador, on 25 June. Yet even Madame Lieven found her well-bred ennui hard to maintain against the Queen's effrontery. Within a few days of her return Caroline was demanding a private interview with her husband. At the end of June, acting on the advice of her radical allies, she went to the theatre, in order to give the public further opportunity of expressing its rapture that she was once more among them.

She was now living off Portman Square, 'a wretched little lodging' by Madame Lieven's lights, but one which quite failed to damp Caroline's spirits. 'I will be crowned,' she told her advisers, as though in touch with some supernatural power. There was in truth little rational basis for such confidence, but her mood proved infectious. The radical press, which commanded all the ablest cartoonists and many of the most brilliant writers, was pouring forth propaganda on her behalf. On 3 August Caroline moved again, courtesy of her old friend Keppel Craven, to Brandenburgh House in Hammersmith. Here every day deputation after deputation of working men would arrive to pledge their loyalty. Written messages of support flooded in from all over the country. Most alarmingly of all, rumour had it that the troops called out to curb the demonstrations in the Queen's favour were openly drinking her health. The King, it seemed, could hardly survive her exculpation; the government appeared hardly less threatened by the prospect of her disgrace.

August 17, when the Bill would be debated, at last arrived, and Caroline appeared as brazen as ever. Though she must have known that scurrilous evidence would be brought against her, she announced at the outset that she would attend the debate in the House of Lords regularly in order to confound the witnesses with her presence. Her drives to Parliament from the house in St James's Square which she had taken for the duration were triumphal progresses. 'For the first time . . . since the early days of her untoward marriage', according to one report, Her Majesty rode in 'an equipage furnished by Government, and suited to her rank in the state', a beautiful coach with six horses. She took her seat in the House of Lords, by another partial account, 'with becoming grace and dignity. She was dressed in black sarsenet, very richly trimmed with lace; a large white veil partially concealed her features, and, falling in a tasteful drapery on her bosom, rendered her figure not merely interesting but highly commanding.'

Creevey, jotting down his notes in the House of Lords, saw her rather differently. 'I had been taught to believe she was much improved in looks as in dignity of manners; it is therefore with much pain I am obliged to observe that the nearest resemblance I can recollect to this much injured Princess is a toy which you used to call Fanny Royds.' (This was a Dutch doll with a round bottom, weighted with lead, which assumed an upright posture no matter how it was set down.) Creevey was sitting behind Caroline – 'such a back for variety and inequality of ground as you never beheld . . . She squatted into her chair with such a grace that the gown is at this moment hanging over every part of it – both back and elbows.'

There is no space in this essay to cover hearings which occupy nearly 1,400 closely printed pages in the record. What emerges most forcibly from the account is the fantastic incongruity of the proceedings, especially during the first weeks while the prosecution lawyers (or, more properly, the advocates of the Bill) were attempting to establish Caroline's adultery with Pergami. The House of Lords was in session, the Queen of England entered, their Lordships rose in respect, the Queen sat down – and then this same august assembly attended to a succession of Italian servants giving evidence of this same Queen's conduct in terms which still shock, even in the liberated twentieth century. The demands of ceremonial were scrupulously fulfilled; the proofs of adultery were assembled in all their immemorial squalor. Their Lordships heard of clothes that appeared in disarray, of clothes that did not appear at all, of bedrooms that had been rearranged for proximity, of tents that had been shared, of sheets that had been stained, of boards that creaked, of two chamber-pots that were not only full but discovered under the same bed. The Princess of Wales, deposed one witness, had her hand 'in the small clothes of Mr Pergami'; Her Royal Highness, confirmed another, who claimed to have seen the happy couple asleep in their carriage, 'held her hand upon the private part of Mr Pergami, and Pergami held his own upon that of Her Royal Highness'.

Exactly what testimony was heard in Caroline's presence is difficult to ascertain, for there were days on which she did not appear. Sometimes, too, she would leave the chamber (their Lordships would rise) in order to retire to a private room where, quite unconcernedly, she would enjoy a game of backgammon with Alderman Wood. She had, she remarked, only committed adultery once in her life, and that was with Mrs Fitzherbert's husband. It was difficult to know whether she was absurdly courageous or completely mad.

Yet, as long as the debate continued, none of the evidence against Caroline shook her popularity. The crowds that supported her remained perfectly indifferent to her guilt or innocence. They cared only that she had been ill treated by her ridiculous husband, and that a detested, reactionary government was endangered by the prevailing storm. 'When she emerges after one of these scandalous sessions,' reported an astonished Madame Lieven, 'she is greeted with respect and enthusiasm, not by the mob – make no mistake about that – but by the solid middle classes who have won England her reputation for virtue and morality.' Madame Lieven had long since abandoned the attempt to be bored. 'We shall only get out of it by blood-letting,' she concluded after picking up wild rumours that the Queen had distributed £9,000 among the troops. 'As it is not my business to be brave, I am feeling thoroughly frightened; and, if anything happens, I shall run away.'

On 7 September, when Caroline travelled down the river in a state barge, some two hundred thousand collected on the banks and bridges to cheer her on her way. 'There was not a single vessel in the river that did not hoist their colours and man their yards for her,' reported Creevey, 'and it is with the greatest difficulty that the watermen on the Thames, who are all her partisans, are kept from destroying the hulk which lies off the H. of Commons to protect the [Italian] witnesses in Cotton Garden.' Six days later Creevey, sitting in Brooks's, heard shouting in the street. 'It was, I may say, the *Navy of England* marching to Brandenburgh House with an address to the Queen.' Thousands of sailors took part in the procession, 'all well-dressed, all sober – the best-looking, the finest men you could imagine ... When the seamen take such a part, the soldiers can't fail to be shaken.'

Moreover, for all the sordid allegations against Caroline, the passage of the Bill of Pains and Penalties remained uncertain. Brougham proved himself a consummate advocate in defence. Caroline had been close to dismissing him before the case, fearing, understandably enough in view of his manoeuvrings during the previous year, that he possessed no real stomach for the fight. At the very beginning of the hearings in the House of Lords, however, Brougham disposed of that criticism in the most effective manner possible, by savagely threatening George IV. He was delighted to say, he announced with hypocritical unction, that he had *at that time* no intention of producing any recriminatory evidence concerning the King's own behaviour; he was perfectly confident of defeating the Bill without adopting such a course. 'But when necessity arrives,' he went on, 'an advocate knows but one duty, and, cost what it may, he must discharge it.' What Brougham meant, he explained in his memoirs, was that he was quite prepared to impeach the King's own title to the crown under the Royal Marriages Act, by bringing forward proofs in his possession that George IV had married Mrs Fitzherbert in 1785.

He showed equal ruthlessness in cross-examining the Italian witnesses. There was, indeed, something almost unsporting in the spectacle of a brilliant Scottish lawyer using his rapier intellect first to expose shortcomings in the evidence of illiterate Italians and then to destroy the unfortunate victims with coruscating sarcasm. The first witness had been a former servant of Caroline's called Theodore Majocchi. His appearance in the House had been a sensation: Caroline had fixed him with a terrible look and cried 'Theodore, Theodore, oh no!' (Or did she, as some thought, actually shout '*Traditore, traditore*'?) Majocchi's evidence at first appeared conclusive against the Queen. Cross-examined by Brougham, however, he was transformed into a shifty dago forever parroting '*Non mi ricordo*', 'I do not remember', in a hopeless attempt to parry the merciless interrogation. A dangerous prosecution witness had become a caricature Italian: '*Non mi ricordo*' became the catchphrase of the season. Brougham also had some success in implying that the Italian witnesses had been bought by the Milan Commission. Interestingly, this was a line espoused by Byron, avidly following events from Italy. 'I hope the Queen will win,' he wrote, '– I wish she may – she was always very civil to me. – You must not trust Italian witnesses – nobody believes them in their own courts – why should you? For 50 or 100 Sequins you may have any testimony you please – and the Judge into the bargain.'

On 7 September the Prime Minister expressed the government's willingness to withdraw the divorce clause from the Bill, evidence of his growing unease about the likely outcome. Some further witnesses from Italy decided, in view of the treatment accorded their colleagues, to remain at home. On 3 and 4 October Brougham's speech opening the case for the defence was an extraordinary *tour de force*: over eight hours he maintained the clarity of his arguments, the elegance of his phrasing and the sharp edge of his wit at the highest level. The performance was all the more remarkable because Brougham, having received his brother's letter from Italy, could have been in no doubt about Caroline's guilt. Nor, in private, did he trouble to disguise his opinions. '*She is pure in-no-sense*,' he would jest at dinner parties. 'I can believe in any folly on the part of that woman,' he remarked in more serious vein at the beginning of September. Creevey, a shrewd observer, believed 'it is not going too far to say that he absolutely *hated* her'. In public, however, Brougham maintained the mask of the tribune of the people bent on the rehabilitation of a much injured woman.

Some of Caroline's friends, Lady Charlotte Lindsay, Sir William Gell, the Hon. Keppel Craven and others, were equally economical with the truth in testifying to the propriety of her life abroad. Less satisfactorily, Lieutenant Hownham, called for the same purpose, was unable to avoid admitting that Pergami had slept under a tent with Caroline on the polacca returning from the Holy Land. Hownham attempted to retrieve the situation by asserting that Her Majesty had never taken off her clothes at night while on board ship. This gave Copley, the Solicitor General, the opportunity to instruct their Lordships that clothing need be no bar to adultery. Caroline had been wearing a morning-gown; Pergami a loose Tunisian robe – 'if such obstructions as these were effectual, what was to become of the population?' As Copley was a well-known lecher his views commanded both amusement and respect. Another awkward moment for the Queen occurred when Denman, Brougham's able colleague in defence, concluded his excellent summing-up by quoting Christ's words to the woman taken in adultery: 'If no accuser can come forward to condemn thee, neither do I condemn thee: go, and sin no more.' This was an odd text to cite in relation to a supposedly guiltless woman, and odder still because Denman genuinely believed in Caroline. As Brougham tersely remarked, 'The fool thinks her innocent.'

This delusion, according to Lord Montagu, was not shared by more than three peers. At the conclusion of the debate, however, the Whig opponents of the government seized eagerly on the view of their leader Lord Grey, who considered that the Queen's guilt had been inadequately established by the evidence, and that in any case a Bill of Pains and Penalties was an inappropriate means of proceeding against her. These doubts were reinforced by the ever-continuing popular hubbub in Caroline's favour: on 30 October, for instance, when the Brass Founders bore a crown in procession to the Queen, Creevey estimated that there were a hundred thousand people in Piccadilly to cheer them on. The vote on the second reading of the Bill on 6 November resulted in a majority in favour of only twenty-eight (123 to 95), which was universally regarded as a moral defeat for the government. Caroline issued a statement in which she 'most deliberately, and before God' asserted her innocence: 'she awaits, with unabated confidence, the final result of this unparalleled investigation'. Madame Lieven saw her coach in Bond Street on 7 November, 'escorted as usual by some hundreds of scallywags . . . The Queen passed by, throwing me a withering glance. I saw two enormous black eyebrows, as big as two of my fingers put together: the contents of two pots of rouge on her cheeks: a veil over everything. She looks completely brazen.'

At least, though, Caroline now had some cause for confidence. When the vote was taken on the third reading, on 10 November, the majority for the Bill was down to only nine votes (108 to 99), a derisory figure considering that Cabinet ministers and government placemen accounted for over twenty of the Ayes. The government dared not proceed with the Bill in the House of Commons, where Brougham might well carry out his threat of recrimination. The

Prime Minister therefore announced immediately after the vote that the Cabinet had decided to withdraw the Bill.

Caroline was sitting in her ante-room close by the Lords chamber when the news of the government's capitulation was brought to her. She uttered not a word: 'she looked fixed and insensible as a statue'. Later, in her carriage, her tension relaxed and she burst into hysterical tears. In the streets her supporters went wild with delight. For three days and nights London (and much of the country besides) was *en fête*: cannons boomed, bells pealed, the whole West End was illuminated. 'They never stop cheering in the streets,' Madame Lieven complained. Caroline was quick to press home her advantage. On 13 November she pledged that she would not go abroad, as she had thought of doing before the abandonment of the Bill; and Keppel Craven, acting as her Chamberlain, demanded that she should be given a palace and establishment worthy of her exalted station. Caroline was determined, though, to keep her radical support. 'If my enemies had prevailed,' she told her sympathisers in the City of London, 'the people, who are now feared, would have been despised; their oppression would have been indefinitely increased.' In future she would 'live for the people'. The Queen attained her apotheosis on 29 November when she proceeded through the streets in triumph to a service of thanksgiving at St Paul's. *The Times* reported that the crowds which lauded her were the largest in the history of the capital. Caroline, far from revelling in the occasion, apparently looked very cross, especially after being forced to leave her carriage open to the cold and fog on her return from the cathedral.

For victory left her quite undeceived. 'No-one, in fact, cared for me,' she said at the end of the House of Lords debate, 'and this whole business has been more cared for as a political affair than as the cause of a poor forlorn woman.' Her judgement proved to be abundantly correct. The service in St Paul's turned out to be the high-water mark of her fortunes, from which the tide of her popularity rapidly began to recede. The country, having supped greedily on sensation for six months, began to rediscover other topics of interest and concern. Whereas in the heat of partisanship it had been obligatory to dismiss the evidence against the Queen, few, in more reflective mood, could believe her fit for her position. Her radical supporters, moreover, were amazed to discover that the government did not fall. Gradually it appeared that the withdrawal of the bill after a narrow majority had been secured was the shrewdest possible political stroke. Caroline was denied both the vindication of acquittal and the martyrdom of persecution; she was neither innocent nor victim.

In the Commons the Tory majority remained secure, so that an attempt made by the Whigs in January 1821 to have Caroline's name re-introduced into the Anglican liturgy was easily defeated. Agitators against the government, with the disappearance of the bill that united them, split once more into squabbling factions. Caroline's potential as a figurehead for the oppressed multitudes was further diminished in January 1821, when she accepted a pension of £50,000 a year. Nor was she likely to gain support in polite society. 'The fact is,' she acknowledged, 'I have lived so long among Turks, Jews, and infidels, that I am not fit for good company.' By February 1821 the Queen, who had been the most popular figure in the country only two months before, could no longer rely on easily earned plaudits, even at the theatre. By contrast, when the King went to Drury Lane and Covent Garden on 6 and 7 February, there were fulsome outbursts of loyalty. 'What is public opinion worth?' wondered Madame Lieven. 'The King ... was received with as much enthusiasm as his father and more – as if he had never instituted proceedings against his wife, as if he were the most virtuous, the most fatherly, the greatest of kings.'

Brougham, conscious of the changed atmosphere, felt obliged to make a solemn declaration in the House of Commons of his belief in Caroline's innocence. (He even changed his line in private. The Queen, he would confidentially whisper, was not an adulteress but a '*child-fancier*': her main interest had been in Pergami's daughter Victorine and not in the man himself.) Caroline herself reacted to her declining fortunes by multiplying the evidences of her instability. 'I trust that in the month of *March* next I shall be in Paradise again, I mean to say in *Italie*,' she wrote to Sir William Gell on 23 January, though at the same time she was negotiating, albeit unsuccessfully, for a fourteen-year lease on Marlborough House. She announced her intention of attending a Drawing-Room at Buckingham House that she might personally present her husband with a petition. She claimed to be gifted with second sight. 'I tell you that in a few months my name will be heard in all the churches,' she informed the Duke of Bedford on 20 February. 'Nothing is needed but courage and patience, and I have both.' Increasingly, such pronouncements appeared only as the pathetic bluster of a deranged woman. There were reports that she was drinking. 'She is sinking apace', wrote Lady Williams Wynn, 'into that entire state of Insignificance which, I verily believe, is to her more mortifying than even disgrace would be.'

In April the Foreign Office received a report that Pergami had just left Paris and was on his way to England. This intelligence, if correct, would certainly have produced the drama on which Caroline throve, but in fact the former courier showed no disposition to leave the comfortable villa at Pesaro, whither he had returned after parting from his mistress at St Omer. Whatever the relations between them had been, they were over. 'If I should go upon the Continent,' Caroline now wrote, '*I should go to a different and new atmosphere.*' Of all the Pergamis that had been in her service none but the Countess of Oldi was in evidence at Brandenburgh House.

Still, Caroline had always been capable of manufacturing her own sensation, and the approach of the King's coronation, fixed for 19 July, provided an irresistible temptation. On 29 April she wrote to the Prime Minister announcing her intention of attending the ceremony. Clearly relishing the resumption of hostilities, she also enclosed a letter to the King. His Majesty was required to appoint ladies 'in the first rank' to bear her train. Also, 'the Queen being particularly anxious to submit to the good Taste of his Majesty most earnestly entreats the King to inform the Queen in what Dresse the King wishes the Queen to appear in, on that day, at the Coronation'. It was a wonderful tease, but Caroline, unfortunately, had no idea of abandoning her campaign at the stage of an epistolary prank. The Prime Minister's letter, in which he bluntly transmitted the King's pleasure that she should stay away from the coronation, was brushed aside. For years Caroline had dreamt of the ceremony in Westminster Abbey as the hour of her justification and revenge. Brougham, who ironically enough had put this idea into her head in 1814, now pleaded that she should desist, but all entreaties were vain. She would attend her husband's crowning, and damn the consequences. Indeed, inspired, as she said, by a vision, she wrote to the Archbishop of Canterbury demanding a separate ceremony on her own account.

'Your Majesty's greatest enemy is dead,' they told George IV about this time, referring to the death of Napoleon. 'Is she, by

God?' the King returned. Caroline, though, was only too evidently alive, and once more taking the popular pulse by visits to the theatre. 'The applause have [*sic*] been much in favour,' she reported with satisfaction. Coronation day arrived. Having somehow possessed herself of a ticket, Caroline appeared outside Westminster Abbey at half-past five in the morning (the early hour being calculated to ensure surprise) and demanded admission. With her, giving a fine example of courtly loyalty under pressure, were Lord Hood and Lady Anne Hamilton. After some wrangling the hapless doorkeeper was compelled to admit that he must allow the Queen of England to enter for the coronation service if she had a ticket. Caroline's attendants, however, were without tickets, and she uncharacteristically ducked the challenge of entering the abbey by herself. 'She flinched,' wrote Brougham, 'I verily believe, for the first time in her life.' At least, though, she had done enough to establish a grievance for propaganda purposes. After presenting herself unsuccessfully at the other doors of the abbey she proceeded to Westminster Hall, where preparations for the coronation banquet were under way, only to have her entry barred by the sentries. 'Let me pass,' she raged, 'I am your Queen, I am the Queen of Britain.' The door was banged in her face.

'The Bedlam Bitch of a Queen', Sir Walter Scott called her after this fiasco, forgetful of the hospitality which, as a younger and less eminent subject, he had enjoyed at Montague House. 'You cannot imagine the contempt she is held in here,' he added. 'I really think she is mad.' Caroline herself, though, did not appear put out by her humiliation at the coronation. She had long inured herself to the disapproval of the respectable, and in spite of some disagreeable cries ('Go back to Pergami') she had been enthusiastically received on her drives to and from the abbey. 'The crowd in the Broad Street of Whitehall was immense,' reported Creevey. 'All, or nearly all followed her and risked losing their places. They crammed Cockspur Street and Pall Mall, &c., hooting and cursing the King and his friends, and huzzaing her.' Back in the house which she had taken for the occasion she gave a merry breakfast party, and prepared for the next stage in the battle. There were plans for a tour of the north, in the hope of rousing support in the manufacturing towns.

Yet, as Lady Anne Hamilton later reported to Hownham, 'she has never had one hour's quiet sleep at a time ever since the 19th.

She exerted herself to keep up her spirits in every way, playing at all sorts of games, dancing and I am afraid taking ether, assafoetida and even laudanum, always saying – "Am not I gay, you see I don't mind it" – but she did mind it! – for it was worse even than taking her name out of the Liturgy – and such an affront that no foreign Court could receive her and that she knew full well. She said to Burnet, "the Doctors know nothing about me, it is here (pointing to her heart) but it shall never come out here (pointing to her mouth)." '

Suddenly, quite unexpectedly, Caroline was dying. Not only was her will broken; she was also suffering from the more prosaic complaint of an obstruction in the bowel. Her health had been unreliable for some time: she had been laid up with 'severe spasmodic attacks' in Geneva on her way back to England; and had also been feeling unwell, notwithstanding her defiant appearance, during the drama in the House of Lords. At the time of the coronation, it was said, she had taken 'nervous medicines & laudanum', which may account for the report that she had looked remarkably well as she drove towards Westminster Abbey. The first public sign that anything was seriously wrong came on 30 July when she went to Drury Lane to see a theatrical re-enactment of the coronation procession. At the end of the performance, an observer noted, 'She got up and curtsied to the Manager in a manner so marked – so wild – with a countenance so Haggard, the disease hanging over her at the moment that the person who saw her do so, without loving her, burst into tears to see Royalty and Pride so broken down and humbled.'

Thereafter her decline was rapid, though she retained command of her faculties until very near the end. She knew she was dying and accepted the fact with all her wonted fortitude. On Friday 3 August Brougham went to see her and attempted some conventional words of comfort as to her probable recovery. 'Oh no, my dear Mr Brougham,' she returned, 'I shall not recover and I am much better dead, for I be tired of this life.' She absolutely forbade any operation. Perhaps she would have done better to forbid any medical attention whatever, for the doctors strove to make up in quantity what they lacked in skill, prescribing enough medicine to physic a hundred people. 'Do what you please if it will be any relief to your mind,' she told them, 'but do not do it for my sake. I have no wish to live: I would rather die.' A heroic fatalism was the last mode through which her indomitable spirit expressed itself. '*Je ne mourrai sans douleur, mais je mourrai sans regret,*' she intoned again and again. 'I never beheld a firmer mind,' recorded Lord Hood, one of the bystanders, 'or any one with less feelings at the thought of dying, which she spoke of without the least agitation, and at different periods of her illness, even to very few hours of her dissolution, arranged her worldly concerns.' Her enemies had finally destroyed her, she said, 'but I forgive them, I die in peace with all mankind'. A saint could not have improved on this example of Christian reconciliation.

On 6 August her mind began to wander, and she spoke much of Pergami's child Victorine and of Alderman Wood's grandson – evidence perhaps, for Brougham's theory that children were always her chief interest. She left some diamonds to Victorine, a bequest that Brougham was careful to keep out of her written will. William Austin was the principal beneficiary of the estate. Extraordinarily, in these last days, Caroline made some belated obeisance towards discretion, giving orders that a diary which she had been keeping should be burnt. Perhaps the truth about her would have remained elusive even without this instruction: fact and fantasy were so intimately intermingled in her mind that it might have been difficult to separate them in her writings. Yet now before the final, the supreme reality she showed a resignation and a confidence that many cool and rational spirits might envy. There was within her, notwithstanding a lifetime's religious indifference, a perfect conviction of a better existence to come; and in truth in her case it would be a bleak afterlife that failed to fulfil such a hope. She died peacefully, 'without a groan or a struggle', at about half-past ten in the evening of 7 August 1821.

The world received the news according to the lights prevailing therein. George IV, reported Croker, 'was uncommonly well and gayer than it might be proper to tell'. *The Times*, out of antagonism to the King, mourned the passing of 'the greatest, perhaps the best woman of her day'. The worldly-wise, with Lord Castlereagh, considered that Caroline's death was 'the greatest of all possible deliverances, both to His Majesty and to the country'. Mr Creevey, by contrast, felt 'an infernal lump in my throat the most part of Thursday', although 'for herself I think her death is not to be regretted'. The pious, like Lady Anne Barnard, hoped that the

Queen's sins would be forgiven her. The sophisticated, like Madame Lieven, found occasion for wit: 'her death at the moment is a mere luxury; for alive she no longer inconvenienced anyone'. The radicals bemoaned the passing of a cause. 'I have never before known what depression of spirits was,' wrote Cobbett, 'but I feel it now.' Perhaps the most telling reaction, though, was 'the loud and lengthened shriek' set up by Caroline's female servants at the moment of her death. The Queen had always expressed the true democracy of the soul in her treatment of underlings.

She had wanted to be buried in the same vault as her daughter Charlotte in St George's Chapel, Windsor, but realised that the government would never permit this. Her will therefore left directions that she should be interred with her father and mother at Brunswick. On 14 August the funeral procession set off from Brandenburgh House to Harwich on the east coast. The occasion provided one last opportunity to muster a display of popular support: for the radicals, it seemed, the next best thing to Caroline live was Caroline dead. Expecting trouble, the government brought out the troops, and ordered that the Queen's cortège should proceed through Hyde Park, and then on a circuitous and northern route that would bypass the City. The mob, however, would have none of this. First it blocked the entrance to the park at Kensington, then made an unsuccessful attempt to stop the procession going up Park Lane. At Cumberland Gate (the present Marble Arch), a more serious challenge was mounted and the troops fired some shots. Two men were killed; a bullet passed through the hat of the coachman driving Caroline's hearse; and, not inappropriately, another shot struck Brougham's coach. Being unprepared to countenance a massacre, the magistrate in charge allowed the cortège through the City, where it was escorted by the Lord Mayor through the packed streets.

It was a wild and disastrous finale to Caroline's wild and disastrous life. At Colchester next day a silver plate bearing the legend 'Caroline of Brunswick, the injured Queen of England' was screwed on to the coffin, as she had instructed in her will. During the night it vanished, later appearing in the possession of Dr Lushington, one of the counsel who had acted for her in the House of Lords. Only the very last scene of all in England, as the corpse embarked from Harwich on 16 August, achieved any dignity. 'It must have been the most touching spectacle that can be imagined', wrote Creevey after hearing Brougham's account, '– the day magnificently beautiful – the sea as smooth as glass – our officers by land and sea all full dressed – soldiers and sailors all behaving themselves with the most touching solemnity – the yards of the four ships of war all manned – the Royal Standard drooping over the coffin and the Queen's attendants in the centre boat – every officer with his hat off the whole time – minute guns firing from the ships and shore, and thousands of people on the beach sobbing out aloud . . . It was as it should be – and the only thing that was so during the six and twenty years' connection of this unhappy woman with this country.'

Mary of Teck

1867–1953

I

'You are the big potato,' Field Marshal Smuts told Queen Mary in 1947, at a Buckingham Palace reception in celebration of Princess Elizabeth's marriage to Prince Philip of Greece. 'All the other queens', Smuts added in disdainful allusion to the several alternative varieties on display at the party, 'are small potatoes.' The Field Marshal's phrasing may not have been quite in Queen Mary's style; nevertheless she found no cause to question his judgement. Her life and example, after all, had helped to set the English monarchy on a new pinnacle of popular affection and respect, while the stern notions of duty which she embodied were the guiding lights of her son George VI, just as they later became the principles by which Elizabeth II would discharge her office.

There is no denying, however, that Queen Mary's personality exudes a certain chill. If her achievement grew out of her almost mystical reverence for the Crown, her failing was that she never experienced another emotion of similar power. In private no less than in public she became an institution, so that distance and reserve characterised even her relations with her own children. They all, to a greater or lesser extent, grew up with neurotic problems, for which the reach-me-down wisdom of the twentieth century has been quick to blame their parents. Mary's quarter of a century as Queen was succeeded by a few months in which the son to whom she could never speak intimately dealt, in the name of intimacy, a contemptuous blow at the monarchy which she held so dear. That the Crown survived the Abdication of Edward VIII with scarcely a blemish might well be ascribed to Queen Mary's strength; that it was ever so menaced has sometimes been attributed to her maternal shortcomings.

Yet the story of Queen Mary's own youth ought to serve as a warning against slick theories of parental determinism. Her background was peculiar enough to explain any extreme of neurosis and folly. If she emerged therefrom as a straight-backed, strong-willed and level-headed young woman, it can only have been because she possessed innate qualities of sense and character. From the human point of view this early period of her life is the most interesting, worth concentrating upon at the expense of the majestic monotony that informed her later years as Queen. To begin with, her parents were such an oddly assorted couple. Her mother, Princess Mary Adelaide, and her father, Franz Prince of Teck, shared an absolute conviction, which Queen Mary inherited, that to be royal is the greatest privilege which life can bestow. Beyond that, however, they had little in common. Most seriously of all, in the royal stakes which they both valued so highly Princess Mary Adelaide was a thoroughbred, whereas the Prince of Teck was a hack.

Princess Mary Adelaide, in fact, had more than breeding to her credit, being a clever, charming woman, who was generally popular on account of the manifold charities to which she lent her patronage. There was, it is true, the occasional dissenter from this view. 'Princess Mary is a spoiled child,' considered Queen Sophie of the Netherlands, 'spoiled by popularity I never understood, except she is popular because she is fat and looks so good humoured but is not.' Such criticism, however, found little support even in the malicious world of society, and none at all among the English people at large. Mary Adelaide's passage through the streets always produced hearty cheers, to an extent that sometimes grated on the sensitive ear of her cousin Queen Victoria.

Mary Adelaide was not disposed to quarrel with the Queen – she was not disposed to quarrel with anyone – but nor did she regard the monarch with any sense of inferiority. She too, after all, was a granddaughter of George III; and she too could reflect that her parents had made a noble sacrifice for the sake of the throne. Mary Adelaide's father, George III's seventh son Adolphus Duke of Cambridge, had lived happily as a bachelor for fifty-four years, but when the death of the Prince Regent's daughter Princess Charlotte threw the succession into the hazard, he loyally obeyed the call to procreation. His marriage in 1818 to a less than ravishing German princess, Augusta of Hesse, produced a boy who for a couple of months was actually heir presumptive to the English throne, until the parallel exertions of the Duke of Kent, an elder brother of Cambridge, yielded Princess Victoria. The Cambridge boy would become not King, but the notoriously reactionary Commander-in-Chief of the British Army in the latter part of the nineteenth century. The old Duke of Cambridge, however, having once accustomed himself to the idea of fatherhood, proved quite undeterred by the settlement of the succession. A second child, a girl named Augusta Caroline, followed in 1822. And then, after a prolonged breathing space, Princess Mary Adelaide made her somewhat surprising appearance in 1833.

The Cambridge daughters found solace for their removal from the steps of the throne in referring to themselves as 'the old royal family', a phrase designed to convey that their pure Hanoverian descent remained untainted, unlike that of Queen Victoria's offspring, by any admixture from Saxe-Coburg. Princess Augusta Caroline of Cambridge, who was both exceptionally sharp-witted and exceptionally conscious of her dignity, observed that her cousin Victoria was 'altogether very jealous of my position in society, as being very popular'. Such reflections came all the more easily because the Cambridge family was far from being overendowed with worldly goods. In Princess Augusta's case that problem was solved in 1843 when she married the heir to the Grand Duke of Mecklenburg-Strelitz. Her younger sister Mary Adelaide simply discovered that money was unimportant and spent accordingly. In consequence she suffered from a constitutional tendency towards debt, though kind friends and relations generally helped to keep the creditors at bay. It proved more difficult, however, to protect Her Royal Highness against the consequence of her other passion, which was eating. Queen Sophie did not exaggerate when she used the word 'fat': Mary Adelaide was mountainous. Those who collided with her on the dance floor – the Princess liked dancing – picked themselves up in a daze. In 1857 the American ambassador, less inhibited than the English courtiers with the facts, reckoned that she weighed about eighteen stone. Thereafter her development was most tactfully described in negatives. 'Mary C. is looking older', noted Queen Victoria in 1866, 'but not thinner.'

Suitors are not easy to discourage in the case of princesses, but Mary Adelaide had found the secret. Her family, however, could not have been more fussy about potential husbands if she had been a peerless beauty. An early candidate, the Prince Napoleon Jerome, known as 'Plon-Plon', the cousin of the Emperor Napoleon III, was dismissed by the Prince Consort on account of having lived a life of profligacy that had 'even disgusted the French'. The widowed King Victor Emmanuel II of Savoy was simply too Catholic. Various English aristocrats were found to lack the necessary royal qualities, while a stream of German princelings failed to come up to the mark. Gustave of Saxe-Weimar was too old; Prince Albert of Prussia was too young; Augustus of Württemberg could 'in no respect be recommended'; no more could Prince Waldemar of Holstein. The Duke of Brunswick proved unwilling. A second Saxe-Weimar prince suffered from *morgue* – and 'German prince's *morgue* which is like no other'. Prince George of Prussia and Prince Maurice of Altenburg were no sooner considered than they plunged into alternative marriages. 'Alas, poor Mary,' the cry went up, again and again, from Queen Victoria, 'I really am in despair about it! It is all her mother's fault for she should have taught her better manners.' Lord Clarendon, no doubt, was nearer the mark when he reflected that no German prince would venture upon '*so vast an undertaking*'. The best hope, perhaps, had been in 1856 when it really seemed that Prince Oscar of Sweden might assume the burden. But the Prince came, he saw – and he beat a hasty retreat.

By her early thirties Mary Adelaide, who was rarely disposed to view life tragically, had reconciled herself to being 'a jolly old maid'. She reckoned, however, without the pertinacity of her relations. It was the Prince of Wales who finally found a willing suitor, in the handsome form of Franz Prince of Teck, a young officer (four years younger than Mary Adelaide) on the staff of the Austrian Emperor. The Prince of Teck's looks had won him the sobriquet of '*der schöne Uhlan*'; nevertheless, in royal terms his antecedents were flawed. His father, Duke Alexander of Württemberg, might have been heir to that principality had he not, in striking anticipation of his great-grandson Edward VIII, forfeited his claim to the throne by contracting a morganatic marriage to a beautiful, and intelligent, Hungarian countess. Franz was the only boy of three children from this marriage, which ended dramatically in 1841 when the Countess was trampled to death by horses at a military review.

As the Prince grew up he found himself in an equivocal position, at once royal and, due to his father's morganatic marriage, not quite royal. He was also poor, and his doubtful status disqualified him from consideration in the marriage market at the stuffier German courts. Queen Victoria, however, once she had got over the fact that the Prince of Teck had been recommended by her abhorred son, took a more liberal view. Always susceptible to the male form divine, she swept away all objections to welcoming the young man in the family. It was particularly fortunate that Prince Franz's looks were of the dark variety. 'That constant fair hair & blue eyes makes the blood so lymphatic,' the Queen wrote to her eldest daughter. 'Dear Alix [the Princess of Wales] has added *no* strength to the family . . . Darling Papa – *often* with vehemence said: "We *must have some strong dark blood*."'

To the general amazement the Prince of Teck, said to be 'a passionate admirer of thin, pale beauties', appeared eager to unite his strong dark blood with Mary Adelaide, a contract that was sealed with all possible speed at a wedding on Kew Green in July 1866. Queen Victoria allotted the newly-weds the rooms in Kensington Palace that she had occupied as a young girl. Here, next year, a daughter was born, and liberally christened with eight names: Victoria Mary Augusta Louise Olga Pauline Claudine Agnes. It was not surprising, perhaps, that Agnes, Teck's preferred choice, came last, nor that the child's mother settled for calling her simply 'May'. This name, after the month of her birth, would only fall into disuse when its holder became Queen Mary. Queen Victoria, who was a godmother, pronounced the baby to be 'a *very* fine child . . . very pretty features & a dark skin'. A year later, however, this favourable impression was modified. Princess May was 'not as handsome as she ought to be'. Worse, by the time that the child reached seven the Queen judged her to be 'very plain'. The Prince of Teck's genes had disappointed: his daughter had fair hair and blue eyes. A second child, a boy called Adolphus ('Dolly'), born the year after Princess May, showed the same lamentable colouring. Only the second and third boys, Francis ('Frank'), born in 1870, and Alexander ('Alge'), born in 1874, would manifest the triumph of the strong dark blood.

Queen Mary is one of those people whom it is difficult to imagine as a baby. Very early in her childhood she appeared as she would continue – capable, studious and conscientious. On one point she was especially firm. Notwithstanding her father's German background, which seemed so clearly reflected in her own penchant for order and discipline, Princess May always insisted that she was 'English from top to toe'. This disposition was only enhanced by regular visits to German relations and by her first acquaintance with French. '*Je puis vous dire aussi le "bon jour", et beaucoup d'autres mots en français*,' she wrote to her Cambridge grandmother, '*mais je serai toujours une vraie petite Anglaise.*' Yet the question of her nationality was never as clear-cut as she liked to imagine. Although she would become the first queen consort in nearly four hundred years whose mother tongue was English, her voice retained a hint of her father's guttural German accent. And the lesson which her parents ground into her before all others was not so much that she was English, as that she was an English *princess*. At no point in her life would she be inclined to shirk either the privileges or the duties of that exalted status. The rogue genes in her family were monopolised by her brother Frank, who achieved the distinction of being expelled from Wellington for throwing the headmaster over a hedge.

Princess May did suffer, however, from one considerable handicap. As a young girl her sterling qualities were largely obscured by her paralysing shyness. Perhaps she was born with this disability; certainly the circumstances in which she found herself would have made it more pronounced. Her mother was an accomplished rattle, quite prepared to talk through day and night together, so that it was all too easy for Princess May to fall into the role of silent bystander. At the same time Mary Adelaide's colossal bulk, which was always attracting sniggers, must have caused acute embarrassment to her self-conscious daughter: when, for instance, Mary Adelaide arrived to watch a dancing class she had to be accommodated on *two* chairs. Again, the young girl's visits to her terrifying old Cambridge grandmother, who was so bent that visitors had to kneel in order to converse with her, inspired a lasting horror of invalids and illness. At the other end of the scale, the required attendance upon The Poor, while it did much to develop Princess May's social conscience, did nothing to diminish her social unease.

The troubles of her parents also left their mark. Mary Adelaide's passion for entertaining meant that, even with only one establishment, the Tecks were always short of money. But Mary Adelaide was by no means content to live in Kensington Palace alone, least of all after she had made the convenient discovery that the effluvia from the Round Pond was bad for her children's health. In 1879 she succeeded in persuading Queen Victoria, very much against that shrewd monarch's better judgement, to let the Tecks use White Lodge, in Richmond Park, as a second home. Its relatively secluded position must have appealed to Princess May; nevertheless, her parents were now living beyond their means in two places at the same time. Mary Adelaide carried this difficult situation off with her usual style. At one of her charity meetings she proposed a special vote of thanks to a local tradesman, 'to whom we all owe so much'.

The Prince of Teck, on the other hand, deeply resented the humiliating position in which he found himself. Mary Adelaide made no attempt to adapt her carefree life-style to his Teutonic notions of punctuality and efficiency; and she would simply laugh off his explosions of fury. 'You can't think', Queen Mary told a lady-in-waiting many years later, 'how tactless my mother was with my father sometimes.' Teck had imagined, when he married, that his brother-in-law the Duke of Cambridge would find him a post in the Army, but the best position he received was Honorary Colonel of the City of London Post Office Volunteers. Not until 1882, when the Prince was attached to Lord Wolseley's staff for the Egyptian campaign, did he hear any call to action; and then 'Francis's impaired vision', as the Duke of Cambridge called it, proved an insurmountable handicap. 'I don't think he enjoys himself out here at all,' the Duke of Cumberland told the Queen. The Prince's main contribution to the campaign was to accuse his batman of stealing his kit. In future, he declared on his return home, he would fight only in the German Army.

So, for the rest of his life, the Prince of Teck was left with nothing to do but to choose wallpaper, collect antiques, rearrange the furniture, work in the garden, and play the piano. He brought considerable talent to all these activities, particularly to interior decoration, an ability which Princess May inherited. She was always his favourite child, treated with sympathy even while he showed himself a martinet with her brothers. But his affection for his daughter did not still his discontent. He began to conceive that he had been forced into his marriage, remarking with venom that he would have done better to marry some wealthy industrialist's daughter. There he was most certainly mistaken, for his dissatisfaction crystallised into an obsession with status and precedence. 'There is a dreadful feud going on between Leiningen and Teck on the question of precedence,' the Queen's Private Secretary reported in 1878, '& I hear that Teck would go nowhere, where there was a chance of meeting Leiningen.' The root of Teck's unhappiness was that, after all his sacrifices, he remained simply His *Serene* Highness. Not until 1887 did Queen Victoria accord him the magic *Royal* status, and under the stress of this disappointment his temper deteriorated further. Princess May's youth was punctuated by his rages, though they were never directed at her.

By the early 1880s the Teck family's debts, at some £70,000, had exhausted both the generosity of friends and the patience of relations. The Duke of Cambridge exerted pressure upon his sister to give up White Lodge: Mary Adelaide responded by having the house redecorated. At Kensington, however, the local tradesmen were threatening to send in the bailiffs, and even Mary Adelaide's insouciance was not proof against the threat of public bankruptcy. In 1883 the Tecks were obliged to submit to a familial scheme whereby credit was provided in return for their undertaking to live on the continent, where, it was optimistically imagined, a more modest life-style might alleviate the financial strain. The Kensington Palace establishment was broken up and the contents auctioned off; White Lodge, to which Mary Adelaide steadfastly refused to abandon her claims, was shut up.

To the sixteen-year-old Princess May, rigorously instructed in the supposedly untouchable mystique of royalty, this turn of events must have come as a profound shock and humiliation. Her previous experience of the continent had consisted of summer holidays in the palaces of her German relations. Now her family was to be relegated to the economical obscurity of a hotel in Florence, where the Prince of Teck's habit of venting his spleen on hotel-keepers cannot have rendered acclimatisation any easier. 'My daughter feels homesick for White Lodge and is often quite melancholy,' the Prince reported. Nor did the delights of Italy provide any immediate consolation. 'We find Florence rather a dull place,' Princess May wrote home to her brother. The houses appeared 'so uncomfortably arranged and so dirty, and the people always smell of garlic'.

Princess May, however, was too intelligent and sensitive to maintain this blimpish indifference to the glories of Florence. Italy is proverbially the place where the inhibited English spirit achieves its liberation, and though this process was never completed in Princess May's case, its effects were perceptible. Hitherto her education had been in the hands of an uninspiring German governess, but now, as scholarly and stimulating guides conducted her through the streets and galleries of Florence, she began to experience the thrill, as well as just the duty, of learning. Very soon the girl who had found Florence dull was spellbound by its beauties, and devouring books about its history. She took Italian and singing lessons; she eagerly tried her hand at painting; she embarked upon her lifelong devotion to the theatre.

Best of all, she was able to meet people on a far freer and easier basis than had ever been possible at White Lodge. Emily Alcock, for instance, an American girl, became 'a great friend of ours', a friend, moreover, with whom Queen Mary would still be corresponding sixty years later. Of course Princess May did not suddenly cease to be shy; she never ceased to be shy. But during this Italian sojourn Thaddeus Jones, an Irish painter who had been taken up by the Tecks, noticed the strength of the seventeen-year-old girl. 'It was easy to perceive', he wrote, 'that, underneath her maidenly reserve, there was developing the quiet determination of the *maîtresse femme*.' Mary Adelaide never ceased to dominate all the conversation, but increasingly it was Princess May who brought order and common sense into the affairs of her unhappy family.

One morning in March 1884 the Prince of Teck woke up with his left side paralysed and his mouth slightly crooked. Mary Adelaide quickly diagnosed sunstroke and continued on her round of pleasure. The doctors experienced the greatest difficulty in convincing her of their own opinion, that the Prince had suffered a stroke. Although he slowly recovered the use of his stricken limbs he would never again be in full and reliable health. Over the next decade he drifted into a premature, if still explosive, decrepitude. With Mary Adelaide exercising her talent for distancing herself from the unpleasantness of life, and with the boys so often away at school, it was left to Princess May to provide whatever solace her father was going to get.

The notion that residence on the continent might curb Mary Adelaide's rate of expenditure had always been dubious, and by the spring of 1886 she had exposed its flaws so effectively that her Cambridge relations began to long for her homecoming. Queen Victoria thought that it might be as well if the exiles did not return to White Lodge, but Mary Adelaide refused to countenance such terms. She came back to England without conceding an inch. Indeed, the only reason that the Tecks did not go straight to White Lodge on their return was that Mary Adelaide would not condescend to live there until it had been – again – properly decorated.

The first important event in Princess's May's life after her return from Italy was her confirmation. Mary Adelaide had withstood pressure from her brother the Duke of Cambridge and from Queen Victoria, both of whom had been anxious that this event should take place about Princess May's seventeenth birthday, as was customary. But the fond mother had no intention of wasting the potential of this occasion while abroad. She knew that an English princess should be confirmed in a royal chapel, and she did not mean her daughter to forfeit a scintilla of her due. Princess May's confirmation in St James's Palace on 1 August 1885 not only made her a communicant of the Church of England: it re-established the Tecks in royal circles after their exile. Next year Princess May was invited to Windsor. Queen Victoria's keen instinct was beginning to divine that there might be more to the Teck girl than immediately met the eye. She still did 'not think May pretty', but she did judge her to be 'a very nice girl, *distinguée*-looking with a pretty figure'.

Princess May herself remarked that she was much too like Queen Charlotte (George III's notoriously plain wife) ever to be considered beautiful. The allusion, however, merely demonstrated that pride in ancestry came before more commonplace worldly vanity. Her appearance had a great deal more to recommend it than Queen Charlotte's. Photographs of Princess May do no justice to her 'wild rose' complexion, to the golden lights in her light-brown hair, to the piercing blue of her eyes. She is said to have been proud of her shapely legs, although inevitably these were assets concealed from the world at large. At least, though, the wasp waist was unmistakable, thrown into relief by the already massive superstructure – Queen Victoria's 'pretty figure'. Less satisfactory was the Princess's hair-style. High on top, close on the sides, with an artificial fringe in the front, it was Mary Adelaide's idea of a fashionable cut, although the style was already *passé* in 1880. Queen Victoria complained that it made women look 'like little *poodles*!' The forehead, she added, 'is always a pretty thing to see'.

The concealment of Princess May's forehead behind a fringe might be taken as a symbol for the way in which her mind and personality remained under wraps. She was an intelligent, presentable girl who wholly lacked allure. Clearly, she was unlikely to inspire a grand passion; yet without passion it appeared questionable whether she would ever marry at all. Insufficiently royal to claim the hand of a prince as of right, she had been brought up to think of herself as someone who should never settle for less. This difficulty was compounded by her family's financial troubles. Poverty not only deterred suitors: it made the Tecks hyper-sensitive about any threat to their status. The Prince, in particular, would froth with rage at any slight, real or imagined, to his daughter. At the same time Princess May was coming increasingly under the notice of her Aunt Augusta the Grand Duchess of Mecklenburg-Strelitz, a woman of decided views, acidulous judgement and ready pen. Aunt Augusta's religion was royalty and she reinforced her niece's devotion to the creed. When the elder daughter of the Princess of Wales became engaged to Lord Fife in 1889, there was much murmuring among the Cambridge clan. 'We are very glad for her because she has liked him for some years,' Princess May wrote to her aunt, 'but for a future Princess Royal to marry a subject seems rather strange don't you think so?'

She herself appeared inclined to be choosy even in the case of royal candidates for her hand. The fertile brain of her grandmother the Duchess of Cambridge was always throwing up potential husbands – the Grand Duke Michael of Russia, the Prince of Anhalt, the Prince of Naples. Princess May met the last of these prospects at a dinner in the Mansion House. 'He is extremely nice, clever, agreeable to talk to, talks English very well & seems altogether a nice boy,' she reported to Aunt Augusta. On the other hand, 'he is terribly short and not beautiful to behold'. That really was being unduly fussy: a doubtful entry to the royal matrimonial stakes could not afford to baulk at mere physical shortcomings. Later Princess May would show herself ready to entertain a far more alarming proposition than the Prince of Naples. What really alarmed her, no doubt, was the prospect of leaving England for ever. Or was Mary Adelaide's mind already dwelling on higher things?

The only alternative to marriage, and one that Princess May pursued for five years after the family's return from Italy, was to continue in the role of dutiful daughter in the strained family atmosphere at White Lodge. Her brothers called her 'the peacemaker'. There was, however, plenty to do besides easing the tension between her parents. Mary Adelaide, a Tory of the old school, responded generously to the sufferings of the London poor during the economic distress of the 1880s. Relief organisations which solicited her help found her generous with both her patronage and her time. She was even more generous with Princess May's time. Foremost among the charities in which the Duchess of Teck involved herself was the Needlework Guild, the members of which produced clothes for distribution to the poor. White Lodge became inundated with such articles, until it seemed that the house had been turned into a draper's shop. Yet Mary Adelaide, though liberally supplied with footmen, housemaids, dressers and laundrymaids, resolutely resisted the appointment of a private secretary. The hard slog all devolved upon Princess May, who managed both to keep chaos at bay within White Lodge and to conduct the interminable petty correspondences that charitable affairs entail. Princess May found letter-writing, whether business or social, a terrible chore, but she did it, as she did everything else, out of a sense of duty. At the same time she accompanied her mother on numerous charitable expeditions – visiting hospitals, attending functions, opening bazaars. There could hardly have been a better training for her subsequent role, remote though such a prospect must have appeared.

Princess May, indeed, was showing signs of becoming that most un-royal phenomenon, a bluestocking. This development was associated with the arrival in 1886 of a new tutor at White Lodge. Mlle Bricka was a French Alsatian of immense ugliness, formidable intellect and radical politics. Though she felt absolutely no instinctive admiration for royalty as such, she soon conceived a devotion for Princess May. Her charge was the pupil of every tutor's dream. 'I suddenly discovered that I was not educated,' Queen Mary later remembered. Her charitable work notwithstanding, she set aside six hours every day for reading under Mlle Bricka's auspices. George Eliot, Carlyle, Froude and Meredith constituted the lighter part of this programme, for it was the Blue Books on social and economic conditions that formed the staple of Mlle Bricka's diet. Princess May devoted every spare moment to her relentless quest for self-improvement, even contriving to get through Motley's *Rise of the Dutch Republic* while waiting for her mother to appear at meals.

Mlle Bricka elicited confidences that hardly matched Princess May's placid exterior. '*Je crois que l'atmosphère à White Lodge est très* depressing, *on y est toujours* guild *et* household worry mad!!!' the pupil wrote in her peculiar mixture of French and English at the end of 1886, '*et les choses importantes de la vie sont entièrement oubliées. Que mes sentiments sont beaux! n'est-ce-pas?*' The important things in life, for Princess May, were increasingly those of the mind; and the most fascinating of studies, she discovered, was the history of her own ancestors, a field which happily afforded more than enough material to last a lifetime. By 1890 Princess May appeared well on the way to becoming a confirmed spinster, whose intellectual resources would more than compensate for the denial of her by no means compelling emotional needs. As for social life, she had neither the inclination nor the aptitude for the gaieties of the London season. Princess May, her uncle the Duke of Cambridge remarked, 'has no conversation whatever'. What the Duke meant, of course, was that she had no small talk, a deficiency that counted for less at country house parties where there was better opportunity to get to know the other guests. Princess May enjoyed doing the rounds of the great country houses. It was even said that she attracted an admirer, Count Thaddeus Koziebrodzki, a Pole. But the man was a Roman Catholic and very far from royal. There could be no question of encouraging him.

It required a full-blown crisis within the royal family to wrench Princess May's existence out of its White Lodge backwater. The emergency centred upon Albert Victor (known as 'Eddy'), the eldest son of the Prince and Princess of Wales and therefore heir presumptive to the throne. It would be foolish, with a hereditary monarchy, to expect the line of succession to embody all human perfections: equally, though, the chances of genetics might reasonably have been expected

to throw up a more suitable prospective king than Prince Eddy. There
were, it is true, one or two points to be made in his favour. He was
not, as has been alleged, Jack the Ripper; nor is it definitely proven,
as has also been alleged, that he frequented homosexual brothels.
Nothing about him was malign. Within his immediate family, indeed,
he was greatly loved – 'dear Eddy', they called him, so 'good', so
'kind', so 'affectionate'. His fellow officers in the Army also liked
him, while women accorded him the full measure of charm and
attractiveness that they are wont to discern in those born upon the
steps of the throne. The fact remained, however, that Prince Eddy was
an imbecile. His tutor, despairing of ever interesting him in anything,
concluded that his condition 'must derive from some affliction of the
brain'. It was also hazarded that his incapacity derived from deafness
inherited from his mother, or, more optimistically, from some mild
form of epilepsy which might pass with maturity. Alas, in 1890, at
the age of twenty-six, Prince Eddy gave no sign whatever of maturity.
He was dissolute, listless, idle and feckless.

Efforts had been made to conceal his failings from Queen Victoria,
but to no avail. The Queen may not quite have plumbed the depths
of the problem, but she knew that Something Had To Be Done
About Eddy. When his parents, concentrating on damage-limitation,
suggested the young man should be packed off on a lengthy colonial
tour with prolonged periods at sea, Queen Victoria countered with
the idea of a journey around Europe. This proposal caused the Prince
of Wales some embarrassment. 'It is difficult to explain to you', he
wrote to his mother, 'the reasons why we do not consider it desirable
for him to make lengthened stays in Foreign Capitals.' Preferring not
to elaborate further, the Prince produced a counter-plan. 'A good
sensible Wife – with considerable character is what he needs most
– but where is she to be found?'

The answer, of course, was within White Lodge. 'Do you suppose
Princess May will make any resistance?' the Prince of Wales's Private
Secretary enquired in August 1891 of Sir Henry Ponsonby, his
opposite number on the Queen's staff. 'I do not anticipate any
real opposition on Prince Eddy's part if he is properly managed
& is told that he *must* do it – that it is for the good of the country
etc. etc.' This sanguine estimate of Prince Eddy's likely reaction was
well founded. Only when, in 1890, Queen Victoria had raised the

possibility of an alliance with Crown Prince Margaret of Prussia had he been moved to protest, for, as even the Queen admitted, the Crown Princess was 'not regularly pretty'. In the absence of positive ugliness, however, the tender passion danced about Prince Eddy's mind with the unpredictable abandon of thistledown on the breeze.

He had not, however, been fortunate in love. In 1889 he conceived an admiration for Princess Alix of Hesse, a German cousin who, though certainly regularly pretty, formed the decided opinion that marriage to Eddy would be a fate worse than death. So she married the future Tsar Nicholas II instead, and discovered death that way. Eddy immediately consoled himself for his disappointment by falling in love with Princess Hélène of Orléans, a daughter of the Comte de Paris, pretender to the non-existent French throne. This time his passion was reciprocated, but the match was impossible on religious and political grounds alike. Queen Victoria, who tended to take a romantic view of her grandson's character, considered that the thwarting of his love would inflict a wound from which it would take Prince Eddy many years to recover. Yet Eddy, even while pursuing Princess Hélène, had been writing love-letters to the beautiful Lady Sybil St Clair Erskine. His easygoing nature made no objection about a further transfer of affection in the direction of Princess May, though the subsequent news of Lady Sybil's betrothal did bring a twinge of regret. 'Don't be surprised if you hear before long that I am engaged also,' he wrote to his lost love, 'for I expect it will come off soon. But it will be a very different thing to what it might have been once . . . but still it can't be helped.' Thus obediently, if unenthusiastically, did Prince Eddy submit to his fate.

And what of Princess May? But for Prince Eddy's position she could hardly have viewed the match with anything but horror. In childhood her shy and retiring nature had always shrunk fastidiously from the rumbustious antics of her philistine Wales cousins. She must, moreover, have known something of the particular disabilities of Prince Eddy. But whereas the Princess of Wales, in her position of strength, had brought up her children to be wholly relaxed about status, the Tecks, as we have seen, clung like limpets to the privilege of being royal. It would have been inconceivable for Princess May to consider even for a moment the possibility of refusing an offer which would in all probability make her one day the Queen of England.

The first sign of what was in the air came in November 1891 when Princess May was summoned to Balmoral, together with her brother Adolphus. Queen Victoria, usually so jealous of her privacy, had suddenly been seized with an uncontrollable desire to get to know her better. The visit proved entirely satisfactory. 'May is a dear, charming girl, & so sensible & unfrivolous. – She was in great good looks,' the Queen wrote to the Duchess of Teck. Mary Adelaide experienced the rapturous happiness of a woman for whom a long-held and far-fetched fantasy had been magically transformed into reality. Her eager prattle was recorded by Lady Geraldine Somerset, formerly lady-in-waiting to the old Duchess of Cambridge and now an acid observer of the Duchess of Teck's triumph. 'P[rincess] M[ary Adelaide] informed me "the Queen has fallen in love with my children! *specially May!* She thinks her so well brought up! *so amusing*" (the very last thing in the world I should say she is!!).'

Prince Eddy, having been shown his duty, somewhat precipitately asked his appointed bride to marry him at a country house party at Luton Hoo in Bedfordshire in December 1891. Princess May, though she contrived some surprise, eschewed any coy attempt at resistance. 'Of course I said yes,' she recorded in her diary. 'We are both very happy.' Such are the circumstances in which a serious and intelligent girl may be brought to rejoice at the prospect of spending her life with a vacuous and dissolute zombie.

The Cambridge family was to be restored to what it had always regarded as its rightful position on the very seat of the throne. Yet the most royalty-conscious of them all, being also the shrewdest, did not deceive herself about what was involved for Princess May. Aunt Augusta, the Grand Duchess, while abundantly sharing Mary Adelaide's now gushing enthusiasm, could not avoid the uneasy feeling that her adored niece was being sacrificed to the Moloch which they all worshipped. For Queen Victoria it sufficed that Princess May was 'a *solid girl* wh. we want'; for the Grand Duchess there was more at stake. She loved her niece too well not to be uneasy. 'Do they care for each other?' she asked Mary Adelaide. 'It is an immense position and has ever been your heart's desire, but it is a serious, great undertaking for poor May, and to fill a Queen of England's position in the present times, a serious matter; she is such a dear, sensible and well endowed creature . . . God grant that he may become worthy of her.'

Princess May began her engagement by gamely detecting signs of improvement in her fiancé: the excitement, she thought, 'has woken him up'. This hopeful assessment of her situation, however, proved hard to maintain. The Prince of Wales kept stressing to his prospective daughter-in-law the need to 'keep Eddy up to the mark'. The Grand Duchess reiterated her concern for her niece's plight: '*all* will devolve upon her'. Queen Victoria wrote to explain that 'the trials in life in fact *begin* with marriage'. In the circumstances it was only to be expected that Princess May's initial euphoria should begin to dissolve. James Pope-Hennessy, in his surpassingly brilliant biography of Queen Mary, to which this account owes everything, produced an unattributed anecdote which indicates that the bride-to-be experienced serious qualms. 'Do you think I can *really* take this on, Mama?' Princess May enquired. The answer, from Mary Adelaide, could hardly be in doubt. But just in case such worries began to multiply, the wedding was fixed for the early date of 27 February 1892.

Whether Princess May could in fact have managed Prince Eddy was destined to remain one of the unsolved riddles of history. With brutal suddenness the whole problem was wrenched from her capable hands. On 4 January 1892 she went down to Sandringham with her fiancé. It was Prince Eddy's twenty-eighth birthday on 8 January; unluckily, though, he developed a slight chill and was unable to attend the celebrations. No one worried much: everybody had had the flu that winter. Even after incipient pneumonia was diagnosed on 9 January there seemed no real cause for alarm. Two days later the doctors pronounced that the patient was 'going on very satisfactorily', as indeed he proved in conversation with his brother and Princess May. By 13 January, though, he was delirious. 'Hélène, Hélène,' he called out again and again, with never a word for his attendant fiancée. The minor indisposition had suddenly developed into a major tragedy. For a few more hours the young man raved inconsequentially before the family assembled in his tiny and stuffy bedroom. Then, early in the morning of 14 January, Prince Eddy was no more.

2

Princess May's brilliant, if daunting, prospects had no sooner been attained than shattered. At the funeral, her father handed the Prince of Wales her bridal wreath of orange blossom to be placed on Prince Eddy's coffin, a gesture that would be immortalised by the inclusion of just such a wreath in Alfred Gilbert's memorial on the Prince's tomb. Whether Princess May's feelings for Eddy the man, as opposed to Eddy the prince, were as evanescent as the flowers or as enduring as the bronze, it is difficult to say. The secret remained locked so deeply in her soul that most likely it was forgotten even by her. In later life she never referred to Prince Eddy. Perhaps she had been fond of him, rather as one may become fond of a wayward child. And his death-bed scene had been harrowing in the extreme.

Yet when the press poured forth its saccharine prose about the romantic idyll of two young lovers being suddenly cut short by the cruel summons of death, it did rather overshoot the mark. Princess May defined her loss more restrainedly to Mlle Bricka as 'some vague dream of something pleasant having passed out of one's life for ever'. Queen Victoria also declined to subscribe to the prevailing cant. She felt as sorry as anyone for Princess May, in whom she had discerned the qualities of a future queen, but she also retained her unnerving capacity to state unacceptable truths. 'You know May never was in love with poor Eddy,' she remarked a few months after the Prince's death. Aunt Augusta went even further, expressing herself 'quite satisfied that May has never been in love and is *most* unlikely ever to be so'. This was one of the many excellencies which she observed in her niece, for whom she felt the most ardent sympathy. The Tecks were now back in their accustomed role of poor relations, and the Grand Duchess was never one to shirk the implications of such a reversal of fortune. The magnificent trousseau that had been ordered for instance: 'who will pay for it and for all the expenses incurred? this is a very serious consideration . . . It is hard enough to lose poor Eddy but to be still more ruined, cannot be expected.'

The return to White Lodge must have been depressing indeed. 'It is so difficult to begin one's old life after such a shock,' Princess

May wrote to her American friend Miss Alcock, 'even reading, of which I am so fond, is a trouble to me & I cannot settle down to anything'. And to Mlle Bricka, in March 1892: 'My father pulls me one way, my mother the other, it is not good to become selfish but sometimes I grumble at my life, at the waste of time, at the *petitesse de la vie* when one feels capable of greater things'.

For Princess May's parents, of course, the death of Prince Eddy had been a shattering blow. Mary Adelaide even confessed that for a moment her strong Christian faith had seemed to waver. By the end of February, however, she had discovered the appropriate note of Christian resignation. 'God is so loving and merciful,' she wrote, 'one feels there must be a *silver lining* to the dark cloud, albeit our tear-dimmed eyes cannot distinguish it.' In truth, her tear-dimmed eyes had already distinguished the silver lining with the utmost clarity.

The Duke of Teck, in the immediate aftermath of Prince Eddy's death, had embarrassed his family by wandering around Sandringham muttering 'It must be a Tsarevitch, it must be a Tsarevitch.' The Prince's meaning was not that his daughter should now become Empress of all the Russias. The reference was rather historical. Had not the Princess of Wales's sister Dagmar been betrothed to the Tsarevich Nicholas in 1865? And had not this same Nicholas died before the wedding could take place? Thereupon, did not Princess Dagmar proceed, in the following year, to marry Nicholas's brother Alexander, the new Tsarevich? Finally, the last chain in the Duke's reasoning, did not Prince Eddy have a brother, now heir presumptive to the throne? Princess May's fastidious mind may have shrunk from so speedy and so naked a transfer of interest. Her mother, though, was not a whit fastidious in such matters; and she possessed powerful allies. The Queen, the Prince of Wales, the entire English nation, were determined that the poor bereaved May of Teck should now marry Prince George. For Mary Adelaide it was simply plain duty to bring about this happy consummation.

A holiday in the south of France was obviously what her family required to help them recover from the gloomy events of the winter, so Mary Adelaide's friend Lady Wolverton was persuaded to rent a villa at Menton in March 1892. It was pure coincidence, surely, that the Prince of Wales had decided to take an apartment nearby on Cap

Martin at the same time; nevertheless, it was a coincidence that did not appeal to the Prince of Wales. Eager though he was for the match between Prince George and Princess May, he had never greatly cared for his cousin Mary Adelaide. To the Tecks' disappointment, Lady Wolverton was prevailed upon to alter her plans and take a villa at Cannes, some twenty-five miles from Cap Martin, rather than at Menton as Mary Adelaide had desired. Nobody can live entirely for pleasure, however, and the Prince of Wales, after a happy fortnight's holiday quite uninterrupted by his tedious cousins, directed his yacht and Prince George towards Cannes. For a few days Prince George and Princess May spent much time together. Of course they had known each other from childhood, had indeed walked hand in hand through the garden at Sandringham during the dreadful ordeal of Prince Eddy's death. But the transformation from cousins to lovers was not easily attained, even at a sovereign's command.

Prince George was a far stronger and more effective character than his brother had been. He was also distinctly more exercised over the choice of a wife. 'The one thing I could never do', he had told Queen Victoria in 1891, 'is to marry a person that didn't care for me.' It was not immediately clear to him how Princess May stood on that score. She was always reserved, and no doubt her mother's shameless eagerness for the match only increased her inhibitions. Two events, however, had helped to clarify Prince George's mind. First, another cousin, the pretty Princess Marie of Edinburgh, whom he had admired even to the point of proposing, announced her engagement to the Crown Prince of Romania. Secondly, in the spring of 1893 his mother took him on a Mediterranean cruise. While in Athens Prince George had some long conversations with his revered Russian aunt, Queen Olga of Greece, who declared herself a whole-hearted admirer of Princess May.

In the matter of choosing a marriage partner, as in attaining religious faith, certainty is often elusive, but by the time Prince George returned from the Mediterranean at the end of April he had made up his mind to take the plunge. And quite a leap marriage to Princess May must have appeared to a young man who had been accustomed to cavorting with a girl in Southsea, not to mention 'a ripper' shared with Prince Eddy in St John's Wood. But Prince George, no less than Princess May, had always been distinguished by his sense of duty.

His proposal was accomplished at his sister's house in Sheen on 3 May 1893. Princess May recorded the event in her usual prosaic style. 'We walked together afterwards (after tea) in the garden and he proposed tó me, & I accepted him.'

The whole business evoked savage reflections from Lady Geraldine Somerset, who could hardly support a second season of triumph for Mary Adelaide. 'It is clear that there is not even any pretence at love-making. May is radiant at her position and abundantly satisfied, but placid and cold as always, the Duke of York apparently nonchalant and indifferent.' (Prince George had been created Duke of York in the summer of 1892.) In so far as Lady Geraldine judged by appearances she was perfectly correct: the young couple did indeed suffer from considerable restraint in each other's company. Their correspondence, however, exhibited a dogged determination to overcome their inhibitions. 'I am very sorry that I am still so shy with you,' Princess May wrote to Prince George shortly after their engagement, 'I tried not to be so the other day, but alas failed, I was angry with myself! It is so stupid to be so stiff together & really there is nothing I would not tell you, except that I *love* you more than anybody in the world, & this I cannot tell you myself so I write it to relieve my feelings.' To which Prince George replied: '. . . Thank God we both understand each other, & I think it really unnecessary to tell you how deep my love for you my darling is & I feel it growing stronger every time I see you; although I may appear shy and cold.'

Evidently both parties did their best to experience the correct emotions. The pity was, though, that the written word would remain for the rest of their lives the sole medium through which they were able to express their very real affection to one another. Still, the wedding, on a matchless summer day (6 July 1893), went off perfectly; and they were not the kind who, having sworn absolute fidelity before Almighty God, could entertain any idea of being false to their oaths. To that extent at least, Queen Mary was more fortunate than the majority of queen consorts.

The Prince of Wales had given his son a house on the Sandringham estate as a wedding present, and it was to this 'glum little villa', as Sir Harold Nicolson called it, that the young couple repaired for their honeymoon. York Cottage was indeed an extraordinary residence for the heir presumptive of the greatest empire in the world. It had been created out of a building originally designed to accommodate the overspill of guests from the big house at Sandringham, and the result would hardly have satisfied a prosperous Victorian solicitor. The exterior appeared to attempt a fusion of Victorian Gothic with Tudor black-and-white. Inside, narrow passages connected tiny rooms, from some of which the light was effectively excluded by laurels growing without. Where the servants slept was a mystery: the Duke of York supposed that it must be somewhere in the trees. The bad quality of the building-work meant that it was impossible not to overhear conversation in the rooms adjacent, above or below. Before every meal the smell of cooking from the basement kitchen wafted through the house. There were few baths. Altogether, York Cottage must have appeared less than ideal to Princess May, who had inherited from her father a real flair for colour and interior design. To make matters worse her husband, no doubt with the intention of saving her trouble, had solved all questions of furnishing and décor by calling in 'Maple's man'.

The Duke of York simply loved York Cottage. Partly, his enthusiasm sprang from memories of childhood days at Sandringham. Also, though, the house itself perfectly suited his character. His early career had been in the Navy, and although he abandoned any active command after his marriage he retained the attitudes of the quarterdeck. In many respects he was a good man, conscientious, honest, as straight as a gun-barrel. These very virtues, however, sometimes caused difficulties. Though he was not deliberately unkind or cruel, he lacked the imagination to avoid being insensitive. His notion of comradeship consisted of the giving and taking of orders, and the interchange of rough, manly chaff. Intellectually he was equally limited, adopting as a defence the posture of a fossilised blimp who gave forth extreme conservative views on all matters of dress and behaviour. No one was encouraged to contradict, or even to disagree with him. His philistinism was a matter of pride, and certainly it appeared to be without a flaw. With one of the greatest collections of pictures in the world available to him, he chose to cover the walls of York Cottage with reproductions, while his study was lined with red cloth originally intended for the trousers of French soldiers. It was only pansies who cared for art.

York Cottage, in fact, was dear to him precisely because it was so ugly. No doubt the tiny claustrophobic rooms reminded him of the shipboard cabins in which he had passed his salad days. They also had the additional advantage of being too small for entertaining.

Princess May's fate appears as a feminine version of Hilaire Belloc's cautionary tale about Charles Augustus Fortescue, who always did what was right, gaining for his pains a rich ugly wife and a house called The Cedars, Muswell Hill. Likewise Princess May had kept the rules, done her duty, worked hard, eschewed frivolity . . . and received her reward. Moreover, in the early years of her marriage the greater destiny that awaited her must have seemed dispiritingly distant. Having committed herself to the sacred calling of royalty, she discovered that her new existence was as mundane, and far more restricting, than her former life at White Lodge. Fortunately she did not know that York Cottage would remain her country residence until Queen Alexandra's death in 1925. She did what she could with it, applying her talents to bring light, air and grace into the rooms. In positive moods she would refer to the results as '*gemütlich*', one of her favourite German words, meaning 'cosy'. But there was little opportunity to exercise her skill for furniture-arranging. 'One should really have in mind a doll's house,' she would say in unconscious anticipation of a future masterpiece.

Although the couple also had a dreary set of rooms in St James's Palace, York Cottage remained very much their spiritual home. The Duke of York's life-style, indeed, accomplished the remarkable feat of making Princess May feel positively skittish in comparison. George V's biographer Sir Harold Nicolson quite despaired of this phase in his subject's life. 'For seventeen years', he confided to his diary (though not to the official biography), 'the Duke did nothing at all but kill animals and stick in stamps.' Prince George was certainly a very good shot, and his stamp collection became one of the best in the world; nevertheless, these activities brought scant amusement to his wife. 'It was so stiff I would have turned cartwheels for sixpence,' Princess May wrote after one shoot. It must have been very stiff indeed.

The proximity of the big house at Sandringham was another blight on Princess May's existence. Relations with her in-laws were always uneasy. Alexandra, the Princess of Wales, adored her children; and although she had been prepared to go along with the general view as to the suitability of Princess May, she could hardly welcome unequivocally a marriage that deprived her of her beloved son. 'There is a bond of love between us', she had written to Prince George just before the engagement was announced, 'which nobody can ever diminish or render less binding – and nobody can, or ever shall, come between me and my darling Georgie boy.' Alexandra was charming to Princess May, as she was charming to everyone, but her goodwill did not go very deep, certainly not deep enough to threaten her own interests.

Prince George, on his side, had from his earliest youth concentrated his entire capacity for affection upon his mother, or 'Motherdear' as she was called by her devoted children. To him it seemed both natural and delightful that his honeymoon should be interrupted after less than a fortnight by the arrival of his parents and sisters at Sandringham. Princess Alexandra would appear in York Cottage at all hours, even at breakfast. Worse, she would insist upon the young couple coming up to the big house, which was just five minutes away across the park. Just as Prince George could not stand Mary Adelaide, Princess May was never at all at home with her husband's family. Their raucous games and their oafish practical jokes – the apple-pie bed, the sticky pear dropped into the pocket, the bicycle pump filled with water – only made her retreat further into her shell. The Prince of Wales acknowledged her virtues and was always polite, but as a pleasure-loving man of the world he had nothing whatever in common with his daughter-in-law.

Indeed, with the notable exception of Queen Victoria, who became more than ever impressed by Princess May – 'so unaffected and sensible, & so very distinguished & dignified in her manner' – the consensus among the royal family held the newcomer to be a tedious, if worthy, bore. 'I do *not* think her clever', reported the Prince of Wales's elder sister, the Dowager Empress of Germany, '– & she is a little heavy & silent – all her thoughts, views and ideas appear to me to be rather banal, commonplace and conventional, – conversationally – but I should say she . . . would certainly never do – or say a foolish thing.' The Empress nevertheless professed to like Princess May 'very much', which was more than Prince George's sisters were willing to admit. Princess Louise could never forget the dubious paternal inheritance. 'Poor May, poor May,' she would sigh, 'with her Württemberg hands.' Princess Victoria was more brutally dismissive. 'Now do try to talk to May at dinner,' she would tell guests, 'though one knows she is deadly dull.' There were commoners who shared this view. 'I have sat next to the Duchess of York for the last three nights,' Sir Henry Ponsonby told his wife in September 1894. 'She is pretty and what you would call voluptuous, but decidedly dull.'

In later life Queen Mary would somewhat defensively claim that those who refuse to give ear to malicious tittle-tattle are invariably judged to be boring. Conversation, in her view, existed simply for the interchange of useful information on subjects deemed to be worthwhile. Irony appeared wholly foreign; small talk remained unattempted; gossip (save with royalty about other royalty) was taboo. 'Before her scandal sits dumb,' Augustus Hare noted in his diary in September 1899. 'She has a quiet but inflexible power of silencing everything which seems likely to approach ill-natured gossip, yet immediately after gives such a genial kindly look and word to the silenced one as prevents any feeling of mortification.' Others responded less generously than Hare, and considered that the Duchess of York gave herself airs. The real problem, though, was that she felt isolated in an unfriendly environment. The daily realities of her existence did not match up to her almost religious faith in royalty. She never lost this faith, but in the first years of her marriage she did react internally against the sacrifices it entailed. '*Souvent mon entourage m'embête,*' she wrote to Mlle Bricka in 1902, '*et je voudrais causer, causer avec vous pour me refraîcher. J'aime beaucoup mes livres et ils me viennent en aide.*'

Yet for all her difficulties with the royal family and society, Princess May did at least have the overriding compensation of gaining her husband's devotion. Prince George never told his love, but he continued, every now and again, to commit it to paper. His direct, uncomplicated nature produced letters that any wife would have been proud to receive. 'When I asked you to marry me,' he wrote to Princess May a few weeks after their wedding, 'I was fond of you, but not very much in love with you, but I saw in *you* the person I was capable of loving most deeply, if you only returned that love . . . I have tried to understand you & to know you, &

with the happy result that I know now that I do *love* you darling
girl with all my *heart, & am simply devoted* to you . . . I *adore you
sweet May*, I can't say more than that.' Sweet May, unfortunately,
could not bring herself to say as much. She valued her husband's
devotion as evidence that she was satisfactorily discharging her duty,
but emotionally she reacted with complacency. 'George is a dear,'
she told Mlle Bricka in the first week of the honeymoon, 'he adores
me which is touching.'

One of the consequences of George's adoration was that Princess
May gave birth to five boys and a girl over the next ten years, though
she always loathed the business of child-bearing. Prince Edward, the
future Edward VIII, was born in June 1894; Prince Albert, who would
succeed his brother as King George VI, in December 1895; Princess
Victoria in 1897; and Prince Henry, later the Duke of Gloucester, in
1900. The mother liked to pretend that her pregnancies did not exist,
a disposition that earned yet more praise from Queen Victoria. 'Dear
May . . . is looking wonderfully well,' the Queen recorded during
the first pregnancy, 'only a little pale & is vy active & *s'arrange
si bien*, with blue lace & other very becoming arrangements that
one sees very little.' Seeing little and noticing less was the correct
procedure to adopt with the Duchess of York at these embarrassing
times. 'She does not wish it remarked or mentioned,' the Empress
Frederick reported during the third pregnancy. After the birth of
her fourth child the mother felt that the time had come to call a halt.
'I think I have done my duty and may now stop,' she told Aunt
Augusta, 'as having babies is highly distasteful to me tho' once they
are there they are very nice.' Nature, however, is difficult to halt in
its tracks. Prince George, the future Duke of Kent, arrived in 1902
and Prince John in 1905 – before finally, at the age of thirty-eight,
Princess May found release.

Notwithstanding the 'very nice' rating which she accorded to her
offspring, her interest in them did not markedly increase after their
emergence from the womb. She was fond of them, no doubt, but
never fond enough to question the established practice whereby royal
children were brought up entirely by hired servants. Delegation was
her preferred system of maternity, to such an extent that the eldest boy
picked up (and retained throughout his life) some most inappropriate
vowel sounds from those who looked after him. Princess May's role

was simply to admire her children for half an hour a day when they were brought – preferably singly – into the drawing-room. This duty she discharged, as she discharged all duties, with punctiliousness. She taught the boys, as well as Princess Mary, to crochet and sew, and gave lectures on the family history, but the task once performed, her mind turned gratefully to other matters. The Empress Frederick, observing her, thought her 'very cold and stiff and unmaternal'. And when, many years later, the Duke of Windsor wrote of having inherited his cultural interests from his mother, he unintentionally emphasised the sparseness of his relations with her. In so far as Princess May registered any attitude towards her young children it was one of distant apprehension. 'David was "jumpy" yesterday morning, however he got quieter after being out – what a curious child he is.' Or again, with some surprise: 'I really believe he begins to like me at last, he is most civil to me.'

Of what went on in the nursery Princess May had no idea. The inadequacy of the first nanny employed by the Yorks was quickly discovered: the unfortunate woman was deemed to have been rude to Mary Adelaide and was instantly dismissed. Her successor, however, merely persecuted the children, so her failings remained undetected for three years. This nanny conceived a sinister passion for the eldest boy; and it is said that, in order to maintain her supremacy over him, she would pinch him and twist his arm before introducing him into the drawing-room, so that the howling child invariably failed to endear himself to his parents. Prince Albert, by contrast, was entirely neglected, even to the point of starvation. One would have thought that such treatment could hardly have passed unnoticed in the cramped quarters of York Cottage, but not until the nanny finally underwent a full-blown nervous breakdown were her misdemeanours revealed.

Princess May's failings as a mother might have mattered less if the Duke of York had been a better father. 'The House of Hanover, like ducks, produce bad parents,' it has been remarked. 'They trample on their young.' Certainly Prince George, forever tortured by the fear that his children might be going off the rails, assumed the mask of a martinet. He shouted at them as though they were recalcitrant cadets under his command, on one occasion making Prince Henry faint from sheer terror. Although Princess May introduced her beloved

Mademoiselle Bricka into the schoolroom, it was the stern father who gave instructions to the tutors and decided that the elder boys should be sent to the brutal naval establishments at Osborne and Dartmouth. Princess May would sometimes try to defend her children against their father, but in the last analysis she was too much in awe of his position. 'I have always to remember', she remarked with her uncritical reverence for all things royal, 'that their father is also their King.' Perhaps she also remembered her own father's tantrums, and considered such behaviour as the routine course of paternity.

If the Duke of Windsor is to be believed, Princess May became another person when her husband was absent. 'We used to have the most lovely time with her alone – always laughing and joking, down at Frogmore or wherever else we might be – she was a different human being away from him.' Such testimony should be treated with caution, for the Duke suffered from an uncontrollable urge to disparage his father which would cause him, later in life, to convey a grim picture of his parents' marriage. 'He [the Duke's father] was foully rude to my mother. Why, I've often seen her leave the table because he was so rude to her, and we children would all follow her out; not when the staff were present, of course, but when we were alone.' There may have been some such incident, but the real trouble was that the York children were in general too far removed from their parents to form any worthwhile assessment of their marriage.

This very considerable handicap apart, the Duke of Windsor's childhood was far from being an uninterrupted trauma. By contemporary accounts he was a high-spirited child, while he himself admitted that the surroundings at Sandringham and at Frogmore House in Windsor were ideal for children. It is no use pretending, though, that there was any warmth in the atmosphere at York Cottage. Even so discreet and reverential a witness as Lady Airlie, who became lady-in-waiting to Princess May in 1902, is obliged to admit that the York children remained emotional strangers to their mother. Physical affection played absolutely no part in Princess May's system; never a hug, never a kiss. Nor was she inclined to tolerate the natural rumbustiousness of youth. 'The children were expected to keep within their own domain,' remembered Lady Airlie. 'I never saw them run along the corridors; they walked sedately, generally shepherded by nurses or tutors.'

This is a sad glimpse into York Cottage, all the more chilling because the children were rigorously isolated from their contemporaries. The only time they came near to leading normal lives was when their parents were abroad and they were left in the charge of their paternal grandparents. Then the tutors and nannies would be shooed away with an impatient wave of their grandfather's cigar, and the spoiling would begin. Princess May feared this influence and wrote anxious if fruitless letters to her mother-in-law stressing the importance of discipline and study. 'I do so hope our children will turn out commonsense people which is so important in this world,' she reflected. 'We have taken no end of trouble with their education and they have very nice people around them, so one feels all is being done to help them.'

As her sons all grew up with psychological problems of one kind or another, one may feel with hindsight that Princess May's satisfaction about their education was misplaced. But complacency had now become an ineradicable feature of her character. No doubt this streak of solid self-regard had always been with her, albeit masked by shyness: nothing less than an indestructible sense of her own worth could have carried her triumphantly through all the difficulties of her youth. Now, as the Duchess of York settled as to the manner born into her elevated role, the note of self-congratulation sounds more and more distinctly, so that the sympathy which flows so naturally towards the young girl rather ebbs in contemplating the mature woman. Yet in part her seamless self-belief developed as a necessary defence against the sneers which she encountered, alike from her in-laws, whom she rightly regarded as far less intelligent than herself, and from the fashionable world which she condemned as frivolous. '*Il parait qu'on s'étonne* "that *I* did it all so well",' she wrote during a state visit to Ireland in 1897, 'but only give me the chance & I will do things as well as anybody, after all, why shouldn't I?'

To this rhetorical enquiry Princess May's detractors might well have replied that she was too stiff, inhibited and unimaginative ever to become a popular figure. Yet she had already begun to present herself in a role that harnessed these very defects to advantage. To the public she did not put herself forward as a creature of flesh and blood; rather she made herself a kind of totem to which the nation might offer reverence. In this capacity her shyness, such a crippling disadvantage in private, served the ideal of distant royalty; her unimaginativeness became a guarantee of absolute dedication, while her lack of humour, sparkle and warmth predicated a dignity that could never be ruffled. The great virtue of the performance was its consistency and integrity: the image would be solid and enduring as a monument. But whereas monuments may be magnificent, they do not necessarily become lovable until time has rendered them familiar.

Princess May herself, it must be said, remained rather more interesting than the image she chose to present. This apparently strait-laced young woman could show herself more broad-minded than any of the sophisticates who derided her. In 1898 a particularly grisly royal scandal gave her the opportunity to show her generosity of spirit. One of the Grand Duchess's granddaughters, Duchess Marie of Mecklenburg-Strelitz, who was nineteen, became pregnant by a footman entrusted with the task of bringing lamps into her bedroom. Possibly the girl was ignorant as much as licentious, for no attempt had been made to enlighten her about the facts of life. Notwithstanding this omission, her parents reacted in the melodramatic manner prescribed for such misbehaviour, barring their child from ever again darkening their door. Only the Grand Duchess herself, of all the German relations, stood by the girl, whom she whisked off to Menton in the south of France. There Princess May also appeared, and made a point of showing open support for the Duchess Marie by taking her out for drives in her carriage.

She also pleaded her cause with the English royal family, winning round the Prince of Wales. Queen Victoria required no persuading: to her it was axiomatic that the poor girl must have been 'drugged'. A similar line of reasoning appealed to the Duke of York, who decided that hypnotism was the explanation for the otherwise inexplicable act. But only Princess May and the Grand Duchess, in many respects the starchiest royalty of all, faced the situation squarely and sought to deal with it as Christian charity demanded. Moreover Princess May's care was not the sort that exhausts itself with the initial impulse. The Duchess Marie's unlucky dealings with men continued when she married a dubious Frenchman called Count Jamatel, who preferred parading his liaison with a Spanish princess to the joys of domesticity. This marriage ended in divorce in 1908, leaving the Duchess Marie ruined financially as well as morally. But Princess May never withdrew her support; and the Duchess Marie did finally achieve some degree of happiness with a second marriage.

As for Aunt Augusta, the Grand Duchess, her long-held admiration for Princess May was lifted on to a new plane. '. . . Nor did I realise or get to know her real character', she wrote some years later, 'until she came to me in 1898, a real Angel of mercy at that terribly sad and trying time for me; then only did I find in her, all that is wonderfully combined in her whole being! the warm heart, the clear, good and quiet judgement in all things, her gentle reserve and yet coming forward when it was right, I not only loved, I respected and admired in her all the great qualities she possesses, then by degrees felt more & more, that she would some day fill her place and be a real Queen as she must be!'

Queen Victoria's good opinion of Princess May also deepened with experience. By the end of the 1890s the Duchess of York had become one of the old Queen's most valued companions, frequently in attendance at Windsor, Balmoral, and Buckingham Palace. 'Each time I see you I love & respect you more & am so truly thankful that Georgie has such a partner – to help & encourage him in his difficult position,' the Queen wrote in 1897. It became all too clear that the Queen preferred this paragon to the Princess of Wales, whom she considered charming but essentially vacuous. This state of affairs, though it can hardly have improved Princess May's relations with her mother-in-law Princess Alexandra, underlined how life had changed for a young woman who, but a few years before, had possessed uncertain royal credentials. When Princess May's brother Dolly married Lady Margaret Grosvenor in 1894, the Duke of Teck raged that the match was far beneath his son, though Queen Victoria, who always had a sound sense of the value of cash, pronounced it 'a vy *good* connection'. As for Mary Adelaide, she died in 1897 secure in the knowledge that, whatever the vicissitudes of her own life, her descendants would fulfil their rightful destiny as kings and queens of England. The Duke of Teck, quite beyond useful conversation in his last years, lingered on until 1900.

Thereafter only Princess May's brother Frank remained as a potential family embarrassment for her, a function which he discharged with gusto. It was said that the Duke of York's sister, Princess Victoria, was attracted to him, but Frank, being a man of hot blood, wholly lacked his sister's sense of the sacred honour involved in marrying royalty. Having fallen heavily into debt he attempted in 1895 to retrieve the situation by placing £10,000 which he did not possess on a racing certainty at 10 to 1 on. Like so many racing certainties this one lost; the Duke of York was required to stump up; and the renegade was dispatched to India. Frank never shared the British passion for that country: in fact he opined that the Almighty must have intended it 'as an example of what to expect in the world below'. His spirits, however, never flagged, and he heard with interest that his sister had been to Newmarket. 'I think I must write and warn her simple soul against the evils of the race', he told his mother, '– I shall send her a betting book as a X-mas pres.' When he wrote to Princess May herself she was at a loss. 'Today I heard from Frank,' she noted, 'a long letter from Mahableshwar, written in his very flippant style which honestly I cannot understand.' She was even less amused when, later, Frank lavished the Teck family jewels on his mistress Lady Kilmorey, a married woman of doubtful reputation.

Princess May was naturally one of those gathered around the great canopied bed in which Queen Victoria died on 22 January 1901. 'The thought of England without the Queen', she wrote, 'is too dreadful even to think of. God help us all.' God had in fact now placed Princess May just a heartbeat away from being Queen herself, and no actuary would have staked much on the longevity of the wheezing and breathless Edward VII. The new King very nearly died from appendicitis before his coronation in 1902. 'Oh do *pray* that Uncle Wales may get well,' Princess May wrote to Mlle Bricka at that time. 'George says he isn't ready yet to reign.' George, however, was most decidedly ready to be Prince of Wales; and his wife was not at all amused when this title was deliberately withheld from her husband at the beginning of the new reign. Edward VII, it transpired, believed that the name Wales was so indissolubly linked with himself in the public mind that there would be confusion should it be instantly conferred upon his son. This was not an argument that made any appeal to Princess May. 'I believe this is the first time that the Heir Apparent has not been created Prince of Wales,' she told Aunt Augusta. 'I dislike intensely departing from traditions.' Fortunately this particular tradition was reasserted before the end of the year.

Princess May also expressed annoyance at Queen Alexandra's dilatoriness in moving out of the Prince of Wales's residence at Marlborough House. It was nearly a year into the new reign before the last of Alexandra's effects had been taken to Buckingham Palace; and another year before Princess May's decoration of her new abode, carried out in decisive rebuttal of the previous owner's taste, was complete. The young Princess of Wales's irritation with her predecessor never really abated, and during the next quarter-century the two women lived in a state of latent hostility, only thinly disguised by oft-repeated but wholly conventional expressions of affection. Neither ever stated explicitly what was in her mind: in Princess May's case that the Queen's laziness, unpunctuality and selfishness rendered her unfit for the responsibilities of her position; in Alexandra's that her daughter-in-law's undeniable worthiness by no means compensated for her impenetrable stiffness and reserve.

In truth Princess May and the new age were irreconcilably at odds with each other. At court the Edwardian era was a time of flashy vulgarity and unabashed pleasure-seeking, in which *nouveaux riches* financiers and women of doubtful reputation found themselves more popular than the paragons of domestic virtue. Princess May instinctively recoiled from what, in an untypically vivid phrase, she called 'the surfeit of gold plate and oysters' that characterised the reign. She could not bring herself to criticise the King, for that would have been blasphemy against the first article of her faith. Nor, indeed, was there anything to complain about regarding the King's attitude to herself. Edward VII not only remained respectful; he acknowledged his daughter-in-law's competence and discretion by allowing her to see State papers, a privilege he never accorded to his queen. On the other hand, when in 1903 Princess May's youngest brother Alexander, much to her delight, married Princess Alice, a granddaughter of Queen Victoria, Edward VII did not dissemble his opinion that the bride could have done better for herself. In his mind the Tecks were still *arrivistes* on the royal scene. It was a reflection perfectly directed at Princess May's most sensitive spot, all the more deadly for being unintentional.

Her sense of exclusion only intensified her inhibitions. She was misjudged, she complained to Mlle Bricka in 1906. '*Il n'y a pas de doute que je ne suis pas populaire parmi de certains gens, pourquoi je ne sais pas, puisque je me donne un mal infini pour plaire, on me trouve trop* "good", *trop* "particular" – *Certes je n'aime pas leurs* "goings-on" . . . [*mais*] *j'ai plus de diablerie en moi, qu'on ne crois* [*sic*].' But Princess May's attempts to portray herself as a witty, amusing, devilish girl at heart never carried much conviction.

Fortunately there was relief from the alien domestic scene. The British, having discovered somewhat to their surprise that they possessed an empire, allotted to the royal family the burden of visiting it. In 1901 the Prince and Princess of Wales undertook a tour of Australia and New Zealand, returning home by way of South Africa and Canada. The natives appeared suitably gratified by the royal presence; and, hardly less important, Princess May in particular enjoyed considerable acclaim. Away from the Edwardian court she seemed to her staff to become a different person. 'Her Royal Highness has quite got over her shyness abroad, and almost enjoys a procession,' her lady-in-waiting, Lady Mary Lygon, reported. 'Her smile is commented on in every paper, and her charm of manner; in fact she is having a "*succès fou*" especially as no-one was prepared for her good looks all photographs being caricatures.' Lady Mary prophesied that the newly confident Princess would 'electrify them at home as she has everyone here'.

That proved to be an exaggeration, but there can be no question of the satisfaction that the star drew from her performance. 'You will see that your humble servant has found great favour with the Australians,' she wrote home to Mlle Bricka, 'rather different to at home where they always find fault with what I do or do not do.' Best of all, perhaps, Prince George showed a touching, entirely unjealous delight in his wife's triumph. 'It was you who made it a success,' he wrote to her of the tour after their return home. 'Although I have often told it you before, I repeat it once more, that I love you darling child, with my whole heart & soul & thank God every day that I have such a wife as you, who is such a great help & support to me & I believe loves me too.'

A visit to the imperial court at Vienna in 1904 also brought its meed of praise. Not merely was Princess May adjudged better-looking than any of the Archduchesses; she had the additional and rare pleasure, in that starchiest of courts, of being praised for the 'ease and charm' of her manner.

It was, however, the arduous tour of India, undertaken by the Prince and Princess of Wales between October 1905 and April 1906, that, more than any other of her travels, captured Princess May's imagination. The unfamiliar landscapes, the exotic Maharajas, the teeming multitudes, the great palaces, the dazzling gems, the mystery of eastern religions, the unchanging laws of custom: all these things fascinated Princess May, and brought her at last, on the verge of middle age, something of the intoxication of youth. Not that her interest in India was exclusively romantic. Typically, she mastered the statistics on rice production, and expressed concern about the oppressed condition of women. For all that, India did evoke in her a deep and lasting affection, though perhaps her pleasure was as much in her position as in what she saw. Can one imagine that simple May of Teck, a dubious and impoverished spinster princess, would have found any more contentment than her brother Frank in the heat and dust of the subcontinent? Yet she would have been a minuscule soul indeed if she had failed to respond to the strangeness and the wonder of a destiny that plucked her from a life of dreary filial duty and deposited her on the very topmost step of an imperial throne. Empress of India! Her apotheosis was now tantalisingly close. To ride in triumph through Persepolis, to appear from across the oceans to receive homage, adoration, worship from a country of four hundred million inhabitants – then a fifth of the world's population: that, surely, was to know what it meant to be royal, however one's in-laws might sneer.

3

Princess May was nearly forty-three, almost exactly half-way through her life, when, on 6 May 1910, Edward VII breathed his last. The problem immediately arose as to what the new consort should be called. 'May' being considered insufficiently dignified for a queen, she perforce reverted to the 'Victoria Mary' of her christening; indeed she had long signed official documents as such. But as George V, in his straight and simple way, disliked the idea of double names, and since Victoria alone was considered scarcely possible so soon after the death of the great Queen, Mary was the style adopted.

But though the title had altered, the public personality remained unchanged, albeit now exhibited at centre stage. The Queen Mary of 1910 was essentially the same production as the Princess May of 1901, and so it would remain until her death in 1953. Even her dress – the long skirt, the toque, the parasol – hardly altered in all those years. This fixed image makes chronology almost irrelevant in assessing her character: what was true of her before the First World War remained true after the Second. So it was that the very idea of Queen Mary came to epitomise solidity and security; so it is also that the second half of her life is of lesser biographical interest than the first. She had become an institution, first; and only secondarily a human being. So many of the common signs of life were missing in her: there was no development, no regression, no internal conflict, no shift of opinion. The woman had, quite deliberately, become the mask. Upon acquaintances was bestowed 'the shy nod that offends so much'; upon any sign of impropriety a glassy stare. In public at least, her smile was dispensed strictly as a bonus.

Naturally, given her position, the effect was formidable. Nancy Astor, who scared a great many people herself, confessed to being in awe of Queen Mary, and of no one else. Only innocence, ignorance and mischance presumed upon her marmoreal dignity. Paul Channon, though an ill-fated Minister of Transport in the later 1980s, enjoyed a brief moment of glory in 1936 when, as an unruly infant, he clutched Queen Mary's nose and pulled at her ear-rings. Rather more embarrassing, when Princess May was in Canada a porter came into her hotel bedroom and, mistaking her seated form from behind as that of a maid, began to berate her for not helping with the work. There was also the occasion when the Queen's ear-rings became entangled in the beard of a plumber who was showing her how the lavatory worked in the Queen's doll's house. Otherwise, examples of lese-majesty are hard to come by.

Queen Mary enjoyed recounting such incidents, for no one could have been more surprised than herself at being taken for an ordinary person. Sometimes her private self seemed entirely lost, an impression reinforced by the extreme banality of language which she used.

Illness was 'too tiresome', the suffragettes 'horrid', the First World War 'too depressing', beautiful scenery invariably 'too lovely'. (The emphatic 'too' was a characteristic of the Cambridge family. Both Mary Adelaide and Aunt Augusta frequently used it; so – they say – does Elizabeth II.) Queen Mary's highest admiration was conveyed by the epithet 'dear' – 'the *dear* Navy', 'dear India'. This was also the adjective which she reserved for royal acquaintances, whereas commoners, it was noticed, were usually referred to as 'poor' so-and-so. Such poverty of expression and blandness of attitude make it easy to understand why Asquith complained that he felt more exhausted after dining with Queen Mary than after a debate in the House of Commons.

The tendency of Princess May's personality to be subsumed in her royal persona was enhanced, in the years after she became Queen Consort, by the deaths of three people whom she had known well in her un-royal past. Her brother Frank died suddenly and unexpectedly in the summer of 1910. Although Queen Mary had never had much in common with this rather disreputable figure, who had always made fun of her earnest ways, she most uncharacteristically broke down in tears at his funeral, almost as if she realised that she would never again in her life experience the kind of easy familiarity which Frank's teasing had implied. Then in July 1914 she suffered another serious blow when her old tutor Mlle Bricka, recipient to the last of many an epistolary confidence, died.

Worst of all, though, was the death of the Grand Duchess of Mecklenburg-Strelitz. Queen Mary had desperately wanted Aunt Augusta to come to her coronation, but her venerable relative felt unable, at the age of eighty-nine, to make the journey to England – unless, as she put it, 'some Aerobike takes me to fly across'. Queen Mary did manage, however, to get to Strelitz herself in the summer of 1912, and she also snatched a few hours with her aunt, their last meeting, out of her visit to Berlin in 1913. These reunions gave great delight to both parties, though Aunt Augusta did not entirely approve of the scenes of welcome at Neu Strelitz station being filmed: 'Fancy, our going *kissing* all over the world,' she wrote afterwards, 'but it is impossible to stop those horrid Kino-men.' Queen Mary continued to write to her aunt in Germany during the First World War, using the Swedish court as intermediary, until the Grand Duchess began to express such fiercely pro-German sentiments that the correspondence had to cease. At least the Grand Duchess returned to her native colours on her death-bed in 1916 (she was ninety-four). She sent a message of loyalty to King George V and passed out of the world with the word 'May' on her lips.

There were precious few people left in the world, thenceforth, for whom 'May' was an option. '*Never make friendships*,' Queen Victoria had instructed a granddaughter, and the principle commended itself to Queen Mary. After the death of Aunt Augusta there was no one at all to whom she could open her whole mind in affectionate confidence, unless, doubtful exception, one counts the King.

George V, in spite of his loving letters, did not care for intimate conversation. Dullness, for him, was a prerequisite of integrity. When H. G. Wells criticised his 'alien and uninspired court', it was only the first adjective to which the King objected. 'I may be uninspiring,' he returned, 'but I'll be damned if I'm an alien.' On his accession to the throne the seedy glamour of the Edwardian court instantly disappeared, to be replaced by the stodgiest conservatism. The fashionable world, being entirely excluded, revenged itself by sneering. Max Beerbohm wrote verses reporting an imaginary conversation about the King and Queen between a lord and lady-in-waiting:

> HE:
> > Last evening
> I found him with a rural dean
> Talking of District Visiting . . .
> The King is duller than the Queen.
>
> SHE:
> At any rate he doesn't sew;
> You don't see him embellishing
> Yard after yard of calico . . .
> The Queen is duller than the King.

In fact, during the first decade of George V's reign the King and Queen did very well to be dissociated from any hint of upper-class glitter. It was a period in which fierce political controversy and alarming social unrest were only extinguished by the horror of the First World War; and left-wing politicians all too easily assumed that the throne was ranged behind the forces of privilege. 'The whole atmosphere reeks of Toryism,' Lloyd George wrote when he stayed at Balmoral in 1911. 'The King is hostile to the bone to all who are working to lift the workmen out of the mire. So is the Queen. They talk exactly as the late King and the Kaiser talked to me . . . about the old Railway strike. "What do they want striking?" "They are very well paid", etc.' Lloyd George, though, was badly mistaken. It was true that the King and Queen were Tories to the extent that they feared the consequences of social upheaval. It was also true that they lacked imagination: 'why, why do you live here?' Queen Mary asked the slum-dwellers of the East End. They did not, however, lack either sympathy or concern.

This was particularly the case with Queen Mary, who had, after all, passed her youth with a mother devoted to all kinds of charitable enterprise. Mlle Bricka, moreover, had left her addicted to hard-headed analysis of social problems, ever since those happy days in 1888 when they had pored together over the report of the Select Committee on Sweated Industries. It is an unlikely comparison, but Queen Mary had the same penchant as Sidney and Beatrice Webb for seeing human ills in statistical terms. Facts were her delight: before undertaking foreign tours, for example, she would conscientiously plough through volume after volume about the countries concerned. Both at home and abroad, however, she also liked to see problems on the ground. In the years before the First World War the King and Queen initiated a new royal policy with a series of visits to depressed industrial areas, beginning in 1912 with a tour of the collieries of south Wales. Queen Mary was too shy to be at ease with working people, but the effort she made, and the practical sense that she displayed, were much appreciated. Perhaps also the genteel poverty of her own youth, though far removed from the distress of those who lacked enough to eat, increased her sympathy for the unfortunate. Above all, she was never a snob, at least not in the ordinary sense of the term. In her mind the royal calling was so far above all others that, with those beyond the pale, it hardly mattered to her whether they were dustmen or dukes.

If there was a class which she loathed it was those who devoted themselves to nought but pleasure. A picture of the idle rich disporting themselves on a beach in the south of France during the 1920s filled her with disgust. 'They would look almost more decent', she expostulated, 'if they had no clothes on at all.' 'I like energy & doing

& seeing things,' she wrote in 1909, 'but the way people fritter away their time & their vitality doing *absolutely* useless things makes me furious.' She herself was never idle. If she sat for her portrait someone must read to her the while; if she had a spare moment she instantly took up her embroidery. A suggestion in some book about her that she was easily bored drew forth an indignant marginal note: 'As a matter of fact, The Queen is never bored.'

It must not be imagined, from what has been said of Queen Mary's social concerns, that she passed her life solely in a succession of good works. The more formal aspects of monarchy greatly appealed to her, in particular those state occasions on which the majesty of the Crown is ceremonially displayed to its grateful subjects. In this connection she helped to sustain George V, for the King concealed behind his gruff exterior an ineradicable diffidence about his fitness for his role. The ceremonial opening of Parliament might not seem too daunting an exercise of the prerogative: the monarch is required to dress in the robes of state, travel down the Mall in a coach, and read a prepared speech to the assembled Commons and Lords. To George V in 1911, however, this was 'the most terrible ordeal I have ever gone through'. Queen Mary, by contrast, rose to such occasions as though she had been born for them, and her mystical belief in the office of the Crown diffused a confidence that her husband badly needed. The King's sense of obligation yielded further expressions of epistolary gratitude, though rarely, to Queen Mary's disappointment, any spoken appreciation. 'I can't imagine how I could have got on at all without you,' George V wrote in October 1910. 'My love grows stronger for you every day mixed with admiration & I thank God every day that he has given me such a darling devoted wife as you are.' There were many who agreed with him. People began to talk of George V and Mary four-fifths.

The rigidly prescribed procedures of state ceremony released some of Queen Mary's inhibition. At the coronation in June 1911 she conveyed by almost theatrical means her sense of what the service involved. As she walked up the aisle at the beginning she appeared to one observer to be 'almost shrinking . . . giving the impression that she would have liked to have made her way to her seat by some back entrance: the contrast on her "return" – crowned – was magnetic, as if she had undergone some marvellous transformation.'

Instead of the shy creature for whom one had felt pity, one saw her emerge from the ceremony with a bearing and dignity, and a quiet confidence, signifying that she really felt that she was Queen of this great Empire, and that she derived strength and legitimate pride from the knowledge of it.' The effect was only marginally diminished by a stand-up fight between Princes Harry and George outside the abbey.

Later in the same year the Durbar in Delhi, at which the Crown's Indian subjects paid tribute to their Emperor and Empress, also proved entirely to Queen Mary's taste. There had originally been some idea that she should be left behind in England, but she soon squashed that notion. The Durbar bore out all her expectations – 'Very grand', she wrote to Aunt Augusta, '& I felt proud to take part in so interesting & historical an event, just the kind of thing which appeals to my feelings of tradition – *You* will understand.' Predictably, when the royal couple returned to England, there were further letters of gratitude and appreciation from the King to his wife.

The King and Queen also enjoyed success on the continent. In May 1913 they made a private visit to Berlin for the wedding of the Kaiser's daughter. Queen Mary relished such gatherings of the royal clan and felt no inkling that this might be the last: in fact she got on especially well with the Kaiser. In the following spring, 1914, there was a state visit to France. Queen Mary had feared a hostile reception – she could never quite trust republics – and was therefore all the more gratified to be cheered to the echo. Contrary to her fears, the French have always been fascinated with monarchy, provided it is not their own. Queen Mary's clothes caused much comment in Paris; and the couturiers anxiously wondered whether the styles of the 1890s might be making a comeback. It was safer, perhaps, to admire her jewels, timeless in their magnificence and dazzling in their abundance. *Soutien-Georges* the Parisians called the Queen, an apposite pun upon *soutien-gorge*, the French expression for a brassière.

Such frivolities, however, were swiftly dissipated by the outbreak of the First World War. Queen Mary never really interested herself in the deeper issues of international relations: in her mind world history was reduced to a series of incidents in the story of her family.

'Poor Nicky of Russia', she would record in 1918, 'has been shot by those brutes of Bolsheviks last week.' It must have been difficult for her to understand, in 1914, how cousin Willy (the Kaiser), who had always been so kind and so charming to her, could possibly have behaved so badly. Another cousin, Count Mensdorff, the Austrian ambassador, received on his departure from England a farewell letter from 'ever your devoted friends and cousins George and Mary'. Only later in the war did popular opinion force the King to abandon such civilised attitudes towards the enemy. George V abjured his German ancestry by assuming the name of Windsor, a move which caused the Kaiser to remark, wittily enough, that he would like to attend a performance of *The Merry Wives of Mecklenburg-Strelitz*. The name Teck also became suspect in England, so that Queen Mary's brothers Adolphus and Alexander became respectively the Marquess of Cambridge and the Earl of Athlone.

However cosmopolitan Queen Mary's loyalty to the royal club, there was nothing in the least equivocal about her dedication to the cause of victory. Despite her German ancestry and (as some thought) her German character – or perhaps because of them – she had never felt the least enthusiasm for the country or its people. 'I certainly do *not* like German,' she had told Mlle Bricka in 1892, and now she clung to her belief that 'God cannot allow those Huns to win'. The national emergency brought out all that was best in her. From the pleasure and sweetness of life she instinctively recoiled: to duty, dedication, hard work and sacrifice she was naturally drawn. During the First World War the mummified figure of state found her true vocation as a practical and efficient worker in the common cause.

The exigencies of war actually appealed to her temperament. All through her life, save occasionally in the purchase of jewels, she practised a rigid economy, and waged a relentless battle against waste. It irritated her, for example, that she was obliged to cast off her long white kid gloves after only one wearing; and the same instinct made her insist on using bars of soap until they had been completely exhausted. On the outbreak of war she eagerly suppressed all luxuries in her own household, and instituted a system of rationing. The napkin-ring, that symbol of middle-class thrift, made its appearance on the royal dinner table. The lawns of Windsor Castle were dug up for vegetables. At Frogmore the Queen personally slaved over her potato plot; at Sandringham she collected horse-chestnuts (required for some arcane purpose in the armaments industry) and sent out parties to scour the estate for scrap. Both King and Queen set an example by becoming teetotal for the duration of the war. The Duke of Windsor maliciously recorded that after a dinner without alcohol George V would retire to his study 'to attend to a small matter of business'. It is hardly possible, though, to believe the Duke, for he also alleged that Queen Mary's 'fruitcup' was sometimes laced with champagne.

Throughout the war the Queen drove herself mercilessly in carrying out her official duties: inspecting troops, encouraging munitions workers, visiting the wounded in hospital. A special interest, most admirable in one who had always shied away from such horrors, was the care of those who had lost limbs or suffered appalling facial injuries. 'I thought I could not do it,' she remarked after visiting a ward of mutilated veterans, 'but of course there is simply nothing one can't do.' That did not mean that she ever came to enjoy such work. 'What a relief,' she told Queen Marie of Romania as they left a hospital together, 'I never know what to say to them.' To the crippled patients, however, her shyness was unimportant beside the fact of her presence. There was, besides, a genuine and affecting humility about her in the company of soldiers who had given so much. 'One felt one could only apologise to the men for being there,' she would muse.

At the end of the war, in 1918, the Queen became Commander-in-Chief of the Women's Army, in the hope that her iron-clad reputation would serve as an impregnable shield against the slurs that were cast on that force's morals. The war also brought her closely into contact with the Women's Trade Union League. This came about as a result of a tremendous expansion of the Needlework Guild, of which, following her mother, she had become President. The Guild developed into a vast organisation which co-ordinated and directed the voluntary work that women throughout the country were engaged upon in order to provide extra clothes for the troops. Queen Mary herself joined in this effort, 'knitting hard against her ladies'. The trouble was, though, that the proliferation of voluntary labour began to put the professional clothing workers out of a job, much to the concern of trade-unionists. Foremost among those protesting was Mary Macarthur, a fiery Scottish socialist not given, up to that time, to speaking with favour of royalty. One meeting with Queen Mary, however, entirely changed her viewpoint. 'The point is,' she announced to her colleagues on her return from Buckingham Palace, 'the Queen does understand the whole situation from the trades union point of view. Here is someone who _can_ help and means to help!' Mary Macarthur was perfectly right. Queen Mary, whose principles naturally inclined towards creating the conditions of self-help, rather than bestowing an indiscriminate charity, became intimately involved with the formation of the Central Committee on Women's Employment, and lent her name to a special 'Work for Women' fund. Mary Macarthur was left hoping that the revolution would not break out in her lifetime, as she would be obliged to rally to the defence of the Queen.

The strain of all the work which Queen Mary undertook in the war noticeably aged her. Whereas in 1908 she had declared that she still felt as though she was twenty-five, by 1918 her hair had gone white and she looked her full fifty-one years. But she had her reward. 'This has repaid us for much hard work and many moments of keen and bitter anxiety,' she told her second son after she and the King had been rapturously received in the victory parades. All over Europe, in Russia, Austria and Germany, the thrones had toppled, but in England republicanism was unable to gain even a toe-hold.

Queen Mary never rested upon her laurels. The royal treadmill had by now become an unbreakable habit. The reader would wish no doubt to be spared an endless list of functions attended and chores performed, but it should at least be remembered that Queen Mary never spared herself. The staple of her life in the 1920s and 1930s remained what it had been in the Great War: public duty and good works. Her mornings were devoted to her vast correspondence, much of it to do with charitable affairs; her afternoons more often than not to some official visit. It is true that there was little sparkle in the way that she worked. She aspired to be dignified and useful rather than to please or charm, for it was never her idea that royalty should stoop to ingratiate itself by any familiarity of manner. George V boasted that he was not 'an advertising sort of fellow'; and Queen Mary followed him to the letter in this as in all things. She never said or did anything extraordinary. If she gave a speech it was a rare event; and the only words she ever broadcast were the twenty-eight which she spoke when she launched the *Queen Mary*. Her ideals were never flashy; they were, however, through unrelenting self-discipline, most effectively realised, unlike the thousand fancies that waft around in less securely anchored minds. If Queen Mary undertook any royal visit there was a cast-iron guarantee that she would be punctual and well informed, that her interest would be genuine, her observations intelligent, her advice practical, and that if any further action was required it would be conscientiously performed. She would, as a Labour politician once remarked, have made an excellent factory inspector.

Her dedication, which appeared so unremarkable in the context of each single event, became something quite extraordinary in the perspective of a lifetime. Most of us can rise to a special occasion. For Queen Mary, however, there were no special occasions, no highs, no lows, simply the same enduring and unchanging commitment to the role which she had espoused. It was not glamorous work. 'A foolish woman said to me, "How gracious she is – every inch a Queen,"' A. C. Benson recorded after watching the Queen perform some routine task. 'Now that was *exactly* what she was not. She had no majesty of mien, or ease or stateliness. She looked a hard-worked and rather tired woman, plainly dressed, doing her best to be civil to nervous people.' Yet this very ordinariness paid dividends. Queen Mary's obvious integrity – what Sir Osbert Sitwell called her 'all-throughness' – lent her rather flat personality an exceptional power. If it was impossible to imagine her being startling or brilliant, it was equally unthinkable that she should ever say or do anything untrue to herself.

Moreover, Queen Mary understood in every fibre of her being that monarchy would survive in a democracy only if it acknowledged obligations as well as privileges. Her service of the state was ultimately a form of enlightened self-interest, so that the uncharitable may discern a hint of self-gratification even in her public work. What was good for the monarchy must ultimately be good for Queen Mary. In this connection it is interesting to find her expressing a high opinion of Catherine the Great of Russia: 'She loved her kingdom. She was prepared to make any sacrifices for it, to go to any lengths – even to commit terrible crimes for it.' That, in Queen Mary's mind, was admirable. There was nothing of the moral philosopher about her, beyond a stoical sense that, willy-nilly, life must go on. 'So many things appear futile, frivolous, waste of time & energy,' she had told Mlle Bricka in 1910, 'yet they must be done as long as the world is as civilisation? [*sic*] has made it, of course one often rebels *mais que faire?*'

No one can deny that on their own terms, which were first and foremost to preserve and strengthen the throne, King George V and Queen Mary scored a solid success. Yet those for whom the monarchy is not an end in itself may, like Queen Mary's eldest son, feel some reservations about the kind of image which the King and Queen presented in the 1920s and 1930s. For the crown helped to sustain an idea of England as a stiff, backward-looking, socially stratified and deeply conventional country, that might more profitably have perished.

It is too readily assumed, because Edward VIII proved so entirely unsatisfactory, that George V's and Queen Mary's intensely conservative interpretation of their role was the only viable course open to them. In fact, English monarchs appear to be able to extract devotion from their subjects on almost any terms short of arousing contempt or precipitating a constitutional rumpus. Edward VII, after all, had been admired for being a card just as much as George V for being steadfast and upright. If, indeed, the English are essentially a stolid, worthy and dull people, the virtues which George V and Queen Mary represented were perfectly suited to their position. The romantic vision, however, might prefer to cull a more exciting national identity from the history books. The English are not condemned to possess stunted imaginations and underdeveloped hearts. On the contrary, in former centuries they have shown themselves capable of poetry, wit, dash, and flair. Wherever the magic flame that might rekindle these qualities may be, it was certainly not at Windsor in the reign of George V.

Queen Mary, of course, could not have changed the character with which nature had endowed her. Being, however, a person of considerably wider interests than George V, she might have been able to let rather more light into the court had she not felt obliged to submit her will so entirely to his. She never contradicted him, and was liable to explode if anyone else did, especially if the offender was a woman. The King wanted to live in a nineteenth-century cocoon, and Queen Mary never doubted that it was her business to minister to this desire. She followed her own independent interests, but as a wife she was content to be a background figure. She never, for instance, showed any disposition to interfere in politics, though she liked to be kept informed and got very angry with Baldwin when she thought that he was withholding information from her. Such was her discretion that George V probably underestimated the extent of her influence. 'Do you suppose that if my wife interfered with me in my work I should pay the slightest attention?' he once demanded. 'Well, sir, a clever woman can help her husband without him being aware of it,' came the brave reply.

For the truth was that George V could not live without her. Separation from the Queen became anathema to him. During their visit to Belgium in 1922 he was given a room the whole palace-length away from her; in the middle of the night she heard her bedroom door open and there was 'his dear, sad little face'. At the Jubilee celebrations in 1935 it was noted that the King's voice would crack with emotion whenever he spoke of Queen Mary. Yet he was never an easy husband. On the contrary, the older he got, the more irascible and pig-headed he became. The least deviation or innovation in etiquette or in dress infuriated him. If his consort's clothes were always out of date, that was because the King decided that they should be. In the 1920s the Queen, eager to make some concession to the prevailing fashion, persuaded Lady Airlie, one of her ladies-in-waiting, to take up her hem an inch or two in order to test the King's reaction. George V's outrage was instantaneous, and the experiment had to be abandoned.

There was virtually no social life at court, save for the odd occasion like Ascot week when every year the same fossilised old fogeys were invited to Windsor for gatherings of killing formality and excruciating dullness. Generally the King and Queen would dine alone together in full fig – he in white tie and wearing the Garter, she always complete with tiara. If any other member of the family was present the King became alarmed. 'We won't talk will we?' he would anxiously enquire. The royal household was run according to regulations drawn up in the reign of George III.

Of course Queen Mary was stuffy too, perhaps even stuffier than George V when it came to upholding court etiquette. She became 'ragingly angry' – shades of her father – when a guest dared to appear at court with a dress slashed up to the knee. She was not amused, either, when the Duchess of Westminster, rather overdoing the obeisance, left the print of lipstick on the royal gloves. 'She gave me one withering look that said all,' recalled the Duchess, 'and I slunk away in disgrace.' Queen Mary spent a lot of time being unamused, rather more than Queen Victoria. Her royal dignity would permit no display of public emotion. On one occasion, so the story goes, she was in an antique shop in the Norfolk town of Fakenham when a bullock from the market suddenly burst into the premises, scattering china and trampling over the furniture. Everyone dived for cover save the Queen, who merely raised her lorgnette to her eyes and held her parasol imperiously out before her. The enraged beast, cowed into submission, was duly led away; the Queen resumed her inspection of the wares on display. The anecdote, however embroidered, does at least convey the truth that no one ever took liberties with Queen Mary. Her attention to formality never relaxed. Even when she went to stay with a friend in the country, a long list of instructions would precede her arrival. There was, for instance, to be a chair placed outside her bedroom door on which her footman could sit all night.

Just occasionally, though, there was a hint of something human still stirring beneath the royal façade. Examples of her wit, admittedly, usually have a slightly desperate air, as though the teller were inwardly convinced that he is attempting the impossible. There was, however, a sly streak in Queen Mary. She took a malicious delight in the occasion when she handed a bishop a dog biscuit to give to the dog beside him, and His Lordship, being rather hard of hearing, gobbled it up himself. Another story shows a rather more subtle relish in another's discomfiture. Sir Osbert Sitwell remembered going with Queen Mary to see a Lady Ailesbury who, as the Queen recalled *en route*, had 'flirted outrageously with my cousin the Grand Duke of Mecklenburg-Strelitz'. Queen Mary did not mean the malefactor to forget this fact. 'I believe you were a great friend of my cousin,' she volunteered on her arrival, with 'an air of undisguised mischief'. 'Yes,' returned the hapless Lady Ailesbury, seeking desperately to turn the conversation, '*and of the Grand Duchess*'.

Queen Mary also, we are told, possessed a talent for mimicry.

She certainly liked going to the theatre. Rather unexpectedly, too, she loved dancing, at which she was appallingly bad. She took an energetic part in the annual ghillies' ball at Balmoral, and even when nearly eighty danced until one in the morning at a family gathering in Sandringham. Lady Airlie, who considered that Queen Mary was of a 'naturally gay and sociable temperament', continually emphasises that in private she could set aside the royal mask. We read of her laughing at jokes in *Punch* 'and even in *La Vie Parisienne*'; of her hopping around the drawing-room at Windsor in a green and white dress in order to impersonate a grasshopper in an after-dinner game; of her singing 'Yes, We Have No Bananas' at the top of her voice, in order (but here Lady Airlie does strain credulity) to shock a particularly staid member of the household. It has even been said, though not by Lady Airlie, that the Queen enjoyed off-colour jokes, providing of course they were told both by and about royalty.

More convincing, though, and more attractive, are the accounts of Queen Mary's fundamental kindness. True, she would cast a wary eye over the many begging letters which she received every day. No one was quicker to detect a fraudulent claim, and she had very little time for the undeserving poor. But where she was convinced of the genuineness of the need and the worthiness of the supplicant she bestowed her charity promptly, efficiently, and often anonymously. The same brisk but benevolent approach is evident in her dealings with servants. She expected their work to be perfectly done, and treated any sloppiness with severity. But if one of her staff was in trouble – a maid pregnant perhaps – she did what she could to help without indulging in any facile moral judgements.

Queen Mary had many social but few intellectual inhibitions. In the 1940s she went to an American play called *Pin-Up Girl* which dealt, among other things, with adolescent sex and venereal disease. The Queen expressed her approval of the manner in which these subjects were handled. She never suffered from any illusions about human nature. 'Fancy telling them to go off and use self-control,' she remarked apropos of the birth-control debate. In many respects the mental climate which she preferred to inhabit was that of the virtuous Victorian free-thinker. She considered, for instance, 'that Buddhism and the Brahmin religions were better than ours in many ways'; and her devotions, though nominally Christian, were addressed to a largely undefined deity. Archbishop Fisher characterised her as 'what you would call Low Church; it's the tendency of all the Royal Family. They come from the continent, you see.'

It was difficult, though, to be a free-thinker when married to George V. The King nursed a deep suspicion of 'eyebrows', as he believed they were spelt. Early in their marriage Queen Mary gave up all hope of educating him. 'With all my love of history you can imagine what a pleasure all this has been to me,' she wrote to the Grand Duchess after a private visit to Versailles, Chantilly and Fontainebleau. 'Alas for my poor George all these things are a sealed book, such a pity & so deplorable in his position.' Travel, indeed, was the King's particular phobia, and after the royal tour of Italy in 1923 he resolved never again to be tempted from England. 'Abroad is *bloody*,' he would say. 'I know. I've been.' It was only doctors' orders that forced him on to a Mediterranean cruise in 1925, and that holiday was a disaster for Queen Mary. Throughout the cruise the King and his sister Princess Victoria teased her mercilessly about her cultural interests and refused to put into port in order to sightsee. Queen Mary was glad to get home. Not that George V's philistinism was any less pungent in England. 'There you go again, May,' he would say when his wife enthused over some piece, 'furniture, furniture, furniture.'

Queen Mary performed an invaluable service in identifying and cataloguing the artistic treasures that were scattered so haphazardly about the various palaces. The work appealed to her innate love of system and regulation. She especially enjoyed a cultural detective hunt: to discover a chair missing from a set, for example; or to light upon some manuscript reference to an object and then track the article down in an obscure corner. Her hobby made her something of an expert on eighteenth-century furniture and china, while visits to museums and country houses became her main source of pleasure, 'much nicer than going out to tea and gossip', she thought. In no sense, though, was she ever a true connoisseur, for she completely lacked the objective approach of the real scholar. 'We prefer the picture to remain as by Nollekins,' she remarked, when informed of a doubtful attribution. Her confident judgements could, in their way, be as philistine as George V's ignorant ejaculations, and rather more damaging in effect. A painting by Francis Danby was destroyed on Queen Mary's orders because she felt that the colours had faded. Again, in a misguided attempt to make a magnificent epergne by Alfred Gilbert even more resplendent she had it gilded all over, thus losing the effect of contrasting metals that the artist had intended.

Her prime interest, in fact, was never in art at all but in the history of her family. A portrait of one of her Cambridge ancestors would hold her attention to the exclusion of any great masterpiece. Even the idea for her famous doll's house, her most notable addition to the royal collection, was first presented to her under the guise of family history, as a means of creating a permanent memorial to the way in which the King and Queen lived during the early twentieth century. In the event the intention was somewhat diluted, and the house became rather the fantasy-creation of its designer, Sir Edward Lutyens. The honour for having originated the project belongs to Princess Marie-Louise, one of Queen Victoria's numerous grandchildren, who also handled the considerable administrative work involved. Once Queen Mary's interest was engaged, however, she followed the construction and furnishing of the house with fascinated absorption. It was her prestige that inspired so many craftsmen, artists and writers to give of their best, turning what might have been simply a passing jest into an enduring, and, in its passionate eccentricity, peculiarly English work of art.

The doll's house represents Queen Mary's interest in the arts at its most fruitful. There was however a darker side to this passion. The Queen gained the reputation of having been a ruthless and avaricious collector of antiques and jewels. Gossip about her predatory techniques abounds: how antique dealers would hide their wares at her approach lest they be forced by an exercise of queenly authority to concede a bargain; how she would send out relations and ladies-in-waiting to haggle on her behalf; or how, visiting other people's houses, she would admire whatsoever caught her eye with such pertinacity – 'I am caressing it with my eyes' – that the unfortunate owners would eventually feel obliged to surrender the coveted piece.

The first thing to be said about such stories is that they are a lot more common than any hard evidence in their support. One may also reflect that if anyone was weak enough to part with a prized possession merely in order to ingratiate themselves with royalty they deserved what they got, which was liable to be a signed picture of the Queen. There can be no question, though, that Queen Mary always took what she was offered, or that she possessed a large sense of what was due to her. It is also true that she never enjoyed parting with cash. As a relation tactfully put it, 'she was generous in spirit but extremely mean about money'.

Suzy Menkes, in her fascinating book *The Royal Jewels*, remarks that the strong-room for valuables in the doll's house occupies a space roughly similar to that provided for the children's nursery. Queen Mary amassed jewels without ever cloying the appetite she fed; she made herself hungry where most she satisfied. There has ever been a certain brand of royalty-worshipper who thrills with excitement at the sight of the object of his devotion swathed in shimmering gems. 'Queen Mary glittered with five diamond necklaces about her neck,' 'Chips' Channon ecstatically recorded. 'She was in blue with literally mountains of jewels.' It was extraordinary, such devotees would insist, how, notwithstanding the plenitude of her adornment, Queen Mary avoided any suspicion of vulgarity. Nothing, apparently, succeeded like excess. 'I have never known any Empress or Queen who could wear a quantity of superb jewels with such ease and simplicity and without appearing overladen.' This kind of comment invites the unworthy, and, alas, the vulgar, reflection that few other queens and empresses possessed such a massive bust on which to display their treasures. Many may find the photographs of Queen Mary's chilling, thin-lipped countenance staring glassily out from the prodigious scattering of sparklers the most resistible of all the images that she presented.

Her penchant for ostentatious display becomes the more distasteful in the light of the lengths to which she would go in order to acquire these baubles. Suzy Menkes tells a sorry tale of how Queen Mary came to possess herself of the Romanov jewels brought out of Russia at the Revolution by the Tsar's mother, the Dowager Empress Marie Feodorovna, Queen Alexandra's sister. When the Dowager Empress died in Denmark in 1928, her jewels were spirited away to England by Fritz Ponsonby, the King's Private Secretary. Ponsonby believed that the English royal family had sold them for £350,000 and put the money in trust for the Dowager Empress's daughters, the Grand Duchesses Xenia and Olga. Xenia and Olga, however, never received more than £100,000. Instead of selling the Dowager Empress's jewels Queen Mary held on to them until 1933, and then, in the depths of the Depression, bought them in for a mere £60,000. For a woman who already possessed the greatest collection of jewellery in the world, it was less than generous. In consequence, the likes of Chips Channon were still more impressed by the Queen's magnificence; and the Grand Duchess Olga died above Ray's Barbershop in Toronto.

There is, indeed, something to be said on Queen Mary's behalf. It is true that George V had given pensions to both the Dowager Empress and her daughter the Grand Duchess Xenia, although there had surely been no suggestion, when these sums were paid, that they were to be treated as credits on account. It is also true that Queen Mary regarded her jewels rather as a family than as a personal possession, and that, far from hoarding her treasures, she could be generous about passing them on to the next generation. These, however, are only peripheral considerations. The crown appeared to acknowledge Queen Mary's sharp dealing when it made a payment to the Grand Duchesses' heirs in 1968.

The obvious explanation for Queen Mary's avariciousness, perhaps too obvious to be altogether convincing, would be that it stemmed back to the humiliations of her youth; that the Queen who dripped with jewels was exacting revenge on behalf of the shy, sensitive girl whose adolescence had been haunted by an awareness of uncertain royal credentials and inadequate family finances. Especially in the petty courts of her German relations, status and prestige had been measured in quarterings and diamonds which Princess May did not possess. From the moment of her marriage, therefore, Queen Mary delighted to show who was now at the top of the heap.

Her covetousness might equally be seen, however, as another symptom of her dehumanised personality. The historian Richard Cobb remembers seeing Queen Mary arrive at the British Museum in 1938. His companion shouted out a loud and embarrassing 'Ave'. 'But the ramrod lady, advancing majestically as if on hidden wheels beneath her grey fur-lined long skirt, looked right through us, as if we had been transparent . . . her very blue eyes betraying no emotion whatsoever, her face, heavily enamelled seen close up, not showing the slightest movement. If she had heard the greeting – as she must have done – her expression registered absolutely nothing.'

Talking to Queen Mary, Chips Channon admiringly recorded, was like addressing St Paul's Cathedral.

Of course this marmoreal quality had its positive side, was indeed an integral part of Queen Mary's image. Her subjects rightly believed her to be as solid as rock, and could not imagine her desiring any pleasure beyond her royal duties. She had always been shy, and after her marriage the formalities of her position, by no means unwelcome to her, further reduced the possibility of any spontaneous or natural expression of feeling. Her interests gravitated towards the dead and inanimate; to the dusty fascination of genealogy, for instance, rather than to the problems of her own children; to objects that might be classified for once and all time, rather than to the shifting uncertainties of the contemporary scene. But human nature, baulked at one outlet, frequently finds another. The emotion which Queen Mary so conspicuously failed to release in ordinary day-to-day contacts was concentrated instead upon furniture, jewels and china. When she spoke of her possessions her eyes lit with an enthusiasm and an excitement that she rarely manifested in her dealings with people.

Queen Mary's acquisitive oddities, though fruitful of dinner-party gossip, never affected her wider public image. To her subjects at large she continued to appear, with good reason, the embodiment of dedication and solid sense. The crowds who turned out in such numbers to cheer George V's Jubilee in 1935 bestowed at least an equal part of their enthusiasms upon his consort. Yet Queen Mary was about to enter a year of three kings, in which she would receive the sharpest jolt of her life.

4

King George V very nearly died from an abscess in his chest during the winter of 1928–29, and thereafter was obviously living on borrowed time. The King's uncertain hold on life increased the popular tendency to regard Queen Mary almost as a coequal sovereign. In her own eyes, though, her position remained entirely subordinate. Lady Airlie even opines that the Queen delighted in the feeling that she could be useful to her husband when ministering to him during his prolonged convalescence. The King had always been lamentably short on personal attentions towards Queen Mary, so that if he ever did compliment her she would blush with pleasure and satisfaction. The written notes of gratitude seem to have dried up in the last years of the marriage, perhaps because the King and Queen were almost always together. There is, however, a touching picture of the two of them sitting together on a bench at Windsor in the autumn of 1935, her hand extended protectively on his knee. In that year, amidst all the Jubilee celebrations, the King gave several hints that he would not survive much longer; and, as ever, he was as good as his word.

The end came quietly at Sandringham on 20 January 1936. '*Am brokenhearted*,' Queen Mary recorded in her diary. Her demeanour, however, remained rigidly self-controlled. She did not forget in her grief that, though kings may die, monarchy endures. No sooner had the breath left her husband's body than she turned to her eldest son, bowed and kissed his hand with a fervent 'God save the King.' Edward VIII later professed to be embarrassed. 'I could not bring myself to believe that the members of my own family, or indeed anyone else, should be expected to humble themselves before me in this way.' Such a statement appears more than a trifle disingenuous in a man whose whole life had been spent in the shadow of the throne. What the remark really conveyed was that the new King had no time for his parents' values.

From his earliest youth he had exhibited a certain diffidence about his royal position. For all his charm, and the dazzling success of the tours that he made as Prince of Wales, the gulf between his personality and the role for which he had been born steadily widened. No doubt the spirit of contrariety was innate, but his childhood cannot have helped. Nor later, when he was a young man, did his parents help reconcile him to his role. There was no social life worthy of the name at court. If the Prince was to have any fun at all he was obliged to seek it elsewhere.

He did not choose well. King George V exaggerated when he complained that his son did not count one proper gentleman among his friends, but there was no denying a vulgar and flash quality about the Prince's life-style, reflected sartorially in the loud checks and suede shoes which he loved to wear. Such things did not greatly matter in themselves: the problem was that in declaring war upon his father's dreary conservatism, the Prince also abandoned George V's high standards of honour and duty. The same kind of reaction against his parents might be discerned in the Prince's love-life. Predictably both Freda Dudley Ward (his mistress in the 1920s) and Mrs Simpson were anathema to George V; equally, with their flat-chested physiques, and their direct, irreverent, sharp, relaxed personalities, they might have been deliberately selected as contrasts to Queen Mary. The key to their success with the Prince (and he became slavishly devoted to both of them in turn) was their ability to create the warm, cosy, *domestic* atmosphere which Queen Mary had been unable to provide, and to wrap him in an affectionate, teasing and familiar intimacy that Queen Mary could never have understood. Too late, in adulthood, he was treated like the wayward but essentially lovable child that perhaps he had always been.

Yet Queen Mary should not be made the scapegoat for the flaws in her son. The Abdication is now such a familiar story that it has become difficult to appreciate just how bizarre the King's behaviour was. No one, not even Lady Donaldson in her excellent and penetrating biography of Edward VIII, has quite succeeded in pinning the man down, so it hardly seems fair to put Queen Mary in the dock for failing to understand in advance what no one has entirely explained retrospectively.

After all, whatever her failings as a mother, her other children appeared to overcome them. Her second son Prince Albert (known in the family as 'Bertie'), in contrast to his elder brother, could hardly have been more unpromising as a boy. Stammering, knock-kneed, sickly, and liable to uncontrollable rages when his lack of ability was exposed, his youth was a succession of disasters. Yet, though it could certainly not be claimed that his parents handled him with sensitivity, Prince Albert never for a moment rejected their values, or ceased in his efforts to win their commendation. Moreover, where the Prince of Wales confirmed his sense of alienation with his devotion to married women who could never be part of his royal life, Bertie found release and salvation by falling in love with a young Scottish aristocrat whom even George V and Queen Mary deemed to be entirely suitable. Indeed, when Lady Elizabeth Bowes-Lyon presumed to refuse her less than glamorous royal suitor – Bertie had a twitch about the mouth and there were rumours of a drinking problem – Queen Mary mobilised herself in support of her son, condescending so far as to shed the lustre of her presence over the girl's home at Glamis Castle. The couple were duly married in 1923. Their eldest child, Princess Elizabeth, a potential queen from the moment of her birth in 1926, became a particular favourite of Queen Mary, who managed to discern a likeness to Queen Victoria. Sixty years on it might be thought that Elizabeth II is rather more like her grandmother.

Of Queen Mary's other children, Prince Henry settled into a career in the Army and into a satisfactory marriage with the Duke of Buccleuch's daughter. 'Don't buy a lot of jewellery in a hurry,' Queen Mary prudently warned him on the announcement of his engagement, 'because Cousin Fredericka of Hanover left you some nice diamond things which can be converted & I have long ago selected for yr wife from my collection.'

The fourth son, Prince George, was potentially a more dangerous character. By far the brightest, as well as the tallest and most dashing of the Princes, he had intensely disliked his allotted career in the Navy, and seemed at one time well on the way to the dogs. As a young man his sexual appetite had been both insatiable and unpredictable. In the late 1920s he had alarmed his parents with his passion for one Poppy Baring; in the early 1930s a large sum had to be paid for the recovery of letters written to a young man in Paris. There were also dark tales of drug-taking. Queen Mary, however, preferred to know nothing of these things. She delighted in Prince George, the only one of her children to whom she succeeded in imparting her enthusiasm for collecting. Besides, his marriage to the beautiful and sophisticated Princess Marina of Greece in 1934 appeared to have steadied him down. Marina was even a match for Queen Mary. 'I'm afraid the King doesn't like painted nails,' the Queen loftily informed her daughter-in-law when she turned up at Buckingham Palace. 'Your George may not,' returned Marina, 'but mine does.'

The youngest child, Prince John, had been both epileptic and subnormal; he was kept on a farm on the Sandringham estate until he died in 1919, at the age of thirteen. As for the only daughter, Princess Mary, her mother had ambitions that she should marry Prince Ernst August of Hanover, who was heir to the Duke of Brunswick and a great fortune. In this respect Queen Mary showed herself to be less modern than Queen Victoria, who had decided by 1869 that 'great foreign alliances' were 'no good'. In the end, however, Princess Mary married the Earl of Lascelles, again with the full approval of both her parents. All the surviving children except one, therefore, were well settled in life by the end of George V's reign; and all of them except one enjoyed cordial relations with their parents.

It is no exaggeration to say that George V came to loathe his eldest son – for his cocky modernity, for his flip views, most of all for his impossible women. Mrs Dudley Ward, 'the lacemaker's daughter' in George V's contemptuous phrase, had been bad enough, but Mrs Simpson, as the King quickly realised, was a far more dangerous portent. The Prince of Wales actually insisted on introducing her to his parents at a Buckingham House reception before Prince George's wedding in 1934, a deliberate hint, surely, that this time he would go to any lengths. Mrs Simpson blandly recorded of this meeting in her memoirs that she had been 'impressed with Their Majesties' great gift for making everyone they met, however casually, feel at ease in their presence'. Few others ever remarked upon this particular skill in King George and Queen Mary, even when they were welcome guests, which Mrs Simpson most emphatically was not. 'That woman in my house!' the King exclaimed in fury afterwards. Mrs Simpson was more honest when, describing the King's steely glance resting upon her at a reception in 1935, she claimed to have felt the 'icy menace' behind it.

One can only regret that this intuition did not carry more weight with her. But Mrs Simpson had too much courage, confidence and ambition to be put off by a few withering glances, even when administered by George V and Queen Mary. Though she obviously recognised the difficulties in front of her, she never permitted herself to see the sheer impossibility of the King of England, the Head of the Church, marrying a woman who had 'two husbands living', as Queen Mary bluntly put the matter. Mrs Simpson, having embarked upon her glorious adventure, meant to see it through to the end. As for the Prince, it was certainly unfortunate that he had fallen abjectly in love with a woman who, while wholly impressed by the monarchy's prestige, believed that she might flout its mystique. On the other hand, Mrs Simpson's bold carelessness about the royal assumptions that the Prince's parents held most dear may well have constituted an essential part of the hold which she exerted over him. The authoritative way in which she removed the picture of Queen Mary from the drawing-room of Fort Belvedere, the Prince's house near Windsor, was far more significant a decision than a mere matter of internal decoration.

George V was in no doubt about how it would all end. 'After I am dead, the boy will ruin himself in twelve months,' he told Baldwin. Yet somehow the old King, who was always so ready with rebukes for the least irregularity in etiquette or dress, could not bring himself to confront his son. Perhaps he no longer cared for him sufficiently to make the effort to save him. 'I pray to God', he said a few weeks before his death, 'that my eldest son will never marry and have children, and that nothing will come between Bertie and Lilibet and the throne.' Queen Mary, of course, would not have considered it any part of her duty – and she rarely acted from any other motive – to raise the dread topic with her son while George V was still alive; neither, it swiftly became evident, was she inclined to broach the subject after her husband's death. 'I have not liked to talk to David [the Prince] about this affair with Mrs Simpson,' she told Lady Airlie in February 1936, 'in the first place because I don't want to give the impression of interfering in his private life, and also because he is the most obstinate of all my sons. To oppose him over doing anything is only to make him more determined to do it. At present he is utterly infatuated, but my great hope is that violent infatuations usually wear off.'

For Queen Mary, indeed, the implications of Mrs Simpson were simply unthinkable. It must have seemed cruelly ironic to her that David, of all her sons, should be the one who now callously threatened to undermine everything she stood for. As a young man he had always seemed, at least for those who looked on the surface of things, ideally suited to the office he would one day occupy. The praises heaped upon him during his tours of the Empire after the First World War had been music to her ears. 'He really is a marvel in spite of all his "fads",' she wrote to George V in 1919, 'and I confess I feel very proud of him, don't you?' The interrogative, perhaps, was already symptomatic of the doubts that George V felt on the subject; nevertheless, in spite of the multiplying instances of her son's vanity, egoism and wilfulness, Queen Mary was able to convince herself, through the assuaging power of distance, that nothing serious was amiss. 'David dined with me in the evening,' she wrote in a typical message to George V, 'we talked a lot but of nothing very intimate'.

Even after the appearance of Mrs Simpson, Queen Mary continued to hope that everything would turn out well in the end. He could not possibly marry the woman; he must see that. And yet . . . and yet, the worried mother could not but observe the most disquieting symptoms. 'He gives Mrs Simpson the most beautiful jewels,' she told Lady Airlie in May 1936. Queen Mary was the last person on earth to miss the significance of that. Still, though, she stopped short of believing that her son had crossed the Rubicon. Her worst fear was that he would ask her to receive Mrs Simpson, an imagining which, according to Lady Airlie, brought 'bright spots of crimson' to her cheek-bones. That was a pity, for both Queen Mary and Mrs Simpson were, in their very different ways, shrewd worldly women; and if, *per impossibile*, they had been able to talk, Mrs Simpson might well have grasped the odds against her. As things were, the King moved towards disaster like a sleepwalker, casting eyes neither to right nor to left. He did not just maintain his loyalty to Mrs Simpson after ascending to the throne; he *flaunted* it. If his intention really was to marry her and remain King he could hardly have acted more stupidly.

In August, when the King went on a Mediterranean cruise, pictures of him with Mrs Simpson were flashed around the world, frequently showing the King clad only in his swimming trunks. The press in England had not yet broken their silence about the affair, yet kind friends abroad made sure that the foreign press cuttings and comments reached Queen Mary. Still, though, she could not act. Edward VIII, on his return, went immediately to dine with his mother, now installed in Marlborough House. Her main concern, apparently, was the weather. 'Didn't you find it terribly warm in the Adriatic?' she inquired solicitously.

Only on 16 November was she finally forced to confront the facts. After dinner that day the King at last told her that he intended to marry Mrs Simpson whatever happened, even if he had to abdicate. A few hours earlier he had told the Prime Minister, Stanley Baldwin, the same thing. How far the King now was from any rational assessment of his situation is illustrated by the fact that he begged his mother to allow him to bring Mrs Simpson to see her. For Queen Mary, though, it must have been almost a relief to be able, after so many months of internal agony, to talk about the crisis. Next day she met the Prime Minister. Normally, Baldwin recalled, these encounters were glacial. 'She had a way . . . of standing at the end of the room when one was shown in at Buckingham Palace; and she would remain there like a statue while you made your bow and walked over a sometimes very slippery floor to kiss her hand.' On this occasion, however, 'she came trotting across the room *exactly like a puppy dog*: and before I had time to bow, she took hold of my hand in both of hers and held it tight. "Well, Prime Minister," she said, "here's a pretty kettle of fish!"'

Queen Mary next saw the King at dinner on 24 November, and again late on 3 December, but she quite failed to influence him. After it was all over, Baldwin would comment that the most astonishing thing about the King's behaviour was the complete absence of moral struggle. 'He had *no* spiritual conflict *at all*. There was no battle in his will . . . no idea of sacrifice for duty.' But how could there be? Once Edward VIII had rejected the religion of royalty on which his parents had based their lives, he had rejected the only moral education that they had given him. Abstract notions of 'duty' carried no weight with him at all; nor, one suspects, did they ultimately mean a great deal to Queen Mary *except in so far as they served the throne*. (Remember her admiration for Catherine the Great; remember the Romanov jewels.) Edward VIII, for whatever reason, quite early in his life cut himself away from the one great rock to which his mother's principles were moored, and thereafter he was for ever adrift, helpless prey to any will that engulfed his own. He could not do his job without Mrs Simpson, he kept repeating, like a player conning his part; he could not do his job without Mrs Simpson, he was going to marry her, he was going to marry her.

It seems that Queen Mary quickly realised that her elder son was, in her terms, a lost cause; at all events her efforts to deflect him from his chosen course were not sustained. She poured scorn upon the proposal that the King should save his throne by marrying Mrs Simpson morganatically. 'Really,' she said, 'this might be

Roumania.' As soon as it became evident to her that the present occupant of the throne had betrayed his sacred trust, she set herself two principal tasks: to limit so far as possible the damage to the crown, and to lend all her support to the next King. Thus, in the last week of Edward VIII's reign, while the nation was agog for news, she carried on her outward life as though nothing was amiss. There was a visit to Sydenham, where the Crystal Palace had burnt down on 30 November; another to Dulwich in order to inspect an aviary. The King might go, her unchanged schedule proclaimed: the monarchy was eternal. 'Thank God we have all got you as a central point,' one of the royal family wrote, 'because without it [the family] might easily disintegrate.'

All her will-power, however, was required to steady the nerves of the Duke of York. Bertie, not to put too fine a point on the matter, was a wreck. On 9 December he went to see Queen Mary and, in his own words, 'broke down and sobbed like a child'. His mother screwed up his courage to the sticking-point, rather as, forty-five years before, her own mother had told her she must go through with the marriage to Prince Eddy. All the same, it was an alarming moment for Queen Mary, and for once her emotions spilled over into her diary. 'Bertie arrived very late from Fort Belvedere,' she recorded of that meeting, 'and Mr Monckton brought him & me the paper drawn up for David's abdication of the Throne of this Empire because he wishes to marry Mrs Simpson!!!!!' Seldom have exclamation marks been so eloquent. 'The whole affair has lasted since Novr. 16th and has been very painful – It is a terrible blow to us all & particularly to poor Bertie.' 'Poor Bertie', a figure in whom she had shown only a peripheral interest these last forty-one years, had instantaneously been elevated, as George VI, into the major concern of her life. By contrast, the Duke of Windsor, as the ex-King became known, was of strictly passing interest. She even tried to dissuade him from making a farewell broadcast. Nothing, now, must detract from Bertie.

Much has been written of the hostility shown by George VI's consort, Queen Elizabeth, towards the Windsors, and of her determination that they should never occupy any position in which they might pose the least threat to the popularity and standing of the new monarch. It is to Queen Mary, however, that one should look for the genesis of this attitude. She made a conscious effort to put on a public front of unconcern in the aftermath of the Abdication; actually, she regarded her eldest son with fury. 'HM is still angry with the Duke,' wrote a lady-in-waiting in March 1937, '& I really think that helps her to bear what she called "the humiliation" of it all.' Another thing that helped her to bear the humiliation was making sure that Mrs Simpson's friends were excised from royal acquaintance. 'The other day in my presence', she wrote with satisfaction to Prince Paul of Yugoslavia, 'Bertie told George he wished him and Marina never to see Lady Cunard again and George said he would not do so. I fear she has *done David a great deal of harm* as there is no doubt that she was great friends with Mrs S at one time . . . Under the circumstances I feel none of us, in fact people in society, should meet her . . . and I am hoping that George and Marina will no longer see certain people who alas were friends of Mrs S and Lady Cunard's and also David's.' Even Winston Churchill, who had pleaded Edward VIII's cause in the House of Commons at great personal cost, temporarily lost favour with Queen Mary.

In 1938 she further relieved her feelings by sending the Duke of Windsor a magisterial and (many will feel) an unanswerable rebuke:

> You ask me in your letter of the 23rd June to write to you frankly about my true feelings with regard to you and the present position and this I will do now. You will remember how miserable I was when you informed me of your intended marriage and abdication and how I implored you not to do so for your sake and for the sake of the country. You did not seem able to take in any point of view but your own . . . I do not think you have ever realized the shock, which the attitude you took up caused your family and the whole Nation. It seemed inconceivable to those who had made such sacrifices during the war that you, as their King, refused a lesser sacrifice . . . My feelings for you as your Mother remain the same, and our being parted and the cause of it, grieve me beyond words. After all, all my life I have put my Country before everything else, and I simply cannot change now.

Queen Mary saw her eldest son again on odd occasions after the Second World War, and once even sent 'a kind message to your wife'. But she never really forgave him.

The Duke, however, was quite incorrigible. For the rest of his life he felt outraged that his wife was not allowed to use the title 'Her Royal Highness'. As for Queen Mary, 'my mother was a cold woman, a cold woman'. 'Ice instead of blood in the veins is a fine preservative,' he wrote bitterly to the Duchess of Windsor when his mother was dying. That, he knew, was the sort of comment that went down well with his better half. But somewhere in the depths of him, behind his jaunty unconcern about what he had done, there lurked a presence that could never be appeased. 'Mama,' he cried as he lay on his own death-bed in 1972, 'Mama, Mama, Mama . . .'

5

With the outbreak of the Second World War, an uninvited and entirely unexpected presence reappeared in Queen Mary's life: the spirit of comedy. The irreverent imp, which had hovered so gratefully over the vicissitudes of the Teck family, never found a secure dwelling in the presence of George V. The King could only see a joke if it was advertised as such; and the soul of wit recoils from regimented displays of mirth. True comedy thrives on characters and situations which are out of joint, on masks that fail to fit, on pretension pricked and humanity triumphant in all its native frailty. One might therefore expect to find plenty of material for the comic spirit at court, where random scraps of mortality are decked in the ill-suiting panoply of status. But George V – it is a measure of his success as a constitutional monarch – utterly depressed the mischievous sprite. Had his court been merely dull, there might yet have been a place for laughter. There was, however, a depth and consistency, even a kind of integrity, about its dullness, which defeated even mockery. Nor did the reign of George VI promise any differently. If the spirit of comedy was ever again to light upon Queen Mary, she would have to be transported into a completely different world. And that was precisely what the war achieved.

It had been decided that, upon the outbreak of war, the Queen Mother, along with primary schoolchildren, their teachers, and mothers with children under five, would be evacuated from the capital. Queen Mary at first resisted her removal. She loved London and felt that it was 'not at all the thing' to leave it in a national emergency. Only with difficulty was she persuaded that her presence in the capital would be an additional and avoidable worry for the government when the German bombs began to drop. Badminton House in Gloucestershire, home of the Duke of Beaufort, was selected to receive her, largely perhaps because the Duke was married to her niece, Adolphus's daughter.

Her hosts were made to feel the honour that was done them. Queen Mary did not intend that her banishment should involve any substantial reduction in the staff that attended her in Marlborough House. 'Oh, how I longed for you to be there when she and about fifty-five servants arrived,' the Duchess of Beaufort wrote to Sir Osbert Sitwell. 'Pandemonium was the least it could be called! The servants revolted, and scorned our humble home. They refused to use the excellent rooms assigned to them. Fearful rows and battle royals [were] fought over my body – but I won in the end and reduced them to tears and to pulp . . . I can laugh now, but I have never been so angry! . . . The Queen, quite unconscious of the stir, has settled in well . . .'

No doubt Queen Mary nurtured the best intentions towards her hosts, but, after nearly fifty years of being deferred to, the role of humble and grateful guest proved beyond her. At table it was ordained, as ever, that there should be at least two feet between Queen Mary and her nearest neighbour; and this arrangement proved to her merely an outward symbol of a general assumption of command. 'I've adopted the house and family as my own,' she told Sir Osbert Sitwell, and so she had, even to the extent of teaching the Duke of Beaufort, as she had once taught her children, how to knit. The Beauforts found themselves squeezed into two bedrooms and a sitting-room, a situation to which they submitted with admirable grace. Only the Dowager Duchess, who lived in a cottage on the estate, seemed to resent the sudden incursion into the county of one who was greater than she.

At first, during the 'phoney war', Queen Mary, who was a townee through and through, would escape from Badminton by making weekly visits to London. These metropolitan outings, however, necessarily became rarer after the events of spring 1940. The German victories in Scandinavia, which signalled the opening of real hostilities, evoked from her a characteristic reaction. 'What a vile enemy, I feel very bitter – Poor Christian of Denmark, poor Charles of Norway.' Subsequently, the fall of France seemed to threaten the spectre of 'poor Mary of Teck', but Queen Mary, though she privately admitted to a fear of falling into the hands of the Nazis, could never seriously believe in the possibility of ultimate success for a leader who spoke German with such an atrocious accent as Herr Hitler. Her argument proved sound enough in the long term; in the mean time, though, the bombing of London and the prolonged struggle in Europe extended her temporary sojourn at Badminton into a continuous five-year confrontation with rural life.

Queen Mary was quite unprepared for such a trial, having spent her first seventy-two years free of any contact with the mysterious processes of the country. She was not, however, the type to repine at any unavoidable crisis, and soon she was bringing the same capacity for study to bear upon agriculture that she had formerly unleashed upon social conditions. 'Oh, *that's* what hay looks like, is it?' she remarked shortly after her arrival at Badminton, when the Duchess of Beaufort drew her attention to a hayfield. Two years later she was making knowledgeable notes about the state of the crops as though she had been a countrywoman born and bred. Every aspect of her surroundings engaged her attention. 'Do hens have fleas?' she unexpectedly demanded one day of the Duke of Beaufort. On being assured that they did she pressed the enquiry still further. 'But do they bite human beings?'

Despite these unpredictable emanations of the scientific spirit on country matters – or had an insect presumed too far? – Queen Mary's heart remained true to her beloved London. As she read of the damage caused by bombing her diary entries became charged with a rare emotion. 'We are all miserable at the destruction of the Guildhall, of so many lovely Wren churches & of so many interesting buildings. I did not realise that I could really *hate* people as I do the Germans, tho' I never liked them.'

The Duchess of Beaufort, meanwhile, was reaching the conclusion that Queen Mary was 'fundamentally very, very German – the two things she liked most were *destruction* and *order*'. Queen Mary indulged both these passions at Badminton with a ruthless concentration of purpose that the Fuhrer himself might have admired. Her campaigns on the Beaufort estate grew out of her perception that life in the country offered opportunities for idleness hitherto unparalleled in her career. To Queen Mary there could have been no more potent incentive to action. Looking around, she immediately detected that the house and estate were under merciless attack from an insinuating and tenacious enemy with which she had already fought several stiff rounds at Sandringham. Ivy! The poor Beauforts had allowed themselves to be gulled by its deceitful charms. Under its seeming fair exterior did it not claw at stonework and strangle trees? Within a few days of coming to Badminton Queen Mary had the gardeners mobilised for an all-out assault on this most dangerous foe. Trees were denuded, walls stripped bare. Alas, though, the roots of the menace were so deep-set that in the following year, rather to Queen Mary's surprise, it presumed to launch a counter-attack. More and more savage, therefore, were the depredations that she ordered.

Nor, she came to see, was the problem confined to the pernicious ivy. Trees, she noticed, all too often grew in unnecessary places, and even when not *de trop* tended to sprout superfluous branches. As for scrub and undergrowth, it could serve no useful purpose whatever. The 'Ivy Squad' was swiftly expanded into a 'Wooding Squad' which grew to formidable proportions. Her four dispatch-riders constituted the solid core of this band, but Queen Mary frequently called up reinforcements from the company of soldiers – there were one hundred and twenty of them – who had been billeted in the Badminton stables in order to defend her against invading Nazis. Members of her household also found themselves dragooned. Every day after lunch, rain or shine, the leader, dressed rather for the galleries of Bond Street than for a foray into the Badminton estate, would march forth her Wooding Squad for further feats of deforestation. The work was rigorous, and there were several casualties. Two chauffeurs were knocked out and a Major Wickham broke his wrist. Queen Mary, who knew the value of example, led from the front, even to the extent of taking a hand with the saw. The ferocious energy which had sustained her multifarious activities as Queen was now channelled into unrestricted arboreal warfare. The end of the day at five o'clock, greeted with relief by the toiling labourers, always came too early for their commander. By 1945 over a hundred acres of scrubland had been cleared.

The Beauforts soon discovered that, if they ever left the house, no tree in the garden was safe. One day the Duchess went out hunting, leaving specific instructions that a certain group of shrubs should not on any account be touched. On the morrow she discovered that they had all been rased. Queen Mary, 'like a naughty child', as the Duchess thought, abruptly forestalled any criticism. 'I'm so glad to see you like my yesterday's work,' she volunteered. Subsequently, battle was joined over a magnificent cedar outside the drawing-room window. Queen Mary, who considered it cut out too much light from the house, determined that it must be felled, and only constant vigilance on the part of the Beauforts prevented the execution of this sentence. It was a relief when, just occasionally, the wooding fury gave way to the search for scrap, an activity that Queen Mary had favoured in the First World War. So long as she stuck to collecting such detritus as old bottles and tins all went well. In the quest for scrap iron, however, her enthusiasm was apt to run away with her. On one occasion a page appeared with an urgent message from a neighbouring farmer. 'Please, Your Majesty, a Mr Hodge has arrived, and he says Your Majesty has taken his plough, and will Your Majesty graciously give it back to him, please, at once, as he can't get on without it!'

Again as in the First World War, Queen Mary was much concerned with economies, stinting herself most conscientiously upon government rations lest anyone should presume to accuse her of enjoying special favours. The napkin ring was once more in evidence at her dinner table, together, this time, with an oilcloth that could be wiped at the end of every meal. When her wooding activities took her to the further limits of the estate she would use a horse-drawn farm-cart in order to avoid wasting petrol. 'Aunt May,' said the Duchess of Beaufort, seeing her drive off, 'you look as if you were in a tumbril.' 'Well, it may come to that yet, one never knows,' the old lady cheerfully replied. Obviously she was thoroughly enjoying herself. By sheer force of character she had succeeded, however eccentrically, in mastering a wholly unfamiliar environment; and shed some inhibitions in the process. Her sister-in-law Princess Alice thought that, after the long years married to George V, Queen Mary rediscovered the marginally lighter touch of Princess May.

Yet, as appears in another memorable vignette which James Pope-Hennessy garnered from the Duchess of Beaufort, the essence of Queen Mary's appeal was that, under all conditions, she remained entirely true to herself. During the first air-raid warning the Duchess was told that the Queen wanted to see her in the reinforced shelter. 'It was a mistake, of course; she hadn't sent for me at all. Well, there I was in the middle of the night, with my hair all anyhow and in a filthy old dressing-gown; and there in the shelter sat Queen Mary, perfectly dressed with her pearls, doing a crossword puzzle. On one side of her was her Lady, who had taken a sleeping pill and kept sagging over to one side. Whenever the Queen said, "High life in six letters beginning with a T, Constance," she'd just grunt "Huh-huh-huh", and flop over again; on the other side of the Queen was her maid, gripping two jewel cases firmly. I never did that again, I just couldn't compete.'

Lady Airlie thought that Queen Mary was 'secretly lonely' in the country, and it is true that she missed the mental stimulation that London afforded. For this reason she looked forward eagerly to the visits of her son the Duke of Kent, with whom she could chat about their respective collecting hobbies. The Duke's death in an air crash in August 1942 was a cruel blow, though one to which Queen Mary reacted with her accustomed stoicism. Four days after the funeral the Wooding Squad was back in action. 'I am so glad I can take up my occupations again,' the Queen noted, 'Georgie would have wished me to do so.' Thereafter Sir Osbert Sitwell would occasionally be summoned to accompany her on expeditions to the antique shops of Bath and Bristol.

Rural existence did not in the least diminish Queen Mary's appetite for public work. Her visits to schools, hospitals and factories continued, while her keen interest in local affairs made her a well known figure in the Badminton neighbourhood. When she went out in her car the chauffeur would be ordered to give a lift to any servicemen whom they met along the way. This could be an alarming experience for the men. 'Do you know who I am?' Queen Mary would enquire, before proceeding to quiz them about their lives. Thus, driving back from Windsor after the Duke of Kent's funeral she met 'a charming young American parachutist, most friendly', as well as 'a nice Sergeant Observer (Air Force) who had taken part in the raid on Dieppe last week'. Of course Queen Mary remained entirely royal. 'Perhaps we should still be one country', she was heard to remark to some American officers at Badminton, 'if my great-grandfather hadn't been so obstinate.' Nevertheless, the majesty of Badminton was quite different from, and far more sympathetic than, the glacial regality of the pre-war years. '*Cheer*, you little idiots, can't you?' Queen Mary had muttered under her breath in 1938 when some schoolchildren gawped at her car. In 1943 she might have given them a lift.

Queen Mary herself recognised the change that Badminton had wrought in her. 'Oh, I *have* been happy here!' she remarked at the end of the war as she prepared to return to London. 'Here I've been anybody to everybody, and back in London I shall have to begin being Queen Mary all over again.' It must be said, though, that the country exile showed absolutely no desire to delay her return to Marlborough House; nor, when she got back to London, did she find 'being Queen Mary all over again' the least bit of a strain. At the service of thanksgiving for victory in St Paul's Cathedral Chips Channon was enraptured to see her again, looking 'magnificent – even beautiful . . . gorgeously arrayed and bejewelled in a pink heliotrope confection'. Henceforward, quite clearly, there would be few crumbs of comfort for the Spirit of Comedy.

Queen Mary knew that her Cambridge genes often bestowed long life, and though now clearly ageing, she never gave any sign of torpor. Even when, at the age of eighty-three, she began to realise that her brain was deteriorating, her will remained intact. 'I am beginning to lose my memory,' she announced, 'but I mean to get it back.' Her working life extended well into her eighties; her interest in her ancestors and their possessions likewise flourished unabated. Amidst the dismal austerities of post-war socialist Britain, her presence evoked memories of the very different country into which she had been born, the most powerful, prosperous and confident nation on earth. Queen Mary herself did not repine: as long as there was a world about her, she found plenty to interest her and something to approve. (Not, however, the 1951 Festival of Britain, which she deemed 'really extraordinary and very ugly'.) Several Labour politicians were counted among her most devoted admirers, and if she ever felt unease at the ebb of the hierarchical assumptions in which she had been raised, she kept it to herself. What did upset her, though, was the break-up of the empire in which she had so passionately believed and which she had so devotedly served. The loss of India caused her an acute pang. 'When I die,' she claimed in uncharacteristically melodramatic style, 'INDIA will be found written on my heart.'

At least, though, the monarchy, which had ever been the alpha and omega of her existence, remained more firmly embedded than ever in the nation's affections. She took immense pride in the achievement of George VI, while the quiet, sensible, strong-willed Princess Elizabeth appeared to her to be in every way a suitable heir. As for Princess Margaret, 'she is so outrageously amusing that one can't help encouraging her'. All through the Princesses' childhood Queen Mary had shown a keen interest in their education, stressing in particular the absorbing interest of family history. Before the war she would take her grandchildren with her to museums and art galleries. Princess Margaret was perhaps the more eager listener, but Princess Elizabeth never failed to muster an expression of polite interest. Queen Mary had been delighted by the put-down which the elder sister gave to the younger when they were all seeing the King and Queen off to the United States in 1939. 'I have my handkerchief,' Princess Margaret rashly ventured. 'To wave and not to cry,' came the stern response from Princess Elizabeth. It is easy to see why this injunction, with its implications of public duty triumphant over personal feeling, appealed to Queen Mary. There is, however, a disconcerting pre-echo of Stevie Smith's famous line: 'not waving but drowning'.

From the early 1940s the *cognoscenti* predicted that Princess Elizabeth would marry Prince Philip of Greece, who was descended from both the Danish and Russian royal families, as well as being, on his mother's side, a great-great-grandson of Queen Victoria. These were credentials bound to appeal to Queen Mary, although, given her difficulties with Queen Alexandra, she may have had some reservations about the Danish inheritance. She approved of Prince Philip who, she did not fail to observe, was exceedingly good-looking and, she thought, highly intelligent.

The marriage, the last great royal celebration of Queen Mary's life, took place on 20 November 1947. The proud grandmother received cheers of love and loyalty from her subjects; 'darling Lilibet' received the diamond necklace and stomacher which Queen Victoria had given to Princess May when she married Prince George fifty-four years before. All, for a moment, was well with the world, and Queen Mary looked supremely happy. 'Saw many old friends, I stood from 9.30 till 12.15 a.m.!!! not bad for eighty,' she noted about the party at Buckingham Palace two days before the wedding. There was only one untoward happening. Mahatma Gandhi sent a loincloth that he had woven himself as a wedding present, 'a horrible thing', as Queen Mary thought, 'a most indelicate gift'. Prince Philip, who had imbibed different ideas from his uncle Mountbatten, presumed to disagree. 'I don't think it's horrible,' he said. 'Gandhi is a wonderful man; a very great man.' Queen Mary passed on in silence. It was no use arguing with these young hotheads.

The birth of Prince Charles, a year later, made Queen Mary a great-grandmother, an event which she marked by a christening present that reflected her relish for family history. 'I gave the baby a silver gilt cup & cover which George III had given to a godson in 1780 – so that I gave a present from my gt grandfather, to my great grandson 168 years later.' In no time at all Queen Mary was discovering a marked resemblance between the infant Prince Charles and Prince Albert the Prince Consort.

One great sadness was yet reserved to her. Ever since the end of the war George VI's health had been precarious. In 1949 and 1950 he underwent two serious operations, the second (though Queen Mary knew it not) being an attempt to remove a cancer in the left lung. For four months the King appeared to be recovering, but on the night of 5–6 February he died peacefully in his sleep. This was the fourth son that Queen Mary had lost, the third by death; and for her brave and true Bertie, who had successfully shouldered the unwanted burden so frivolously bequeathed to him, she had developed a special admiration. Even in her shock and grief, however, the proprieties of monarchy still sustained her. No sooner had the new Queen arrived back from Africa, where she had just begun a five month tour, than Queen Mary went to see her. 'Her old Grannie and subject', she insisted, 'must be the first to kiss her hand.' A few days later Chips Channon saw a 'small and fragile' Queen Mary at George VI's lying-in-state in Westminster Hall: 'I was very sorry for her as she must have known and realised that she is next'. Possibly, though, she was regretting that she had not been the last. 'I suppose one must go on until the end,' she remarked with an uncharacteristic trace of despair to a visitor.

And that, of course, is what the indomitable old woman did. 'My 85th birthday!' she noted on 26 May 1952, 'hundreds of letters, cards etc. arrived – we tried to deal with them – I felt very much spoilt & had a nice day in spite of my great age.' Later that summer Harold Nicolson went to see her about his biography of George V. She stared fondly at a picture of her husband as a young man: 'how like he was', she mused, 'to my poor silly son.'

The past was her true domain now, notwithstanding her benevolent regard for the new reign. In February 1953 Queen Mary drove into Hyde Park and watched as workmen began to erect the stands for the coronation on 2 June. Her beloved Aunt Augusta had attended the coronation of King William IV in 1830; now she herself, whose Cambridge grandfather had been born in 1774, had become the embodiment of that sense of continuity and tradition by which the throne is ultimately sustained. She was not, however, destined to see her granddaughter crowned. At the beginning of March her health started to deteriorate sharply. The summons of eternity found her concerned that the coronation might have to be postponed on account of her funeral: lucid to the last, she left firm instructions that this should not occur. In the event death came without prejudice to the royal schedule. On 23 March Queen Mary could still ask a lady-in-waiting to read to her – a book about India, as it happened. A day later she had entered a kingdom where, just possibly, the claims of the English monarchy do not press quite so hard.